# HEMINGWAY AND HO CHI MINH IN PARIS

# HEMINGWAY AND HO CHI MINH IN PARIS

## THE ART OF RESISTANCE

DAVID CROWE

Fortress Press

Minneapolis

HEMINGWAY AND HO CHI MINH IN PARIS
The Art of Resistance

Cover image: Eiffel Tower and park, Paris, France, Library of Congress 1909.
Cover design: Laura Drew, Drew Design

Print ISBN: 978-1-5064-5570-9
eBook ISBN: 978-1-5064-5571-6

For all the students over the years who saw me not only as their professor but also their friend.

# CONTENTS

offer here two ways to help readers navigate this unusual biography of
two young men and a city.

First, if they are like virtually every person I have ever told about
this book concerning Ernest Hemingway and Ho Chi Minh, readers
will be quick to ask, "Did they know each other?" For a time I answered,
"No, there's no record of a meeting." After thinking further about the
possibilities, I learned to answer, "They lived only three blocks apart
and shared a market street that ran between their flats. They read a lot,
and they both published many articles and stories in Paris. One year,
Ho lived a couple doors down from the Hemingways' maid and her
husband, who were also Ernest and his wife Hadley's dear friends. So
Hemingway and Ho probably knew of each other, and they might even
have met briefly, but I'm afraid there is no record of that meeting."

What I want to say—I hope without any real defensiveness—is that
this book is not about how the two men affected each other. That would
be a short book indeed. It is about the more complicated story of how
Paris affected both of them, and affected them similarly, in the same
Left Bank neighborhood and during the same few years. I began writing
with only a vague sense of these similarities, but my research surprised
me again and again with the depth of these shared experiences and the
men's resulting shared commitments to justice.

Next, readers should know that Ho Chi Minh's and Hemingway's
years in Paris overlapped only partially. Ho lived there before Hemingway, from 1919 to 1921, and Hemingway lingered in the city after Ho
left it, from 1923 to 1928. So, reader, be prepared: The first part of the

book is about circumstances that led the men to bring similar burdens with them to Paris. Then there are a few chapters focusing mainly on Ho—though there are parallel events and experiences in Hemingway's life to uncover. A number of chapters concern the men living near each other and performing very similar work in a neighborhood called la Mouffe. Then, finally, there are a few chapters mainly about Hemingway—though there are parallel events and experiences in Ho's life to uncover. Notably, a few of Ho's later interactions with Parisian institutions (revolutionary cells, publishers, and the League of Nations) were from a distance, all the way from Russia and then China. Few readers should find this confusing, but I want to be clear and, I hope, helpful about the book's organization.

Finally, there is the problem of Ho Chi Minh's many pseudonyms, which include the name Ho Chi Minh itself. Readers may find it helpful to know that throughout this book, I will match Ho's many traditional and pseudonymous names to the appropriate historical moment. At his birth in 1890, Ho's parents gave him the "milk name" of Nguyen Sinh Cung. Following Vietnamese tradition, at age ten he was given another name, Nguyen Tat Thanh. This should have been Ho's name throughout life, but he chose to use many pseudonyms. When he left Vietnam at age twenty-one, he took the pseudonymous nickname Ba, dropping the given name Thanh for all time. He worked under the name Ba in Marseille, Boston, New York, London, and many colonial ports of call for a few years, and then moved to Paris around 1918, adopting the dignified symbolic pseudonym Nguyen Ai Quoc, or Nguyen Who Is a Patriot. For a brief time in Paris he used the sarcastic pseudonym Nguyen Ai Phap, or Nguyen Who Hates the French. Finally, in 1944, as emerging leader of the Vietnamese nationalist movement, he began to sign official documents with the name Ho Chi Minh, or He Who Has Been Enlightened. He kept using that name until his death in 1969. He used other pseudonyms more briefly, usually to escape official notice, but we will not trouble ourselves with those names. At bottom, if you are reading about Thanh, Ba, or Quoc in this book, you are reading about the future Ho Chi Minh. But even this knowledge is nonessential, as each chapter is marked with the relevant year and name.

# JOINING THE RESISTANCE IN PARIS

T his is the story of two young men who came to Paris to join a resistance movement that had been going on since the end of the previous
century, a modern arts-and-politics movement that had accelerated
sharply as the Great War ended in 1918. These young men knew that in
postwar Paris a search was underway for new political, artistic, and journalistic practices that might sweep away the oligarchs, profiteers, corrupt
politicians, colonial overseers, extreme nationalists, and casual bigots who
had united to prosecute and prolong the first-ever world war. Like other
hopeful modernists who came to Paris just after the war, they hoped to
join with those who would dismantle a system of empire that was then
bleeding dry Europe's laborers and colonial subjects. These two young
men hoped for the birth of a new freedom for people like themselves—
smart, talented, humane, and hopeful, but seemingly consigned by the
powers that be to the role of mere cannon fodder.

≡ ≡ ≡

One of these men came to Paris determined to become an important
writer. Soon, he decided to write as a modernist, which meant doing justice to the new theories of Friedrich Nietzsche, Karl Marx, and Sigmund
Freud—recent liberators in the theological, political, and sexual realms.[1]
This young man wanted his writing to be existentially, politically, and
psychologically realistic. He wanted to add his testimony to those who

wrote about the challenges of living as a newly liberated person in a suf-focating, pious Victorian culture, burdened with smug Christian confi-dence and a strong tendency toward violence.

He brought to Paris a unique viewpoint: he had nearly been killed in a battle with the soldiers of empire. He had not yet completely overcome the shock and outrage resulting from that trauma, so he found himself often angrier and more argumentative than his peers.

Over the course of the next three years, he would study in French libraries, visit galleries with friends, and attend a Parisian salon that was really a kind of debating society for modern ideas. There he learned about avant-garde arts such as Dada, surrealism, jazz and other black arts, Stravinsky, the *Ballet Russe*, cubism, vorticism, and the new French love of abstract art generally. On his own, he read Shakespeare and Dick-ens and Dostoevsky. He made friends who encouraged him in his writ-ing, including French anti-war novelist Henri Barbusse, who showed him how to write acerbic accounts of recent violence from the point of view of the victim.

During this time of learning, he worked as a reporter, covering peace conferences that we now know actually scripted both another world war and the many local ethnic-nationalist conflicts of the 1920s and 1930s. He worked as a fiction writer too, but there was a serious snag. Stun-ningly, one day this apprentice writer's manuscripts were stolen. At first depressed and enraged at the loss, he soon took the opportunity to begin the painstaking task of learning to write a different, more modern prose. He began to write vivid prose poems about the suffering of the century's refugees and reluctant combatants, and this writing went well. He found an audience. Eventually he gave up journalism to dedicate himself to his more literary art, and because of the new literary circles he now ran in, he began to edit and publish in a modernist little magazine, a sort of bohe-mian pamphlet for small audiences. Once his readership was large enough to make him known internationally, he was able to consider leaving Paris for greater things. Before long, he found that a book he had written had earned a broad international readership. He had become regarded not just as a writer but as a revolutionary new thinker redefining his culture.

This young writer was Ho Chi Minh.[2]

Another young man came to Paris a committed Communist (the capital C is his). For more than a year before arriving in Paris, he worked hard to promote a sweeping, worker-centered socialism, an anarchic, lib-ertarian set of governing policies designed to redirect power from the elite citizen to the ordinary one. Indeed, while still living in his home country, he wrote socialist workers' propaganda as a full-time job. He believed emphatically in one big union of international workers. He voted communist in national elections. He viewed the new Russian revolution as a hopeful event, possibly about to become, he thought, the greatest fulfillment of democracy the world had yet seen. He did not believe that it was the destiny of the working class to become shock troops for a violent revolution, but he did see laboring men and women as fierce, durable, and crafty—a potent force for worldwide reforms. He believed that if workers were to reduce the power and unearned wealth of the people we now call "the one percent," forces for justice would have to learn to use creative coercion.

He was interested in a Parisian experiment newly underway—the practice of using art and propaganda in explosive combinations to raise into consciousness, and maybe into possibility, serious changes to an unjust and broken world. The bohemian artist-radicals practicing this art seem to have found the most peaceable form of creative coercion available to the right-minded. Wisely, these bohemian provocateurs mul-tiplied the effect of their efforts by forming cliques and schools and alli-ances and movements dedicated to refining and promoting their arts. A fiercely independent young man, he did not want to join any such school, but he was interested in talking with these artists about their hopes and goals and crafts.

This young man brought to Paris a unique viewpoint: he had nearly been killed in a battle with the soldiers of empire. He had not yet com-pletely overcome the shock and outrage resulting from that trauma, so he found himself often angrier and more argumentative than his peers.

He treated Paris as his university. From a variety of friends he learned about avant-garde arts such as Dada, surrealism, jazz and other black arts, Stravinsky, the *Ballet Russe*, cubism, vorticism, and the new French love of abstract art generally. On his own, he read Shakespeare and Dickens and Dostoevsky. He made friends who encouraged him in his writing, including French anti-war novelist Henri Barbusse, who showed him how to write acerbic accounts of recent violence from the point of view of the victim.

Before he had been in Paris for two years, this young man's communist commitments had altered. He was no longer a pro-union, Marxist tough. He was interested in the artists who split off from the dadaist satirists of Western civilization, who were mostly hilariously nonpolitical, to become the surrealists. He knew that these artists were more serious about communism than the comical dadaists were. The surrealists even wanted to join Lenin's Third International, a momentous decision because it meant they were ready to contemplate, if not carry out, armed revolution. Our young man found these surrealist arts intoxicating, and the artists fun to be with, so he began to drink with them, to learn their doctrines about the possibility of sweeping social change, and to purchase their weird and unsettling art—the pieces he could afford, anyway, by not buying new clothes.

During this time of learning, he worked as a reporter, covering peace conferences that we now know actually scripted both another world war and the many local ethnic-nationalist conflicts of the 1920s and 1930s. He worked as a fiction writer too, but there was a serious snag. Stunningly, one day this apprentice writer's manuscripts were stolen. At first depressed and enraged at the loss, he soon took the opportunity to begin the painstaking task of learning to write a different, more modern prose. At first he wrote vivid prose poems about the suffering of the century's refugees and reluctant combatants, and this writing went well. He found an audience. Eventually he gave up journalism to dedicate himself to his more literary art, and because of the new literary circles he now ran in, he began to edit and publish in a modernist "little magazine." Before long, he found that a book he had written had earned a broad international readership. Once his readership was large enough to make him known internationally, he was able to consider leaving Paris for greater things. He had become regarded not just as a writer but as a revolutionary new thinker redefining his culture.

This young communist was Ernest Hemingway.

≡ ≡ ≡

Ho Chi Minh and Ernest Hemingway were actually unacquainted brothers-in-arms. They probably never met, mainly because of the racism and elitism that normally kept menial Vietnamese workers in Paris from befriending American expatriate artists. But these two had something more important in common than, say, a brief conversation in their la Mouffe neighborhood. They shared humane ideals, a hatred of injustice, and curiosity about processes of change. They also had severely wounded psyches. When they arrived in Paris, Ho probably in the first weeks after the Great War's conclusion in late 1918 and Hemingway definitely a few months later, in December of 1921, they came in order to join in a kind of revolution. That is, they were dedicated to developing talents they knew they possessed so that they could make a material difference in the lives of injured-people, those who, like them, had suffered want or indignity or physical harm. They hoped to help sweep away those elements of the traditionalist Victorian society that had pushed the world into cataclysmic war.

Both were invested in reforming governments and economies they thought inhumane. They were convinced that the powers behind empire had started the war under a false flag. The war had not been launched to preserve democracy or to end all wars, as some of its apologists claimed. It was actually a morally dubious attempt on the part of privileged men to retain their power and to increase their profits. These powers that be then had managed the conflict so ineptly that millions upon millions had died—about seven million civilians and ten million military personnel—and for nothing more than a slightly different and wholly temporary European balance of power. Both Hemingway and Ho were determined to resist that cynical and violent world with all their talents. If the art they created in the course of this work gave them some personal meaning and widespread reputation and, in Hemingway's case, even material profit, so much the better.

Ho and Hemingway were in a uniquely parallel situation. Both had been raised in deeply devout, idealistic households, and then both experienced the deep shock of near-fatal encounters with the empire's military forces. Indeed, both may have arrived in the City of Light still suffering post-traumatic shock. Certainly both felt desperately angry and anxious when they moved to Paris: angry about the waste of war and anxious about the future of civilization. They were especially concerned about the Great War's wasted young people, the colonial subjects and common soldiers who had been told during that war that it was their responsibility to die gladly and readily for empire. *Dulce et decorum est pro patria mori*, the pious motto went: "It is sweet and becoming to die for one's country." Ho and Hemingway thought differently. They wanted to turn their talents— and thanks to excellent secondary educations and extraordinary international experiences, they had truly impressive talents—to help build a civilization that did not turn so readily to killing or, less drastically, to the routine domination and exploitation of the least powerful. They wanted to learn how to live, and live meaningfully. And so, they began to study the arts of modern resistance—resistance to this universe of killing, mainly, but also to the worldview and economic system behind the killing. No stage in this learning was more important than the months they spent as unknowing neighbors in la Mouffe, a neighborhood grouped around the short market street rue Mouffetard on Paris's Left Bank.

The empires on both sides of the Great War revealed something about the traditions we call the West when they sent their young male citizens, and not a few women and colonial subjects, into the Belgian and French and Balkan mud to suffer and kill and die by the millions. To many observers, the promiscuous killing exposed the lie that the Christian West was especially reasonable and civilized. And if all of Western civilization could be legitimately questioned, then so could doctrines and traditions and constitutions and economies. Already in 1919 Russia's Czar Nicholas had fallen out of power, losing control of Russia to a revolutionary party called the Bolsheviks. In the early 1920s, few knew what the Bolsheviks or their governing councils, called Soviets, were really about. Some predicted the totalitarianism to come, while others hoped for a new society that celebrated and supported the working man and woman. At the war's end, Ho and Hemingway saw that other nations were teetering toward revolutionary change too, perhaps even Germany and Italy. Some observers at the time believed that the French and English empires would also eventually fall into the hands of the workers, as Marx had predicted.

Neither Ho nor Hemingway hoped for quite so chaotic a near future. Both cherished the values of constitutional democracy during the Paris years, yet both also saw that ordinary European laborers and even Asian and African colonials just might be on the verge of startling change. Workers seemed poised to flex their muscles in negotiations with the executive class, pushing for a greater share of profits and securing better working conditions, while colonial subjects seemed about to gain full citizenship in their own nations, to be free of the economic exploitation of European empires. Ho and Hemingway spent their days in Paris in their own ways, working for and promoting this more egalitarian future for the politically powerless, the stateless, and the colonized. Even as they doubted that Bolshevism was the answer to working people's problems, they were interested in the Russian experiment. Much of bohemian Paris was similarly interested and had set out on the audacious project of seeing whether those frightening revolutionary energies—everyone knew about the bloody phase of Bolshevik assassinations and reprisals—could be harnessed for something more peaceable and creative. They avidly explored Paris's more humane models for revolutionary change.

It was a moment for a smart, young person to become an agent of change, a definer of a better way, a modernist, or even a revolutionary.[3] Ho and Hemingway were certainly not alone in realizing that the Great War had revealed a smug, murderous side to Western civilization. In the immediate postwar years, in cities across Europe such as Berlin and Zurich and Vienna and Paris, the very word *civilization* was undergoing revolutionary redefinition. So-called modernist artists, writers, philosophers, and political revolutionaries, many of them motivated by their own faiths, worked to propose and promote a new way. These modernists took seriously the writings of Marx, Nietzsche, Freud, and even Einstein, finding in these men's theories the foundation for a more egalitarian, psychologically astute, relativistic world, consonant with their deeply held beliefs, yet leading, they hoped, to more widespread material justice.

Ho and Hemingway were primed to become modernists. Ho grew up a racially denigrated servant of the system of European privilege called colonialism. He saw his father and other elders endure insults and injuries from French colonial managers and leaders. He also witnessed Frenchmen perpetrating racist assaults on his Vietnamese friends and neighbors, both at home and during his world travels. These outrages included beatings of innocent laborers, sexual domination of young women, and taxation of poor servants and farmers who had no say in their system of government. He knew that his unluckiest fellow colonials often suffered far worse abuses, such as murder, rape, and sadistic torture—all essentially permitted by a legal system that served the French but not the Vietnamese. A smart and talented young man dedicated to Confucian teachings, Ho knew that he was not simply to resist these criminal acts but was to resist the immoral political and economic systems that made them possible.

Hemingway, by contrast, was the son of a respected suburban physician and church elder. As the child of such a father, he enjoyed his own privileges, including excellent schooling and idyllic summers at the family's lake home. Yet his first job out of high school, reporting for a Kansas City newspaper, showed him the desperate lives of other, less fortunate Americans. He witnessed crimes that arose from hunger, and cruelty that arose from anti-immigrant bigotry. When he went to war as a Red Cross volunteer, he met men from Europe's working classes who as civilians had had no choice but to perform degrading work and, when drafted, were forced to serve as pawns in a rich man's war. He realized that fighting for the survival of empires, even joining that fight as a compassionate noncombatant as he had, was deeply problematic and perhaps even wrong. Like Ho, he came to realize that his faith put demands on him as well. Having been trained in Protestant Christian doctrines and then having undergone a wartime conversion to Catholicism, he felt called not just to resist specific acts of unkindness or violence but to resist the political and economic abuses that made them possible. Ho and Hemingway followed differing logical and theological paths to their realizations, but their conclusions turned out remarkably similar. When cruelty, hunger, and denigration arose from specific political and economic systems, those systems, they realized, had to be resisted and reformed.

≡ ≡ ≡

This conflict between traditionalist Christian-capitalist values and leftist egalitarian alternatives is with us still, of course, though the conflict does not feel modern anymore. Almost exactly one hundred years after modernism began in earnest, we endure what historian Adam Hochschild astutely calls a "clash of dreams"—represented for him by pro–Great War patriots clashing with anti-war dissenters. In the postwar world there were other new or renewed clashes that should sound familiar to us. There was a struggle going on between those who were content to see the world divided between rich and poor and those who viewed basic income and retirement and health care as civil rights; between those who believed in the theories of ethnic European racial superiority and those who worked for a just and color-blind society; between those who viewed non-Christians as enemies and threats and others who embraced an inter-faith world; between those who viewed war as a useful tool for securing a certain kind of society and those who chose to make war on war because they were repelled by the idea of young people dying for an expanded consumer society and yet more wealth for the already super-rich.[4]

These are the modern versions of the two sides from which Ho and Hemingway had to choose. In interwar Paris, the clashing of these two worldviews had just begun, or rather, had entered an early acute phase. The traditionalists and imperialists felt both beleaguered and especially empowered during those immediate postwar years. They felt beleaguered in 1919 because they were accused of having started the first world war[5] for fiscal reasons, and perhaps saw signs that their power might soon wane, yet they also felt especially empowered because their empires had survived the war, and as the winning side, which of course included the French, they anticipated reparations profits. If, as many supposed, the war had mainly been an excuse for these powerful anti-progressive conservatives to quash labor unions, end women's suffrage campaigns, forestall pending banking regulations, and silence anti-colonial liberals who called for colonial reforms, then they had succeeded for a time, as wartime ramped up patriotic defense of the status quo. Yet the powers that be must have realized that their gains had been temporary and obtained at an obscene cost, and now they faced renewed pressure from these modernists and reformers.[6] Arguably, the most creative and avid of these resisters and reformers lived in Paris, which is something Ho and Hemingway intuited as they decided to live there.

Some of these progressives believed furthermore that the United States, which was a nation born in an anti-colonial moment and there-fore supposed to despise imperialism, was complicit in this exploita-tion of the common citizen. Hemingway's best Paris friend and fellow American novelist John Dos Passos was one such person. He believed the theory of the rich man's war and the poor man's fight so deeply that in his novel *1919* he created a character who condemns the war, calling it a transparent effort to save the American Morgan Bank's huge loans to the European Allies. In his own words in another more experimental passage, Dos Passos offers up this sarcastic prose poem in his James-Joycean modern style:

(Wars and panics on the stock exchange,
machinegunfire and arson,
bankruptcies, warloans,
starvation, lice, cholera and typhus:
good growing weather for the House of Morgan.)

And in another passage, he offers this ominously relevant addendum to the story of the oligarchs' lies in supporting the war:

oil was trumps.[7]

Access to raw materials such as crude oil was only one hidden motive of the imperialists. Sending European workers and colonial subjects into the trenches would be an added bonus. If Europe's governing elites had their way, those childish, dusky, and rebellious upstarts would learn who was boss.

We might call them Victorians, these pro-empire Parisians and their international allies, even though as post-revolutionary Frenchmen they despised royalty and certainly didn't love the English or their nineteenth-century queen. They were Victorian in the sense that they loved and supported empire, believing the colonial mission to be benign and just and scripturally warranted. These were the kinds of elders who urged young people to salute their flags and to respect traditional sources of authority in government, church, and society. In their view, the brash veterans and other youngsters, the clamoring women and the childish colonials especially, needed to learn their place in the order of things, needed to learn to accept the wisdom of the white, male leaders whom God had placed in charge. Before and during their Paris sojourns, both Ho and Hemingway endured instruction from such people.

Even before the war, as their consciences were forming during their teen years, both chafed under this Victorian instruction. This is where our story begins, in a moment prior to their woundings, during Ho's and Hemingway's final months living at home as sons of their parents. Both were lucky to have loving, attentive, and instructive parents, but both also underwent some troubling cultural training during their youths. Parts of the story are abhorrent. Ho, for example, claimed to have witnessed a group of French colonial managers laughing with glee as they watched Vietnamese harbor workers under their orders trying to secure boats in a storm. These callous Frenchmen continued to laugh as the workers drowned. When driving in Vietnam, French colonizers ran down old women because, they said, the French built and owned Vietnam's roads, so the roads were for the French. Such events come from the dark side of the civilizing mission, the deadly, viral form of Victorian paternalism.

Hemingway experienced the Victorian mind at work too. During his teen years, and especially after he returned home from war, he felt alien in his own home under the constant, exclusivist Christian preaching of his parents. They were so rigid about this that once, during his Paris years, they wrote him to condemn stories in which he had written sympathetically, but certainly not crudely, about Greek war refugees trudging in the rain away from the homes from which Turkish forces had just expelled them. The elder Hemingways viewed such Mediterranean foreigners as filthy and ignoble and therefore an inappropriate subject for their son's writing. While Ernest was still a boy, he recalled in later life, they treated Ojibwe people living near their lake cottage with similar dispatch, if not contempt. It wouldn't be the last time they made such a cold, dismissive judgment about people they supposed to be non-Christian and who were nonwhite. Hemingway may have felt that in telling the story of suffering refugees, he was honoring the gospels his parents had taught him to respect, honoring especially Jesus's encouragement that we heal the sick and minister to the needy. After experiencing his parents' hostile indignation toward those refugees, he realized he would have to make his own way, both with his writing and with his faith.

In Paris, Ho and Hemingway made their way into a much more complicated moral, ethical, and political world. As we will see, in Ho and Hemingway's neighborhood in Paris's 5th Arrondissement there were many nominally nonviolent but determined revolutionary cells ready to give them instruction—some Moroccan, some Chinese, some

Indochinese, some native French, and some even American, all plotting demonstrations and provocations to unsettle the status quo. A few of these cells planned acts of terrorism—bombings, armed insurrections, and revolution in Paris's streets—but most were more peaceable, viewing the new arts themselves, and the reformed attitudes they were supposed to prompt, as a route to a more modern, just society. Ho and Hemingway found that they would have to make choices about what kind of resistance, reform, and revolution they were willing to endorse—willing, indeed, to give their lives to. Specifically, they would decide whether the true revolutionary took up the rifle or the pen. Or both.

From 1918 to 1923, Ho belonged to one of the nonviolent cells, an Indochinese group called the Annamite Patriots, whose members had varying ideas about the way to liberate Vietnam (then called Annam in French colonial speech) from the French. He and his comrades could be heard many nights in loud, heated debate about the efficacy and moral correctness of their evolving commitments. Ho's voice, French police agents reported, was usually the loudest and most frantic. The Annamites were divided over the crucial question of whether to remain reformist French socialists or to become internationalist communists— that is, whether the world they knew then might be changed peaceably through legislation or only through social disruption and the threat of violence. Hemingway had to trouble the same questions. He also spent part of those years in political argument with his revolutionary literary cell. His mentors, Ezra Pound and Gertrude Stein, both preferred rightist, authoritarian governments. Pound promoted paranoid economic theories about the scourge of Jewish moneylenders, and would one day broadcast fascist propaganda on the radio for Mussolini, while Stein claimed in the middle 1930s that in the United States only authoritarian Republicans guided by their instincts were "natural rulers." She added that "there is no reason why we should not select our immigrants with greater care, nor why we should not bar certain people and preserve the color line."[8] Hemingway struggled to find a way to keep learning from these two mentors about developing a concise prose style, conveying complex psychological states, and valuing the power of the literary image, but he could not endorse the bigoted judgments or the fascism. In Paris, as we will see, he allied himself with certain new friends in the art scene and tried to imagine adapting his own art and views to their ethic of radical progressive politics linked to humane, individualistic, and artistically and politically creative liberty.

For both Ho and Hemingway, to be whole and human was to side with low-wage workers and the politically dispossessed. Ho's notorious communist affiliations, which began in Paris, make this obvious. We have been slower to realize Hemingway's commitments to the egalitarian society. Recent scholarship indicates that Hemingway not only sided with the poor farmers and laborers on the left during the Spanish Civil War, which we knew, but that he actually worked for the Soviets as well, beginning in 1940, not as a spy or seditious informant but as a kind of propagandist for workers' rights. He also provided material support for Castro's Cuban rebels.[9] Of course, he risked his life reporting from Europe during the Second World War, and his reports sided generally with American GIs and the Allied invasion. He believed so much in the Allied cause that he violated protocols for news reporters in combat zones, taking up weapons and fighting alongside GIs in their campaign across Normandy. So, it would be a mistake to view him as a communist dupe or as a traitor to the United States. Yet, as we have seen, it was Hemingway, not Ho, who came to Paris calling himself a "Communist." We will have to see what he meant by that word.

Ho and Hemingway came to Paris searching for political solutions to social problems they had witnessed. They also planned to work on talents they possessed, which for Ho meant improving his speaking and debating skills, which he had already begun using on behalf of his people in Vietnam, and for Hemingway, improving his writing about comic and tragic human striving in a baffling modern world. They soon discovered, as young people do, that their learning in the City of Light would lead them to tasks and projects and skills and commitments and goals they could not have imagined on the day they arrived. Paris surprised them with its wealth of ideas—its modern and traditional art galleries, its incredible university and public libraries, its salons for literary and philosophical debate, its established and upstart magazines, its dozens of French and American newspapers, its anti-colonial and pro-worker ferment, its anarchic schools and cliques of social theorists, its female beauties and potential life partners, its ancient churches and temples offering renewal. Without knowing about each other at all, it seems, Ho and Hemingway were about to begin studying strikingly similar curricula. The result would be both fame and infamy for each man as he prepared to leave Paris and found himself strangely well prepared to speak to the world about its pressing problems.

# 2

## WOUNDED STUDENTS OF EMPIRE

### THANH IN 1908 AND HEMINGWAY IN 1918

H o Chi Minh was twenty-nine when he arrived in Paris, and Hemingway was just twenty-two. But, coincidentally, each was only eighteen when his journey to Paris began, years before either one of them had the faintest thought about one day living in France. Before either could even consider a move to Paris for its revolutionary mentors, its anarchic arts, its anti-colonial cells, its journals and newspapers covering international relations, and its competing ideologies, the two devout, idealistic young men would have to encounter the deadly cynicism of European empires making war, sometimes under the banner of peacemaking, civilization-building, and democracy-saving. Ho and Hemingway would have to be disillusioned, which is the classic state for any modernist—because, of course, disillusionment with current ways prompts the effort to imagine a better, more modern way.

They had these disillusioning encounters, Ho in 1908 and Hemingway in 1918, on two terrifying days when each young man was nearly killed by defenders of empire. Ironically, Ho and Hemingway nearly lost their lives to young men very much like themselves, patriots in uniform who bore them no grudge but who had simply been enlisted into the defense of beloved nations and traditions. Later we will see that in the wake of these traumas, the shock and outrage Ho and Hemingway felt confused and disabled them for a time, leading each into his own period of weariness and purposelessness. Later still, those unwelcome feelings of post-traumatic shock would turn, at least partly, into something else. The pain was there, but so was a growing determination to resist the values of empire, to rebel against the universe of killing, to work for greater economic and racial equality. And this became the motivating energy for their moves to Paris and the work they did there. These raw emotions that the men felt immediately, and the sense of revolutionary vocation that the two felt later, can best be explained as a reaction against the Western idealism, both religious and intellectual, that they had been trained into by their parents, teachers, and other devotees of empire. What is remarkable is how painful this training was, and how desperate were the situations into which it led Ho and Hemingway before they began to think about a life in modernist Paris.

Both Ho and Hemingway were born into deeply devout homes. Ho was raised a Confucian and Hemingway a Congregationalist Christian. This early religious training would prove double-edged for both young men. Trained into sincere faithfulness and doctrines, if not the practice, of nonviolence, they found themselves unprepared for the cynical waste of war and police-state tactics. They knew that killing was going on around them, of course, but they were understandably stunned and terrified when it seemed their own lives might be the ones wasted. Even before becoming modernist revolutionaries, they were moved to sympathy with the expendable, the wounded, and the already-wasted dead. Perhaps their youthful religious training had something to do with this sympathy, a broader wish to enlarge and improve the neighbor's life, or perhaps both merely yearned for others to avoid pain they had experienced. In any case, both of them moved away from their parents' obviously devout ways.

Yet, they altered rather than abandoned their faiths. Throughout their adult lives, both Ho and Hemingway retained the deep humanism of their faiths' teachings, and there are signs that they even retained belief in their faiths' mysteries and mysticisms. It is not too much to say that both developed and acted upon what we would now call an interfaith understanding and ethics. During their Paris years especially, Ho and Hemingway supported a form of universal social welfare that they found consonant with a religious idea common to their faiths: both Confucianism and Christianity teach a form of nonerotic love that insists we should treat others as we wish to be treated. It was a difficult principle to live by during the trials of colonialism and Great War battles.

≡ ≡ ≡

Ho Chi Minh was born in 1890, his parents giving him the traditional "milk name" of Nguyen Sinh Cung. His father, Nguyen Sinh Sac, was a well-known and locally important Confucian scholar.[1] By the time the boy was ten, when he received his adult name, Nguyen Tat Thanh (which means "he who will succeed"), he was steeped in the Confucian values of benevolence, honesty, conscientious loyalty, altruism, knowledge, faithfulness, and proper worship.[2] Thanh embraced these values sincerely, and they helped him work with and understand his French neighbors in Annam. Under the French, the colony of Indochina (present-day Laos, Cambodia, and Vietnam) was a nominally Christian land. The first colonists in the sixteenth century were Portuguese missionaries, but their influence quickly waned when French Catholic missionaries arrived in the mid-nineteenth century. Their arrival set up the situation that would allow for French economic and military control of Indochina beginning in 1858, when the Vietnamese crown endorsed the harassment of these missionaries and expelled a number of priests. In response, French gunships opened fire on Da Nang, supposedly to put a stop to these anticlerical activities. But clearly, the Da Nang incident was France's excuse to dominate Vietnam militarily so that it could also dominate the people economically.

There are many troubling and horrifying instances of this domination, both in Ho's life and across Vietnam more broadly. Yet, in spite of French misdeeds, the Catholic mission in Vietnam must have been compelling and convincing, at least to some Vietnamese *indigènes*, many of whom became Catholics. (In fact, there were four hundred thousand Christians in Vietnam just before colonialism began.[3]) Even today there is at least one Catholic church in the center of any sizable Vietnamese town. Indeed a Catholic cathedral stands at the heart of Saigon, right next to a colonial-era post office now decorated with a huge portrait of a grandfatherly Ho Chi Minh, while Hanoi's cathedral is just down the street from the "Hanoi Hilton," or Hoa Lo Prison. In spite of government suppressions of religion and the fact that the Vietnamese rightly associate Catholics with the South Vietnamese, whose army and government were almost entirely of that faith, there are still more than five million Catholics in Vietnam.

Yet for Sac and his son, Confucianism did not always blend perfectly with French Catholicism. The two faiths may have included a similar sense of faith, hope, and charity leading believers, hopefully, to a similarly gentle personal disposition and a commitment to social welfare, but Sac and his son Thanh believed that Confucius taught Eastern nationalism rather than Western Christian submission. Both father and son are remembered in Vietnam and around the world as especially kind—we think of the statues of Uncle Ho (as many Vietnamese call their hero) in Vietnam, such as the one outside the Rex Hotel in central Saigon, the gentle old revolutionary suffering the children to come unto him—but both also ended up resisting the French Catholic missionaries in Vietnam who schemed with French colonial managers to subdue and control the Vietnamese. Sac cared deeply about his son's moral and patriotic growth. He took young Thanh to funerals of Vietnamese patriots who died resisting the French—occasions when both father and son wept at the sacrifices—and sent him to Confucian teachers who taught him to rise above an official career and "try to understand the inner content of the Confucian classics in order to learn how to help your fellow human beings."[4] Then one day, Sac unwisely ordered one hundred lashes of the cane for a landlord who had been cheating Vietnamese tenants. As a result of this brutal punishment, this landlord died, and Sac suffered the consequences. He lost his job and his chance at further Confucian study. He was lucky to lose only his job, not his life.[5] This conflict so close to home troubled Thanh, yet the Confucian core values he had imbibed helped him emerge from his boyhood especially idealistic, patient, cooperative, and kind-hearted. He was also unusually literate and, thanks to his father's troubles, unusually aware of the need to comply with French norms.

Thanh's French teachers saw these qualities, so in 1907 they admitted him to an elite Western-style school for the training of imperial bureaucrats. We do not know whether Thanh was really there to advance a career in colonial management, as his teachers believed, or to exploit the French by turning skills earned through their Western education to revolutionary resistance work. For an answer to that question it is necessary to know how much his father's revolutionary friends were mentoring and influencing him at the time, which the historians, working with scant biographical information, continue to debate. We do know that Thanh was an exceptional student. One biographer notes that he "earned the respect of several teachers for his tireless curiosity, quick wit, maturity, and talent for writing." A French teacher wrote on an essay the young man had written, "Thanh wrote his paper on the writing of verse; he is an intelligent and very distinguished student."[6]

Ernest Hemingway was raised with similar religious seriousness. He was born in 1899 to Congregationalist parents—though his mother later became attracted to Christian Science—in conservative Republican Oak Park, Illinois, a first-ring suburb of Chicago then sandwiched between a huge city to the east and farm fields to the west. Hemingway's father practiced as a physician in the suburbs and around the family lake cottage in Michigan, and his mother, a would-be operatic diva, taught music lessons in a special room in the house she designed and had built mainly for her needs. It would be difficult to exaggerate the piety of the Hemingway household. As we will see, even after Hemingway returned from war a wounded veteran who had volunteered to serve in the Red Cross, his mother chided him about his laziness and his failure to get a steady job, writing to him, "[You are] neglecting your duties to God and your Savior Jesus Christ." Hemingway does not appear to have been especially devout as a youth, but he certainly imbibed the values and the rhetoric of Victorian Christian patriotism. From his Red Cross posting in Italy he once wrote to his family, "When a mother brings a son into the world she must know that some day the son will die. And the mother of a son that has died for his country should be the proude[s]t woman in the world, and the happiest."[7] *Dulce et decorum est*, he argues, *pro patria mori*.

Ho and Hemingway came by their intelligence and idealism honestly. One could hardly find more sincere ideals than those taught in the colonial Vietnam and Midwestern America of their day. At Ho's Quoc Hoc National Academy in Hue and Hemingway's Oak Park High School, students read classical works written in cultivated, proud, colony-holding empires. Hue's National Academy trained promising Annamites for service in the colonial bureaucracy, so literature and language instruction were almost entirely in French. Overt defenses of colonialism were rare in the curriculum, but there was a pervasive sense of French cultural superiority. As many of Hemingway's biographers have noted, the Oak Park High curriculum emphasized English imperial literature and history—almost to the exclusion of an American tradition. (In his English classes Hemingway read Tennyson and Coleridge but not Hawthorne, Emerson, or even his later hero, Mark Twain.) So Ho's education was imperialist Francophile, while Hemingway's was imperialist Anglophile. In both Ho's and Hemingway's schools, training for a useful career began with cultural literacy, and with principles and values rather than the contemporary model emphasizing a foundation of mere communication and critical-thinking skills.[8] Indeed, Ho's and Hemingway's high school educations were nearly as rigorous as a good liberal arts college education is today.

Thanh's French teachers in Hue recalled his precocious understanding of French Enlightenment thinkers, classic authors such as Descartes, Diderot, Rousseau, and Montesquieu,[9] all of whom celebrate the benefits of a deeply curious intellect and commitment to reason freed of ancient superstitions. This list of authors reveals an emphasis on post-Revolution secular reason, though with a nod to theology in Descartes and even to anti-colonialism in Diderot, who argued that colonial domination was evil and would inevitably corrupt the Europeans who practiced it, a surprising essay to find in a colonial curriculum. In the Indochinese colonies, French primary schools taught students a litany of French moral maxims drawn from the works of Voltaire, Chateaubriand, Thierry, Michelet, Cicero, St. Augustine, Jonathan Swift, and Benjamin Franklin. Thanh also had courses in geography, literature, science, and history—so, taken as a whole, these are the array of various disciplines that elite colleges still call general education and still offer as part of that process of liberation from error and superstition that we call the liberal arts.[10]

In his high school days Hemingway read more Shakespeare than most English majors read today in good college courses, and his training in rhetoric was so extensive that he was assigned four books on the history of the English language alone. This is not to mention the grammar book, dictionary, thesaurus, and study of etymology his rhetoric teacher also required. He read Chaucer, Spenser, Milton, Pope, Macaulay, Carlyle, Austen, Brontë, Dickens, and other English greats. He read Plutarch and, as Ho did, Benjamin Franklin.[11] And these are only his English courses. (Unfortunately, his literary scholars tend to care only about these.) We know because he bragged in a letter that he also did

well on a Cicero exam in "ancient hist."[12] We also know that he had the
math and science skills he would need to get into the universities that
interested him, Illinois and Cornell, and that his father, founding member of the local Agassiz Club, taught him lessons in natural history.[13]
Both at school and at home, Hemingway was steeped in Bible stories and
principles of Protestant theology.

Both young men were educated into a certain kind of cultural conservatism, but we should not exaggerate the threat of such a traditionalist
training. An education like Ho's and Hemingway's can be liberating as
well as coercively traditionalist (or "hegemonic," as some cultural critics would put it today). Hemingway and Ho and their teachers understood, it seems, what general education is for. If young people like our
two revolutionaries were to become effective citizens, leaders, debaters,
parents, spouses or partners, voters, worshippers, and stewards of their
own minds and bodies, they first had to become whole persons. They
needed to become idealists willing to rise above mere training designed
to lead to their advancement and comfort. Because career training is not
an ultimate good, their teachers felt they also needed to consider ideas,
ideals, values, and faith in otherworldly meaning as basic ingredients of
personhood. For both young men, this is exactly what happened. Their
educations took.

Ho and Hemingway had very similar existential choices to make
during the time of their schooling. By design, the *indigènes* of Hue and
the elders of Oak Park wanted Ho's and Hemingway's educations to turn
them into useful, patriotic citizens. The problem with such a goal is that
patriotic citizenship can be uncritical and can lead to needlessly deadly
projects. If Ho and Hemingway accepted such an education uncritically,
they would have had to support the empires that gave them instruction,
through loyalty to the colonies on Ho's part and through patriotic service
in the Great War and continued support of the West's elective conflicts
on Hemingway's. Lucky for them, Ho and Hemingway rose above the
stated aims of their educations, as the best students do, to seize a more
personal, immediate, and urgent education. They learned for themselves
what it means to be human, to care about social equity and peace.

But these wonderful educations were nearly wasted.

It was May of 1908 when Ho realized that leaders of empire found
him mortally expendable. Known then as Nguyen Tat Thanh, his given

adult name, he had been studying French literature and history for about a year at the Quoc Hoc Academy for promising *indigènes*. His classmates knew him to be especially bright, and teachers praised him, as we have seen. But he was also known for asking probing questions, and increasingly, he was showing sympathy for political dissidents, specifically a group of peasants and intellectuals who had taken to cutting their hair to demonstrate their rejection of feudal traditions. These dissidents were called Short Hairs, and they liked to chant a rebellious poem:

> Comb in the left hand,
> Scissors in the right,
> Snip! Snip!

> Cut out the ignorance,
> Do away with stupidity,
> Snip! Snip![14]

It's hardly "We Shall Overcome," but Ho Chi Minh remembered and cherished this chant many years later. He seems to have been fascinated by a burgeoning protest movement then afoot in Annam, the central highlands around Hue, Da Nang, and Hoi An. Intellectuals were opening nationalist schools for Vietnamese people, even urging peasants to exercise nonviolent direct action by withholding required tax payments from the French and by voicing public displeasure at such coercive French colonial policies. Peasants began to protest not only taxation without representation but also forced labor requirements. Apparently, Thanh was fully aware of and supportive of these activities. He was becoming a dedicated student in classes and an emerging rebel on the streets.

One day that May, a few thousand peasant protesters showed up in Hue, crowding the streets of the beautiful, tropical imperial city with its grand citadel reflected in the lazy Perfume River. A local mandarin led troops to suppress the protest. The peasant rebels captured him, placed him in a bamboo cage, and brought him the next day to the French *resident supérieur*. The caged mandarin was at the head of a very large crowd of angry, defiant peasants. Seeing the protest gathering in the wide, parklike avenue and grassy shoreline along the Perfume River in central Hue, Thanh realized that he could be a help to both parties in this conflict. For the first time, but certainly not the last, he showed that he was a believer in negotiated settlements that would be fair to all. As a Confucian he had been taught the concept of *Rén*, the innate wish to enlarge and improve your neighbor's life and to despise misdeeds that tend to harm the other. He had also learned to love the family, to respect authority, and to serve the community. Here was an idealist's opportunity. He could translate the peasants' demands so local French officials could better understand them and so the peasants' demands would get a proper hearing. Surely, Thanh seems to have thought, an accommodation could be worked out between the two parties, and their dispute could be settled peaceably.

It was a near-tragic decision. Just as Thanh moved to the head of the demonstration outside the main colonial administrative building, and just as he had been invited inside to help with negotiations, a French officer ordered his men to charge the demonstrators and beat them back with batons. The beatings were indiscriminate, and some French troops opened fire. Many Annamites were badly hurt. Even though Thanh had been treated as a respectable negotiator-translator just moments before, he, too, was beaten, struck repeatedly, his life definitely in danger. Soldiers exceeded their orders that day. Some French soldiers shot and killed Vietnamese peasants running across the new steel bridge spanning the river, the same bridge American Marines fought to control during the Tet Offensive of 1968 and that tourists cross today on their way to the Hue Citadel from their comfortable hotels on the opposite bank.

Once the violence waned, Thanh's troubles had only begun. During the chaos, he had been recognized, identified as a "tall, dark student" of the National Academy. Because Annamites who made political trouble had no future in colonial offices, and because the French believed insubordination of any kind had to be put down harshly, Thanh was immediately and permanently expelled from school. He was lucky to avoid a prison sentence—not that he deserved one. In any case, he was no longer welcome in French educational and managerial circles, so he had no choice but to wander Vietnam for a few months, pondering his complicated and apparently bleak future. Eventually, he hatched a plan for a truly international education abroad in various forms of resistance and freedom-fighting. But he had help making his decision. His lifelong travels and the desperate political education he pursued in Paris, Moscow,

Canton, and Hong Kong began with his 1908 beating at the hands of French officers in Hue.

≡ ≡ ≡

Hemingway had an even more serious brush with death in the Italian wartime trenches of 1918, where he, too, learned how little European empires valued his life. He was Lieutenant Hemingway at the time, an American volunteer in Italian uniform working for the international Red Cross. A few months after the United States entered the Great War in 1917, he had volunteered to serve as an ambulance driver with the organization. He would have preferred to fight, but he would not be old enough to volunteer for American military service for another year, and he feared that with a weak eye he would not pass a physical examination anyway, even if he waited and the war continued that long. He felt he had to get to wartime Europe. Once the American phase of the war began and he saw other young men entering into service, he found working as a beat reporter on the *Kansas City Star*, his job since the fall of 1917, to be empty and bland. Yet it was not just sophomoric adventure Hemingway was after. His choice to help the wounded with the Red Cross, saving lives, indicates a wish for meaningful purpose as well as masculine adventure. Like Thanh, young Hemingway was an idealist who was capable of selfless behavior.

Upon arriving in Italy for his Red Cross assignment, Hemingway was shipped out to the mountain front just north of Venice. There the Italians, associated with their British and French allies in the Triple Entente, faced their neighbor Austrians, who had joined with Germany in the Central Powers. On July 8, 1918, near the Piave River in a contested region of the Dolomite foothills, Hemingway rode a bicycle to the communication trenches that he would walk along to reach the main battle trenches at the front.[15] As his Kansas City friend and fellow ambulance man Ted Brumback reported in a letter home, "Ernest was not satisfied with the regular canteen service behind the lines. He thought he could do more good and be of more service by going straight up to the trenches."[16] Hemingway went to the battle trenches to hand out Red Cross cigarettes and candy to Italian troops, who were manning the lines facing the enemy Austrian soldiers. The task seems trivial to us today, and might have seemed so to Hemingway at the time, but the presence of any American would remind the Italians of America's recent entry into the war, hopefully boosting their morale. They needed the boost if they were to continue fighting. There were rumblings of mutiny in the Italian regiments, especially among the troops with communist sympathies.

Hemingway tells the story of his actual wounding in *A Farewell to Arms* (1929), where he gives the experience to an American commander of Italian ambulances named Lieutenant Frederic Henry. As he recalled that day in 1918, he had just settled down to a simple meal of cold pasta and canned meat with a group of Italian soldiers when an artillery barrage and mortar attack opened up. "Through the other noise," Hemingway writes,

> I heard a cough, then came the chuh-chuh-chuh-chuh—then there was a flash, as when a blast furnace door is swung open, and a roar that started white and went red and on and on in a rushing wind. I tried to breathe but my breath would not come and I felt myself rush bodily out of myself and out and out and out and all the time bodily in the wind. I went out swiftly, all of myself, and I knew I was dead.[17]

He was wrong about that. He was not dead, and he soon came to. He discovered to his horror that the explosion had blown off one of his kneecaps, so that it hung on to his shin by a shred of skin. He was partly buried in the earth of his collapsed trench. Italian soldiers around him had died instantly, one with his legs blown off. Nearby, other young men— still alive, though barely—lay half-buried in the collapsing trench. In the next few minutes some of them lived and some died. Hemingway was fortunate to make it to an aid station where competent physicians were at work. Years later, Hemingway would claim that he had been baptized a Catholic as he waited his turn for emergency treatment, a sign that he was both a devout Christian and worried for his life that day.

How badly this near-death experience wounded Hemingway's psyche is a debated question, but there were definitely lasting effects. Throughout his life, he portrayed his characters' and his own anxieties and insomnia as direct results of wartime trauma. Yet he remained a traditional patriot in full support of the Allied cause—at least for a time. In late 1919 or early 1920, home from the war and beginning to dream of a career as a writer, he wrote a story titled "The Woppian Way," in which his hero, a boxer prior to going to war, joins a unit of the Italian shock troops called the *Arditi* and eventually kills Austrians in hand-to-hand combat.[18] It is a kind of warrior's fantasy. He also wrote to his parents about the deep sincerity of his military service: "There are no heroes in war. We all offer our bodies and only a few are chosen, but it shouldn't reflect any special credit on those that are chose [*sic*]. They are just the lucky ones."[19] Echoing Matthew 22:14 here ("For many are called, but few are chosen"), Hemingway utters a classic Victorian piety about a young man's willing sacrifice for the nation. However, this humble and self-forgetting patriotism was about to evaporate. Soon he would meet politically radical friends in Chicago and would witness the economic and emotional troubles his fellow veterans were suffering, even after such willing service to the nation. Then he would be ready for his education in Paris to begin.

No example of his evolving attitudes is more famous or more important than the "big words" passage of *A Farewell to Arms*. In this scene, Frederic Henry, just before his wounding by that trench mortar shell, talks military strategy with an Italian friend, a patriotic young man who at one point expresses his hope that the terrible fighting in Italy that year had not been "in vain." Henry does not contradict his friend, but the language is a problem for him, given the reality he has seen in the trenches. "I was always embarrassed by the words sacred, glorious, and sacrifice and the expression in vain," Hemingway's autobiographical character admits privately to us and to himself. "I had seen nothing sacred [in this Great War], and the things that were glorious had no glory and the sacrifices were like the stockyards at Chicago if nothing was done with the meat except to bury it."[20]

Clearly, sometime between 1920, when Hemingway wrote about the goodness of patriotic self-sacrifice, and 1929, when he wrote his masterpiece novel about the waste of war, he had undergone a profound change of heart. We can and will chart that change, which involved his choice of Paris for its revolutionary arts and politics, and his gradual realization that the nation-state had no right to waste young men's blood or exploit the loyalty of its citizens.

During those very same years, Ho was to undergo a similar change of heart. He would choose Paris for more nakedly political reasons, mainly because the city was the capital of French colonialism, a system Ho knew he needed to understand if he were to resist its logic. Yet he would learn a lesson too, similar to the one Hemingway learned—that a genuinely humane nation-state had a deep responsibility to lengthen, strengthen, and enrich the lives of ordinary people. This was an ideal that would emerge from youthful woundings, post-traumatic shock, and resulting disillusionment.

# 3

## THE SEED OF EUROPE AND INDOCHINA

### THANH IN PREWAR VIETNAM AND

### HEMINGWAY IN POSTWAR AMERICA

After their woundings, both Hemingway and Ho lived among Victorian imperialists—Ho aboard ships traveling the world to many ports of call, and Hemingway spending a pair of years in Michigan and Illinois trying to find his postwar feet. As a result, both came to realize, or realize more sharply because of their shock and pain, the toxic nature of empire. Neither man knew it yet, but in prewar London and Paris and Greenwich Village, certain intellectuals were already noting a deep dishonesty and widespread bigotry in Western attitudes. The modernist poet Ezra Pound, for instance, was already calling the toxic, dishonest element of this culture "Victorian slither." (He did not mind the bigotry.) By that phrase he meant a kind of basic dishonesty in prewar life, a smug overconfidence that needed to be excised from postwar life, and a self-congratulatory love of abstractions and pretensions and patriotic pieties that clouded judgment and, horrifyingly, paved the way for even more wars of national honor and economic precedence. Hemingway was to call this slither the "big words," as we have seen, and Ho, while living in Paris as Quoc, railed continually in speeches and magazine articles against French colonial lies and pretensions. Both of them were to learn that Victorian slither, with its commitment to official mendacity and its chronic love of violence, was the enemy.

≡ ≡ ≡

Hemingway's home life just after his return from the Great War was all about Victorian slither. This we gather from many of the excellent short stories he wrote during his Paris sojourn. His domineering, pietistic mother appears in many of his early short stories, not to mention in his letters to friends and family during his young adult years, and so does his weak father, whose Christian ethics and good sense kept him from confronting his wife about her domineering ways. Grace and Clarence Hemingway were far from soul mates, but on one matter they agreed wholeheartedly: there was a way to be a good Christian, and that way had much more to do with good manners, conventional life goals, and an obedient spirit toward parental and governmental authority than it did with, say, healing the sick, feeding the hungry, or loving one's neighbor. The stories in which his parents appear, especially those Hemingway wrote in Paris during the 1920s, are a window into the Victorian mindset as he experienced it.

Perhaps the best of these stories, at least for our understanding of Hemingway's growing frustration with his Victorian training as a young adult, is "Soldier's Home," which he published in 1925 after a burst of writing we now know was his emergence as a major literary talent.[1] The story, with its ambiguous apostrophe (the soldier *is* home, or this house is the soldier's *home*, or this damaged soldier should be in a therapeutic *soldier's home*), tells the tale of an American Great War veteran's first weeks home from the war. It is clearly necessary to read the story as a response to a postwar world of veterans returning home, but it is also a window into certain American values of the staid, pious, self-deluding kind. In this story, Hemingway exploits the distance between Harold Krebs's experience as a very young war veteran and his parents' contrasting innocence as parochial Americans who, like many others in early twentieth-century America, did not want to know the truth about combat, lest their pieties and patriotism be disturbed.

Harold, we are told, went to "a Methodist college in Kansas,"[2] and his deeply conventional parents must certainly have approved of the choice, with its hint of *in loco parentis* strictness. Even in these postwar days, and even though there is a wartime photo revealing that, while in Europe, their son consorted with women his hometown neighbors would judge "fast" (the community, Krebs recalls, recently judged "fast" even local girls who bobbed their hair), Krebs's parents refuse to regard him as a self-regulating adult.[3] They ration his use of the family car, show little interest in his wartime experiences, and monitor his progress toward the one proper life goal: combining marriage to a good woman with a remunerative career. They treat him like an indolent teenager, and while he tries to overcome a strange ennui he has felt since arriving home from the war, he willingly accepts that role—to their irritation. He spends his days sleeping in, reading library books on the family porch during early afternoons, and then walking to a dark, cool pool room for some afternoon fun. In the evenings, he practices his clarinet and reads some more. These innocuous activities seem to be his way of resisting his family's goals for him while taking care not to offend them too deeply, lest he cause a real conflict to erupt.

Krebs's habits are hardly those of a libertine or a lost soul, but he has his parents worried. Perhaps they can tell, as the reader can, that he has suffered some mental injury during the war, that his lassitude and blunted emotions have an origin in combat terrors and stresses. Krebs actively avoids any talk of meeting women or taking steps toward a career. He is obsessed with his own tendency to lie about his combat experiences, either to entertain friends with battlefield tales he knows about but did not actually experience, or to conceal just how much he enjoyed meeting the demands of combat, including, presumably, killing or trying to kill. In his mental distress, he talks to himself in a kind of repetitive singsong: "He did not want any consequences. He did not want any consequences ever again. He wanted to live along without consequences."[4] His parents have other ideas: "The boys [in our town] are all settling down," Krebs's mother tells him in the story's moment of crisis. "They're all determined to get somewhere; you can see that boys like Charley Simmons are on their way to being really a credit to the community."[5] Her doctrines, we see, are certainly Victorian. She believes in conforming to the community's view, forged in church, of what it means to be worthwhile. He is to be a conforming member of the then-emerging consumer society.

The story ends with two cleverly parallel scenes that illustrate the emptiness of both Krebs's retreat from life decisions and his parents' Victorian dream of what it means to "be a credit to the community." First, Krebs's favorite little sister cajoles him into coming to watch her play a game of indoor softball. She teases and cajoles Krebs until he admits, at her insistence, that he loves her best. Then she insists on his attending her game to watch her play. This coercion seems innocent and sweet enough until, in a subsequent scene, Krebs's mother begins to use the same technique to pursue larger game. First she offers Krebs the car to use on certain evenings so that he will begin to meet the girls who will make him settle down to work. "We want you to enjoy yourself," she assures her son. "But you are going to have to settle down to work, Harold." She reveals to Krebs that his father is waiting in his downtown realty office for him to visit so that they can have a talk about careers. When Krebs tries to end the conversation before his mother is ready by asking if she is finished, she shows us where her daughter got her cajoling ways. "Don't you love your mother, dear boy?" she asks.

Krebs, nauseated by lies he has told already and unwilling to tell one more, replies simply, "No." And his mother, who has no wish to understand this refusal to play her game, who has no impulse to explore the genuine underlying mixture of familial love and psychological need for independence and postwar hurt that prompted his unkind answer, bursts into tears. She cries so hard that she cannot, or will not, reply to his apologies. Eventually she tells Krebs that when he was a baby, she held him "next to [her] heart." He in his turn begins to call her Mummy. She insists that Krebs pray with her. He is too embarrassed to comply, so she does the praying. While she utters her prayer, Krebs thinks about the one final scene of this kind he will have to endure before he can move to Kansas City for an independent adult life. It will be a showdown with his father about going to his office, which Krebs has no intention of doing, no matter what plans his parents have hatched for him or how much they pressure him to conform to local ways.[6]

We know that this domineering, coercive, and blunderingly pietistic parenting was modeled after Grace and Clarence Hemingway's ways. Indeed, in creating the Krebses, Hemingway may have soft-pedaled his parents' coercions. Our best example of their Victorian attitude concerns a story I mentioned earlier, the one about their reaction to Ernest's story of Greek refugees fleeing their settlements in Turkey after Kemal Atatürk's forces expelled them. I noted the dismissive and perhaps chauvinistic character to their distaste for the story. As it happens, their reaction was even more stunning and more revealing of the Victorian mind in post–Great War America.

In the story Ernest wrote after witnessing desperate refugees on a reporting trip to Anatolia, which is actually a brief prose poem of fewer than 150 words, Hemingway depicts the sad caravan of refugees, focusing his viewer's attention on one young woman who is giving birth on a moving farm cart: "There was a woman having a kid with a young girl holding a blanket over her and crying," he writes. The sentence fragment he offers next, "Scared sick looking at it," makes us wonder whether it is the young girl or Hemingway's narrator who is more frightened by this medical nightmare.[7] For reasons I have suggested, possibly a distaste for nonwhite, non-Christian others and certainly a preference for stories with clear spiritual lessons, Clarence found such stories ignoble. He wrote to Ernest, "The brutal you have surely shown the world. Look for the joyous, uplifting, and optimistic and spiritual in character. It is present if found." Then he admonished his son: "Remember God holds us each responsible to do our best." Ernest seems to have felt that he had done his best to show compassion for suffering neighbors. In any case, he did not follow his father's advice. He continued to write evocative and provocative stories communicating the trials of living hungry and cold and lonely in the conflict-riven modern world created by powerful men's decisions in distant cities. That had become his Parisian *métier*.

When Hemingway received his father's letter, he was upset by his parents' lack of understanding and support. But luckily for him, he never learned the full extent of their distaste for his work. As one recent biographer of Hemingway's first wife discovered, "[Clarence] Hemingway wrote a friend that he'd rather see Ernest dead than writing in raw detail about such vulgar subjects as war and fleeing refugees."[8]

Here was the Victorian world in full flower: spiritual superiority united with flippant talk about how and when the young should live and die. Surely Clarence Hemingway used hyperbole when speaking of his son's life this way. Surely Ernest's sin, writing about Balkan refugees, was not a mortal one in his father's eyes. Yet the attitude implied by the remark is shockingly coldhearted, seemingly unloving. The most alarming thing about wishing your son dead in the interest of family or community honor is that the sentiment syncs with wartime rhetoric. As Hemingway's "big words" passage makes clear, pro-war Victorians saw their sons' deaths as vain only if the battle causing that death was lost. But if the war itself was essentially vain, and if the young men who died on its battlefields really died to secure profits for governing and business elites, then there was no way to die sweetly and becomingly for one's country or one's neighbor's liberty. Dr. and Mrs. Hemingway were not likely to consider such a possibility. Judging by his callous remark, Clarence was one of those who sent sons into the trenches of a dubious war without examining closely the justice of the conflict, and judging by his lack of sympathy for Anatolian refugees, he was also one who felt little sympathy for suffering colonial laborers in distant lands—so long as those colonials were hearing the holy Christian scriptures.

The war precipitated a dramatic rethinking, especially in artistic and literary circles, of this kind of parenting and teaching. The English war poet Wilfred Owen made this rethinking the foundation for his tragically brief career as a poet. He knew about the waste of Europe's sons, and he worked hard to tell the world about the problem. Before he died leading his men across a canal in Northern France during the final week of the Great War, he wrote some startling poems about insights he had gained while serving at the front. During a 1917 wartime rest in a treatment center in Craiglockhart, Scotland, which Owen took as a cure for shell shock, he came under the care of a physician who discovered that the young soldier loved writing poetry. Dr. W. H. R. Rivers encouraged Owen to write new poems about the war as a kind of psychoanalytical treatment, an attempt to purge or master some of his worst memories of battle. The result of Owen's subsequent writing is a beautiful series of poems expressing love of comrades in arms on the one hand, and hatred of war on the other. Many of us encounter these poems in school and, if we are lucky, hear them sung in Benjamin Britten's beautiful *War Requiem*.

One of the best of these poems is "The Parable of the Old Man and the Young," a retelling and updating of the biblical story of Abraham and Isaac, which turns on God's strange command that Abraham kill his son in an act of ritual sacrifice. Abraham is released from this horrible task once he proves his trust in God. The poem places that tale of a father's willing sacrifice of a son, blessedly interrupted by God, into the trenches of the Great War, and with a different conclusion. In Genesis 22, the horrible sacrifice of a son is halted by a just and loving God, who provides a ram as a substitute sacrifice. Owen's version of the Old Testament story offers a caustic new ending that indicts the wartime generals and governing elites. It is a satire on their Victorian overconfidence in their goodness:

> So Abram rose, and clave the wood, and went,
> And took the fire with him, and a knife.
> And as they sojourned both of them together,
> Isaac the first-born spake and said, My Father,
> Behold the preparations, fire and iron,
> But where the lamb for this burnt-offering?
> Then Abram bound the youth with belts and straps,
> and builded parapets and trenches there,
> And stretchèd forth the knife to slay his son.
> When lo! an angel called him out of heaven,
> Saying, Lay not thy hand upon the lad,
> Neither do anything to him. Behold,
> A ram, caught in a thicket by its horns;
> Offer the Ram of Pride instead of him.
>
> But the old man would not so, but slew his son,
> And half the seed of Europe, one by one.[9]

With savage, accusatory irony, the kind both Ho and Hemingway were about to learn from Paris's avant-garde artists, Owen makes his point. He reminds us in our complacent patriotism that the old men who sent European boys to their deaths in huge numbers between 1914 and 1918 knew Genesis 22 perfectly well—indeed, regarded the story as part of Holy Scripture so essential, so precious that it ought to be taught to the world's unchurched in, say, the rice paddies and rain forests of Indochina. These old men should therefore have realized, Owen implies, that God's wish is to spare the young, not to waste or merely spend their lives in wartime. Meanwhile, the Great War was so wasteful of precious lives that individual daily attacks sometimes killed more British or French or

German boys—or boys from the colonies—than the fifty-eight thousand American servicemen and -women who died in the entire Vietnam
War. And those many boys may have died, on any given day between
1914 and 1918 at the Somme or Passchendaele or Ypres, for just a few
yards' worth of gained ground and no real strategic benefit.

We see the same old-man's arrogance and misdirected piety animat-
ing the French colonists who gained control of Indochina in the late
nineteenth century, which means that Ho suffered under the pressures of
Victorian cant as much as Hemingway did. Our source for this information is Ho's own writing during the Paris years, a series of documentary
essays describing ongoing living conditions in colonial Annam. Thanks
to those stories and a few other sources, it is possible to conclude definitively that during his days in colonial Vietnam and during his time in
Paris too, Ho was shown repeatedly that his life as a colonial laborer was
as casually expendable as Hemingway's was as a volunteer in wartime
trenches. Probably much more so.

Historians regard the French *mission civilisatrice*, or civilizing mission, in Vietnam as a Victorian program for the promotion of Catholicism and, because of France's own Enlightenment revolution, the
promotion of advanced modern science—all in one coercive package.
This was the pretense, at least. The French who most wanted to civilize
the Indochinese had little regard for the elaborate and developed civilization they found in Vietnam when they arrived, a sophisticated and
proud culture the Vietnamese had developed and fought to protect long
before relenting to the French, who governed by superior force of arms.
While there must have been well-meaning French educators and priests
and nuns and managers in Vietnam, all too many of the French colonizers wanted to exploit the Vietnamese for economic gain and, it seems, to
gain sick psychological satisfactions from the bullying of the locals with
unkind acts of racial and religious superiority.

Unlike these openly supremacist French colonial businessmen in
Vietnam, colonial officials tended to avoid direct, racist talk about the
Vietnamese, or, as they called them, Annamites. They wanted instead to
create the illusion of high-minded intentions, so they sent coded messages, the kind we now call dog whistles, employing a subtler rhetoric they distributed in a variety of venues and media. Historian Alice
Conklin helpfully lists them: "world's fairs, national symbols and

commemorations, the military, domesticity and the home, government circulars, law courts, legal codes, school textbooks, imperial propaganda, the new social sciences, marriage and paternity debates, missionary societies, health manuals—and the list goes on." She suggests that these "are seen as so many sites for the constant reinvention and assertion of notions of French civilization and the colonial need for it."[10] Conklin is speaking here about the role of propaganda in what Marxists call ideology: the ongoing creation of an attitude, a belief structure so embedded in the unconscious that it is invisible to us, like the air we breathe. The task of ideology, defined this way, is to keep the status quo unquestioned and undisturbed so that those who benefit most from current practices continue to reap those benefits. Ideology of this kind is far more insidious than the more overt pieties Hemingway attacked, though their foundation and purpose are similar. During the time of French colonialism, citizens back home in the metropole needed to be shown that they were righteous, just, helpful, and dedicated to a noble future, both for themselves and for their dusky, primitive adoptees (as many of them thought of colonial *indigènes*) in the Far East or the Caribbean or North Africa.

The 1907 World's Fair in Paris is a startling example of this training in Victorian colonialism. Traces of the fair remain more than one hundred years later, a kind of "junkyard of French colonial history," according to one writer; a tragic theme park filled with symbols and souvenirs of the colonial project.[11] In the Bois de Vincennes, a giant park just outside the ring road to the east of Paris, not far at all from Ho and Hemingway's old neighborhood of la Mouffe, is the *Stade de Baseball-Pershing*, a baseball stadium named after the general who led American forces in the First World War. Right next to the ball field is the *Jardin d'agronomie tropical*, or Tropical Gardens, now a few weedy acres holding a scattering of decaying and burned-out pavilions. Only the Indochinese pavilion has been restored, for some reason: a cream-painted brick building resembling a greenhouse, decorated with pink horizontal stripes and topped with a dome. The building gleams white among the weeds and peeling paint of the oriental gates and grass-roofed African huts and broken statuary of the 1907 colonial exposition. Above the building's great double door is a Greek Revival frieze with "*Indo-Chine*" declared in giant letters.

Some scholars call this garden a human zoo because in 1907 French organizers animated their pavilions and displays about Laos, Tunisia, the

Congo, and other French colonial lands with living representatives of each colony. These native Southeast Asian and African people were displayed in typical, or rather stereotypical, clothing and home settings. One visitor writes that witnessing Indochinese people in conical hats, butchering a dog for their next meal, was an odd sight in a Parisian park.[12] Postcolonial scholars concede that these indigenous colonial performers were paid, and that they volunteered to go to Paris in order to be on display. They were not slaves. But the *indigènes* could not have known that they were going to be dressed and displayed and even bodily measured as though they were freaks, rare specimens of formerly unknown species.

Or that they were going to be improperly cared for. Twenty-seven of the *indigènes* died of disease and failure to acclimate during the term of their display. These dead *indigènes* were buried in a park then called, ironically, the *Jardin d'acclimitation*—so named because agronomists were curious to see whether tropical species such as palm trees and bamboo could in fact acclimate and grow successfully in hothouses in the gardens, surviving the European climate. Historians are particularly offended, and rightly so, that social scientists of the time failed to condemn the exhibition or its methods, not even after the large number of deaths by disease. On the contrary, these researchers gathered data, such as measuring Annamites' cranial circumferences, to support racialist theories then in vogue, theories that placed the French and their Enlightenment science and Christian seriousness at the top of an evolutionary pyramid. Colonial subjects were to be found, of course, just above apes and other quasi-sentient animals—and far below colonial bureaucrats.

The young man in Vietnam's central highlands named Nguyen Tat Thanh, the future Ho Chi Minh, did not experience French colonialism as a carnival performance or even as a mere political and economic disadvantage. Under colonialism, he was less than fully human. He would never vote for his representatives in government nor be free to raise his voice in protest over a shift in policy or practice. He would never receive a professional-level education in Annam, because only an inferior imitation of French universities was available to the indigenous people there. Even though he was on his way to receiving an elite secondary education designed by the French administrators to equip young Vietnamese with excellent managerial skills, he would never supervise a Frenchman— even if he was allowed to complete that education, and no matter how

much talent and good judgment he displayed. As historians Pierre Brocheux and Daniel Hémery show, French colonization was built on the
dubious idea that France had the duty "to bring modern civilization to
backward people."[13] The French believed that people of color around the
world were pagan, which is to say uncivilized and incapable of spiritual
response to the world. This was the assertion of French premier Jules
Ferry in a series of speeches in the mid-1880s, which shaped what Brocheux and Hémery call the "code of colonial conduct" shaping colonialism into the next century. Ferry argued

> that the superior races have a right because they have a duty. They
> have the duty to civilize the inferior races. . . . In the history of
> earlier centuries these duties, gentlemen, have often been misun-
> derstood; and certainly when the Spanish soldiers and explorers
> introduced slavery into Central America, they did not fulfill their
> duty as men of a higher race. . . . But, in our time, I maintain that
> European nations acquit themselves with generosity, with gran-
> deur, and with sincerity of this superior civilizing duty.[14]

Ferry's code essentially states that genuine European gentlemen teach and
lead the "inferior races" outside of Europe, never stooping to exploit them.
    Under this code, the colonial subject, even a young man like Thanh,
who had read Montesquieu and Rousseau and was deemed by his French
literature teacher to be "an intelligent and very distinguished student,"[15]
was to be treated like a child. The French tended to state this claim
directly. There is the example of the labor recruiter who "described the
coolies as credulous, improvident children." And there was the Christian idealist who claimed that the French "usually disembarked in Indochina determined to be on the best possible terms with the Annamese,"
but after the usual series of "small misunderstanding[s]" accepted the
master-and-servant relationship as best. Far from seeing the best in the
Indochinese, even early in their Southeast Asian experiences, the French
colonialists operated by a stereotype of the Indochinese, a developed
and extended one about the characters of the people in different regions.
According to these stereotypes, Laotians were "heedless and sensual,"
Cambodians were "passive and not particularly sharp," the Annamese
were "intelligent, proud, and secretive," the Chinese were "active and

shifty," and the Malabar were simply "deceitful." This kind of chauvinism obviously made dignity for colonial subjects impossible, and stood in the way of fair and genuine opportunity.[16]

Brocheux and Hémery describe the experience of Vietnamese students who had studied in France and then journeyed back to Indochina alongside French citizens. Once their ship had left European waters and crossed the Red Sea, the French behaved more coolly toward Vietnamese university graduates. As the historians note, a sense of colonial social hierarchy began to be reasserted through language, as "*tutoiement* (use of the familiar/disrespectful second-person address *tu*)" began to be heard when the French spoke to the Vietnamese, rather than "*vouvoiement* (the formal/respectful *vous*)." Whether you were a "rifleman or a physician," Hémery and Brocheux continue, you could be addressed over-familiarly and disrespectfully.

Humiliations are one thing. Murders are another. During his childhood and youth in Vietnam, Thanh witnessed far worse than personal insults. French colonialists in Indochina felt great freedom to beat their Indochinese workers, even those in white-collar positions. Sometimes these beatings were fatal—even though the offense was simply alleged laziness, or tardiness in completing a task, or even refusing a French man or woman a better seat at the cinema. Brocheux and Hémery, whose *Indochina: An Ambiguous Colonization: 1858–1954* (2009) is an excellent, readable history of Indochinese colonialism, know that the testimony of *indigènes* may be suspect, so as further evidence they offer the words of a French lawyer named Georges Garros.[17] Garros tells about a typical colonial situation, one that seems based in particular fact: A colonist's "farmers" (read: field-hands) run away. Furious, the French landlord patrols his property with his Chassepot rifle in hand. A "peaceful *ta dien* [farmer], innocent of any wrongdoing but looking something like a 'marauder' to the 'lord of the place,'" skirts the property. The rifle goes off—by itself, claims the landlord—killing the Vietnamese farmer. The French landlord must go to trial, but the process is rigged and thus predictable: "Legal intervention, involuntary homicide, eight days in jail, suspended sentence." The French landlord goes back to his work, Garros writes, and to his rifle. Needless to say, "the Annamese does not understand this solution."[18]

This is the kind of story that tells us why Ho's relentless pursuer during his Paris years, Minister of Colonies Albert Sarraut, once warned his compatriots in Indochina, using alienated and inadequate language that focuses on French benefits rather than Vietnamese justice, "Watch out for racial verdicts!"

Ho Chi Minh witnessed even worse crimes. After his expulsion from the National Academy, Thanh took a number of jobs in a wandering journey southward toward Saigon, where he eventually caught his ship for France. One day a Vietnamese port city he was visiting was hit by a typhoon. As biographer William Duiker tells the tale, "French officials ordered Vietnamese dockworkers to dive into the water to salvage ships." This indifference to Vietnamese lives is appalling, but the situation then turned even more tragic and surreal. "According to Ho Chi Minh's later account, many Vietnamese died in the process, to the apparent amusement of Europeans watching from the shore."

In another terrible story from his travels, Ho recalls African men in Dakar sent to their deaths by drowning in nearly identical circumstances.

> The French in France are all good. But the French colonialists are very cruel and inhumane. It is the same everywhere. At home I have seen such things happening in Phan Rang. The French burst out laughing while our compatriots drowned for their sake. To the Colonialists, the life of an Asian or an African is not worth a penny.[19]

Long before the Great War, we see, the French colonial administrators sent sons of empire carelessly to their deaths, just as carelessly as their national leaders sent all the sons of Greater France to their deaths in the trenches, in the skies, and on the seas during the war. Daughters of empire were at mortal risk in the colonies too, prone to alcohol and opium addictions and diseases associated with prostitution, all products of social demoralization. These addictions often led women into unwanted careers as *con gai* sexual companions, or as simple prostitutes.

Nguyen Ai Quoc and Ernest Hemingway were about to learn that the only way to make this suffering known to postwar citizens of Paris and eventually to a larger world was through documentary journalism and expressive art, and they quickly learned how to produce both. Their styles would be different, and eventually, so would their aims. Quoc would produce the better propaganda, more impersonal and shockingly documentary, while Hemingway would produce the better art, including, as we will see, artistically crafted news stories for the *Toronto Star*. Some of the young men's readers may have found their writings vulgar, as Hemingway's father did, but between the two of them, Hemingway and Quoc produced something like the brash new art that was called for during the Great War by Dada founder Marcel Duchamp:

> The war will produce a severe direct art. One readily understands this when one realizes the growing hardness of feeling in Europe, one might almost say the utter callousness with which people are learning to receive the news of the death of those nearest and dearest to them. Before the war the death of a son in a family was received with utter, abject woe, but today it is merely part of a huge universe of grief, which hardly seems to concern any one individual.[20]

Hemingway and Quoc both addressed a huge project, each in his own way—helping the people living in the so-called Western civilization to heal the universe of grief they had created, to admit their errors, and to learn to love their sons again rather than wishing them dead.

# 4

## DOWN AND OUT IN LONDON

### BA FROM 1911 TO 1918

It is time to return to Ho Chi Minh's story, a tale of his wanderings from Vietnam to the United States—a destination we can confirm with only one brief letter and a postcard sent from Boston in 1912—to England, his last stop before Paris. The tale about the London period, from 1914 to 1918, is especially telling. It becomes apparent that Ba, as Ho was known during the Great War, grew serious about poverty and hunger while living in London, partly because he was cold and hungry there himself during that time, but also because he had important lessons to learn about wage disparity and workers' rights from some very surprising others.

≡ ≡ ≡

Ho—or Thanh, as he was then called—was expelled from the National Academy for promising *indigènes* immediately after the Short Hairs protest had been put down. The day after the turmoil along the Perfume River in Hue, a group of French investigators figured out who the tall, dark young man near the head of the protest really was. They showed up at the academy at nine in the morning expecting to find that the perpetrator, Thanh, had fled, but were surprised to find him in his seat in the classroom. Though he had hid out at a friend's house the night before,

Thanh had apparently concluded that he had done nothing wrong and should not be in any kind of trouble. But the officer in charge disagreed, declaring, "I have orders to request that this troublemaker be dismissed from school."[1]

Thanh was dismissed on the spot, which meant that he had not only lost his future as a colonial manager—or a colonial manager with a secret mission to destabilize the colonial administration, perhaps—but he had also lost his room and board. With no intention of returning to his childhood home, he was on his own now, and homeless.

After wandering southward for a number of months, in the fall of 1910 Thanh took a teaching assistant's job. He seemed to be finding his footing as an ordinary laborer in the French colony, but in early 1911 he left the job suddenly, and under a political shadow. There were rumors that Thanh had left because French officials had discovered his where-abouts and had placed the school under surveillance.[2] It seems he had begun to seek out anti-colonialist friends of his father's. Somehow, the French got wind of these activities, so Thanh was forced to leave his teaching post without explanation during the middle of a term. A French Indochinese police report of the time warned that Thanh "is strongly sus-pected of complicity" with two known Annamese dissidents, Phan Boi Chau and Phan Chu Trinh. (The police could not have been far wrong because Trinh would one day become Thanh's roommate in Paris, where the latter called himself Quoc.) After leaving his teaching post, homeless and indigent once again, Thanh worked odd jobs while making his way down the coast to the Paris of the Orient, the cosmopolitan city of Sai-gon. From there his journey to France and to fame would begin.

In June of 1911, in one of those fortunate accidents that lead many of us into our callings, Thanh signed on to work as a cook's assistant on board the *Amiral Latouche-Tréville*, a steamship sailing from Sai-gon for French ports. It is difficult to know how carefully Thanh had thought out his decision to leave Vietnam. He may have been sent abroad for an education in resistance by those nationalist rebels who knew his father, or he may have simply followed his wanderlust and disgust for colonial injustices.

Many years later, Ho told a story about sailing from Vietnam that first time. Nominally, the story is told by a friend of Thanh's in Saigon, Tran Dan Tien, now regarded by scholars as fictitious. One day, Tran

Dan Tien bought Nguyen Tat Thanh some ice cream. "He was astonished," Tran reports, "because it was the first time he had ever eaten it." Then the young men have an important conversation:

> "Hey, Lê, do you love your country?"
> Astonished, I replied, "Well, of course!"
> "Can you keep a secret?"
> "Yes."
> "I want to go abroad, to visit France and other countries. When I have seen what they have done, I will return to help my compatriots. But if I leave alone, there will be more risk if, for example, I get sick. . . . Do you want to come with me?"
> "But where will we find the money for the voyage?"
> "Here's our money," he said, showing me his two hands. "We will work."[3]

For the next few years, he would work, and work hard—throwing out trash, peeling vegetables, shoveling snow, and generally scrambling for a meager living. So began a journey that would lead to the presidency of North Vietnam.

Any work on board the ship would have been good enough. He was desperate to escape from French Indochina, with all its injustices and indignities, and he wanted to learn some way to fight colonial power. Going by the minimalist pseudonym Ba, which would be his name until he made Paris his home at the Great War's end, he traveled the world aimlessly until August of 1914, when he settled in London because the war had begun to make work as a sailor who made long visits to interesting ports too risky.

Along the way, Ba even visited the United States in 1913. He may have lived in Harlem for a time, though his claim to have heard a speech there by Marcus Garvey, the Jamaican Black Nationalist and civil rights leader, has never been definitively confirmed.[4] It is the kind of detail—two great justice-centered nationalists of color meeting accidentally years before achieving their greatest notoriety—that our sources, his communist propagandists in North Vietnam, might have been tempted to invent (as they invented his late-life virginity and chaste marriage to the Vietnamese people). It is also impossible to confirm that Ba traveled in the

American South, where he supposedly witnessed a lynching and came to understand the racial pathologies of turn-of-the-century America. He may or may not have seen a lynching, but would not have required such an unsubtle illustration of American racism to grasp its character and importance. There were thousands of lynchings across the United States in the first two decades of the century, many of them covered by newspapers around the world, and racist provocations were common in the American cities Ba apparently visited.

What we can confirm is that he lived in Boston in 1913, and that he parlayed his experience as a shipboard cook's assistant into a job as baker and kitchen assistant in the city's best hotel, the Parker House. This was an important step in his personal growth, allowing him soon to find work in London and then to move on to Paris. While at the Parker House he must have made serious strides in his understanding of Western food and its preparation, moving as he did from galley boy on a steamship, washing pots and pans and throwing out the garbage, to under-chef in the bakery of a fine-dining restaurant catering to Boston's wealthy elite. By legend, Ba was a baker, and if so, he would have learned to make two American classics invented and still available and celebrated at the hotel: Parker House rolls and Boston cream pie. His new work surely required discipline, meticulousness, high energy, and artistry, talents he would turn to other purposes later. He must have learned a lot of English too.

We do not know why Ba left the Parker House, or precisely when, but most biographers agree that by 1914, the year the Great War began for Europeans (the United States would not enter the war until 1917), he was in London. There, he claims in his late-life memoirs, on the strength of his professional cooking experience in Boston and a brief stint at a modest London restaurant, he again found work in an important kitchen, the one serving the restaurant of the Carlton Hotel. His boss there was known as "the Chef of Kings and King of Chefs," and was the inventor of Peach Melba and of hollandaise and Bordelaise sauces, author of the *haute cuisine* bible, *Le Guide Culinaire*—Auguste Escoffier.

Our sources for this phase in Ba's life are admittedly dubious. Late in his life, while calling himself Ho Chi Minh and battling American forces in Vietnam, Ho and his North Vietnamese propagandists circulated and promoted the story about his time during the Great War working for

Escoffier. We do not know whether Ho did in fact work for Escoffier, or whether his writers embroidered a true story about his work in a hotel restaurant kitchen in London, or whether they made the story up out of whole cloth. Many of Ho's biographers accept the Escoffier employment as basically true, possibly because the tale is worth exploring and would have taken great imagination to invent. In any case, the tale tells us a great deal about Ho's political views as they were crystalizing during the war, as he worked with hungry laborers, many of them colonial emigrants like himself, while serving the comfortably sated super-rich. No propagandist invented the wage disparity then prevalent in London, and Ho had to learn about unionization and solidarity somewhere.

In his ghostwritten memoirs, Ho Chi Minh tells about the day when, as lowly Ba the busboy, he first talked with Escoffier at the Carlton and seized the occasion to perform a remarkable feat. Supposedly, he pricked the great chef's conscience:

> Each of us had to take turns in the clearing up. The waiters, after attending the customers, had to clear all the plates and send them by means of an electric lift to the kitchen. Then our job was to separate china and silver for cleaning. When it came to Ba's turn he was very careful. Instead of throwing out all the bits left over, which were often a quarter of a chicken or a huge piece of steak, etc., Ba kept them clean and sent them back to the kitchen. Noticing this, the chef Escoffier asked Ba: "Why didn't you throw these remains into the rubbish as the others do?"
>
> "These things shouldn't be thrown away. You could give them to the poor."
>
> "My dear young friend, listen to me!" Chef Escoffier seemed to be pleased and said, smiling: "Leave your revolutionary ideas aside for a moment, and I will teach you the art of cooking, which will bring you a lot of money. Do you agree?"

Ho then offers the moral lesson of this scene in the rhythms of the King James Bible:

> And Chef Escoffier did not leave Ba at the job of washing dishes but took him to the cake section, where he got higher wages.

It was indeed a great event in the kitchen for it was the first time the "kitchen king" had done that sort of thing.[5]

If "that sort of thing" means listening to his lowest-paid workers and assisting them in getting better wages and benefits, then, as we will see, this was hardly the "first time" for Escoffier. It turns out that he was a much more complex man than Uncle Ho wanted to admit in Vietnam War propaganda.

Like Ho, Escoffier was a genuine revolutionary, one of those impressive figures who can deftly ride a wave of change in social life. The King of Chefs capitalized on a moment in the late nineteenth century when *haute cuisine* shifted from the luxurious private dining rooms of royal and noble families to fine restaurants catering to old money and new money alike. His diners included aristocratic courtiers on the one hand and powerful industrialists and financiers and entertainment stars on the other. Like our present day, this Gilded Age or *Belle Époque* was a time of enormous wage disparity between the working and the executive classes. In this world of stark class differences, Escoffier's restaurants filled a perceived need: they provided a place and a form of consumption that allowed the economic elite to confirm their special, godlike status. In one sense, Escoffier's dining rooms were like today's stadium luxury boxes. They were reserved for the super-rich, a place where they could feel apart and above and could flaunt their ability to consume conspicuously. The goal, then as now, was to spend a great deal of money on very brief and essentially trivial moments of pleasure—to show that you could.

Escoffier tells us directly who dined in his restaurants, such as London's Savoy and Carlton, and Paris's Ritz: "At the dinner hour, one could see . . . the richest people in England and the world, princes and princesses, dukes and duchesses, great barons of the banking world, political figures, ministers, and also great artists, writers, journalists, theatre stars, etc."[6] Among the customers, Escoffier's obvious favorites were "the great diva Nellie Melba"; actress Sarah Bernhardt; the Prince of Wales, Albert Edward; and, until he began to make war on France in 1914, Kaiser Wilhelm II of Germany.[7] Escoffier served these luminaries absolutely amazing meals, which he describes proudly in his memoirs. It is interesting to imagine Ba, the future Ho Chi Minh, working and moving about in such an opulent restaurant—the thin young student from a two-acre farm in central Vietnam, trained in Confucius and Montesquieu, acquainted with the hungry and downtrodden, baking treats to be carried out into a room gilded in gold and sparkling with crystal.

Escoffier has an amusing habit as a writer. He likes to describe a posh event—say, a dinner the Prince of Wales once gave to guests in town for an important royal wedding—and then to offer the full menu centered on its own page:

### Menu for the Dinner
### Presided over by the Prince of Wales

*Melon Cantaloup*

*Tortue Claire Saint-Germain*

*Truite Saumonée Royale*

*Whitebait à la Diable*

*Mousse de Jambon au Velouté*

*Epinards au Beurre*

*Selle d'Agneau à la Broche*

*Haricots Verts à l'Anglaise*

*Pommes de Terre à la Crème*

*Suprêmes de Volaille en Gelée à l'Alsacienne*

*Cailles Souvarow*

*Salade de Blanc de Romaine*

*Asperges d'Argenteuil*

*Biscuit Glacé à l'Ananas*

*Fraises au Maraschino*

*Laitances*

*Café Turc*

*Vins: Amontillado*

*Milk-Punch*

*Bercasther Doctor, 1874*

*Brown Cantenac, 1888*

*Pommery Brut, 1884*

*Moët Cuvée, 1884*

*Château Léoville Poyferré, 1878*

*Grande Fine, 1865*

*Groft's Old Port, 1858*

*Curacao Marnier, Extra Sec*[8]

It is impossible to imagine what it must have been like to consume a meal like this—one that included sauced dishes of turtle, trout, white fish, ham mousse, and saddle of lamb, accompanied by potatoes in cream, jellied chicken, quail, half a dozen vegetables, more than one dessert course, and a battalion of wines, punches, ports, and liqueurs. When Escoffier cooked your dinner, and when the Prince of Wales offered it to you, surely you would not pick at any of the dishes or leave some of them untouched while you displayed your ready wit to your dining partners. Surely you ate what you could and then waited until the waiter carried away your burden of gluttony.

Incredibly, Escoffier laments in his memoir that such a menu represents a concession to patrons who no longer have the stomach or time to eat a proper meal. He recalls the days when diners sat down to a banquet ready and willing to spend real time at table, much more time than the paltry couple of hours gentlemen and ladies spent dining in his day. In former times, when Escoffier was young and *service à la française* was the norm, twenty to thirty elaborate dishes would be placed on the table all at once, in grand, symmetrical displays anchored by an architectural, confectionary *pièce montée*, which might be a royal sugar sculpture of the Arc de Triomphe or a topless goddess holding aloft lanterns decorated with parrots. For hours waiters would serve the diners whatever they wished to taste from this buffet. After a time, the first twenty or thirty dishes might be carried away and replaced by new ones, elegantly and symmetrically arranged on a great table once again. The dishes might be replaced once or twice more during the evening. When dessert was served, there might be another twenty or thirty sweet dishes placed on the table, and the marathon of eating continued.

Now, the old man grumbles, a meal might consist of "only" soup, a fish course in a wine and butter sauce, two roasted meats with potatoes and seasonal vegetables served with *sauce béarnaise* or hollandaise, a roasted fowl flavored with truffles and served with a rice pilaf, and two or three desserts with assorted handmade candies. Escoffier reports that in each of his London restaurants he used 150 pounds of butter per day, more than a pound per patron. Even so, the meals he prepared struck him as conspicuously light.

And what was Ba's reaction to this kind of epicurean excess? We simply do not know what he thought about the economic foundation of his work in Escoffier's kitchen. In the index to Escoffier's memoirs, between *"History of the Isle of Dominica"* and "Horse meat, consumption of," we find no "Ho Chi Minh." Escoffier's memoir does include a marginal note declaring, without naming a source, that on the night in 1914 when Germany invaded Belgium, kicking off the Great War battles that would ultimately threaten Paris, Ho Chi Minh, "the future communist leader of North Vietnam," prepared the vegetables for a dinner shared by two future English prime ministers, David Lloyd George and Winston Churchill. But this scene is implausibly specific and ironic—with its picture of the communist Ho Chi Minh preparing conservative capitalist Winston Churchill's vegetables.

We ought to be interested in more than such delicious trivia. Here we have Ba working for low wages in the midst of rich and powerful national and cultural leaders, the very people who launched and then publicly supported the Allied cause in the Great War. Historians tell us that once Ba arrived in Paris, he often served his roommates a simple workers' meal of sautéed fresh vegetables seasoned with soy sauce and set on rice, washed down with jasmine tea. This simple fare was an improvement upon the diet of his fellow Vietnamese back in French Indochina. Growing up, he ate what most malnourished Vietnamese colonials ate. For breakfast there was a bowl or two of rice or yams cooked in water, and at noontime, a meal of rice with fresh and pickled vegetables, soy and fish sauces. On rare good days, there might be a bit of fish. In the evening, his people ate more of the plain rice or yams. In his highlands province of Vietnam almost no one could afford to eat fish, so his people were called the "wooden fish people." By tradition, they carried a carved wooden replica of a fish in their pockets when traveling, so that when they visited a street-side food stand and ordered the only meal they could afford, rice seasoned with a sprinkling of fish sauce, they could place the wooden replica fish onto the rice and trick other diners nearby into thinking that they had purchased a full meal.[9] It was a way of saving face, of avoiding the shame of being chronically hungry and poor.

Meanwhile, in London, Ba must have felt outrage at the waste and conspicuous consumption he saw at Escoffier's Carlton. Historians see signs, if not definite historical documentation, of Ba's training in London in unionization and other techniques for championing workers' rights. These associations with union leaders mean that during his time in Escoffier's kitchen, Ba would have begun to critique the Great War effort and the absurd wealth of the one percent. He looked to the revolution brewing in Russia for its promise of the workers' control of economies, a shift that just might topple the corrupt institution of colonialism and the extreme wealth of Gilded Age imperialism.

We know that Ba's life was hard in 1914 and 1915, when he worked extremely menial jobs in London before landing the Carlton job. (Indeed, Ho's life was hard long after he landed that job as well.) He complained in letters to friends that his first London job, sweeping snow at a school, was very uncomfortable for a kid from the tropics: "I sweated all over and yet my hands and my feet were freezing. And it was not easy to break up the icy snow, for it was slippery. After eight hours' work I was completely exhausted." His next job as a boiler operator was also awful: "It was terribly hot in the basement and terribly cold outside. I did not have enough warm clothes and therefore caught cold."[10] His next job, as busboy and dishwasher at the Carlton, required him, as we have seen, to throw away food that was so refined he could never hope to purchase it for himself or his friends. He claims to have objected to this waste and to the negligent disregard for the hungry poor, but his emotions may actually have run hotter; he may have been sickened by it.

Ba was one of a growing number of manual laborers in London then beginning to demand better treatment. Restaurant workers went on strike in 1910 and 1913, just before Ba arrived there. These men protested the long hours they worked, the filthy conditions, and the lack of holidays from work. Ba never participated in such strikes because he was in England while the country was on a war footing. Under pressure from hawks and patriots, rebellious workers set aside most agitation during the course of the war. In the years just prior to the war, labor leaders and leftist sympathizers such as suffragette leader Emmeline Pankhurst were willing to go to prison for the women's vote and for fairer distribution of wealth. But once the war began, many of these agitators ceased agitating and, in some cases, such as Pankhurst's, became so fervently patriotic and anti-German that they joined other women in taunting young Englishmen with the infamous white feathers, handed to men in street clothes to accuse them of cowardice. Some of Ho's biographers point to the prewar strikes and other forms of agitation in wartime London as the original prompts to his own political consciousness and his initial interest in Marxism. The idea is plausible. Both during the war and after, England's labor unions debated whether to adopt communist methods and whether to form an English Communist Party. After October 1917, they debated whether to support the Bolsheviks in their violent, revolutionary takeover of Russia. They wondered whether England was ripe for such a revolution, and if so, whether their lives would be improved if they governed themselves.

It is difficult to imagine Escoffier sympathizing with the strikers, much less viewing socialism as a valid form of social and economic organization. After all, his profits depended upon the continued existence of a very wealthy leisure class with the taste and means to purchase meals in his restaurants. Yet it turns out that Escoffier was not merely a profiteer. If we want to understand Escoffier's actual political commitments, including those Ba might have learned from, and even his deep emotional relationship with food, we have to look back to the 1870s, when his beloved France went to war with the Prussians and he became a prisoner of war. This war was a dress rehearsal for the Great War in the sense that it was an attack by militarist Germans on nominally peaceable France. When fighting broke out in 1870, Escoffier was already an accomplished chef in a chic Paris restaurant that catered to the aristocracy, Le Petit Moulin Rouge. In his memoir, he rages about the treacherous beginnings of this war. He writes, bitterly, "Just as the wolf needs no excuse to devour the lamb, certain politicians need no real reason to decree their carnage— they just make up a reason (for example, the falsified telegram that led to the 1870 war)."[11]

Here Escoffier refers to a treacherous and falsified telegram that prompted Germany and France to declare war on one another, mainly over the question of national honor and the possession of the ethnically blended Franco-German Alsace and Lorraine. As this dubious war began, Escoffier quickly found himself responsible for preparing the food for the officers and men of a frontline division. He was a patriot, and he took his military work seriously, doing everything he could to secure and prepare nourishing food for his officers.[12] In the Franco-Prussian wartime chapters of his memoir he recounts threatening a French farmer with reprisals if he did not make his well available to his unit, as it was the only well nearby where fresh water could be found. Escoffier knew, he tells us, that fighting all day in the summer weather, both men and horses must have "suffered horribly from thirst," and he was determined to do his best to provide them with clean and ample water. He writes of hoarding supplies once it became clear that his division would be surrounded and under siege in Metz. Eventually he had to cope with the end of those supplies. By September he was serving his unit horsemeat, not to answer French tastes but because his division's supply lines had been cut off. Horses, fed meagerly on the leaves of trees because no other feed was available, were the only meat there was to eat. He served "horse stew one day, braised horsemeat the next, macaroni horsemeat the next, horsemeat with lentils the next."[13] His most touching passage is about his encounters with dying horses, some of which had been worked nearly to death during the siege and were now too thin and unwell to butcher and serve to his men. He writes, "I will never forget the sad sight of the few skeletal horses, all that remained of what had been the magnificent division of the Guard, dying in pools of water and trying to rise with difficulty as I passed them. They turned eyes on me that could have been human in their ardent and vital supplication."[14]

"Ardent and vital supplication": Escoffier was a Victorian armed with all those florid rhetorical habits that Hemingway called the "big words." He was also a Christian idealist and pietist who resisted cynical or nihilistic or even relativistic conclusions. He had a tendency to romanticize, yet he served the commanders of his division with passion and care.

Escoffier knew the truth about war. Once his division surrendered, he experienced deprivations that typically only his cooks and busboys knew. As a prisoner of war, Escoffier and the other men confined in Metz had nothing to eat but watery soup made of rotten potatoes. That changed when he secured another cooking job, this time for another French general, the one who in a few months' time would command the forces that put down the Communards in Paris: Marie Esme Patrice Maurice de MacMahon, First Duke of Magenta, had been Governor-General of Algeria and so was a fierce defender of colonialism.

Now Escoffier's economic awakening began. During the time he was MacMahon's staff *chef de cuisine*, Escoffier watched the general take command of French government troops in Versailles, where a provisional government had been formed after France's surrender to the Prussians. MacMahon then marched to Paris to put down the Commune, a revolutionary group trying to spark an insurrection during the time of political instability. "This meant," writes Escoffier, "that the prisoners of war arriving home from Germany had to fight once again, this time not against an outside enemy but against their fellow Frenchmen who disrupted order and organized the incredible insurrection that terrorized Paris for two months, and whose final curtain was at the Père Lachaise cemetery."[15] Here he refers to a time called Bloody Week, when MacMahon's forces slaughtered around 150 of the final remaining Communards. It was an event that Ho remembered, once Escoffier told him about it. French troops loyal to the government stood the final few rebels against a wall in Père Lachaise Cemetery and executed them by gunfire—an event that Ho Chi Minh later went out of his way to mourn and remember at that very wall during his time in Paris.

The massacre in Père Lachaise was a very modern moment. In essence, what happened that day is that Catholic, rural, aristocratic, and traditionalist France defeated secular, Parisian, working-class, socialist France—in a way that left no doubt about who held power and would use that power most ruthlessly. To describe the result of Bloody Week another way, Escoffier's customers defeated his employees—at least those employees who were desperate for better wages, more time with their families, and freedom to express their political wishes, including perhaps the wish to force the government to quit sending their sons to Indochina and other colonies to strong-arm the *indigènes*.

The near civil war leading to the defeat of the leftist Commune is etched in French minds, partly because of anecdotes about eating during and after the fighting. During their own civil wartime siege, the working people of Paris grew desperately hungry and had to overcome their distaste for eating their own pets. They saw signs around the city for "Feline and Canine Butchers." One resident of Paris reported to a London newspaper that he "had a slice of Spaniel the other day," a meal that made him feel "like a cannibal."[16] According to modern calculations, during the siege Parisians consumed 300 rats, 65,000 horses, 5,000 cats, and 1,200 dogs.[17] It is no wonder that Escoffier loved choice, elegantly prepared food with an ardent passion and willingly served the aristocrats who, in his mind, had preserved order in his beloved Paris, handing the city back to its established political and social hierarchy.

Ba must have worked with men who had endured these times, and with others who heard about the hunger and despair from friends and family members. Because he worked in a French kitchen in London employing more than fifty men, many of them French and French colonial, he must have heard the stories of many former soldiers and wartime laborers. Because these laboring men were also tutored by their trade unions, they knew who held the power, and who was in desperate financial need, and who deserved some help. So it is completely within character for Ba to have suggested to Escoffier in 1914 that the table scraps from his restaurant might be reserved for hungry families in wartime London, families suffering through food rationing.

However, for readers who get all the way through Escoffier's memoir, Ho Chi Minh's moral tale falls apart. Reading those memoirs, we discover that Escoffier had already come up with a charitable plan for his food scraps in the 1890s, decades before Ba arrived on the scene in his Carlton Hotel kitchen. Not only that, but Escoffier had also proposed a pension scheme for his employees at least five years before he met Ba. In a 1910 pamphlet on "the suppression of poverty," which Escoffier distributed to his employees, the chef declares that "socialist theories . . . are basically indisputable and just."[18]

Escoffier put his money where his mouth was. When nuns called Little Sisters of the Poor came to the Carlton during the war, asking for coffee grounds, tea leaves used just once, and crusts of bread cut from toast, Escoffier—a Catholic himself—gave them more. He found fresh, clean food to donate. "Some days I could add to their modest provisions the respectable gift of 150 to 200 quail left over from the previous night's dinner. Indeed, we removed the white meat from these quail to serve to our customers, but each carcass still had two legs on it!" Escoffier encouraged the nuns to serve the quail to "old-age pensioners" with rice pilaf, according to his recipe. In his memoir, Escoffier not only describes the care he took in keeping the quail parts fresh, placing them "in an enamel pail reserved for this purpose" and "then refrigerated," but he tells of buying the nuns a horse to pull their wagon as they made their rounds to the Carlton and other destinations.[19]

It is clearly unlikely that Ba had much to teach Escoffier about feeding the hungry poor. Indeed, it is much more likely that Escoffier signed Ba up for a retirement pension and taught him how to change workers' living conditions legally. Perhaps surprisingly, the King of Chefs believed that good nutrition and a secure retirement were basic human rights. He lived, he tells us, by what he called a simple "formula [that] revolution-ized the ancient world: 'Love thy neighbor as thyself.'"[20]

Escoffier had unusually sweeping and practical ideas for demon-strating love of the neighbor. He believed that all of France could afford a social security insurance system like the one he offered his employees, if French voters would only reduce some of the huge budget for what he called "an armed peace." He feared that French militarism must inevita-bly lead to another war, and he was concerned about the poor people he saw around him, especially those who were too weak or poorly trained to perform his kitchens' menial jobs. He asked a compelling question about such people, whom others might call the undeserving poor: "Must they suffer until their last dying day for want of schooling, for not hav-ing begged protection from those currently in power, or for [not] having had enough confidence in themselves to want to take advantage of their youth and freedom?"[21]

These remarks show us the other side of the Victorian coin. The rigid, superior pietism that led Dr. and Mrs. Hemingway to their insuf-ferable and sometimes cruel speech, to their domineering parenting of their son and rejection of his calling as a writer, their sense of moral superiority and contempt for his career describing human suffering so that his readers might think to work for justice—this pietism some-times expressed itself in compassion and a sense of responsibility for the other's welfare.

When the elderly Ho Chi Minh helped his North Vietnamese ghostwriters to contrive the story of his tutoring the great Escoffier, therefore, he must have felt at least a bit guilty. He probably knew in his heart that during his London sojourn, which encompassed nearly the entire term of the Great War, he had learned from both leftist workers and his capitalist boss. Indeed, we will see clear signs during Ba's Paris years, when he called himself Quoc, that he was open to both radical, revolutionary solutions to the West's injustices and inequalities, the kind he enforced in Vietnam during the 1950s and 1960s, and to reforms we might now call liberal. These included the kinds of legal reforms that Escoffier promoted wholeheartedly for his own workers and his London neighbors. Even Quoc's discovery of the writings of Lenin, which found a way into his heart during the Paris years, did not crowd out the idea, the hope, that the prevailing governments of empire might correct and heal themselves, willingly and legally. This is a lesson he learned in London, apparently, and tested in Paris.

☰ ☰ ☰

The next time we meet Ba, in June of 1919, he is calling himself Nguyen Ai Quoc. He is living and working in Paris and has joined the French Socialist Party. He is preparing to write for their periodical *L'Humanité*. Remarkably, he is also preparing to present his "Demands of the Annamite People" to President Woodrow Wilson and other leaders of the victorious Western nations at the Paris Peace Conference. Clearly, he is an assistant chef and busboy no longer. Quoc has joined a group of anticolonialist resistance workers debating just how far they will have to go to get their friends and families back in Vietnam a decent, nourishing, dignified life.

If we want a satisfactory story for how this incredible personal evolution happened, we will be disappointed. We will find ourselves again sifting the truth from the propaganda and the outright lies, but not because our information comes from Ho Chi Minh's communist ghostwriters. We are forced to accept information from agents of the French police, who regarded Quoc as a potential terrorist and tracked his every move in the City of Light.

# 5

## LABOR UNREST IN CHICAGO

### HEMINGWAY FROM 1918 TO 1921

After a few months in Milan recuperating from his wounds, Hemingway made his way home to the United States. This Italian sojourn was, all in all, a pleasant, rather than painful, time for him because during his hospitalization he fell in love with a nurses' aide who helped take care of him, a pretty American woman named Agnes von Kurowsky. She returned his affection, for the time at least. Their affair (which is the right word because their fraternization was forbidden by military policy and everyday ethics of the time) would later become the central plot of Hemingway's 1929 masterpiece, *A Farewell to Arms*, which is also our best source for the seemingly torrid nature of their love relationship. During the months of Hemingway's recovery in the summer and fall of 1918, the two of them not only accompanied one another to the horse races at San Siro and to drinks and dinner dates in the glorious Milan Galleria, but (if the novel is truthful) adjourned afterward to a shared hospital bed once the other nurses and aides had gone to their own rooms for the night. Both Ernest and Agnes believed they were in love. Back home in Oak Park in early 1919, Hemingway was congratulated and feted for his exemplary service during the war—exemplary because he had acted bravely and suffered bodily during his Red Cross service of Italian troops. But Hemingway still saw a future for himself and Agnes. He knew he had found not only the woman of his dreams but also the lovely Italian city to which the two of them would return to work and play.

Soon, however, Agnes wrote to say that she had met a truer love of higher rank, a rejection Hemingway absorbed as a body blow. Then, predictably, he began to find his parents' rules and ample advice and Victorian slither in Oak Park hard to take. So he decamped to the family cabin on Walloon Lake in northern Michigan, where he mainly bummed around with friends during two summers and, as we will see, took temporary work during winters. He still thought of Milan as the city where he would live one day, hopefully as a successful writer. Like Ba, he was dealing with his post-traumatic shock by withdrawing from civilization and its discontents.

Hemingway removed his Italian officer's uniform only to don his lake clothes, unable or unwilling yet to take on more mature responsibilities. As we have seen, his parents could only imagine a very conventional future for their son, one that involved working for good wages, marrying a good girl, and living the pious manners of a good turn-of-the-century Congregationalist homeowner and churchgoer. So they regarded Hemingway as an adolescent and treated him that way. Not surprisingly, he found this treatment maddening, since he had served honorably in the war, risking his life to boost the morale of frontline fighting troops and to give them medical aid to those who were wounded. He had willingly placed himself at mortal risk to support America's allies and had nearly lost his life during this mission. While he bled from war wounds back in July, he had adopted the ancient and beautiful Catholic faith as his own, yet he had not become a simpleminded pietist. He had experienced sexual freedom with Agnes in Milan just after this conversion and believed that he had found a woman to love who was as adventurous and intellectually freewheeling as he was. He had also met people who made their living in opera halls, and others who painted, and still others who made a living writing poetry and fiction. He had seen that there were many more ways to live a fulfilling and meaningful life than those his parents cared about.

Hemingway had no desire any longer for a conventional life in Oak Park, Illinois. Yet he soon found that his consoling days with lake friends and ecstatic moments with northern Michigan's more willing teenage girls did not re-create the joys he had experienced with Agnes in Italy. More than sexual dalliances he needed love, and more than ample free time he needed a meaningful career and access to the deeper feelings found in art and faith. He found himself on a kind of desperate search for these things, and for a time, he dreamed of a move to the freedoms of Europe. But first he would have to endure a number of months under his parents' thumbs.

Shuttling between Illinois and Michigan, Hemingway experienced 1919 and 1920 as a series of distressing personal and cultural shocks. A brakeman on a train he hitched to Seney, Michigan, noticed the limp he had earned in Italy and referred to him as a "cripple." His post-traumatic shock gave him a fiery temper and bouts of ennui. He found himself speaking cruelly and crudely to his parents. (He did not really respect them, but he had no wish to hurt them either.) He wrote a few stories for American magazines, but they were rejected. Then he worked for a time on an autobiographical novel, but he was not proud of the manuscript.

It had grown difficult for Hemingway to love his city or his country. In July, there were race riots in Chicago, which led to violence he deplored and the deaths of dozens. (It is uncertain whether he deplored the racism or only its consequences.) Newspapers began to report that nearly two million veterans like him were out of work, even in an economy that was heating up fast, and the executive and investment classes did not seem to care. In October, Prohibition became law, a depressing event for a young man who had recently enjoyed Milan's local wines and liqueurs and, more generally, Europe's enlightened and moderate attitudes toward drink and the lightly regulated personal life. Hemingway was also informed enough to realize that Prohibition was part of a larger agenda on the part of pietist white Anglo-Saxon Protestants. In taking beer away from immigrant Germans and wine from immigrant Italians, and in closing the bars and saloons that women were frequenting for the first time (mostly young women who managed their own sexual lives and called themselves flappers), these WASPs were fighting a war against modernity, against greater freedom for women, and against a welcoming tolerance toward the faiths and ethnic ways immigrants were bringing to America's shores. It began to seem to Hemingway that the democracy that his friends had fought for and that he supported with the Red Cross at real risk to his life was basically violent, often corrupt, and badly misguided.

Then Hemingway's luck began to change. A war lecture he gave to an audience in Petoskey, Michigan, a small town near his family's lake home, impressed a wealthy woman in the audience, a Mrs. Connable of Toronto, well-to-do wife to the Canadian head of the Woolworth dime store chain. Soon she hired him as companion to her disabled son Ralph for the winter of 1919–1920 so that she and a daughter could spend time sunning themselves in Florida. Once Hemingway began working for the Connables, he found he felt a bit better. Scheduling outings for Ralph, who was only a year younger than himself, was a job that Hemingway met with some energy, charm, and good judgment, and the outings left hours in the day for his writing and even some leisure. Working as a social companion was not a vocation he could embrace, either permanently or for any length of time. Still, his light duties as companion gave him time to send out feelers and stories to the local *Toronto Star* newspaper. He felt he might be about to get back into a newswriting career. Thanks to his few months working on the *Kansas City Star* after high school, newswriting was Hemingway's one professional skill at the time, and the great writers of the previous generation—London, Dreiser, Crane, Twain, and others—had all come to literature through newswriting and journalistic entertainment pieces rather than through university training.[1] Hemingway planned to take the same path.

In spending time in Toronto and getting to know the *Star*'s editors, he was luckier than he could have known. Not only was Hemingway about to resume work on his true vocation, writing about the world's pain in both journalism and fiction, but he had also found a paper that within a few months would place a reporter in Paris to cover the war's diplomatic aftermath. Hemingway had a chance to be that reporter. But first, if he was to own the skills and attitudes that work would require, he had some growing up to do.

≡ ≡ ≡

If only we could turn to as wonderful a political and economic parable in the Hemingway scriptures as the one Escoffier provided for Ba. There is an awakening, however, if not a parable. Hemingway was about to undertake a transitional vocational period between the wartime trenches and postwar Paris. This period began with the months he spent on the near north side of Chicago, writing pro–farmer-laborer propaganda for a magazine called the *Co-Operative Commonwealth* and living in an apartment with a group of men who loved politics and the arts. This period, beginning in October of 1920, was crucial to his life, in part because this was when Hemingway met an older but still enticing young woman named Hadley Richardson, who was visiting town from her home in St. Louis. This crucial phase ended in November of 1921 when he and Hadley, by then newlyweds, took a train to New York to board the SS *Leopoldina* for Le Havre, the port and train connection for Paris.

Hemingway's fans like to focus on his and Hadley's mutual courtship, which is sweet, interesting, and important. But in order to know what kind of young man came to Paris in 1921, we also need to meet the second- and third-most important people Hemingway met in Chicago: Isaac Don Levine and Sherwood Anderson, two men who put Hemingway's incipient resistance and apprentice artistry on a main line to Paris. If we care to know about Hemingway as a humanitarian, indeed as a kind of radical Christian living out a theology of care and resistance to oppressions, then we need to recognize how Levine, a newspaperman who had covered the Russian Revolution, talked with Hemingway and his roommates about revolutionary politics, and how Anderson, one of the first American modernists, talked with them about the best, most freethinking, and most compassionate modernist art and writing of 1921.

≡ ≡ ≡

During his own time of emotional recovery, Hemingway began to interest himself in the Wobblies, the International Workers of the World or One Big Union, and he demonstrated his allegiance to IWW values by voting for Socialist Party of America candidate Eugene V. Debs in the 1920 presidential election.[2] We can imagine how Ernest and his Republican parents must have been getting along in those days, with his radicalism and their conservatism. Soon enough, in the late summer of 1920, he grew weary of his parents harping on him to get a steady job, so when in a moment of pique they denied him rent-free use of their unoccupied lake cottage, he cut economic ties with them, if not the emotional and filial ties he continued to try to maintain, and moved to Chicago. Although he made the move reluctantly, it turned out to be a great stroke of luck. Without this move he would not have met his future wife, he would probably not have learned that Paris was the place for him to become a writer, and he certainly would not have gained introductions to some of the key people in Paris who would teach him to write and help him to publish.

We know about Hemingway's political awakening in Chicago because of a confession he made to friends later in life. He told these friends that when he arrived in Paris in December of 1921, he was a "paid up Communist." He made this surprising admission to F. Scott Fitzgerald in a letter he wrote in the early 1930s. "Have you become a Communist like Bunny [Edmund] Wilson?" he asks Fitzgerald. (Wilson, editor and book reviewer for *The New Republic*, was one of Fitzgerald's friends from his college days at Princeton.) "In 1919-20-21 when we were all paid up Communists Bunny and all those guys thought it was tripe—as indeed it proved to be—but suppose everybody has to go through some political or religious faith sooner or later."[3] He goes on to suggest that disillusionment is important to a developing young mind, which means that a period of idealism is important too: "Personally would rather go through things sooner and get your disillusions behind you instead of ahead of you." Keneth Kinnamon, the best scholar on Hemingway's politics, suggests that we should "interpret this statement as humorous hyperbole." But Kinnamon also wisely suggests that the remark in the letter to Fitzgerald "does confirm other indications of [Hemingway's] early sympathy with the revolutionary left."[4] Kinnamon goes on to cite Hemingway's 1920 vote for Debs and the sympathetic stories about Marxist revolutionaries he drafted in Paris, stories we will later examine as part of Hemingway's development as a modernist writer in 1924.

Our best bet for understanding what Hemingway meant by "Communist" in the months leading up to and early on in Paris is to consult the doctrines of the International Workers of the World, Debs's One Big Union. According to the long-standing "Preamble to the IWW Constitution," there is an employer class and a working class, and the two have "nothing in common." Indeed, the "Preamble" declares that the two classes are in natural conflict: "There can be no peace so long as hunger and want are found among millions of the working people and the few, who make up the employing class, have all the good things of life." It is the responsibility of the working class to repair this unjust condition with constant effort "until the workers of the world organize as a class, take possession of the means of production, abolish the wage system, and live in harmony with the Earth." This declaration would seem to imply that the employing class and the working class must inevitably end up in physical combat, but the "Preamble" then reminds workers that one mistake of ordinary skill-specific trade unions—teamsters or pipefitters or teachers or the like—is that they fail to see that workers and employers have common interests. Presumably, both the employer class and the worker class want robust industries that offer good jobs to laborers while also protecting the earth. However, there is one unmistakably aggressive aim for the IWW: "It is the historic mission of the working class to do away with capitalism." Hemingway called the Debs presidential platform "Communism," and in this sense he was right—there was his deep hostility to capitalism as a system of abuse and undeserved advantage. And for the Wobblies, this anti-capitalist aim was modernist to the core: "By organizing industrially we are forming the structure of the new society within the shell of the old."[5]

Especially in Hemingway's day, which came after some violent confrontations between Wobblies and pro-employer factions in the far West, the Wobblies employed mainly nonviolent methods to accomplish these ends. They promoted the idea that the IWW could tolerate and accommodate trade union membership, so long as a key Wobbly doctrine prevailed: that an injury to one worker was an injury to all. This meant that a given trade union would sometimes have to set aside a particular fight for advantages in a certain workplace in order to support the larger cause of workers' rights across the world. This was a necessary doctrine because broad worker solidarity and willingness to withhold labor is the only real power the working class has, according to the Wobblies as they paraphrased Marx. Wobbly members went about producing this solidarity through a model of workplace democracy in which workers elected their own managers. Under this system, managers would be much less likely to side with management, the employing class, in any dispute.

Notably, the IWW officially welcomed immigrants, women, Asian workers, and black workers into its ranks.[6] Hemingway probably had no problem with this policy or practice, indeed with any Wobbly doctrine. He was a lifelong practitioner of casual personal prejudice (we will see some bigotry in his Parisian writings) and principled tolerance. He was the kind of guy who, a few years later, would call a Jewish friend a "kike" but name two Jewish lesbians, Gertrude Stein and Alice B. Toklas, his son's godparents.

Hemingway admired Debs for his "honesty" and for his willingness to go to jail for his anti-war beliefs. This honesty that Hemingway liked can only have been Debs's directness about the nature of capitalism and its remediation through worker power. The IWW showed a certain willingness to use force, as well as democratic practices, in the workplace. For example, Wobblies did give in to the practice of violence in 1916 and 1917, when they intimidated a trade union of mine workers in Scranton, Pennsylvania. But Hemingway had no real problem with such methods. He was anti-war, to be sure, but not pacifist or physically passive, and he believed that workers should fight for their rights. He was personally disposed to aggressive competition. His favorite sport was boxing, and he liked nothing more than bloodying an opponent's nose. Aggressive violence he thought proper if absolutely necessary.

But the Wobblies always emphasized, and still do today, that workers can get what they want, including an entirely new society pitched much more to their benefit and to the good of the earth, by organizing and striking, not by pummeling enemy reactionaries or, worse yet, shooting them. We will see the same impulse in Quoc's turn to communism as in Hemingway's. Both of them believed, at least during the Paris years, that communism should be elevated to governing and economic power, but only through voting, through workers expressing their governing power via existing democratic structures rather than revolutionary violence and a temporary descent into chaos.

That is one of the ideas Hemingway found reinforced one day in Chicago when an expert on the Russian Revolution came to talk with him and his friends in their apartment. On January 9, 1921, *Chicago Daily News* reporter Isaac Don Levine came to a friendly lunch at Hemingway's Chicago residence, an apartment on East Division Street that Hemingway and his bachelor roommates called the Men's Club. Levine apparently knew one of the roommates, Y. K. Smith, brother of a long-term Hemingway lake friend, Bill Smith. Kinnamon notes that Levine gave the young men "a favorable account" of the Russian Revolution.[7] The discussion piqued Hemingway's interest, prompting him to read Levine's book *The Russian Revolution* (1917) soon after the day of the luncheon.

Typically, the Hemingway biographies treat the Levine luncheon as a mere matter-of-fact occurrence, as in this passage from the very good James Mellow biography:

Frequently, there were guests for dinner. Writing to his mother, Hemingway informed her that Isaac Don Levine, the *Daily News* correspondent in Russia, had been there for a midday dinner. Levine was an excellent fellow "and gave us the cold dope on Rooshia." Then the group went to a concert by the pianist Benno Moseiwitch [*sic*] at Orchestra Hall.[8]

There seems to be an assumption here that Hemingway did not much care about Russia, no more than he might have cared about the Russian pianist who played Rachmaninoff downtown that evening. Mellow does not even mention Hemingway's decision to read Levine's book. Michael Reynolds does, though he, too, minimizes its impact: "Immediately Ernest began reading Levine's *The Russian Revolution*, which Hadley allowed did not interest her." Reynolds is so tied to his thesis, which is that Hemingway's politics was permanently shaped by his youth among Oak Park Republicans, that he declares, "Hemingway's interest [in the Russian Revolution] was academic; after the conservative years of Oak Park, it would take something closer to home to create much sympathy in him for the proletariat."[9]

But if Hemingway told the truth about being a "paid up Communist" in 1920 and 1921, and if his work with the Co-Operative Commonwealth group was about hating profiteers, then this is a faulty leap of logic. Hemingway certainly did care about the proletariat, and he had just spent two summers showing his parents and friends how little he cared about "the conservative years of Oak Park." He drank and tomcatted with the local girls of the Michigan lake country and made smart remarks to his conservative parents. They picked up on his anti-Victorian message. One day in 1920, after he had treated his mother rudely at a lunch she prepared for him and a friend, his Victorian mother wrote him an annihilating letter. The conflict this letter epitomized quickly became the main reason for Hemingway's move to Chicago.

Clearly, this was not a conflict between a conservative Republican son and mother. She had heard rumors that Ernest was consorting with sexually willing women in the area, including a local Chippewa girl, a match she and Ernest's father didn't believe had been made in heaven. Predictably, a real family crisis brewed. As his July birthday approached, Ernest decided to show a bit of defiance, refusing to cash a check his father had sent him as a twenty-first-birthday present. Then one day Ernest invited one of his freewheeling lake friends over to his mother's cottage for a meal, which his mother, Grace, had offered to prepare. Ernest apparently spoke crudely at the table and also failed to thank his mother properly for making the meal. He was duly scolded. In a letter from Oak Park that was clearly prompted by a report from Grace in Michigan, Dr. Hemingway wrote his son that "no gentleman need use common vulgar words in any ordinary conversation." He advised Ernest, who had been wounded in battle only a few months before, to get over his need for consoling fun. He should conform to local habits and "work at good wages." The doctor was not above name-calling: "Try not to be a sponger," he wrote to his son. Then he announced that Ernest was no longer welcome at the family cottage. He urged Ernest to "look this matter square in the face as an honest boy."[10]

Later that summer, Grace wrote her son an even more reproving letter. Apparently she had taken some time to work up an adequate metaphor for the situation, and she used it with some relish: A mother's love, she writes, is like money in a bank. She has obligingly and dutifully paid out her children's withdrawals, especially little Ernest's. "The Mother is practically a body slave to his every whim," she explains. She lists the repayments Ernest might have deposited into his personal account of her love as he grew older: apologies, "services willingly done," "interest in Mother's ideas and affairs," "flowers, fruit, candy." She reproaches Ernest for making no such deposits, and then concludes the letter with emotional blackmail in the form of an impossible ultimatum:

> Unless you, my son, Ernest, come to yourself, cease your lazy loafing, and pleasure-seeking—borrowing with no thought of returning— stop trying to graft a living off anybody and everybody—spending all your earnings lavishly and wastefully on luxuries for yourself— stop trading on your handsome face, to fool little gullible girls, and neglecting your duties to God and your Savior Jesus Christ—unless,

in other words, you come into your manhood—there is nothing before you but bankruptcy: *You have over drawn.*[11]

It does Ernest no credit that from this time on he often called his mother "that bitch." Grace's directions for earning a place in Oak Park's conservative circles—earning regular wages in order to buy candy for Mother and perform duties for his Savior Jesus Christ—apparently offered little to attract Ernest.[12] He was about to show more interest in the proletariat, which he may have considered closer to Jesus's actual work anyway.

A few months later Hemingway read Levine's book on the "Rooshian" Revolution, and we are left to determine how he actually reacted to it. We should probably take Hemingway at his word. As we have seen, he wrote to his mother (they seem to have reached some kind of rapprochement by the winter of 1921) that Levine had told him "the cold dope" about the revolution. Judging by Levine's rhetoric in his book, we should assume that *The Russian Revolution* was anything but fair and balanced. Levine could hardly be more positive about the revolutionaries, especially Kerensky's Mensheviks, who envisioned a more liberal Russia than did the Bolsheviks they then battled. In a chapter titled "The New Russia," Levine lists the many benefits of the czar's overthrow: Workers and soldiers lived more dignified lives. Women were treated as equal citizens. Corrupt actors had been rooted out, especially lingering criminal Romanov relatives of the deposed czar. The possibility of a truly just democracy was on the horizon. Russia appeared to be the worker's paradise that many leftists of the day dreamt about.

Levine is positively ecstatic about the provisional prime minister, the liberal socialist George Lvov: "A man of the highest aristocratic extraction, Prince Lvov was a democrat to the last fiber of his being." He describes the Minister of War, Alexander Kerensky, as "a young lawyer [whose] passion for justice knew no limitations."[13]

Levine describes post–Czarist Russia as a kind of utopia, especially for the soldiers who had refused to kill enemy fighters of the German/ Austro-Hungarian Alliance during the Great War, but had decided to make revolution at home instead. This, it seems, is what communism meant to young Hemingway: "The soldiery was granted complete religious freedom, free speech, uncensored communication with their homes, delivery of all kinds of printed matter, abolition of servile terms in addressing officers, complete abolition of corporal punishment, and many other reforms that infused a new life into the army."[14] This "new life," this democratic modernist's dream, had not just improved Russia but made it a model for the entire world:

> The new Russia thus began a rapid and intensive march along the path of progress and democracy. Should no external or internal mishaps overtake her, Russia was in a fair way to emerge *the freest, the most democratic, the greatest nation on earth—a true and fitting leader of all humanity toward true democracy, liberty, justice, and international peace.*[15]

It is not that Hemingway swallowed this pro-Menshevik hyperbole whole. Far from it. Hemingway probably believed that becoming a "Communist" in that year simply meant that he supported much broader worker rights and economic equity, not a route to paradise. A careful reader, he certainly must have noted the darker cautions occasionally cropping up in Levine's book. In the last chapter of *The Russian Revolution*, Levine strikes some ominous notes. There was a menacing figure named Nikolai Lenin, he warns, who threatened the free world's hopes for a Republican Russia, a state combining personal liberties with a universal social welfare system. Lenin's authoritarian fervor threatened all this liberality. As we will see, concern with the meaning of Lenin's leadership was a preoccupation in 1920s Paris.[16] During their time in Paris, Ho Chi Minh and Ernest Hemingway would both be forced to confront Leninism and its likely meaning—the future it would script for that day's most hopeful of nations, Soviet Russia.

Then, just as Hemingway's political education was launched, his literary education began in earnest too, as he learned much about the tenets of literary modernism from Sherwood Anderson. And in addition to literary matters, Hemingway learned from his new bohemian friend that political revolutions meant more than replacing one leadership model with another, one form of regulating work and making profit with a different form. He learned that political revolutions must also be cultural and even psychological revolutions. Anderson helped Hemingway see that embracing modernity, which certainly had a political dimension, might also involve changing one's consciousness, conscience, taste, life-style, faith, and ideas about love, relationships, and family. Hemingway was about to learn from Anderson that becoming a modernist meant becoming a new person in search of a new society.

Lucky for us, Anderson wrote a detailed memoir of his Chicago days. He loved Chicago, where he found many like-minded modernist friends. As a freethinker, he loved the liberty of big-city life, which for him was a welcome change, maybe even a life-saving alteration. A decade before, he had been a successful Ohio businessman with an attractive family, but his natural bohemianism and freethinking stood in the way, he believed, of genuine faithfulness to a wife and family. He often concealed sexual affairs during those days, and he spent hours writing instead of tending to his substantial paint business. Then, in November of 1912 he suffered a nervous breakdown. He ended up wandering for four days in a fugue state, unable to remember who he was or whom he knew.[17] The story of the next few months is too complicated to summarize easily, but soon Anderson had abandoned his family and his business. He had moved to Chicago to begin writing full time. There he fell in with a group of writers who, with him, became known as leaders of a "Chicago Renaissance," including Theodore Dreiser, Floyd Dell, and Carl Sandburg.[18]

Anderson also became associated with two of America's greatest modernist little magazines then published in Chicago: Harriet Monroe's *Poetry: A Magazine in Verse*, which is still published in the city, and Margaret Anderson's *The Little Review*, which moved to Paris in 1924, just in time to publish Hemingway's earliest modernist prose there. Monroe and Anderson became two of Sherwood Anderson's dearest friends.[19] On the pages of their magazines and a couple of others headquartered in Paris, literary modernism was being born. The movement's doctrines were published there, and young men like Hemingway were hoarding copies, studying them intently, taking in the stated and implied aesthetic of modern writing. Anderson published continuously in Chicago's third major modernist little magazine, Scofield Thayer's *The Dial*, which was published in the city until 1918. In 1922, *The Dial*, then located in New York, published the greatest masterpiece of high modernism, T. S. Eliot's epic collage-poem *The Waste Land*. It is no coincidence that young Hemingway would one day publish in all three of these little magazines. He came to hate *The Dial* for delaying that publishing relationship, he thought, for far too long, but these three little magazines, which he admired early on, were part of his Sherwood Anderson DNA and the roots of his modernism.

In 1920, critic and public intellectual H. L. Mencken declared Chicago the "Literary Capital of the United States." During the previous few years, Ezra Pound published dicta for the authentic free verse poem in *The Little Review*, essentially inventing the poetic form of the twentieth century. Soon, all of the finest English and American poets published in that magazine and in *Poetry*. Anderson was one of them. He also published two well-received books during the 1910s, gaining some attention in modernist circles, then in 1919 had his breakthrough moment. He published his masterpiece, *Winesburg, Ohio*, which would become a model for Hemingway's first American book, *In Our Time* (1925).

When Hemingway met Anderson in early 1920, the older writer was riding high. He had turned his bourgeois failings in Ohio into revolutionary personal and literary success in Chicago. The angst and alienation that had plunged him into that fugue state a decade before had become an urgent personal reason to explore psychoanalysis. His marital infidelities had become the ground for explorations of sexual liberty and identity. And his contempt for the commercial American audience connected him to a network of modernist publishers attempting to find a new, freethinking audience that wanted a newly frank truth instead of stale, sentimental Victorian slither.

In his memoirs, Anderson celebrates Chicago as a kind of mecca for artists who wanted to write something new, fresh, compelling, and true:

> And that's what Chicago is to me. I went there, from a small Ohio town, as a very young boy, saw my first play there, felt all of the terror and loneliness a small town boy must feel pitched down alone in a great city. I was a laborer there, went from there to join the army, gradually made friends, walked restlessly Chicago streets at night, became in love with Chicago women, wrote many of my best stories there, hung over the old wooden bridges that formerly crossed the Chicago River, watched the gulls float over the river, got out of the ranks of labor and became a business man, began to scribble and was less and less good at my job, chucked the job and

wandered away, came back to try again. It was in Chicago that I first knew other writers and was interested in literature.[20]

He then lists Hemingway among the fascinating writers he met in Chicago, many of whom (Ben Hecht, Floyd Dell, Arthur Ficke, Carl Sandburg, Edgar Lee Masters, but not Hemingway) became known as members of the "Chicago School." He calls his time in Chicago a "Robin's Egg Renaissance," but notes that he and his literary friends did not let the egg hatch properly. "It fell out of the nest," he writes. "It may be that we should all have stayed in Chicago." If they had hatched that egg, the stories people tell about writers strolling the avenues of Paris might have been tales of writers striding "up and down Michigan Boulevard until this very day."[21]

Anderson does not simply recall Jazz Age Chicago as a community of writers, editors, and publishers. He notes that he first learned about homosexuality in Chicago. There he first realized that men could be sweetly attracted to one another. He realized for the first time that "sex was to bring a new dignity," and that, unfortunately, "on all sides of us there were men and women living the lives of married men and women without love, without tenderness." After he wrote his *Winesburg* stories, shaping them into a psychologically realistic and sensitive collage-novel, he endured harsh criticism for his views on free love. Friends failed to defend him in print. He once received a letter from a woman who had sat next to him at a dinner years before and who now reported, "I do not believe that, having been that close to you, I shall ever again feel clean." He received many such letters, and he even encountered women who spat on him and shouted condemning epithets. Still, he felt that in Chicago he had found "what every man and woman in the world wants"—a genuine calling to the work he was meant to perform: "When it happened," he writes, "when for the first time I dared whisper to myself, perhaps sobbing, that I had found it, my vocation, I knelt in the darkness and muttered words of gratitude to God."[22]

Hemingway needed to meet a writer like Anderson. Though he had been writing since his high school days, passing up a university education to apprentice as a reporter with the *Kansas City Star* and then eventually writing for the *Co-Operative Commonwealth* magazine after returning to the States, Hemingway knew how to craft sentences but knew essentially nothing about the literary life. His tastes ran to broadly comic and sarcastic writers, Ring Lardner first among them, and he was steeped in Kipling and O. Henry. But these comic and sentimental models for writing were not going to help him have his say about resisting a violent and unjust world. And he knew nothing at all about magazine and book publishers, how to submit manuscripts, how to acquaint himself with the kind of writing then in demand, how to establish professional connections with other writers and editors—in other words, how to make a living as a writer. These are things he learned from Sherwood Anderson during the first days of their friendship.

The two of them met over dinner at the Men's Club.[23] One of Hemingway's roommates wrote copy at an advertising firm that also employed Anderson, who when he wasn't writing psychoanalytically informed fiction of sexual longing was writing ads intended to sell tractors. We have no record of the conversation that evening, but Hemingway seems to have employed his natural gift for self-promotion. Anderson came away from the dinner liking Hemingway and wanting to support him in his quest for a writing career. "Of course he likes you," Hadley wrote in reply to Hemingway's letter describing their meeting. She had already taken on the role of Ernest's Babbitt, her indefatigable boosting matching her willingness to read psychoanalytical sex studies he had begun mailing to her. We do not know just what Anderson communicated to Hemingway about the writing life, but we do know that Ernest soon began reading Turgenev in addition to Lardner and the little magazines in addition to the *Saturday Evening Post*, and he began generally to distinguish literary from popular writing.

Before long, Ernest suggested to Hadley that their mutual purchases of lire for a move to Italy might have to be exchanged for francs. Anderson knew the leaders of the modernist movement in Paris, which he had visited recently, and he was willing to introduce the Hemingways (as they were soon to be known) to these tastemakers, particularly to Gertrude Stein and Ezra Pound. It would be possible, in other words, for Hemingway not only to receive a quick education in modernist writing, including lessons from the virtual inventor of free verse poetry (Pound) and the foremost expert on the corollaries between modern abstract art and writing (Stein), but possible also for him to enter into a relationship or near connection with almost every single important publisher of avant-garde writing on both sides of the Atlantic.

Hemingway had found his vocation too. Just before he left Chicago in late 1921, he was a newly married, ambitious, unpublished writer of fiction with a sideline in free verse poetry. He was an anarchic leftist who believed that a sweeping and benevolent socialism might be achieved through agitation, organization of workers, and the ballot box. He was essentially a Wobbly, a protégé of Debs who believed, as the recent presidential candidate did, that workers of all crafts and in all industries might unionize in common cause and, as a result, become a force oligarchs and capitalists and their governmental allies would have to reckon with. Eventually, the capitalist powers that be would have to share power with the One Big Union, which was radical enough to remake society and to avoid stupid, cataclysmic wars, yet rational enough to have no wish to achieve their goals through blood-soaked revolution.

The only remaining political question for Hemingway was whether armed revolution was right or necessary—a question both he and Ho were about to take up in Paris as the reality of Lenin's leadership of the Bolsheviks came into clearer view. On the literary side, there is a bit more uncertainty. Probably Hemingway came to Paris knowing the things Anderson told him—that Pound and Stein would train him in a freethinking, sexually frank, socially reformist, psychologically complex, highly experimental literary prose.[24] He had much more to learn about this focus and the literary style and methods it would require—and much more to learn about how a modern new literature could become a window onto a new, more just and clement existence for himself and for others in his generation.

Ho may have come to central London, and Hemingway to the Near North Side of Chicago, emotionally down and out, in a deep state of unrest. But both left their interim cities feeling tremendous hope. They were ready to seize educations and vocations that, just a few months before arriving in London and Chicago, they didn't even know existed.

# 6

## A JUST AND LASTING WAR

### QUOC IN 1918 AND 1919

S ometime in the last months of 1918, probably just before the Great War ended, the London busboy and kitchen assistant Ba decided to move to Paris. He had political reasons for his move across the Channel, specifically the Paris Peace Conference just then about to get underway. The conference was to be a yearlong summit meeting, an occasion for world leaders to redraw the world's postwar map and decide who would pay reparations to whom, but Ba saw that the summit also offered representatives of colonized people around the world opportunities to make pleas for national independence. At the very least, they could argue for improved civil rights and economic equity. Ba also had personal reasons for his move across the Channel. Mainly, he was lonely for friends and fellow countrymen. He wanted to talk with people in Vietnamese and French, which were his first two languages, rather than in English, which was his third and the one in which he was least fluent. He was eager to bring to Paris his recent learning about unionization and social welfare schemes. And finally, but not least importantly, he looked forward to visiting Paris's libraries and galleries and salons. He knew that he had a lot to learn and that Paris, as the capital not only of France but of French culture, had a lot to teach him. He did not know the half of it.

It is possible that all of Ba's travels, up to and including this trip from London to Paris, had been scripted for him as training experiences for anti-colonialist work. Some suspect this because he was about to move into a Left Bank apartment with men who had founded an organization called the Association of Annamite Patriots. This group was led by an old acquaintance of Quoc's father's named Phan Chu Trinh, who was known to have corresponded with Ba during the London years. (We recall that Thanh's correspondence with Trinh lost him his brief teaching assistant's job.) Some scholars believe that Trinh helped recruit Ba much earlier, perhaps when the boy was about to enroll in Hue's Quoc Hoc Academy. Thanh's father and Trinh may have wanted to get the boy into the school for an education in French language, believing he would be better prepared to argue and fight for Vietnamese rights, including the great right of national independence, if he did. But in his memoirs, Ho characterizes the decision as his own. He tells that when he was just entering his teenage years, he "first heard the French words for liberty, equality, and fraternity." These words made him want to "learn something about French civilization to explore what lay concealed behind those words."[1] The truth is, the boy probably had help from mentors and teachers in forming this goal. If so, then surely they also guided Ba in his choices of the cities he visited between 1911 and 1918, and the things he learned and people he met during that time.

Whether or not Ba was a kind of secret agent biding his time in London, he certainly had exchanged letters during the war years with Phan Chu Trinh, who was a known nationalist rebel. A Mandarin scholar converted to the ideals of Western democracy, Trinh had helped plan the 1908 anti-tax protest in Hue—or so the French believed—in which Ba had nearly been killed. The French sent Trinh to prison for his role in the Hue protest, then released him in 1911 and allowed him to travel to France. They regretted their decision. Trinh had become a hardened anti-colonialist, radicalized by the French and their egregiously undemocratic mastery of his life. It infuriated him that during the war French employers could choose their colonial workers by race, as though their racist preferences were innocent and sanctioned. He hated the French for assigning to most of the few colonials allowed to stay in France after the war the hideous and dangerous job of collecting bodies and clearing unexploded ordnance from the abandoned trenches—work that was also a violation of traditional Vietnamese beliefs that ghosts were angered by improper treatment of the dead. He resented being monitored by the

Ministry of Colonies, a bureaucracy that seemed to have no interest in increasing justice in Vietnam. On the contrary, the Ministry's agents treated *indigènes* as natural criminals and national traitors.

In his hatred of the French, Trinh may even have contacted the German government ministers as the war began, seeking their support for an independent Vietnam in exchange for useful information he might provide. Certainly the French suspected him of treasonous acts, so they put him in a French prison for a year. These problems almost led to Ba's arrest in London, or at least to an interrogation. When Ba sent Trinh letters and postcards from London during the war, French agents intercepted them. These agents asked the English to track down this strangely articulate Indochinese menial, this young kitchen worker who was in touch with politically radical friends in Paris. But English agents could not find Ba at the address the French provided. Lucky for him, he remained free to debate charitable methods with Escoffier, to discuss unionization with his fellow kitchen workers, and to otherwise learn and grow. As the war ended, Trinh was also watched by French agents, but he and other rebels were occasionally able to meet Annamite comrades in their homes or in out-of-the-way Left Bank cafés to discuss the liberation of his nation. He had assembled the group of Vietnamese émigrés who called themselves the Annamite Patriots. It was this community of anti-colonialist Indochinese that Ba wanted to join, and it was Trinh he wanted, for now, as his mentor.

And so, in 1918 Ba left London for Paris.[2] As he crossed the English Channel toward the Calais ferry harbor, he decided to change his name to Nguyen Ai Quoc, Nguyen Who Is a Patriot. Apparently, he had an inner sense that he was a special person, his fate somehow tied to that of his nation. As his ship docked, he no doubt noticed Vietnamese compatriots, the kind of working men he had worked with in prewar days, when he, too, worked aboard ship and on the docks. Unloading luggage and freight, refueling the ship, and helping passengers to the customs shed, these men were too busy to spend much time with Quoc, as he now called himself. But whether he knew any of them personally or not, he must have been very glad to see them. He hoped his total isolation among mostly white Europeans was now over. Paris, his new home, was going to offer him many more chances to meet the people who not only knew his language but also shared his resentment at working as virtual slaves for the selfish French. Some of these new friends, Quoc knew, also hoped for a new nation freed from French colonial control, and he would work with these people, and for their rights.

Almost immediately after meeting Quoc and getting to know him, his new roommates recognized his poise and his skill with languages. Soon they appointed him spokesman for their movement, indeed for the entire nation-in-waiting they called Vietnam. (The French, who called the colony Annam, actually outlawed the name Vietnam, which was preferred by most *indigènes*.[3]) For the first time in his life, Quoc found himself preparing to speak for the Vietnamese people—the first and probably only job he really wanted.

≡ ≡ ≡

As a new resident of Paris, Quoc soon discovered there was a larger community of Vietnamese living there than he had realized—around two thousand people, scholars propose today, or perhaps as many as three thousand. He was to learn that this was actually a sharp decline in the number of Vietnamese residents in the city. Just a year before, at war's end, there had been around fifty thousand Vietnamese soldiers, nurses, and war workers in the country, many of them in and around Paris. (By way of contrast, there were fewer than forty thousand French and other European colonizers living in Indochina and managing the colonial project.)[4] Most of the Vietnamese in France had been demobilized in late 1918 and early 1919 and sent home—in some cases, forced home—to Indochina once France was no longer on a war footing. Such repatriation policies had later repercussions. Many of these veterans of the European theater of the world war would one day teach the fighting skills they learned in Great War trenches to the Viet Minh of the French Vietnamese war and to the Viet Cong and North Vietnamese regulars of the American Vietnamese war.

The few remaining Vietnamese in Paris just after the Great War's end were not easy to find because they were scattered about the city and rarely congregated. Only a few were easily discovered living close to the Seine on the Boulevard Saint-Michel. These were the Vietnamese students at the Sorbonne. Eventually they would recognize the power of Quoc's arguments and come over to his side, but in 1919 Quoc and his mentors had little to do with them, mostly because these students were from wealthy pro-French families with homes in Saigon. The students spoke French, dressed and acted like the French, and embraced European values. This behavior was a requirement for those who wanted permission to pursue an elite French education. The rest of the Vietnamese in the city were uneducated workers, toiling away alone or in small numbers in kitchens, boiler rooms, photo shops, and other places where the work was menial. Quoc would eventually work as a photo retoucher and lacquerer—one of many Indochinese laborers who applied lacquer to household objects or even airplane wings and fuselages, which were then made of lacquered fabric. It was boring work he performed merely to make money to live on, to support his comrades, and to meet Indochinese workers in the city. This particular work also allowed him to set aside time to develop the skills of anti-colonial resistance and the broader learning he was certain would help him shape a vocation.

The Indochinese were often treated poorly in Paris, as Quoc soon knew. There were deeply rooted French prejudices about the people who came to Paris from the colonies. The Algerians and Tunisians were considered strong and slow-witted, so they typically performed hard manual labor, digging up cobbles in the streets or repairing and servicing trucks. Laotians were considered simply indolent, so they struggled to get jobs. The Chinese and Annamese were considered clever, though a bit devious, so they often worked as household servants or cooks, because those professions required men to learn subtle manners and precise recipes for French dishes. Keeping their stereotype of Asian deviousness in mind, French employers watched their Annamese employees closely. French women who returned from stints living in Annam told tales of Annamese servants drinking the household liquor when their employers were out on the town, or simmering a piece of dog meat in the family soup and then eating the meat in the kitchen while, in the dining room, the French family sipped a broth they had no idea was so disgustingly (to their minds) contaminated. Few of these French women had evidence for such misdemeanors. Many of them listened to the suspicions of other *colons* and passed the tales along as fact.

The French called all Vietnamese "Annamites," but the word is a misnomer. The Vietnamese in Paris were just as likely to have come from any of the French colonial administrative regions, intentional divisions of a formerly unified Vietnam. (The French knew the principle of "divide and conquer.") There were Tonkin, the northern region around Hanoi; and Annam, the central highlands comprising the long, narrow, alpine middle region of the country; and Cochinchina, the southern region including Saigon and the bulge of the Mekong Delta. Students usually came from cosmopolitan Cochinchina, while workers usually came from more parochial Tonkin—yet another reason those living in Paris had no early solidarity as Vietnamese colonial subjects. The two groups spoke with different accents about very different ways of life.

Almost as soon as he arrived in Paris, Quoc entered into an intense and sometimes difficult comradeship with Phan Chu Trinh and another older roommate named Phan Van Truong. Both were Confucians of Quoc's father's generation, so he respected them as elders—at first. They became his mentors and guides in the process of his becoming an informed socialist, which they approved because, as members of the French Socialist Party, they believed in worker-centered policies achieved through legal governmental reforms. Following their lead, Quoc joined the FSP just a few months after arriving in Paris. Later, the two older men would have difficulty with Quoc's growing interest in Lenin and Bolshevik communism, which sought to turn left-leaning voters into revolutionaries willing to seize power and control of the state. The elder roommates worried that Quoc was feeding a dangerous interest in armed revolution or in total worker control of the economy, while Quoc believed that he should be free to explore any route to Vietnam's liberation that showed promise. Like Hemingway, he had read that the Bolsheviks were creating a worker's society based in mutual care. He was sure he could explore Bolshevism's benefits without becoming a rigid ideologue or moral monster.

Trinh and Truong's apartment at 6 Villa des Gobelins, which was in a laborers' neighborhood of the Left Bank, became Quoc's first Parisian home. There he prepared simple vegetable stir-fries with soy sauce for his comrades, who included Phan Chu Trinh, Phan Van Truong, and an indeterminate number of younger men. He made sacrifices for them and accepted their sacrifices, and together they argued for hours over political doctrines.

Unfortunately for the true Vietnamese nationalists at the Gobelins flat, the group was also infiltrated by Vietnamese men who spied for the

Ministry of Colonies and who made Quoc their special focus once he emerged as a vocal leader, which was almost immediately. For the next few years, Quoc would have to work hard to distinguish his loyal friends in the house, the true Vietnamese patriots, from the double agents who worked to contain him as part of an effort to keep Indochinese colonies under French control.

≡ ≡ ≡

Sometime in early 1918, Quoc and his friends would have read a document called the Fourteen Points in London's and Paris's newspapers. Crafted for the American president Woodrow Wilson, the Fourteen Points was devised by 150 advisors called the Inquiry and was written under the leadership of a Wilson aide named Colonel Edward M. House. The proposals, or points, sought to place postwar negotiations onto an idealistic, justice-minded foundation. Wilson's Inquiry group seems to have believed, naïvely enough, that Europe and its colonies could be sensibly reorganized in one fell swoop in the aftermath of the war, with new and revised national boundaries enclosing distinct ethnic and language groups, each ethnic group governing itself. Wilson called this self-determination. When Quoc and his comrades learned in late 1918 that the greatest peace conference of all would be held in Paris, and that Wilson would be one of the attendees, they surely grew excited about the opportunities the Fourteen Points and the conference offered them and their nation's people. They wanted nothing more than for the Vietnamese people to determine their own nation's fate.

Quoc was mainly interested in the fifth of Wilson's Fourteen Points, which concerned the colonies. It called for "free, open-minded, and absolutely impartial adjustment of all colonial claims, based upon a strict observance of the principle that in determining all such questions of sovereignty the interests of the populations concerned must have equal weight with the equitable claims of the government whose title is to be determined." The Annamite Patriots saw that the Americans had used the word "sovereignty." They had not merely implied that colonial people might someday govern themselves. Wilson had stated clearly and boldly that the colonies should achieve national independence as soon as possible. The prospect of sweeping colonial reform was thus on the peace conference table.

But the Annamite Patriots still had subtle calculations to make. The liberation of all colonies was hardly a foregone conclusion. The American position in Point Five was unlikely to receive support among the nations destined to lose access to Vietnam's raw materials (rubber, rice, and more) and, most crucially, its population. Quoc was a canny student of the international scene, so he probably knew even as he read the Fourteen Points that France would cling to its colonies in Indochina, unable to relinquish the profits and prestige the colonial economy brought its leaders. He may have realized, too, that because Germany was more populous than France, and because its population was growing faster, France needed its colonies as a source of laborers and soldiers both. As the wartime service of the fifty thousand Indochinese soldiers, nurses, and laborers had shown, a colony could play an important role in national security. It was essential for French security that the nation retain men ready for service in the armed forces, enough young men to match the number Germany could put into uniform. There were not enough French boys living in the metropole in 1919, so for this and other reasons, France expected to retain its colonies—not just as territory to plunder, but as a hedge against national annihilation.

There were problems on the anti-colonial side too. Quoc probably felt, for example, that there were no real equitable claims the French might possibly make. From his point of view, the French civilizing mission was unnecessary in the first place. After all, the Vietnamese knew that they were holders of an ancient and developed civilization. Furthermore, the French had voided any moral claim to a role in Indochina by turning the civilizing mission into an oppressive occupation and exploitation of people the French, clearly, had no real interest in educating or assisting.

However, if immediate national independence as described in Point Five seemed unlikely, there was, Quoc saw, a more modest opening for his people. Thanks to Wilson's and the Inquiry's proposal, an emphasis would be placed on Vietnamese claims for once, over against the clamoring claims of the victorious but war-weary ethnic French, who felt they deserved, and who clearly planned to push for, a period of undisturbed prosperity.

As the peace conference opened, the Annamite Patriots saw an urgent and immediate task before them. They needed to acquaint President Wilson with Vietnam and its situation, especially its lack of uniform rights under the law. They hoped he would come to recognize French Indochina as a perfect example of the kind of colony that should become a nation under Point Five. Quoc knew that American support for Vietnamese independence might be the engine for national independence. The Annamite Patriots might not reach that supreme goal in 1919, but initiating a long-term alliance with the United States might begin to build pressure on the French. Such an alliance might generate a longer-term process leading one day to a peaceful, prosperous, independent Vietnam.

≡ ≡ ≡

According to some historians, at the Paris Peace Conference in June of 1919, Nguyen Ai Quoc walked briskly and anxiously up and down the hallways of the French Foreign Ministry on the Quai d'Orsay wearing formal diplomatic garb, a morning coat and striped pants, imperfectly fitting because he had rented the outfit for the great occasion. How he gained entry to the building is not quite clear, though surely the formal attire helped. Quoc wanted to deliver copies of a document he and his friends called "Demands of the Annamite People" to French Prime Minister Georges Clemenceau and to members of the French National Assembly. He was especially eager, of course, to deliver the demands to President of the United States Woodrow Wilson.

Because Quoc and his colleagues in Paris believed in constitutional rights in 1919, they had taken care to craft the "Demands" document so that it read like another key Enlightenment set of demands: the American Declaration of Independence. Quoc hoped the "Demands," which focused on what the Americans called "unalienable rights," would touch Wilson's patriotic heart. They hoped the document would make him feel like a minuteman at Lexington or Concord whenever he thought about the Vietnamese suffering under taxation without representation. Perhaps then Wilson could convince French President Clemenceau, British Prime Minister David Lloyd George, and Italian Prime Minister Vittorio Orlando, who with Wilson made up the Big Four, that colonialism was wrong in the deepest human sense.

Quoc and his friends clearly believed that colonialism was a human evil that needed to be destroyed. Yet all that the Annamite Patriots demanded in their document was a kind of Vietnamese bill of rights, an assurance that if the Vietnamese must remain colonial subjects, as it seemed they would, then they should receive fair and humane treatment under French law. Specifically, they called for just a handful of reforms:

1. General amnesty for all native political prisoners
2. Reform of Indochinese justice by granting the natives the same judicial guarantees as [are] enjoyed by Europeans
3. Freedom of press and opinion
4. Freedom of association
5. Freedom of emigration and foreign travel
6. Freedom of instruction and the creation in all provinces of technical and professional schools for indigenous people
7. Replacement of rule of decree by rule of law
8. Election of a permanent Vietnamese delegation to the French parliament, to keep it informed of the wishes of indigenous people[5]

Quoc felt that he and his new comrades had done all they could before the peace conference to promote these demands. Apart from the planned appeal to President Wilson, they had also arranged to have the "Demands" printed in the leftist newspaper *L'Humanité* and to have a French labor union print and distribute six thousand copies around Paris's neighborhoods. The hope, apparently, was that sympathetic readers in the larger public would increase pressure on the presidents and prime ministers, pushing them toward support for basic civil rights for the Annamite people.

When Quoc delivered the "Demands" to American aides that summer, specifically to Colonel House, he received a note of reply from a lower-ranking assistant:

Monsieur,

Colonel House has charged me with acknowledging reception of your letter of 18 June, 1919, and to thank you for the copy that you enclosed of the Note of Claims of the annamite [*sic*] people on the occasion of the Allies' victory.

Sincerely yours,
Arthur Hugh Frazier
Embassy Counselor[6]

In his late-life memoirs, Ho claims that House himself replied with a polite note of receipt, and that later in the day House followed up with another note assuring Quoc that the "Demands" would be brought to the attention of President Wilson. Historians have never found the letters that would corroborate Ho's claim. However, Frazier's note, which does exist, provides evidence that Colonel House had in fact read Quoc's "Demands" and received his request for a meeting. Neither President Wilson nor House knew that just weeks earlier the author of this note, Nguyen Ai Quoc, had been calling himself Ba and working as a busboy in a London restaurant. That intelligence, it seems, would have made a meeting either much less likely—or, if the Americans had time to pursue their wonder, much more.

It is certainly astonishing that a Vietnamese busboy with some experience in baking and snow shoveling and perhaps participating in a London restaurant workers' union would have the confidence to walk the halls of the Quai d'Orsay ministry and the Versailles palace in the summer of 1919, delivering insistent documents to world leaders who were busy working to negotiate an end to a world war. It is even more amazing that he would address an American president and French ministers and parliamentarians with demands. We simply do not know how he came to view himself as Wilson's peer, or how this expatriate busboy came to believe he represented all the Vietnamese people. Perhaps Quoc's surprising confidence raises a more general question, which is how anyone comes to believe, as Ho and Hemingway clearly did, that they had something important to say to the whole world.

The rest of the story is anticlimactic. As the summer wore on into the autumn, Quoc and the Annamite Patriots began to realize they were not going to get the hearing they had requested. Neither House nor Frazier nor any other member of the American delegation followed up with further contact. Probably Quoc and his friends should have expected this result. All they had to do was look around them to see that their pleas for improved conditions in Indochina would be considered minor by men who were trying to remake Europe. Wilson, Clemenceau, Lloyd George, and Orlando had to work out a way to restore Germany to full nationhood, while forcing the German people to pay reparations to the winners of the Great War. Under pressure from the French people, they felt they had to weaken the German military and make certain that its industrial capacity turned to peaceful projects. They had to contain Bolshevism, though they didn't know at that moment what the revolutionary movement really meant or where it might be headed. They also had many European national boundaries to redraw, hopefully without sparking new wars.

In seeking attention to Vietnamese problems, the Annamite Patriots were in intense competition with other colonies and oppressed peoples. Eyewitnesses to the conference note that the Quai d'Orsay's hallways were packed with pleaders from the world's less powerful nations and from incipient ones such as Vietnam. Apart from the Annamites, there were representatives of the Irish Republic, Palestine, Korea, and even, according to American eyewitness Harry Hanson, a group of black officers of the YMCA pleading for justice for all people of color. Lawrence of Arabia was there, dressed in English military garb topped with a draping Arab headdress. He proposed a great, new pan-Arab nation. Bulgaria, Austria, and Hungary, now freed from their former empires and associations, were represented there as sovereign and independent nations. We can imagine the slight young Quoc in his over-large morning suit, weaving among these other pleaders, seeking out listeners, trying vainly to be heard.

Finally, as the summer waned, the Annamite Patriots gave up their hopes. The ongoing Paris Peace Conference was turning out not to be the political triumph Quoc had hoped for, nor even a few modest steps toward Vietnamese dignity and autonomy. He could only shrug, go get a library card, and start studying political philosophy and working on his debating skills. He was not the only attendee to encounter severe disappointment. The conference was a debacle for Wilson too, as he returned to the United States and to a hostile Republican congressional caucus that he had neglected and insulted for far too long. He launched a frantic tour of the US, making speeches promoting the Treaty of Versailles with his League of Nations proposal, pushing for congressional approval. In October, completely exhausted by these efforts, Wilson was incapacitated by a stroke. Dealing with a weakened president, Congress did not ratify the League of Nations proposal. Leaders on both sides of the aisle were skittish about creating the League because its members were to be granted the power to commit the United States to another war without Congress's approval.

Quoc probably didn't care about Wilson's humiliating defeat. By that fall, Quoc would have noted that League policies were actually designed to perpetuate colonialism, not end it. According to mandates approved in Paris that summer, only Palestine, a UK possession, and Syria, a French possession, were deemed nearly ready for independence—and those peoples would have to wait a long time for that independence to be realized, at the end of the Second World War more than twenty years later. Vietnam, Haiti, India, Tanganyika, Togoland, Kamerun, New Guinea, German Samoa—these and many other colonies were regarded as too primitive to raise an army and govern themselves, so the empires would continue to administer them. These lands would have to fight and connive for their freedom a generation later or more, sometimes long after the empires were weakened by another world war.

≡ ≡ ≡

In late 1919, a new phase of learning began for Quoc. He had been hopeful about the peace conference, perhaps too much so. Now he began to struggle with the realization that the Vietnamese had very little bargaining power when they met with leaders of the empires. It seemed that powerful nations were not moved by logical demonstrations, no matter how reasonable, nor by merely moral arguments, nor by stirring bills of rights. Quoc must have considered the option of giving up bargaining and negotiating altogether. He knew that this was what the workers of Russia had done when they saw that the czar's government had no real interest in good-faith reforms. Harnessing their outrage, these workers fomented a successful revolution, swept the czar and his governing assembly aside, and took the governance of Russia into their own hands.

But this was not Quoc's calculation—not yet anyway. In 1919, Quoc's friends and the police informers tell us, he was reading the novels of fellow FSP members such as Romain Rolland and Henri Barbusse, writers and reformists who mainly called for more humane policies and conditions for the working classes and who expressed sympathy for veterans of battle. He seems to have set aside political agitation for the time being, in favor or a more patient approach, a time of deep reading and learning that might help him become a better negotiator and, more importantly, a stronger framer and promoter of civil rights proposals. As the Paris Peace Conference wound down that fall and early winter, Quoc began to spend his time practicing his French and his debating skills at a Right Bank salon called the Club du Faubourg. He also entered into political discussions in cafés and private homes, began to acquaint himself with the doctrines and personalities constituting the French Socialist Party, and started to read the political magazines that would soon feature his own bylines.

The founder of the Club du Faubourg, socialist eminence Leo Poldes, remembered noticing Quoc at the club for the first time. His is one of the few portraits we have of Quoc and his appearance and demeanor in Paris:

> It was at one of our weekly meetings that I noticed this thin, almost anemic *indigène* in the rear. He had a Chaplinesque aura about him—simultaneously sad and comic, *vous savez*. I was instantly struck by his piercing dark eyes. He posed a provocative question; it eludes me now. I encouraged him to return. He did, and I grew more and more affectionate toward him. He was *très sympathique*—reserved but not shy, intense but not fanatical, and extremely clever. I especially liked his ironic way of deprecating everything while, at the same time, deprecating himself.[7]

Given that club meetings often drew in excess of two thousand attendees, it is remarkable that Poldes noticed Quoc at one of his thrice-weekly debates.

The spirit of the gatherings was just what Quoc liked. One attendee noted that at the club "absolute freedom of speech" was an accepted ethic: "A Jesuit and a Bolshevik may take one debate," this member wrote, "and the rigid upholder of faith and dogma or the revolutionary is equally assured of a hearing."[8] Women were also welcome members and debaters. Though debates could become heated, Poldes's equitable chairmanship assured everyone of a respectful hearing, and many meetings were noted for high spirits and laughter. Quoc quickly made good friends, and he took reading tips from club members, so that soon he was reading Shakespeare, Tolstoy, Dickens, and, of course, Barbusse. Notably, these are writers who work on readers' emotions, who call their readers to sympathy for the weak, the disadvantaged, and the downtrodden.

He tried to read Marx but found the great theorist of historical materialism and revolution difficult to follow and completely uninformed about the colonial world. Quoc once joked that he mainly used his copy of *Das Kapital* as a pillow.[9] In other words, he was not especially interested in historical processes theorized by Marx, the inevitability of class conflict and of the proletariat's eventual control of governments and economies. Quoc cared more about the work that novelists and documentary essayists do—illustrating the lives of suffering people and crafting scenes and situations that brought readers into a feeling of compassion for the disadvantaged and demoralized. One sign that Quoc's aims were very practical rather than ideological at this this time, and that he had an artist's sense of audience and performance, is that he turned key tenets of the Annamite Patriots' "Demands" petition into a ballad for his less-literate Vietnamese compatriots to sing each day, a mnemonic and hymn to democratic liberty.[10] Clearly, he loved the Vietnamese people more than he loved Marx.

As for the problem of too little negotiating power that had become apparent at the peace conference, Quoc had another idea. He realized that he, too, could become a compelling writer, and that if he did, he could help bring the Vietnamese people living in Paris and in his homeland into a feeling of national and political solidarity. He could help the Vietnamese know their own history, see their present condition, and realize they could put pressure on French leaders to negotiate with them for improved lives. He could teach people to agitate by offering informed argument, telling about the abuses and outrages they suffered, withholding their labor through workplace strikes, and, if need be, fighting for their rights and for the birth of a new nation in the country they loved. Together, they could and would make the French listen to them.

For his part, he would also turn his improving language skills to political writing, including, soon enough, the very same literary forms that most interested Hemingway: political fiction and documentary journalism. As he worked on these skills, he would meet active members of Paris's vibrant arts movements who would provide him with models, mentors, and comrades he had never heard about before arriving in the City of Light. They would bring him to yet another evolution in his art of resistance.

# 7

## FIGHTS AND FOOLISHNESS

### QUOC IN 1919 AND 1920

O n September 6, 1919, while the peace conference was still in session but the Annamite Patriots' concerns were dead in the water, Quoc received an invitation for a meeting at the Ministry of Colonies. Specifically, he was invited to the offices of the former Governor-General of French Indochina, now Minister of Colonies, Albert Sarraut. Quoc may have been surprised that an actual minister of the government wanted to meet with him, but he was not surprised that his existence had been noticed by the Ministry. Certain comrades in his circle had taken surreptitious photographs of him recently, and they had begun asking him questions about his history and opinions. It had dawned on Quoc that he was being monitored and investigated, treated as a threat or agitator, and that some of his Vietnamese friends were actually agents for the Minister of Colonies.

Quoc went to the meeting, probably with some trepidation. We do not know the substance of his conversation with Minister Sarraut, except that the general atmosphere of the meeting must have been tense but polite, judging by Quoc's follow-up note: "Since you were kind enough to tell me that you were disposed to talk frankly," Quoc wrote with some asperity, "I am taking the liberty to ask you to indicate to us [the Annamite Patriots] what has already been accomplished regarding our eight demands." Quoc noted that he and his comrades had seen precious little progress themselves. He enclosed a copy of the "Demands" and invited further discussion. Then he concluded the note with "the assurance of my profound respect."[1] This is the language of diplomacy—more polite than circumstances might require, firmly restating a position, open to further engagement.

Yet, instead of continuing talks with Quoc or any of his colleagues at this time, Sarraut ratcheted up his monitoring, assigning two police agents the task of tracking Quoc hour by hour and noting his political activities. Seeking information from Vietnam too, Sarraut wrote to the Governor-General of French Indochina, who had just replaced him in May of 1919, and learned from the reply that Quoc was in fact Nguyen Tat Thanh, the young translator identified on that deadly 1908 day in Hue when a tax protest had to be violently suppressed with gunfire. Sarraut seems to have given his people instruction that, from now on, when they met with Quoc he was to be treated as a rather annoying expatriate laborer rather than a representative of a colony of France. Like some of our own leaders in the West today, Saurrat would not negotiate with perceived terrorists. There would be no further open talks about justice for the Vietnamese people with this Thanh or Quoc fellow, whatever he was calling himself now. There would be only taunting, cajoling, and bribing—treatment Sarraut apparently thought the "excessively sly Annamite" (as he once called Quoc) clearly deserved.

For now, Quoc's mode of resistance was to fight in a forthright and sincere manner for rights he read about in the French Rights of Man and the American Declaration of Independence, rights he understood to be his simply by virtue of his humanity. The "Demands" document made that clear. He certainly considered revolutionary change necessary in France and Vietnam, and other places where colonization and other injustices made people suffer. But he clung to the hope that this revolution could be a peaceable one, achieved through ordinary political pressure on government leaders, who would see the necessity of reforms and, as a result, pass them into law and institute them.

In other words, he believed in the legal processes of elected governments. Because this political doctrine was the socialist line in France at that time, and because the United States was still founded upon its anti-colonial doctrines, the French Socialist Party and the United States of America were Quoc's great hopes in 1919. The US would remain a beacon for the future Ho Chi Minh for at least another twenty-five years. The French Socialists would lose his trust in less than two years' time. Quoc was about to learn that to resist oppression did not necessarily require sincerity or a transparent personal disposition. It was possible to be ironic, sarcastic, secretive, provocative, and even a bit mad.

≡ ≡ ≡

Both Hemingway and Quoc made a turn to documentary journalism in 1920. Hemingway had learned in Kansas City before the war that to document a nation's social life was an important civic act. Readers in a good society needed to know how their neighbors lived, especially those whose lives were most troubled and deprived. He wrote many vivid stories on his Kansas City police reporter's beat, covering the economically destitute and disadvantaged as well as the more cynical wrongdoers who perpetrated most of the city's crimes. Thanks to his good luck in meeting publishers and editors at the *Toronto Star* in 1920, he was beginning to think about returning to reporting, financing a career as a novelist with some ready work as a correspondent. At about the same time, Quoc was determined to develop new skills in the wake of the peace conference disappointment. A gifted writer and thinker already, as his French teachers in Vietnam had told him, he, too, trained for work as a politically engaged reporter. He saw that Parisian magazines such as the FSP organ *L'Humanité* invited the kind of audacious truth-telling that he now saw as necessary. In 1920, on two different continents, Hemingway started writing for the *Co-Operative Commonwealth* magazine and Quoc for *L'Humanité*. Both would tell the truth as they saw it in order to move people to concern and sympathy for the people who most deserved and needed the fruits of resistance and reform.

The Paris avant-garde would change all that. In 1920, with Quoc but not Hemingway as witness, a new arts-and-politics movement had arrived in Paris and was beginning to make waves. It was called Dada, a silly name whose meaning was not at all clear. The word means "hobby-horse" in French, but also seemed to be baby talk. Dada was nevertheless the name chosen by a group of extremely bright artists and philosophers from France, Romania, Germany, Switzerland, and the United States for their school of art and protest. All of them felt extreme disgust at the waste and absurdity of the recent war and wanted desperately to expose and heal the madness somehow. So this polyglot group launched a new arts movement from a cabaret in Zurich. The internationalism was part of the point, as the dadaists were anti-nationalist. They were also anti-bourgeois, so their art sought to offend the ordinary citizen who lived by conventional values. As early member Hans Arp put it, the dadaists were "revolted by the butchery of the 1914 World War" and began making art as a form of resistance to its deadly values: "While the guns rumbled in the distance, we sang, painted, made collages and wrote poems with all our might."[2] There was an inartistic and sarcastic quality to this art. Instead of a bust in marble, a sculpture might be a pig in military uniform hanging from the ceiling. Instead of an evocation of shimmering light on a water's surface in oils, a painting might be a mustache drawn on a cheap copy of the *Mona Lisa*.

Yet clearly, even if Dada had childish qualities, it was a thoroughly adult enterprise. The dadaists believed that art, even infantile art, was liberating. There was direct and clear satire in such artworks, of course—assaults on the unthinking reverence often conferred upon men who served in uniform, or on the hushed respect that art usually received. But the dadaists believed that art, even and especially juvenile art, also sometimes emerged from a deeper place in the subconscious than civic words and acts did, and furthermore, art was capable of revealing and then exploring the irrational, the mad, the dreamlike aspects of human existence. Dada sprang from the idea that it was civilization that was mad, not strange new conceptual artworks. The Great War had proved that. Nothing could be more mad than the battles of Passchendaele or the Somme.

Within a few months Dada would be an important model for a new kind of resistance, which both Quoc and his soon-to-be new neighbor Hemingway would find fascinating and, eventually, useful. Quoc and Hemingway were going to learn an important lesson from Dada, and then from its successor movement called surrealism. They were to realize that journalistic writing, with its calm logic and sincere wish to describe conditions accurately for the benefit of the community, was not nearly provocative enough. Nor was it psychologically astute enough to understand or convey the insane quality of Western culture. Nor was it provocative enough to move conventional minds to consider unconventional new practices.

≡ ≡ ≡

In February of 1920 Dada held a soiree at the Club du Faubourg. Quoc either attended or heard much about the event. We do not know just what kind of performance—they called them "manifestations"—the dadaists André Breton, Louis Aragon, Francis Picabia, and Tristan Tzara put on for the club members, but all of their events had a particular anarchic style. The very first Dada event in Paris, in early 1920, had been simple fraud. The dadaists rented a huge hall, the Grand Palais des Champs-Élysées, and advertised a presentation by the day's great American film star Charlie Chaplin. On the night of this presentation, thousands who had purchased tickets took their seats. They waited and waited to listen to the inventor of the Little Tramp. As time passed and the presentation grew alarmingly late, no one made an announcement about the delay or requested patience. Finally, the wait was unendurable. The audience members realized that Chaplin was never going to show and that they had been duped. Some of the angriest traded insults with the dadaists.

After this strange introduction, Dada events grew in popularity. The highlight of one evening for a packed crowd of thousands in a large Paris theater came when Tzara read a parliamentary address from a newspaper while clanging bells drowned out his voice. This spectacle was followed by Breton carrying a huge copy of the *Mona Lisa* onstage, with pencil mustache and Van Dyke beard added. Defacing a Leonardo was shocking and funny to most, probably, but not shocking enough for Dada. Also appearing on the painting were the huge, readable letters: "L.H.O.O.Q." The French audience recognized these familiar initials for "She's got a hot ass." As the audience tired of these anarchic displays, they objected in the French manner, hurling food and coins at the Dada performers.

Some audience members simply gaped at such craziness, others were quickly offended, and still others gradually realized that something interesting and communicative was going on. Even Paris's hipster progressives tended to find such antics offensive—at first. It was not unusual for a Dada evening to end with the audience rising from their seats to kick and strike the performers (or manifesters) until the police intervened. Yet these audience members presumably also went home to their flats after the melee, talking about what all this Dada nonsense really meant. Many of them must have realized, upon reflection, that the dadaists at the very least raised an important and compelling question: whether it is always best to be polite listeners to the solemn orations and un-ironic expressions of traditionalist art, literature, or politics. After all, the great Western culture these traditionalist institutions sprang from had just spent four savage years fighting in the mud, killing their own and each other's citizens by the tens of millions. For the dadaists and other more radical resisters, even logic and right behavior now seemed suspect—because logic and right behavior had led to Ypres, Gallipoli, mustard gas, the hell called no-man's-land, men without jaws or noses or legs, and to the generals who sent men into battle to die in what everyone knew were the scheduled final minutes of the war.

Some Dada efforts, Quoc saw, meshed more fully with his own mood and interests. Around that same time, the Dada artists published a journal, *La Littérature*, which included "automatic writing," unedited spontaneous prose supposed to emerge from an unfettered subconscious. The idea was that the subconscious was free of society's unjust rules, and a freed subconscious was a much better route to justice than codified laws and traditions emerging from solemn lessons. So writers should simply let the words flow and avoid editing, polishing, or correcting themselves. Quoc may have taken the lesson to heart. His own brief documentary essays on colonial outrages, which he published in local leftist magazines beginning that year, often have an immediacy that is enhanced by angry, inartistic, and sometimes even sloppy writing. Some of the events Quoc describes even seem a bit unlikely, as we will see, so he was catching on to the kinds of freedoms the dadaists modeled.

Not everything about Dada was childish. There was often a more serious character to Paris Dada, which a recent art catalog captures nicely:

> The spectacles of Paris Dada, but also many of the individual paint-
> ings and literary works, exhibit a profound violence: physical hurt,
> damage to language, a wounding of pride or moral spirit. This
> violence, which may seem uncharacteristic of French sensibility,

is often explained as nihilism or anti-aesthetic provocation. The attacks are more pointed than that, however, for they are caustic rather than annihilating.[3]

The caustic is what Quoc caught on to. Within a few months, he would publish descriptions of atrocities in Vietnam that included the raping of old women, the cold-blooded killing of children, and the roasting of human bodies—horrifying crimes perpetrated by French soldiers who were considered national heroes at home.

Marcel Duchamp's works, which many Parisians first encountered in 1920 and just after, provide perhaps the best examples of this caustic impulse. Even before the war, Duchamp was famous—or infamous—for his highly experimental and non-representational art. The best-known of these was the cubist painting *Nude Descending a Staircase, No. 2* (1912). This painting, a series of loosely grouped, shoebox-lid-sized, tan-flesh-colored planes organized to represent a human body descending a staircase in time-lapse, is nearly understandable as an act of representation. With a small act of imagination, you can actually see a nude person of no definable sex or identity descending a staircase. Yet in its day, specifically the 1913 Armory Show in Manhattan, this painting caused a great stir—one that Ba might have read or heard about, because he, too, was in America at the time. Outraged critics saw nothing but chaos in Duchamp's painting. They were accustomed to seeing recognizable human bodies in art, whether realized photographically in the pre-Raphaelite English style or more sketchily and luminously in the impressionist French style. These styles were permissible to traditionalists, but Duchamp's struck many as outrageous. Viewers in Manhattan groped to understand and describe Duchamp's blurred, flowing, collage-like image. One critic writing for the *New York Times* famously described the painting as "an explosion in a shingle factory," and cartoonists made the picture famous in America through ridicule. One cartoon from the pages of a March 1913 edition of the *New York Evening Sun* is titled "Rude Descending a Staircase"—a Duchampian cubist representation of pushy New Yorkers on the subway stairs at rush hour. Another from the *New York American* in February shows a little boy gazing at *Nude Descending a Staircase*. The little cartoon tyke says to his father, "Papa, buy me that puzzle." Wide-eyed Papa is too shocked by the picture to reply.

Undaunted, Duchamp soon began to experiment with even more caustic "ready-mades," ordinary objects connected with basic human processes turned into art. The most famous of the ready-mades is his *Fountain* (1917). The sculpture is actually a porcelain urinal, disconnected from plumbing pipes, its back resting on a display table rather than mounted onto a wall. Usually photographed so that we face the water connection on the usual top of the urinal and the drain in the middle of the bowl, we see the urinal's bowl as a vertical curving shape (some have seen the hooded Virgin Mary in its curve), and the drain holes as a triangle of perfect little circles, one above two above three. Duchamp signed the outer edge of the urinal in crude black paint with a pseudonym and accurate date, "R. Mutt 1917." This work says to viewers something like, "Screw you and your aesthetic pretensions, your commitment to beauty, your prudish morals, and your love of war. Let's think about the art of waste for a minute." Such artwork clearly resists the solemnity of ordinary ethics, which are, after all, usually framed by people in power, who can readily manipulate the economy and civic institutions.

Quoc hardly seems to have been the type to admire childish nihilism, and he had no real interest in artworks that commented on the nature of artistry, even if those works raised questions about the French cultural heritage—which, as he knew, could combine *liberté, égalité,* and *fraternité* with government-sponsored *criminalité.* Still, the timing was propitious. Just as Quoc began to reconsider his own methods in light of the Paris Peace Conference failure, he was introduced to this pointed, intentional, radical form of political provocation that had recently begun fascinating, offending—and changing—audiences in Paris, sometimes audiences numbering in the thousands. We have reason to believe he took notice: Around this time he began telling the police agents in his circle— perhaps mistaking them for honest friends and colleagues, or perhaps not caring whether they carried his sentiments to Minister Sarraut—that he needed to discover provocations that would raise sharply the profile of Indochinese suffering and freedom-fighting efforts. The Annamite people, he said, needed to make "a lot of noise" in an effort to provoke Parisians' consciences. "We need fights and foolishness to get attention," he said.[4] Dada was nothing if not intentional foolishness, with both aesthetic and political goals.

≡ ≡ ≡

Agents reporting in from the Annamite Patriots' home at 6 Villa des
Gobelins that year said that money was short and tension was high.
Though he would continue to represent Annamite interests at conferences and summits, Quoc had launched a new career as a writer. He
had begun publishing anti-colonialist diatribes in left-leaning journals,
including *L'Humanité*. Most of these essays simply pointed out, in an
outraged tone, that the Indochinese were denied basic civil rights, were
forced to purchase quotas of drugs and alcohol, and were often paid little
or nothing for work they could not refuse. This is a representative passage from July of 1920:

> English, German, and French capitalists are all equal, as are their
> crimes, but for the fact that the capitalists of other countries at least
> have the modesty not to dress up their egoism with the pompous
> phrase of "Civilizing Mission." But behind the three colours of lib-
> erty, equality and fraternity, France introduces alcohol, opium and
> prostitution to all of her colonies and sows misery, ruin and death
> along with her ill-gotten riches.[5]

There was no real artistry or extreme provocation yet. The last sentence
in the passage is not even logically coherent. This is Quoc working tire-
lessly in his still-intact sincere and scholarly mode. At this time in 1920
he had begun an even more daunting scholarly task: writing a long, vivid
history of French colonialism, with all its injustices. To that end, Quoc
studied in the Bibliothèque Sainte-Geneviève next to the Pantheon
most days, reading everything he could about both the mythic and real
aspects of the colonial enterprise. A police agent reported that Quoc had
recently read thirteen books on colonialism in the library, so we know
that the Ministry of Colonies was well aware of his composition of this
study. Agents even tracked activity on Quoc's library card.[6]

Judging by the sarcastic tone and indecorous subject matter Quoc's
essays began to display during the next few months, including horrific
descriptions of rape and murder and bodily mutilations of his people
(which we will review), he underwent at this time a significant change as

an artist, propagandist, and revolutionary. He began talking with Club du Faubourg members and other local Parisians about the provocative new arts in town. He started thinking about writing dramatic satire. His magazine stories became more strident, and those that documented colonial abuses became almost sickeningly graphic. Quoc was to become a provocateur, almost but not quite as antic as the dadaists.

Meanwhile, because he could not or would not work for money during this time of extremely hard anti-colonial work, others were paying Quoc's rent and other expenses. His older mentor Trinh selflessly worked at photograph retouching, a *métier* Quoc would take up himself within a few weeks, and Truong provided paid legal counsel to Indochinese and French defendants in military courts. These two colleagues earned enough money to pay the rent, and they provided funds for the group's simple meals, which Quoc prepared. As we know, he was an expert at the preparation of vegetables and soy sauce served over rice—about the only approximation of Asian cooking the group could produce from French markets and one or two tiny Asian groceries. The Annamite Patriots were clearly exhausted and underfed. One union member who met Quoc at this time noted that he was "as frail as a sparrow," even though he "burned with the zeal of a Crusader."[7] Agent Edouard reported from the Annamites' house that all the men suffered from bronchitis or, he suspected, tuberculosis. He wrote that "they lack the means to lead a healthy or comfortable life," so in his view they did not pose an immediate threat to French colonialism.[8] With hindsight we think, *Not yet anyway.*

☰ ☰ ☰

Quoc and the Hemingways were just months from becoming neighbors in la Mouffe, a workers' neighborhood on a Left Bank hilltop only a short climb from the Notre Dame Cathedral. Once the Hemingways did move to la Mouffe, Ernest faced many of the same quandaries Quoc did just after he arrived. He was treated as a non-entity for a time, and had to earn his stripes as a Parisian modernist. He took instruction from experienced elders, but found himself unable to accept their worldview completely. He wrote documentary journalism with occasional forays into opinionated sarcasm, especially about the wealthy. He was surprised at the wild arts scene in Paris, but, like Quoc, he did not reject the strange logic of the avant-garde. Instead, also like Quoc, he showed interest, learned what he could, and eventually made the arational and caustic his own too. In the interest of his new vocation, he suffered certain hungers. All of these things he endured because he was, like Quoc, a modernist and a revolutionary.

# 8

B y the end of 1921, which was still just over a year away, Quoc and Hemingway would be revolutionary neighbors in Paris, sharing the same cafés and shops on the sloping rue Mouffetard, chilly and pretty in its Christmas decorations, its displays of candy for French kids and wines and liqueurs for their parents. They would also share a hopeful interest in the Russian Revolution, with an eye toward the notions of justice that concerned them both—an end to colonialism for Quoc and an end to deadly lives for working people for Hemingway. But first, in the final year or more leading up to their time living near each other in la Mouffe, they would both have to choose Paris. Quoc lived there already, of course, while Hemingway was in Chicago trying to decide which European city suited him best. Yet in a real sense both of them were strangers to the qualities of Paris that would help them fall in love with the city. They were about to enter the ferment of arts and ideas and political positions and friends and rivals that would help them to make the city their own modernist university.

During the months leading up to that Parisian Christmastime, Quoc and Hemingway were upset and anxious about personal problems. Indeed, the two young men grappled with exactly the same two key decisions in their lives in late 1920 and throughout 1921. First, they needed to discover the best way to make their arts of political resistance powerful and effective, especially within their own gifts for writing and leading others. And second, they needed to decide whether it would be best to commit to a life with a woman who was willing to share a revolutionary life at the intersection of art and politics.

If Hemingway's letters to friends in the months before he sailed for Paris are any indication, his political commitments were sincere, certainly, but less than a burning passion. For the time being, he was far more concerned with courting Hadley Richardson, attending Chicago's concerts and plays, and getting together with friends to discuss books or talk with interesting guests.

He was not apolitical. Certainly he had personal reasons for supporting the Debs thesis about the Great War—namely, keeping himself and his friends from being called up for service in another useless war. But in 1921 he was less an angry Wobbly demanding revolutionary change for American society than a bemused propagandist for the Co-Operative Society, which had the more modest aim of producing farmer-labor solidarity. He believed in the work, which involved promoting cooperatives that would unite farmers and workers into more powerful political and economic blocs. If they were united in this way, these laborers could not be so easily pushed around by the investor class, and they could do more to set their own favorable prices. "Some said it was not the American way," Michael Reynolds writes. "Some said it smelled of socialism."[1] If so, then it was right up young Hemingway's alley. He was making his own American way, and if other citizens joined him in wanting more attention to workers' needs, so be it. Yet even this work Hemingway conducted with cool dispatch and some irritation with his bosses, as they gave him what he regarded as silly task after silly task. (Their business would collapse under the shadow of fraud soon after Hemingway left it.) He would have to reach Paris before this rather cool interest in revolutionary change, this calmly principled solidarity with the laboring class, would become enough of a passion to enter strikingly into his writing and become one of his literary and personal preoccupations.

In the meantime, it took Hemingway a number of months to court Hadley. It is clear from their passionate letters that the two fell in love within a month of their first meeting in the autumn of 1920, so their courtship was more about imagining a future together than deciding that there should be one. Ernest seems to have found it especially important to establish two things: first, they would be avid and freewheeling sexually, in accordance with certain modern psychoanalytical books he had been reading; second, they would live an unconventional life as expatriates in Italy. Though Hadley had been raised as he had, in a bourgeois but cultivated Christian home in a Midwestern city, a place where a young wife looked forward to putting her best silver in a drawer the day she moved into a new home, she willingly signed on for Ernest's plan to move to Italy, with regular sojourns to other interesting destinations in Europe.

The two of them had met just before the presidential election, in October, at the apartment of mutual friends Y. K. and Genevieve "Doodles" Smith. Modernists themselves, of a sort, the Smiths had an open marriage and felt free to take lovers—a detail they did not share with Hemingway until after he condemned Doodles for an affair he learned about later that year. Hemingway liked hanging out with the Smiths, and even lived with them happily for a time that year. They were unconventional and arts-minded like he was—as their invitations to the Menshevik journalist Levine and Lost Generation writer Anderson indicate. Y. K.'s sister Kate was Ernest's lake friend (and possible lover, as a story he wrote in Paris suggests) and Hadley's classmate in the Mary Institute of St. Louis.[2] Kate kindly invited Hadley to Chicago that fall because Hadley's mother had recently died and Kate thought a trip might be a welcome diversion from her grieving. Hadley's father, a wealthy pharmaceuticals heir, had died years before, so that meant she was now fully independent and financially secure too. She had full access to a trust fund that would yield perhaps $2,000 per year. As Hadley began to become serious about Ernest, which happened sometime between October and Christmas of 1920, her very protective sister urged her not to reveal the existence of this trust fund to him or to any other beau. It would be better for men, she argued, to appreciate Hadley for virtues other than her money. After all, if the trust income was not quite enough to pay for decent room and board in most economies (it would be in Paris), it was a desirable supplement to any young man's entry-level income, certainly to Hemingway's income as a journeyman writer.

Hadley certainly had charms other than her money. Men and women alike found her attractive. She had traveled in Europe as a youngster and was part of a family that supplied funds and leadership for St. Louis's civic life. She was kind and funny. She played along with Hemingway's boyish baby talk, nicknames, and malapropisms, such as his calling her Hash and using *male* for "man" and *mort* for "kill" and *yence* for "making love." Yet she was not a kid but a serious adult, age twenty-nine to his twenty-one. As Hemingway makes clear in his late-life Paris memoir, *A Moveable Feast*, Hadley was unfailingly supportive of his work in Paris. She was also a talent in her own right at the piano, a willing companion on the road and in bed, eventually a loving mother, and even a modernist—which is to say that she embraced with few complaints an expatriate lifestyle based in unconventional new theories about families, women's roles, and societal revolutions.

By December of 1920 Hadley had high hopes of a deep and continuing relationship with this writer and Great War veteran from Chicago. For his part, Hemingway kept telling her that he loved her deeply, yet he displayed signs of certain hesitations about the relationship. He wrote that month to tell her that a failure to kiss her goodbye at the train station a few weeks earlier should not be misunderstood. He simply wished he could say "good night" to her instead of "goodbye." (His sexual urges were a major topic in their correspondence.) He explained that a tight budget was the reason he had declined her invitation to join her in St. Louis for that Christmas, and he made certain she knew how much he loved her nevertheless: "'Course I love you—I love you all the time—when I wake up in the morning and have to climb out of bed and splash around and shave—I look at your picture and think about you—and that's a pretty deadly part of [a] day as you know and a good test of loving anyone."[3]

The two of them visited each other's homes during the succeeding spring and early summer, and they talked about their future together. They committed themselves to buying lire for a life together in Italy. Hemingway wrote letters to an editor named John Bone in Toronto, exploring the idea of the *Star* taking him on as a full-time foreign correspondent. He exaggerated his time on the *Kansas City Star*, telling Bone that he had been there in 1916, when in fact he had still been at Oak Park High, writing for the school newspaper. Bone apparently replied in a positive if noncommittal way, yet, oddly, Hemingway allowed the opportunity to pass for many months, probably because he and Hadley were still discussing alternate plans. Then, in June an announcement appeared in the *St. Louis Post-Dispatch* reporting that Hadley Richardson of the city and "Ernest Miller Hemmingway" [*sic*] of Chicago were to be married in the autumn. They chose September 3 for their wedding day.

Hadley had committed herself to a young man who was just then undergoing a certain kind of maturation and intellectual evolution. It was that January that Hemingway met Sherwood Anderson at the Smith apartment and became aware of the "Robin's Egg Renaissance" in Chicago, the writers' movement involving Anderson, Ben Hecht, Carl Sandburg, Floyd Dell, Edgar Lee Masters, and others. The books these people wrote might have changed Hemingway's prose and his approach to human story, bringing badly needed dignity and psychological realism to his writings, but he was not ready for that kind of learning yet. He still regarded publishing in the *Saturday Evening Post* as his goal, not in *The Little Review* or *The Dial*, so he still wrote comic entertainments rather than studies of postwar conditions or new insights into the human character prompted by psychoanalysis. He must also have known that the *Post* paid thousands for a good story while the modernist little magazines paid nothing at all.

He was getting part of the modernist message though. When a female lake friend wrote with concerns about his marrying so young, he replied in late July that he had no intention of taking up a conventional domestic life:

Sure I know how you feel about my getting married—course I'm too young by the calendar and would seem terribly funny to be married and horrible to be domesticated and settled into a dead rut of seed [dollar] getting and maybe children having and all that.

He had another life in mind:

Good chance that it'll be just two people that love each other being able to be together and understand each other and bum together and help each other in their work and take away from each other that sort of loneliness of [*sic*] that's with you even when you're in a crowd of people that are fond of you.[4]

With its loving and aware partnership, its lack of conventional gender roles, and its vision of making the wider world their home, this was a far cry from Hemingway's parents' marriage. Hadley was apparently on board with this vision, as well she might have been, because it suggests a kind of modernist egalitarian love marriage based in mutual appreciation and commitment to creative work and edifying adventure. Anderson was at the bottom of this vision. His hero of *Winesburg, Ohio*, a lonely young reporter and would-be writer named George Willard, could have written its cadences of hope and longing.

Throughout the spring and summer, Hemingway sent out stories based on his wartime experiences in Italy. He wrote in a broadly humorous style that could not in any way capture the true experiences of soldiers in the trenches. The editors at *Red Book* and the *Saturday Evening Post* rejected the stories quickly, and Hemingway's revisions did not lead to later publication. As Reynolds aptly observes, those editors were doing the future Hemingway a favor. In Paris, he would craft a style, a method, and a sympathy for suffering people that he had not yet dreamt about in Chicago in 1921, and it was better not to have a trail of stories in another less mature and corrupt style dogging him.

Because Ernest and Hadley chose the Michigan lake country for their wedding, trying to escape the bourgeois wedding conventions of either Oak Park or St. Louis, their 450 invitations yielded only about thirty attendees on September 3. But they did not care. They were eager to be alone together, to get to the Hemingway cottage (the family called it Windemere to recall the haunt of the English lake poets) for a quiet and inexpensive honeymoon.

Sometime just before the wedding, Anderson had convinced the two of them to go live and work in Paris. It was there, he argued, that loving and bumming and working and defeating loneliness could best be accomplished. There were things worth learning in that city, and tutors ready to lend support and deeper understanding. Anderson even offered to introduce Hemingway to two of the most important modernists—people Hemingway had never heard of before that summer—Gertrude Stein and Ezra Pound. The modernist educations of Ernest and Hadley Hemingway were about to commence.

Hemingway quit the *Co-Operative Commonwealth* job after taking three weeks off for the wedding, two of them paid.[5] In late October he wrote to John Bone again, following up on Bone's casual offer the previous winter of a foreign correspondent's job. Hemingway must have written that he was ready to take the job. (We do not know because all we have is an unfinished partial draft of the actual letter he apparently sent.) Shortly after Thanksgiving, Hemingway had a written agreement in hand. He would set up base in Paris as a "roving correspondent for both Star papers."[6] He would be paid well for his stories and would receive travel and per diem expenses too. By this time, Hadley had revealed that she had a steady income from her trust fund, so both of them could enter into this adventure with far less financial insecurity. They would have enough to live on, no matter how Hemingway's reporting and fiction writing sold. The Hemingways were ready for Paris.

≡ ≡ ≡

Meanwhile, Quoc was beginning to realize that his efforts during the 1919 Peace Conference had been disappointingly inartistic. He had not found a way to be heard by the men who held the power, the Big Four and their aides. In the first weeks of 1920 it began to dawn on him that sincerity alone was not going to pierce the complacency shielding the consciences of Allied leaders from revolutionary ideas. French leaders preferred to consider the ongoing project in the colonies a settled question, and the American President Wilson had left town preoccupied with too many domestic political problems of his own—such as his failure to build a coalition of political allies for his League of Nations proposals.

If he was going to unsettle French minds, Quoc would need to become much more provocative. He began to pay attention to the provocations that seemed to work most effectively in Paris in those days, from French laborers' May Day marches and general strikes to international bohemians' showings of the new abstract arts, including the brash dadaist art. The ideas of these artists had an anarchic quality, yet most of them did not merely want to tear down the institutions of Western civilization, no matter how corrupt and venial the war had shown that civilization to be. These artists, writers, and political revolutionaries wanted to preserve the beautiful works and ideas of the West while bringing about a new fulfilment of the West's democratic and cultural ideals. This campaign would require the nonviolent cleansing of all Western heritage bent toward domination and exploitation. This sorting of the beneficent from the immoral traditions of Western culture was essentially the modernist project. Even the dadaists wanted to escape the logic of super-aggressive capitalism with its hawkish self-defense ethic, but not the larger logic of human responsibility and care.

Quoc was concerned that there was too little attention paid to the ills of colonialism among these bohemian people. However, he had seen hints of an awakening. People understood that Picasso's primitivism, for example—such as the African masks that lent such a disturbing quality to his masterpiece *Les Demoiselles d'Avignon*—was an homage to the dignity of people suffering under colonial rule. Quoc was furious about the human zoos and working conditions his compatriots had to endure, so he was searching for a movement or a body of ideas in Paris that more directly addressed the evils of colonialism.

Quoc's work during the Paris Peace Conference had earned him a measure of respect in the Parisian anti-colonial community. Though he had been an invisible member of the French Socialist Party before the summer of 1919, by the autumn of that year he could count as friends Marcel Cachin, the editor in chief of *L'Humanité*; Leon Blum, later to be a three-time prime minister of France; Jean Longuet, Karl Marx's son-in-law; and Henri Barbusse, the first novelist to expose the deplorable conditions in wartime trenches to a large French audience. He met important media figures at the Club du Faubourg, including the writer Colette, the actor and singer Maurice Chevalier, and Émile Coué, founder of Couéism, with its famous positive autosuggestion: "Every day, in every way, I'm getting better and better."[7]

Thanks to the club, Quoc was indeed getting better. There he learned about abstract art, twelve-tone music, the doctrines of French socialism, and the cadences of proper French prose. By this time, perhaps the summer of 1920, Quoc had begun working intermittently as a photo retoucher, one of those jobs the French believed the frail, gentle Indochinese were fitted for. In this work, all he was required to do was create realistic red lips and glowing cheeks on black-and-white photographs of French children and newlyweds. He settled into a daily life that involved both study and reasonably remunerative work.

He also seems to have made friends with a woman named Marie Brière, a French dressmaker and a member with him in the French

Socialist Party. We know absolutely nothing about the relationship, except that Marie later reported information about Quoc to agents who identified her as his former mistress.[8] A few historians have proposed that she and Quoc were very close, even in love, but the evidence for such claims is thin. If she was his love interest, the relationship would have been active during the middle of 1920, just as Quoc was beginning to reevaluate his commitment to socialist reformism through legal channels. Unlike Hemingway, Quoc seems to have placed his politics before his wish for female companionship and partnership. Perhaps his attitude toward women at this time is an index to his increasing political radicalism. According to a police file, he broke up one friend's marriage because the wife in the couple would not "give up her entire salary to the [anti-colonial] cause, do the family washing on Sunday, and obey her husband blindly."[9]

As for his own personal life, Quoc was far too busy and far too distressed to pursue a meaningful relationship. Throughout that year, he exhausted himself laboring away on his history of Indochinese colonialism. He called the book *Les opprimés* (*The Oppressed*). As he brought home sources from the library and sat each day to write the truth about colonialism in Vietnam, his handwritten manuscript pages for the book began to accumulate. Then one day he returned to his flat to find the manuscript gone. There were signs that thieves had taken it, right off his desk. Quoc suspected government agents were the perpetrators, perhaps even roommates or friends, because the thief or thieves seem to have known exactly how complete Quoc's manuscript had grown before taking it. They had waited until the manuscript was nearly finished to spirit it away and destroy it, an incredibly cruel thing to do to a writer. In the aftermath of this shock, Quoc would not abandon writing as a primary activity of resistance, but he would take much better care of his manuscripts. He would turn to magazine articles for the time being, returning to this history of recent French colonialism only after he had left Paris and the den of vipers he lived in.

Then, with Marie apparently present, Quoc made a major step toward becoming Ho Chi Minh.[10] In December of 1920 the two of them, as card-carrying socialists, attended a congress of the French Socialist Party in Tours, France. (I wonder: Did they feel comfortable sitting with each other on the train to Tours, a mixed-race couple journeying together through central France?) There, Quoc renounced his membership in the French Socialist Party and cofounded the French Communist Party. He became a communist that day largely because he had recently read a 1919 essay by Vladimir Lenin titled "Theses of the National and Colonial Questions." This essay addressed colonialism as a great injustice, an illegal and immoral prop keeping Western capitalist nations in good economic order. As part of his argument, Lenin reversed the Marxist orthodoxy declaring that revolution could only begin with urban industrial workers who had pre-existing solidarity and access to weapons stored in nearby military barracks. He argued that Russian and European communists should view the colonies as a likely source for revolutionary allies, and that revolutionaries should begin building solidarity and Marxian awareness there.

Quoc saw that this thesis granted him and his colonized people a great role in revolutionary processes, but more important to him, the thesis virtually assured the colonies of their autonomy and liberty if they hitched their fate to a successful Bolshevik-Soviet cause. Lenin's essay had a profound effect on Quoc, as he admitted:

> There were political terms difficult to understand in this thesis. But by dint of reading it again and again, finally I could grasp the main part of it. What emotion, enthusiasm, clear-sightedness, and confidence it instilled in me! I was overjoyed to tears. Though sitting alone in my room, I shouted aloud as if addressing large crowds: Dear martyrs, compatriots! This is what we need, this is the path to our liberation.[11]

Not long after this emotional outburst, Quoc arrived with Marie in Tours for the congress of French socialists. He knew that there was going to be a discussion of Third International, an organization of communists with a plan for revolutions that would lead to communist societies across the earth, and he knew that he was now obliged to support this plan.

Many progressives felt that the Second International, formed in Paris in 1889 and imagining a bloodless revolution leading to worker control of economies and nations, had failed. In 1914 its adherents, mainly socialist labor unions from European countries, had supported the war, allowing nationalist patriotism to trump their principled self-interest.

Lenin now believed that support for war among the unionized workers exposed a weak, antimilitarist, reformist element in the membership of the Second International. Now, he wanted a more serious platform.

Quoc had narrower reasons to support a Third International: "As for the Second International, it is not concerned about the colonial question," he wrote. Now, with Russia under communist control and Germany teetering toward revolution, Lenin's prediction that revolution would sweep across Europe, perhaps even to the distant shores of the United States, seemed more realistic to Quoc—and to many others. As Margaret MacMillan nicely puts it, "Europe had been a place of unsatisfied longings before the war—of socialists hoping for a better world, of labor for better conditions, of nationalists for their own homes—and those longings emerged again with greater force because in the fluid world of 1919 it was possible to dream of great change—or have nightmares about the collapse of order."[12] Many of the more hopeful workers now regretted the naïve patriotism that had caused them to stop campaigning for wages, benefits, and political power so they could fight for their countries. They came to Tours in search of new options too. So in December of 1920 Quoc journeyed to the Eighteenth Congress of the French Socialist Party in Tours with a plan: either to change the FSP or to leave it.

It was Christmas Day, an ordinary working day for nominally secular French socialists, when Quoc addressed the congress as the delegate from Indochina. In a grand old indoor horse-riding hall that Duiker describes as "festooned with portraits of the old socialist war horse Jean Jaurès and banners proclaiming the unity of the working class throughout the world," Quoc took his place along the rostrum among Europe's most famous leftists.[13] It was a fraught meeting. At one point two police agents stormed toward Quoc during a plenary meeting. In an act of canny nonviolent direct action, the other delegates, nearly all European and thus less likely to be beaten by police, surrounded slim young Quoc. They kept the police away from their fellow delegate until they gave up and left the hall. Quoc then took the floor and made his pleas for attention to the problem of colonialism. He accused some delegates of betraying indigenous people living in France's colonies. As he spoke, he aggressively shouted down reformists, including his friend Jean Longuet, who interrupted to defend their records on colonial questions. "Silence, the Parliamentarians!" he shouted angrily.[14] He also engaged in the central debate of the congress, on the effectiveness and realism of reforms versus revolutions. He found himself caught between his two French mentors, Marcel Cachin and Longuet, both fellow members of the Club du Faubourg and close acquaintances since at least the peace conference days of 1919. Quoc sided with Cachin, believing that a certain French interpretation of communism yet to be defined offered more realistic methods for sparking and winning revolutionary change, as Bolshevik Russia had just proven.

The Tours Congress crested when the socialists voted on whether to join Lenin's Russian Bolsheviks and the German Bolshevik party in approving the Third International, also known as the Communist International, or Comintern for short. At that moment, Quoc changed his life, siding with the 3,208 delegates who joined the Comintern and its dream of revolution. With his vote, he helped defeat 1,022 others who remained committed to socialist reforms within the existing legal and governmental systems. Like Hemingway earlier that year, Quoc became a communist alongside thousands of his comrades in what many (especially anti-communists) must consider a deeply ironic way: through a democratic vote. Within days of this vote he returned to Paris to join more than thirty thousand Parisians in a rally to celebrate the promises of the Third International.[15]

But Sarraut was about to lay ruin to Quoc's hopes. He was about to show how determined France was to retain control of its colonies, how adamant, how cruel, and how devious the French were willing to be in resisting reforms that might lead to Indochinese national independence.

☰ ☰ ☰

Quoc still held out hope that the American people hated colonialism and would one day help put the system to an end. Like Hemingway, he hated the status quo but still saw America as a force for justice, a set of ideas and ideals. And free speech was the Americans' most important tool. So Quoc behaved like a good citizen of a liberal democracy, even after becoming a communist. Notably, while he lived in Paris, Quoc never incited violence, never organized so much as a public protest, never even helped organize a strike. The only real pressure he exerted on French officials was rhetorical, a few public speeches and the many essays he wrote mostly for *L'Humanité*, and for two other journals, *La Vie Ouvrière* and *Le Paria*. The titles of these journals tell us what Quoc was working for during his Paris years: humanity, the life of the worker, and an end to the plight of political and economic outcasts. Quoc may have signed on for the Third International alongside Lenin's Bolsheviks, but he was no Bolshevik himself.

Sarraut was not a hardliner or ultra-nationalist either, and he may have wanted the best for Indochina's *indigènes*—so long as they remained colonial subjects. When he was appointed Minister of Colonies in January of 1921, he quickly became known for his impatience with arguments for Indochinese independence. He believed in the colonial relationship. But he was also known for pushing reforms he thought would actually fulfill France's mission to civilize the *indigènes*. In 1923 he published his statement of colonial policy, "*La Mise en valeur des colonies françaises*," or "The Development of the French Colonies," which explained what he had been working to accomplish as Indochina's governor-general, a role he filled from 1912 to 1914 and from 1917 to 1919. "*La Mise*" also laid out what he wished to accomplish as Minister of Colonies. His goals mainly involved modest reforms, giving the Indochinese access to education and freedom to publish opinions in the press.

When Quoc wrote to the Human Rights League in 1921, offering a copy of his "Demands of the Annamite People," a League official replied with a summary of his consultation with Sarraut's office: "They say that you haven't taken into account the reforms accomplished by M. Sarraut." Quoc was encouraged to make his complaints "with more precision." What this correspondent really meant, of course, was that Quoc should accept the logic of present-day colonialism. Liberty of the press in Indochina had already been accomplished, this official wrote, and liberty of education was on its way. In fact, these reports of progress were exaggerated. Everyone knew that colonial managers still freely beat Vietnamese workers. The idea that these workers would soon be free to choose an advanced education was laughable.

Meanwhile, Quoc's relations with Sarraut were evolving into something personal, a kind of bitter feud. Sarraut now had Quoc monitored around the clock, presumably a very expensive precaution. French agents in Paris began to treat Quoc with the contempt they felt he deserved as a traitor to Greater France. When Quoc went to a hospital in 1920 to have an abscess on his elbow treated (yet another sign that he may have had tuberculosis), policemen deliberately destroyed his peace, trying to photograph him in his hospital room. Quoc's nurses barred the way into his room, refusing entry to police agents and their photographer, honoring principles of universal care and protecting their patient, the frail young Annamite man with the bandaged elbow.

In August of 1920 Sarraut wrote to a prefect of police that Quoc "has no right to meddle in our politics under an assumed name." It was a hypocritical legal stance. If Quoc did not have a right of dissent, of course it is only because none of France's colonial subjects had any real civil rights. Any white French citizen could casually change his or her name—and many did, such as Marie Cocotte, who was about to become the Hemingways' Paris maid, and whose real surname was Rohrbach— and could voice political opinions freely.

In September of 1920 the irritated Sarraut called Quoc into his offices for another audience. This time he gave a subordinate, M. Guesde, the task of interviewing Quoc. When Quoc visited Guesde's office, he was irritated to discover that an even more minor functionary was actually to conduct the interview. This M. Pasquier tried to conciliate Quoc, offering vague and noncommittal help with his requests (or "demands") to the French government. When Quoc replied that he only wanted his eight "Demands" granted, his set of basic civil rights within a continuing colonial relationship, Pasquier, according to Quoc's own record of the meeting, simply changed the subject. Clearly, Quoc saw that reform through diplomacy was at a dead end.

Early in 1921 Nguyen Ai Quoc was summoned to Sarraut's offices again, this time to meet with the Minister of Colonies himself. Sarraut seems to have believed that he could reason with Quoc, could teach the young communist how unrealistic his hopes were. Sarraut argued in this meeting that no Southeast Asian peasant society could assemble a working government or organize armed forces for its national defense. "If France returned Indochina to you," Sarraut argued to Quoc, "you would not be able to govern yourselves because you are not sufficiently well armed." Though it is obvious that if France had cared about its Indochinese brothers and sisters as much as it claimed, the nation could easily have supplied the materiel and military guidance needed for the Vietnamese to defend themselves, Quoc argued that Japan and China had both managed on their own in the past generation to leave behind their colonial pasts and become "nations of the world." Both had achieved more than respectable militaries and functioning governments. Just as Pasquier had, Sarraut addressed this argument by changing the subject. Quoc must have been exasperated as his arguments were treated as childishly naïve.

Around this time, Sarraut and his lieutenants discussed whether to deport Quoc to Vietnam. They concluded that it was better to monitor Quoc in Paris than to send him back to Indochina. Perhaps to keep Quoc's resistance efforts in Sarraut's lap rather than his own, Governor-General Maurice Long argued that if Quoc could travel, he might foment Vietnamese revolution from anywhere in Asia—as eventually he did, from China and Hong Kong. "A Nguyen Ai Quoc unmasked and kept under surveillance by the Metropolitan police—" wrote one of Sarraut's men, "we can not wish for better than that."[16]

By summertime of 1921 Quoc had recovered his health, but he faced other challenges. In July he took a terrible beating at the hands of police agents. He had attended a commemoration of the Paris Commune of 1871 in Père Lachaise Cemetery, where the Commune met its end. The event was a chance for Quoc and his comrades to honor the sacrifice of an earlier generation of communists in their struggle to secure reasonable rights for the working people. In May of 1871 French government forces, some of them fed by Escoffier, were mopping up a final assault on the Communards. French forces, humiliated by their recent defeat at the hands of the Germans, now took out their frustrations on their fellow French. On this May day, the final few Communards, numbering about 150, had barricaded themselves in the cemetery. After the two sides fought among the tombs for a few hours, French military forces gained the upper hand. They gathered up their prisoners. Then they lined up the last remaining 150 Communards against a wall in the cemetery and, ignoring French law and due process, massacred them by rifle fire. In spite of the outrage and passion such memories evoked in Quoc and other modern leftists, the memorial gathering in the cemetery was a peaceful one. There was no plan to incite a riot or any other public disturbance. Yet police broke up the commemoration violently, with batons and other weapons. Quoc was one of those who was badly beaten.[17]

As Quoc recovered from his cuts and bruises once again that month, debates at the Villa des Gobelins apartment became more heated. One shouting match lasted from nine in the evening until the early morning hours. Soon Quoc moved out, first to a friend's flat and then to a small room of his own far across the city.

This move surely increased Quoc's loneliness and sense of political isolation, and these effects were hardly accidental. The agents following him, who had Vietnamese names but were known as Jean, Edouard, Devillier, and Désiré in police reports, must have worked hard to erode the morale and sense of comradeship at the Villa address. Quoc found life on the Villa des Gobelins so inhospitable that spring that he moved from the southeast corner of the Left Bank to the northeast corner of the Right Bank, into a slum hotel on the Impasse Compoint. (*Impasse* means "blind alley.") And he had lost the financial support of the Patriots. Soon an ad appeared in *La Vie Ouvrière* (*The Worker's Life*) that read, "If you would like a lifelike memento of your family, have your photos retouched at Nguyen Ai Quoc's. A lovely portrait in a lovely frame for 45 franc."[18]

Quoc's move to 9 Impasse Compoint must have been emotionally difficult for him. His life had grown even more straitened. His photo retouching business earned him barely enough to pay for food and the rent on a room so small that it could contain only a bed and wardrobe. His apartment had no running water, so he washed himself in a basin and cleaned his clothes in the yard. He read by an oil lamp, and because his tiny room had no heat, each evening that fall and winter he warmed a brick in his landlady's furnace, wrapped it in newspaper, and brought it to bed with him. He ate only twice a day, a bit of salted fish or bread and cheese.[19] It is no coincidence that this is the moment when, according to police records, the lonely, cold, and hungry Quoc began asking for dates with pretty customers at the photo shop, including a woman named Miss Boudon, whose beauty moved him so much that he asked her out twice.[20] Among other things, he seems to have needed company and emotional support.[21] Agent reports show that he did still return to the Villa for meetings and discussions, and never truly cut ties with Truong and Trinh, who still admired his patriotism, if not his impatience.

As the deprivation and harassment continued that fall and early winter, Quoc's politics and his methods changed. He began to seek out allies and to focus more sharply on colonialism as a worldwide institution rather than a specifically Indochinese problem. He came to see colonial *émigrés* in Paris as a power base. Indeed, he began to choose Paris—by choosing its most dispossessed people and the arts-and-politics movements that sided with them.

In October he attended the first meeting of a new group, the Intercolonial Union, inaugurated by a Malagasy lecturer at the School of Oriental Languages named Stephen Oju Oti. The Union's purpose was to study the politics and economics of colonialism in order to dismantle the system. Quoc's involvement represents a new stage in his political consciousness. Now he sought to build solidarity among expatriates from all the French colonies. Quoc became the group's treasurer. Because it soon became clear to members of the Union that Quoc was also a talented propagandist, they urged him to publicize their efforts. So Quoc followed the modernist script by starting a little magazine. (We have seen that there were little magazines trumpeting modernist literature in Chicago and New York, but they abounded in Paris as well.) In April of 1922 the journal *Le Paria* emerged as the newsletter of the Union. It was more than a newsletter, though. It was also a brash modernist journal filled with manifestos and vivid stories and all the serious reformist intention that Parisian readers of the 1920s had come to expect. As we will see, the rhetoric of *Le Paria* expressed outrage at colonial injustice, reminded colonial subjects of the abuses they and their families had suffered, and provided Parisians in general with a window on the utterly hypocritical and abusive *mission civilisatrice* that many of them naïvely supported.

Quoc finished out the terrible year of 1921 fending off another arrest attempt, this time in Marseille, where he was attending the First Congress of the French Communist Party in December. Two plainclothes policemen tried to apprehend him on a street outside the conference hall. Quoc managed to break their grips and enter the hall, where once again his comrades and fellow delegates escorted him past the policemen to a hiding place. He stayed there until he was able to escape the city and return to Paris.[22]

≡≡≡

The Hemingways arrived in Paris in December of 1921. Ernest and Hadley had enjoyed their sail across the Atlantic on the SS *Leopoldina*, and they quickly found a serviceable hotel in Christmastime Paris, the Jacob d'Angleterre in Saint-Germain-de-Prés, which Anderson had recommended as "clean and cheap." On December 23, Hemingway wrote to Anderson, "Well here we are. And we sit outside the Dôme Café, opposite the Rotunde [*sic*] that's being redecorated, warmed up against one of those charcoal brazziers [*sic*] and it's so damned cold outside and the brazier makes it so warm and we drink hot rum punch, hot and the rhum [*sic*] enters into us like the Holy Spirit."[23] They celebrated a quiet and rather lonely Christmas together in the hotel.

Anderson had sent them to Paris with three letters of introduction. He wanted them to know Gertrude Stein and Ezra Pound, who could teach Hemingway modernism, and a lesser-known American named Lewis Galantiere, who was a problem-solver and could help them with practical matters. Just after Christmas, the Hemingways presented their letter to Galantiere, who worked for the International Chamber of Commerce in Paris and was thus part of the large American colony in the city. The Hemingways shared a dinner out with this new friend and began to get the lay of the land. Hemingway nearly wrecked the budding friendship that evening, breaking Galantiere's glasses in a post-dinner boxing match that was supposed to be casual. (Boxing matches with Hemingway, who loved the sport and took special pride in his prowess, were never casual.) But Galantiere forgave Hemingway, perhaps because he liked Hadley and felt sympathy for her. Soon enough, he had found the Hemingways their first apartment, a cold-water walk-up with bathrooms on the stair landings at 74 rue du Cardinal Lemoine. The apartment was in a workers' neighborhood, on the Seine side of a city square called the Place Contrescarpe. At the other end of the square was the entry point to the market street, the rue Mouffetard. At the bottom of the downward-sloping rue Mouffetard, with its charcuterie shops and wine stalls, was a neighborhood where Vietnamese immigrants lived—including Quoc, who was about to return to his comrades, including the agents who tailed him.

Ernest and Hadley were welcomed immediately by sympathetic, generous, and like-minded people—all Americans. Some, including Stein and Pound, became his professors and mentors. Others, such as Bill Bird, founder of Three Mountains Press, and aspiring novelist Robert McAlmon, became his buddies and opponents in tennis matches. Sylvia

Beach's Shakespeare & Company bookstore would become a mailbox, lending library, credit union, and home away from home, and Beach herself, a dear friend. Ernest quickly felt at home in his Paris neighborhood, and he no longer regretted giving up his earlier plan to live in Italy. He loved the many cafés in the neighborhood—comfortable rooms where it was considered perfectly appropriate to purchase a cup of café crème, get out your notebook, sharpen your pencil with a pen knife and drop the shavings onto your coffee saucer, and write for hours. Hadley was happy too. A dedicated artist herself, she was attracted to the idea of practicing her piano with uninterrupted professional dedication. She played a borrowed piano for hours every day, and when she was finished, she joined Ernest in a café for a nice drink. She had grown weary of predictable Victorian St. Louis and had wanted to return to Europe, which she had visited and enjoyed as a seventeen-year-old. She was perfectly ready to live as an expatriate, for now, and was sure she would not miss being a housewife in an ordinary, bourgeois American home. She was wrong about that, as it happens, but she did not know it in 1921.

In choosing Paris, the Hemingways had chosen vocations as world-aware artists in a modern mode. Gone were Victorian patterns of career and marriage, the patriotic conformism and rigid gender roles. Ernest and Hadley came to Paris as partners, if not wholly equal ones, expecting to learn from Pound and Stein how to make revolutionary art. They knew they would learn from great modern artists such as Picasso and Stravinsky too, even if they only got to see the pictures and listen to the symphonies. Anderson had told them as much, but even he underestimated Hemingway's charm. Indeed, Ernest and Hadley would soon know almost all the great artists of the city in their time and would become part of the fabric of what has become known as Lost Generation Paris.

Hemingway and Quoc made their political decisions and revisions of the 1920s amid a heated debate about the meaning of the Russian Revolution. For every Lincoln Steffens—a reporter friend of Hemingway's known for his muckraking journalism—who returned from Russia in 1919 to declare, infamously, "I have seen the future, and it works," there was a Winston Churchill noting, presciently, "The essence of Bolshevism as opposed to many other forms of visionary political thought is that it can only be propagated and maintained by violence."[24] (Was that not true of democratic capitalism?) Of course there were probable reasons for these differing opinions. Muckraking reporter Steffens had slept in dank, crowded American tenements among the poor and had high hopes for a more just society, while Churchill was dressed by a valet in London townhouses and estate homes, dined at Escoffier's Carlton, and came from a landed community of privilege dedicated to its own survival. These were two men unlikely to understand each other very deeply and quite likely to reach differing political commitments. They weren't alone in this partisan sorting. As more than one historian has noted, there seemed to be no moderate position on Bolshevism in 1919 and 1920. "The debate on Russia," Christopher Lasch writes, "had become a struggle between those who wanted to recognize the Bolsheviks and those who wanted to beat them into submission, a struggle from which a moderate man could only retire in confusion."[25]

In 1920, Hemingway and Quoc hoped, and even voted, to see the Russian experiment through. Or rather, they voted to see some part of Bolshevism's restructuring of society attempted and tested in their own homelands, hopefully nonviolently and humanely—a quasi-utopian dream that was still thinkable at that time. They did not see Stalin on the horizon, not in 1920. As Lasch notes, in the early 1920s, "what began [in Russia] as a democratic revolution had become a communist revolution, and the communist example . . . would appeal mightily to underdogs everywhere."[26] As a colonial subject with no real future in his own country, Nguyen Ai Quoc was one of these underdogs, and as a working man with a love of the arts making do on a shaky income, so was Ernest Hemingway.

# 9

## POUND AND THE ECONOMY

### HEMINGWAY IN EARLY 1922

In early 1922, the Hemingways quickly met members of the literary colony of Americans who lived, like the Vietnamese students at the Sorbonne, along the Boulevard Saint-Michel or clustered around the Luxembourg Gardens, one side of which runs along the Boul Mich. These artists, composers, choreographers, and writers, some of whom we now call the Lost Generation, were not difficult to find. All anyone had to do was walk from the gardens a few blocks south or uphill away from the Seine on the Boul Mich, then west on the Boulevard du Montparnasse. After a few blocks they would arrive at a grouping of popular cafés, the Rotonde, the Select, and the Dôme. (The same cafés and bars are still there, not much changed except the clientele—and the prices.) These cafés were housed on the ground floors of Paris's traditional, elegant, buff-colored, six-story mansard buildings, with their lovely old wrought-iron balcony railings, yet they glowed untraditionally with their bold neon signs. In 1921, the tables clustered around the doors of these cafés, on the extra-wide sidewalks of Paris, were crowded with artists of every kind. Hemingway quickly saw that many were not artists at all, but really frauds wasting time, but he enjoyed getting to know the truly hardworking craftspeople working on serious ideas. He and Hadley frequented the cafés often, but they were more curious than many of the other customers, so they also explored Paris further afield. "Everywhere [Hemingway] turned," biographer Michael Reynolds writes, "there was something new to learn, and turning with him was Hadley, always close, eager to move in whatever direction his interests led: piano concerts, gallery openings, late night spots drinking and early morning breakfasts afterwards among the fresh produce at Les Halles."[1]

In that day, the cafés were both very French and very American, catering to those who wanted to sit in the French manner at a little, round marble-topped table outdoors as well as to those who wanted to stand with an elbow on the *bar américain*. It was pleasant, but it would be like this for only a couple more years. Partly thanks to Hemingway's own international fame and the stories and novel about Paris he would write later that decade, the cafés became so crowded by the mid-1920s that he could not work in them. He was irritated when a table he had previously found free was occupied by a bohemian poseur or, worse yet, an American tourist. It turns out that Americans in Paris were both a blessing and a curse for Hemingway, as he tried to write about America in France. It did not help that as early as 1924, before Hemingway had even published an American novel or short-story collection, a guide to Paris listed him as an attraction to see in the Latin Quarter. His brief journey to that celebrity status was about to begin—but so was a journey to his authentic artistry, his ability to create human dramas that showed the crying need to build a better society.

Many think that Sylvia Beach's Shakespeare & Company bookstore was the hub of expatriate Americans in Paris, almost all of whom practiced radical new art forms, opposed the censorship of James Joyce's *Ulysses* (1922), quoted T. S. Eliot's *The Waste Land* (1922), celebrated varied sexual identities, met in salons or at cocktail parties to discuss art, revered Pound and Stein and Picasso, attended Dada manifestations, and read little magazines. But the few dozen Lost Generation artists and their followers and chroniclers were not, as we are often led to believe, the most influential American expatriates in the city in the 1920s. If anything, the Lost Generation artists had to struggle to be heard over the voices of the more commercially minded Americans of the Right Bank, who lived mainly in the 16th and 17th Arrondissements, just west of the Arc de Triomphe, and worked mainly in the 1st and 2nd, around the grand Opera Garnier.

Americans in 1920s Paris had no reason to feel alien, because they had actually built their own American town in the very center of the city. This group of forty thousand non-literary American Parisians felt at home with their two houses of worship, the great stone American church ministering to general Protestants on the Quai d'Orsay and the even larger Gothic American Cathedral ministering to Anglicans and Episcopalians on the avenue George V. The congregations of these churches, average Americans abroad, were proud of their grammar schools and prep academies, their English-language library, their hospital in the suburb of Neuilly, their daily newspapers reporting American news in the English language, their gymnasium ("It differs from the French gymnasium in having fresh air."[2]), even their own restaurants and grocery stores catering to American tastes. A recent social history of interwar Paris tells us just how American life could be in the city:

> Like all immigrant communities, even in the land of haute cuisine, Americans had their cravings. So there was Sam's Place on the Boulevard des Italiens, where you could get pork and beans or club sandwiches, or the Chicago-Texas Inn near the Eiffel Tower, run by a black Pullman-car chef, advertising authentic hot biscuits and corned beef hash. An American grocery store near the Madeleine advertised its "all American cereals" (Grape Nuts, Shredded Wheat, Puffed Wheat, Cream of Wheat), along with grape juice and popcorn.[3]

Hemingway probably ate at Sam's, because it was located among the American newspaper offices, where he met other reporters for scheduled talks once a week in 1922 and 1923. And he probably laughed at the bizarre geography in the name of the Chicago-Texas Inn.

Americans hardly had to interact with the French at all on the Right Bank. Non-literary expats belonged to the YMCA or YWCA, went to American Legion meetings, frequented the American Library, and if they had the right pedigree, accepted membership in the Daughters of the American Revolution. Even on the Left Bank, the Hemingways could go days at a time without speaking French if they wanted to, and when they wearied of brioche for breakfast, they could grab the box of Grape Nuts.

Between the low prices caused by postwar inflation, the American bars and restaurants and shops, and the ready access to friends from America, early days in Paris were going very well for Ernest and Hadley Hemingway. Their income stream might have felt shaky at first, but as we will see, Hemingway began writing and selling news stories and travel pieces right away in early 1922. They felt flush enough to travel to Switzerland in January, trading Paris's rainy gloom for alpine sunshine, and returning to Paris in mid-February. That was when they decided to take advantage of those two remaining letters of recommendation Anderson had sent with them to France. The first letter had put them in touch with Lewis Galantiere, who found them their flat. Now they needed to meet Ezra Pound and Gertrude Stein. It was lucky for Hemingway that he did. During the spring of 1922, and perhaps for a brief time after, these two tutors caused a revolution in Hemingway's writing. It is no exaggeration to say they gave him a literary future. But he also learned, to his regret, that he would have to supply the sympathy for the downtrodden and dispossessed.

≡ ≡ ≡

Pound and Stein were quite simply the gatekeepers of the American literary avant-garde at that time. Stein was known mainly among the Parisians as an arts maven. She was not only an avid collector of post-impressionist modern art—cubist and expressivist art that gave up impressionism's prettiness to raise painterly questions (is it the real world or ideas in paint?) in bold colors. She was also a writer who brought expressivist methods to that craft, creating stories that kept calling attention to themselves as artificial and raising artsy questions (does language create a world or merely sounds?) in repetitive phrasings. Pound was known in Chicago, New York, and London, as well as Paris, because he was an irrepressible theorist, always vying for attention in the little magazines of those cities and laying down rules for modern writing. He practically invented free verse poetry on the pages of those magazines, submitting to the editors both poems and rules for making poems. If size of audience is a measure of literary quality, Hemingway would soon surpass these two mentors. He was far more sensitive than they were to popular taste. Still, it's natural to wonder what direction Hemingway's talent and art would have taken without Stein's and Pound's help. For under their tutelage, Hemingway's writing shifted from a characteristic ironical overstatement to a more memorably characteristic emotionally charged understatement. Both overstatement and understatement remained present in Hemingway's writing throughout his career, but he is at his best when the arrogant bluster and sarcasm recede and the quiet, stunning images and dialogue emerge to sketch the sad, modern human condition.

Anderson's letter to Stein declared that "Mr. Hemingway is an American writer instinctively in touch with everything worthwhile going on here."[4] Yet as a developing writer, Hemingway badly needed something other than his instincts. His blustery, sarcastic pre-Paris stories explored psychological complexities, and they dealt with sex and sport and war in a frank way that Victorian literature almost never did. This may be the "instinctive" modernity Anderson wrote to Stein about. But Hemingway's writing was unsubtle and inelegant. He subtitled one tale "The Woppian Way," the word *wop*, of course, a juvenile slur on Italians, and he was capable of writing sentences like this one: "For as an Opera Singer must be continental, and a corporation soulless, so must a pug be Hibernian."[5] He needed both a more sophisticated style consistent with his modernity and a way to address his hurt and alarm, his sense that the war had destroyed core values he had been raised to honor. He needed a way to show ordinary patriotic citizens, of America and France especially, that the war had also destroyed his personal peace and, by extension, the personal peace of other men and women like him. Hemingway, like the diplomats, government ministers, and radical reformers of his day, including Quoc, needed to construct an artistry of awareness, self-diagnosis, and peace-seeking. Taken together, these qualities would enable his resistance—his campaign against capitalist privilege, complacency about human suffering, and the habits of aggression.

Hemingway did construct that artistry, and the process began in February of 1922, when Ezra Pound and his wife, Dorothy Shakespear, replied to Anderson's letter by inviting the Hemingways to tea. Pound's interests were varied, and he sometimes wrote brilliant poetry. He had many friends. Pound endeared himself to people, as some of us do, by being inept at certain things. Speaking once as Pound's boxing coach and sparring partner, one of his roles in that winter of 1922, Hemingway said that he was embarrassed to let others see Pound boxing.[6] English novelist and expatriate Ford Madox Ford said that Pound played tennis like "an inebriated kangaroo."[7] Pound built chairs and tables for his ramshackle, under-heated studio in Montparnasse that show up in archived pictures as gracelessly crude objects, two-by-fours and six-inch planks nailed together at 90-degree angles, slung with low-hanging, awkward sheets of canvas. Ford said getting out of one of these chairs made him feel like a horse trying to right itself after falling on a slick cobblestone street.[8] When Hemingway first met Pound, it was this endearing bohemian goof he met, though Hemingway quickly realized that this goof had a profound sense of poetic excellence and literary heritage. He also had some troubling prejudices, which Hemingway would have to confront soon enough and deal with throughout their lifelong friendship.

Hemingway and Pound drank lots of tea that afternoon they first met and began an intense face-to-face friendship that, once Pound left Paris for Italy later that year, became a lively and testy lifelong correspondence. Between Ernest's trips to peace conferences, which were about to begin at John Bone's request from Toronto, and Pound's stays in his beloved Rapallo, there was very little time for instruction and discussion in 1922 and early 1923. However, for a few weeks in the summer and fall of 1922 Hemingway lounged in the awkward sling chairs and looked at pictures in the studio Pound shared with Dorothy, who was a modernist painter and (both Hadley and Ernest thought) a real beauty. Because Pound was a "village explainer," as Gertrude Stein acidly and aptly put it, we can be sure Hemingway did a lot of listening to Pound's theories—anti-Semitic economic theories on the one hand and modernist aesthetics on the other. Hadley recalled being surprised at how rapt and respectful her brash young husband usually was in Pound's presence.[9] At least at first.

Hadley believed that her husband's discussions with Pound yielded lasting principles for his writing, if not his economics: "I believe some of the ideas lasted all his life," she said in a late-life interview. But what ideas? The single principle Hemingway was willing to confess was to "distrust adjectives." That is hardly a revelation. Most college composition instructors teach the principle that parades of adjectives are distracting and best replaced with more concrete description. Luckily, however, we can reason out this remark. To distrust adjectives is one of Pound's imagist dicta, directions for producing elegant rather than ordinary free verse poems and for producing images that function first as legitimate concrete objects, then, and only then, suggesting a metaphorical meaning as well. During the 1920s, among a school of half-willing poets such as Hilda Doolittle, Amy Lowell, D. H. Lawrence, and other lesser lights, as he thought them, Pound launched free verse poetry with a series of his own and others' brief, elegant, concrete, and demotic poems. He insisted on the language that people actually speak, and he cut every single extra word. He was, in fact, particularly hostile toward nonessential adjectives: "Use no superfluous word, no adjective, which does not reveal something," he wrote in one of his manifestos, printed in one of those Chicago little magazines that Hemingway may have read before coming to France.

Pound's facility with his own imagist dicta is best illustrated by his poem, only two lines long, "In a Station of the Metro" (1913). Pound claimed it once grew to thirty lines, but he cut and condensed to the two we know, which is a very imagist evolution for these lines:

The apparition of these faces in the crowd;
Petals on a wet, black bough.[10]

The poem is based on the Japanese haiku or hokku. In fourteen words, Pound conveys a moment in which a rider of the brand-new Paris Metro, opened in 1900, experiences the subway's mechanical rush in the subterranean dark, the impersonal mass experience of commuting to and from work. This subway rider then suddenly sees the faces of other commuters as beautiful and ephemeral. The petals imply faces, because both are oval and lovely. The "wet, black bough" implies this ephemerality: the lovely petals we see against a wet, black background must have been detached from their blossoms by a driving rain, or perhaps by their aging fragility. With his lovely image, Pound suggests that the modern world has not entirely extinguished human beauty, spirit ("apparition"), or compassion for our burden of mortal consciousness. Even amid our busy working lives, we can still recognize the beauty of human individuality and the sadness of death and decay. It is a brilliantly compact poem in lovely rhythms and sounds and expressions.

After publicly transcending imagism in 1914, moving on to a more spiritual theory of artistic energies called vorticism (which, thankfully, does not concern us), Pound turned the sprawling early versions of *The Waste Land* into the first long imagist poem. Instead of two lines, *The Waste Land* goes on for 433, yet the author, T. S. Eliot—with Pound's help— retains imagism's indirection and allusiveness and elegance and depth. To Eliot's bruised gratitude, Pound cut half of the poem's original lines, many of them impersonations of particular European workers and bourgeois characters. These impersonations fit the poem's early working title, drawn from Dickens's *Our Mutual Friend*: "He Do the Police in Different Voices." In the now-published typescripts of the poem, marked up with Pound's advice, we see entire pages, presumably days' worth of writing, if not weeks' worth, eliminated with a simple line scrawled from a top corner to the opposite bottom corner of a page. We get indications of approval for certain passages expressed by a mere line in the margin. We get ambiguous, gnomic judgments: "Echt" (German for "real"), or "too easy." The best notation appears beside a passage Pound apparently judged as having a too-iambic rhythm. "Too tum-pum at a stretch," he writes in excellent schoolboy cursive.[11]

Though Hemingway never gave Pound the chance to edit his own writings so radically, at least to our knowledge, the poet's imagist traits are still fundamental to his mature, modern prose style. So is imagism's hostility to Victorian slither, that tendency we have seen for Victorian types to speak in abstractions, to label things noble or glorious. During the next few months, Hemingway tried his hand at poetry-writing. With Pound's help he even placed a few of these poems in Chicago little magazines. But they are not good poems and do not matter here. What does matter is that Pound's tutoring of Hemingway in imagist technique brought new discipline and maturity to Hemingway's stories. He learned how difficult it is to write clear, simple, concrete sentences that convey a subtext. He began telling people that writing had become so difficult for him that he could only write a few sentences in a day's hard work.

We can be sure Pound tried to take over Hemingway's career, to make the young American a mere disciple of vorticism or whatever theory was roiling his mind in that day. In his role as agent/editor for a number of modernist little magazines, namely *Poetry, The Little Review, The Dial,* and *Blast,* Pound took great license in marketing his friends' work. Hilda Doolittle was reportedly shocked during tea with Pound in the British Museum tea room one day in 1912 when he showed his appreciation for one of her spare new poems by trimming and editing it in her presence. Then he signed "H. D. Imagiste" at the bottom of the page. She had no idea what an "Imagiste" was. Pound then sent the poem to the editors of *Poetry* in Chicago, a prestigious magazine then as now, and a new poetic movement was born with H. D. as a founding member. Pound had treated Doolittle brusquely, but if calling herself an "Imagiste" got her poems published, she was all for it.[12]

And we can be sure Pound taught Hemingway about the proper function of a spare, modern new literature. In *Poetry* in March of 1913, Pound laid out tenets he regarded as authentically imagist. It just happens that these dicta perfectly describe Hemingway's brief stories of 1923 and after:

1. Direct treatment of the "thing," whether subjective or objective.
2. To use absolutely no word that does not contribute to the presentation.
3. As regarding rhythm: to compose in sequence of the musical phrase, not in sequence of the metronome.

These are characteristics of the best short modernist poems, but Pound was interested in much more than style or other textual features. To paraphrase these precepts:

1. Poets need to render the world, including human feeling, with accuracy.
2. They need to do so in the fewest well-chosen words possible.
3. And they need to develop an ear for subtle, musical phrasing, and facility in writing such phrases.

Beyond these cautions, Pound believed that poetry, and specifically the image, had an almost spiritual psychological power. "An 'Image,'" he writes in the opening of his essay, "is that which presents an intellectual and emotional complex in an instant of time. It is the presentation of such a 'complex' instantaneously which gives that sense of sudden liberation; that sense of freedom from time limits and space limits; that sense of sudden growth, which we experience in the presence of the greatest works of art." For Pound, mediocre writing was not just a sin against the language, but also a sin against meaning, intellectual growth, and personal liberation. "It is better," he declares, "to present one Image in a lifetime than to produce voluminous works."[13]

Hemingway got the message. It is no coincidence that just after meeting Pound for the first time, he began writing prose poems—concrete, vivid little slices of life in elegant prose. Hemingway's 1920s prose poems about war or postwar refugees or political murders or (after a trip to Spain) bullfights are typically fewer than two hundred words long. Though Pound's imagist tenets seem to apply mainly to poetry—especially the third, with its condemnation of metronomic rhythm—each also describes an important aspect of Hemingway's early writings. First, Hemingway learned to describe the subjective and objective "thing" with precision and realism. In one prose poem, which we will consider soon, he uses fewer than fifty words to describe a Great War soldier's shock combined with pride at finding himself able to kill young men who seem all too much like himself.

Secondly, Hemingway learned to make concision the hallmark of his prose. This was not natural to him. He came to Paris with a story in manuscript that opened with this knowing and baggy sentence: "If you are honestly curious about pearl fishing conditions in the Marquesas, the possibility of employment on the Trans Gobi Railway, or the potentialities of any of the hot tamale republics, go to the Café Cambrinus on Wabash Avenue in Chicago." After meeting Pound, Hemingway rarely produced another such sentence, and then usually only in his travel nonfiction and magazine reporting, where he allowed himself the know-it-all stance he wisely eliminated from his best fiction.

Thirdly, Hemingway learned to hear the beautiful sentence, so that his prose began to seem not only terse but elegant and elevated. Using repetitions "in sequence of the musical phrase," he soon learned to turn impersonal newspaper reportage into a kind of poetry. He could provide glimpses of emotionally charged young minds contemplating the existentialist realities of life—death, suffering, and thwarted purpose, things the profiteers seemed not to care about. In showing these things to the world in elegant, elevated language, he could resist the bureaucrats who sent young people to their deaths, or the arch-capitalists who consigned them to poverty and made them labor like animals.

Hemingway would come into his imagist powers in the summer of 1923. Mussolini had been Italy's prime minister for about a year, and in the fall of 1923 an upstart politician in Munich named Adolph Hitler tried and failed to start a coup d'état in an effort now known as the "beer hall *putsch*." There was a new kind of violence afoot in Europe, and a new kind of hatred and denigration of the weak. Hemingway wanted to offer resistance to this new movement called fascism. He wanted to show that even demoralized young people of his day cared about human liberties and the possibility that compassion rather than hate might govern the world. By 1923, partly thanks to Pound, he had the prose style to accomplish this important task.

The prose poems currently available to us as Chapters I through XV in *In Our Time* (1924, but composed much earlier) include bullfighting scenes, arrests and executions of street criminals in prewar Kansas City, streams of refugees he had seen in Greek and Turkish borderlands, the execution of incompetent Greek ministers from the year before, and more specimens of international violence.[14] The most moving and important are scenes from the Great War. Two are particularly important for our understanding of what Hemingway learned about good writing from Ezra Pound. Chapter III and Chapter IV are brilliant imagist poems, most of their meaning arising from implications we can deduce from the voices of two young soldiers, one sensitive and the other less so, who speak about battlefield experiences. These prose poems show Hemingway at his best, employing a modernist sympathy for the cannon fodder that he never matched in any other book over the course of his long career. There is simplicity in the telling of these prose poems, but a complexity in psychological and moral meaning. This is the writing of a modernist revolutionary.

The Chapter III prose poem is spoken by a British officer stationed around Mons, northeast of Paris, just across the Belgian frontier. We can date the vignette's fictive moment to August of 1914. Hemingway's original readers knew very well that for British troops, Mons was the first battle of the Great War. These Brits had just crossed the Channel into Belgium to support the French, who were involved in a precarious defense of Paris and of their nation as a whole. British troops stumbled into the path of the advancing German 1st Army at the Mons–Condé Canal. Though the British "Tommies" were badly outnumbered and completely inexperienced, the green, young soldiers fought stubbornly for a number of days in August 1914 before falling back nearly to the outskirts of Paris. There they regrouped, while the French shuttled reserve troops from the city to the battle lines, heroically and picturesquely, in hundreds of brightly painted city taxies. Then came the Battle of the Marne; then Paris's relative safety was restored; then the trenches were dug; then the long-term stalemate and trench warfare that characterized the Great War began.

In the vignette, in a few carefully distilled sentences, Hemingway captures the sense of a young officer's initiation into war in those kinds of days. In its entirety it reads this way:

> We were in a garden at Mons. Young Buckley came in with his patrol from across the river. The first German I saw climbed up over the garden wall. We waited until he got one leg over and then potted him. He had so much equipment on and looked awfully surprised and fell down into the garden. Then three more came over further down the wall. We shot them. They all came just like that.[15]

It may not seem like it on first reading, but this is an amazing performance. First, Hemingway is able to communicate the speaker's military rank, and thus his responsibilities, through his expressions. Only a seasoned officer, and a British one, would call a fellow soldier "young Buckley." We can conclude that the speaker is also relatively young, because he is a field officer. Next, Hemingway communicates the officer's existential sympathies. This soldier at first seems to be a calculating and emotionless killer, one who casually "potted" German young men when given the chance—and a rather unsporting chance at that, because these Germans were unable to use their own weapons while climbing over a wall. And then we notice the halting sentence, "We shot them." The casual epithet "potted," which he used just before, has now become the frank and mature "shot." Finally, we hear the nightmare terror this soldier felt as the situation continued to unfold, one German after another unthinkingly crawling over the wall to his death—with our speaker doing the killing. The Germans do not even know that they are in danger, as indicated by the surprise on their faces when they are shot. "They all came just like that," our stunned officer says. Some might say that the

Edenic setting in a garden is heavy-handed, but it is not. Hemingway's British officer is undergoing an elemental fallout of innocence. Yet there is still complexity. Readers get to use their own values to assess and theorize just what kind of innocence, and just what kind of fall. Surely the reader must contemplate what it means to send young men into this kind of deadly and guilt-inducing situation. Hemingway does not resist the soldier's vocation as national killer in this ambiguous portrait so much as he questions it.

In the next prose poem, Chapter IV, Hemingway gains even more meaning through contrast with the Chapter III vignette. Chapter IV is labeled "Mons (Two)" in *The Little Review* (though never afterward in its subsequent publications), so we know we are witnessing soldiers in the very same battle of initiation. We meet yet another British soldier, another officer. His rank we can deduce because of his upper-class idioms. He describes a similar experience in battle, but with a very different attitude:

> It was a frightfully hot day. We'd jammed an absolutely perfect barricade across the bridge. It was simply priceless. A big old wrought-iron grating from the front of a house. Too heavy to lift and you could shoot through it and they would have to climb over it. It was absolutely topping. They tried to get over it, and we potted them from forty yards. They rushed it, and officers came out along and worked on it. It was an absolutely perfect obstacle. Their officers were very fine. We were frightfully put out when we heard the flank had gone, and we had to fall back.[16]

We recognize the key similarities to the Chapter III vignette. There is the wall or barrier. There are the soldiers climbing over a wall to their deaths. There is the easy killing, expressed as "potting" the enemy. Most importantly, there is the voice of a man attempting to control overflowing emotions, his sympathy for the "very fine" German victims who were tragically caught in this deadly situation yet who remained willing to perform their duty.

We see—or rather, hear—that the young officer of Chapter III is different from the officer of Chapter IV. Though both have done their duty, each of them harbors very different feelings about the killing. The Chapter III officer recognizes a personal humanity in his German victims, specifically the surprise on their young faces as they die trying to enter a place they had assumed was safe. And that officer has trouble describing the moral weight of the situation he has taken part in. The Chapter IV officer, on the other hand, is delighted with his killing machine. He is able to recognize good soldiering in the Germans, specifically their "very fine" officers (he's siding emotionally with the employer class, not the working class), but he does not grapple with their deaths or woundings, or with the moral weight attached to the way he and his men are trying to kill them. He is thrilled at the opportunity to kill the sons of Germany, and "put out"—an entirely inadequate expression for a soldier's proper feeling witnessing the deaths of brave others—when he must stop as a flank attack is threatened. The officer of Chapter IV is capable and professional and can honor the Germans who die, but he is still infected with the Victorian virus, the extreme nationalism and ready willingness to kill for ideals.

Hemingway did not come to Paris with this kind of writing in hand, and even in the Left Bank's extraordinary literary community there were no models in prose available to him for this kind of intense distillation of feeling and meaning. He learned this technique from Pound, applying to the prose sentence what the poet taught about the poetic line. Pound's doctrines about the image were fundamental to Hemingway; he adopted them whole. On the other hand, it is Hemingway, not Pound, who adds the essential ingredients: the situations, the voices, the dialects, the rhythms, the implications, but mainly the compassion. The compassion is what Quoc and Hemingway came to Paris to express because demonstrations of compassion represent resistance to cruelty. They sensed that modernism was invested in the authentic feeling and psychological complexity of ordinary modern people. These ordinary people believed that they lacked the power to refuse useless wars or to campaign for better pay or conditions, but that is only because they had not yet encountered the arts of liberty and solidarity. Quoc and Hemingway were just beginning to learn those arts, and they knew that if they developed such an art fully, they would be doing their part to resist the universe of killing.

≡ ≡ ≡

But Paris was not all about liberty and solidarity among laborers. Quoc and Hemingway also had to resist the blandishments of reactionaries and totalitarians, and Pound was one of these. Though he was a friend and mentor of Hemingway's, he was also one of his very real moral threats, for Pound was a fascist and an anti-Semite. He loved Mussolini and hated Jews. He promoted a theory of Western economies that blamed Jews for many of Europe's pathologies, its poverty and wars especially. Under the influence of a crackpot economist named Major Clifford Hugh Douglas, he believed that Jewish bankers or moneylenders exploited Europe's workers. The Jews, he said, paid too small a wage, reaped huge profits for themselves, and then launched iniquitous wars in order to protect their interests, to make the world safe for profit-taking. Hemingway makes fun of this side of Pound in his late-life memoir, *A Moveable Feast*, though he respects Pound's literary and limited personal virtues enough to conduct this satire through quiet, even gentle implication.

In *A Moveable Feast*, Hemingway tells us all we really know about his reactions to Pound during that crucial first year together in Paris. He begins his chapter on Pound, "Ezra Pound and His Bel Esprit," with this charitable sentence: "Ezra Pound was always a good friend and he was always doing things for people."[17] To illustrate Pound's generosity, Hemingway tells the tale of Pound's "Bel Esprit," his fundraising campaign intended to give his genius friend T. S. Eliot more writing time. But first he offers a broad hint at his method for accepting and rejecting Pound's theories. He credits Pound with introducing him to Dada painter Francis Picabia's works, a few of which hung in the poet's rue Notre-Dame-des-Champs studio, along with at least one of Wyndham Lewis's cubist paintings. There were Gaudier-Brzeska sculptures, including at least one of Pound himself, and many other art objects on a shoulder-high shelf that ran around the whole room. Hemingway writes that he did not think Picabia worthwhile in early 1922, but he did later. This is his way of confessing that he had things to learn from Pound in 1922.

The many Japanese paintings that dominated Pound's room, on the other hand, left the young Hemingway cold. Even after understanding them better with Pound's help, he tells us, they still "meant nothing" to him. "There was nothing I could do about it," Hemingway writes. Here he hints in this introductory paragraph that Pound's tastes, theories, and instruction were decidedly mixed, that they had to be sorted by an active, critical mind for acceptance or rejection. The dadaist Picabia deserved Pound's hype, Hemingway implies, while perhaps the Japanese artists did not. And then there were the economic theories.

Hemingway had the good sense to reject Pound's economics. As his chapter continues, Hemingway makes a few digs at Pound's expense, teasing the poet for his lack of good judgment in accepting Douglas's implausible theories. For the most part, though, Hemingway remains amazingly kind to his former mentor, considering that as Hemingway wrote *A Moveable Feast* in the late 1950s, Pound was world famous as a fascist propagandist who had just barely avoided execution for treasonous acts during World War II.

While living as an American citizen in Rome during the war, Pound had made radio broadcasts critical of President Roosevelt, mainly attacking the president for his supposed collusion with Jewish bankers who were then supposedly profiting excessively from the war. Pound made the broadcasts because he loved Mussolini almost as much as he loved drawing attention to himself, and he wanted to be of assistance to *Il Duce*. Pound's broadcasts were recorded, transcribed, and studied in the United States. In one of them, an April 1942 radio broadcast to the people of Rome, he made the depth of his corruption clear:

> Don't start a pogrom, that is, not an old style killing of small Jews. That system is no good whatsoever. Of course if some man had a stroke of genius and could start a pogrom UP AT THE TOP, there might be something to say for that. But on the whole, legal measures are preferable. The sixty Kikes who started this war might be sent to St. Helena as a measure of world prophylaxis.[18]

In 1942, there was a man "UP AT THE TOP," of course, who held similar views. In January of that year Adolph Hitler ordered a military aide, Reinhold Heydrich, to convene a planning meeting in a villa at Wannsee, outside Berlin. There these planners devised the Final Solution, the plan for exterminating all of Europe's Jews. Pound seems to have supported the "prophylaxis" of concentration camps. It is not clear what he really thought about the mass killing that occurred when concentration camps became death camps.

Pound's comments about the United States in the broadcasts were judged seditious, and once the Allies took Italy from the Nazis in 1944, he was arrested, tried, and declared insane. During his virtual imprisonment in St. Elizabeth's, a Washington, DC, mental hospital after the war, Pound was careful to express his anti-Semitism as a matter of legal process for individual criminals. He argued that the Holocaust was unnecessary and unwise. It would have been better to go after indicted Jews one at a time, Pound thought, through the courts—as though Germany's courts did not serve the Final Solution or apply the unjust laws of the Reich and its Italian satellite. When he was finally released both from St. Elizabeth's and from the threat of a new treason trial, Pound fled the United States and sailed to Italy, where he was returning to make a final home. Seeing photographers at the docks, he defiantly gave the Nazi salute. He seemed to show no moral growth at all.

But in 1922 Hemingway showed a great deal of both aesthetic and moral growth. As he sipped tea in Pound's bohemian flat on the curving rue Notre-Dame-des-Champs, which would become his own street in just a few more months, he could have no idea about this wretched future. Nevertheless, he was wise enough, even as a twenty-two-year-old newlywed, to convert Pound's deadly teachings to more humane ends. He used Pound's imagist dicta to write brief, elegant, and precise modern stories alert to the complexity of prejudice, hatred, violence, and economic exploitation. He turned Pound's instruction to alternatives born of empathy. As his childhood training in the gospels urged him to do, he entered into imaginative sympathy with those in need of care, feeding, and healing—no matter their faith. He chose as his subjects soldiers in battle, refugees cold and afraid as they fled their homes, government ministers facing execution for failed plans, and criminals facing execution. Hemingway and Quoc were about to spend the next few months waffling about the correct methods for resisting oligarchy and the abuse of laboring people. Sometimes they would embrace communism and sometimes socialist solidarity leading toward legal reforms intended to improve workers' lives. Sometimes they would simply express despair in a cynical and noncommittal way. But they never learned to love totalitarianism.

# 10

## MISS STEIN AND THE CÉZANNE SECRET

### HEMINGWAY IN EARLY 1922

I t was March of 1922 when Anderson's third and final letter brought Gertrude Stein to the Hemingway home. She climbed the four flights of stairs to the apartment, passing on each landing the "Turkish" toilet—a flushable basin in the floor—knocked on the door, and entered the cold-water flat. Ernest and Hadley discovered that she was a rather large, grand older woman, imperious in manner and utterly confident in her artistic theories, yet charming too. During this meeting in the tiny apartment, with its piano occupying the dining room, dining table in the bedroom, and total lack of a sitting room, Stein sat on the bed and read some of Hemingway's work. The manuscripts he gave her included the sexually frank "Up in Michigan," his best and most modern story at that time. In the denouement to this short story a boarding house maid in a small Michigan lake town loses her virginity to the attractive but drunken local blacksmith. The encounter on the planks of a wooden dock in chilly fall weather is painful for the young woman, and she is at best partly willing. In modern language, it is date rape. Stein pronounced the story "*inaccrochable*," French for "un-hangable." For Stein, the story was like a pornographic painting even a sophisticated patron of the arts doesn't want to display in the sitting room for every visitor to see.[1]

Indeed, Stein found all of Hemingway's work undisciplined and unfocused. She told him that day to "begin over again and concentrate," the kind of double entendre she was known for.[2] With this remark, she was urging Hemingway to focus his mind, certainly, but also to distill his material into a more honest, straightforward moment in human time. The lesson in concision echoed Pound's instruction, which of course Hemingway was hearing at the same time. This was the modern way in the literature of Paris, a style and method that rejected Victorian rhetorical excesses and obvious, morally overdetermined meanings. Just as modern architects such as Mies van der Rohe, Le Corbusier, or Frank Lloyd Wright were stripping Victorian bric-a-brac from their houses, inside and out, to produce simpler, more elegant, and (to their minds) honest structures, modernist writers worked by simplified and distilled implication and image. They respected readers enough to allow them to sense the carefully calibrated moral content in a story. The idea in literature, as in architecture, was to show concern for modern people, especially working people, by offering them a rational, satisfying, peaceable new way of life rather than ancient traditions of European elitism that, it seemed, inevitably led to conflict.

After her first meeting with Hemingway, Stein invited both Ernest and Hadley to her flat at 27 rue de Fleurus, near the western edge of the Luxembourg Gardens, and she kept on inviting them to come see the paintings she had collected. One or both of the Hemingways ended up going there often. It was an ordinary, if spacious, flat with a parlor in need of a fresh coat of paint, but hanging in that parlor were incredible works of art Stein and her brother had purchased from Picasso, Matisse, Cézanne, Gauguin, Manet, Toulouse-Lautrec, and many more of Paris's best artists of that generation. Hemingway felt amused sympathy for Hadley during those visits to rue de Fleurus because Toklas nearly always took her aside so that Gertrude could give him his day's instruction on the serious matters that concerned literary geniuses and abstract painters. Toklas, on the other hand, tended to discuss cooking and housekeeping with Hadley. While Hadley was grateful to have a maid-of-all-work named Marie Cocotte helping her, Toklas employed both French girls from the country who looked for men to marry and Vietnamese men who took too many drugs and drank too much and showed up for work surly and tired. She told Hadley how to manage difficult servants from the French countryside or the colonies. Hadley saw that, unfortunately, it boiled down to treating all of them like slow-witted moral children and complaining about them bitterly.[3] This was something she would never do to her friend Marie.

In many meetings at the Stein-Toklas apartment during the next few months, Stein tutored Hemingway on the meaning of cubism and other modern arts, which at bottom attempted to question the status of the familiar and ordinary. While many abstract paintings seemed to ask compulsively, "Does art exist?" they also asked a much more important question: whether all givens in our world, such as the economic and governmental order, were legitimate and inevitable. Modern art questioned whether things as they are really existed or, rather, ought to persist permanently as currently constituted. Questioning the status of traditional art, with its renderings of recognizable people and objects and rooms and landscapes, the modern arts also questioned society itself. In 1922, Hemingway and Quoc both imbibed this message from the Parisian avant-garde, Quoc from the dadaists at the Club du Faubourg and Hemingway from Stein in the parlor that she had turned into a gallery of the modern abstract arts.

Stein showed Hemingway how her own writing extended the cubist experiment onto literary ground. Stein's language experiments, like her favorite works of Picasso or Matisse in that amazing parlor of hers, sought insights through play with patterns rather than through representation of a familiar, realistic world. She tried to bring to literature that unsettling quality of Dada, cubism, twelve-tone music, or Diaghilev's choreography. She did not want her readers to become comfortable; she wanted to produce in them an unsettled alertness, the poise of a thoughtful revolutionary. (Not that her revolution would be anything like Debs's, as we will see.) Hemingway apparently listened to Stein's celebration of post-impressionist theories in painting and writing, and he learned from her. He saw that his own newly spare prose lent itself to deeper psychological meanings, and even to the dreamlike qualities her own repetitions and odd sentences tended to create and suggest. He saw that his own writing could be concrete, tactile, and realistic, as he wanted it to be, yet still be involved in this project of questioning the ordinary that Stein taught.

Then, gazing at Stein's collection of modern art, he saw on his own what he really wanted his writing to accomplish. Glancing around her drawing room, where he was soon invited to come and look at pictures whenever he liked, whether Stein and Toklas were home or not, he was drawn to Paul Cézanne's portrait of his wife, *Madame Cézanne with a*

*Fan*, and also to one of his landscapes with human figures, titled *The Bathers*. He recognized in these works both investment in modernist experiments—there were large patches of paint that made little attempt to model Madame Cézanne's face or dress, and the bathers had a vaguely cartoonlike quality—and yet a more direct than usual respect for the lives of ordinary, bourgeois working people and for the recognizable world they occupied. As he tells us in his late-life memoirs, Hemingway immediately set out to make his writing like Cézanne's paintings. But first he had to absorb the benefits and endure the excesses of Stein's instruction. Before long, he would struggle to deal with Stein's right-wing theories—a challenge almost as difficult as dealing with the blandishments of his new fascist friend, Ezra Pound.

Stein devoted her long novels of the 1920s to self-conscious language games rather than to the rendering of intriguing human situations. This is ironic because at the same time, her hero and artistic mentor, Pablo Picasso, evolved from his cubist phase toward more complex artistry. During 1921, for example, he produced both the synthetic cubist *Three Musicians*, which depicted stock characters from French pantomimes, a mime and clown in bright clothing and a monk playing instruments, a picture composed almost entirely of uniformly colored rectangles and trapezoids in primary colors on a totally flat plane. This was the cubist game, which minimized social meanings in favor of esoteric questions about painting reality. Yet he also painted *Three Women at the Spring*, a depiction of stout women in flowing dresses, their skin and the folds of their clothing carefully shaded and presented in three-dimensional space, only their oddly beefy hands and feet seeming at all unrealistic. This was a painting that showed some care for women and the daily work they performed. There was genuine human sympathy in this picture.

Stein seemed stuck that year in the formalist rather than humane mode. This sentence from *The Making of Americans*, a book Hemingway claimed to admire and helped to publish during the Paris years, illustrates Stein's cubist emphasis:

> It happens very often that a man has it in him, that a man does something, that he does it very often that he does many things, when he is a young man when he is an old man, when he is an older man.[4]

Clearly, Stein did not care how people really talk about "what a man does"; she is trying out repetitions, perhaps to test her audience's patience or perhaps to bring to consciousness the beauty of language's sounds. She certainly saw herself as a revolutionary. Critics who admire Stein's work note that she created an oblique language of lesbian love, which was, of course, a real contribution to an emerging and expanding sense of justice and propriety in 1920s Europe. But her work was not always about love or about women's dignity during this period, and she seems disinterested in issues other than the nature of art and the subconscious energy of sexuality. She seems to ignore vital issues such as the nature of war and peace and justice. She never, for example, turned her cubist fervor to a work such as Picasso's *Guernica* (1937), his shocked reaction to Hitler's bombing of a Spanish city, or any of his other works concerned about human suffering, including anti-colonial works of the 1920s.

Lost Generation memoirist Malcolm Cowley links Gertrude Stein to Dada, listing her as an experimenter with Dada-esque obscurity. "She seemed, indeed, to be writing pure nonsense," he writes, "and yet it was not quite pure: one felt uneasily that much of it could be deciphered if only one had the key."[5] If she were in fact dadaist in any real way, then we can at least attribute her nonrational writings to that project of revealing society's endemic madness.

But when Gertrude Stein introduced Hemingway to Picasso's and Cézanne's works in 1922, and to other artists who turned out to be less important to his work, she probably did not emphasize issues of Dada-esque liberty from routine or opportunity to dissent from service to the nation-state. She probably did not emphasize the hope that shocking, experimental performances could also liberate others from their mental oppressions, nor did she likely tell him that an avant-garde artistic response to racism and oppression of working people could cause audiences to ponder a different and better kind of society. Her sense of resistance had a different character. She was a social conservative who regarded Republicans as the only "natural rulers" in the United States. Stein hated FDR, supported the fascist Franco in Spain, and, as the Second World War began, loved Vichy leader and Nazi collaborator Marshal Philippe Pétain, whose anti-Semitic writings she translated. Janet Malcolm also suggests, in the very carefully vetted *New Yorker* magazine, that during the Second World War the lesbian Jews Stein and her lover Alice B. Toklas may have

been spared deportation and total loss of property—the penalties suffered by most American Jews living in Vichy France—because they were
friends with a collaborator, Pétain advisor Bernard Faÿ. Malcolm suggests
that Stein and Toklas may have collaborated themselves, if only through
unusual friendliness with Nazi officers.[6]

Other scholars have noted that in her 1945 wartime chronicle, *Wars
I Have Seen*, Stein repudiates fascism and celebrates liberal freedoms:
"The one thing that everybody wants is to be free," she writes, "not to
be managed, threatened, directed, restrained, obliged, fearful, adminis-
tered, none of these things. . . . The only thing that any one wants now
is to be free, to be let alone, to live their life as they can, but not to be
watched, controlled and scared, no no, not."[7] However, this may have
been a hard-won lesson she learned while witnessing yet another world
war, not a lifelong commitment of hers, not something she shared with
young Hemingway during their brief time as friends almost twenty years
before the Second World War began.

What Hemingway took from Stein's work, mainly, was her discovery that certain kinds of repetitions and rhythms had a mesmerizing
effect on readers. Her theory was that by refusing to write the kind of
prose many of us delight in, the kind that disappears under our eyes,
she would raise questions about literature's character and purpose. So,
in her stories, she refuses to let us move into the action or situation of a
story, living it without consciousness of the language that describes that
situation. Instead, she offers poems and prose poems and even long novels that persist doggedly in remaining language, just as Picasso's cubes
pointedly remain paint on canvas no matter how much they suggest
persons or objects. Malcolm presents this example, a poem from *Tender
Buttons* (1914), inspired, she tells us, "by Cubist still-lifes":

Out of kindness comes redness and out of rudeness comes
rapid same question, out of an eye comes research, out of
selection comes painful cattle. So then the order is that a
white way of being round is something suggesting a pin
and is it disappointing, it is not, it is so rudimentary to be
analysed and see a fine substance strangely, it is so earnest
to have a green point not to red but to point again.

With this style, Stein courted accusations that her writing was monotonous, meaningless, trivial, and careless. Yet there is something complicated going on.

Hemingway himself accused her of carelessness, but not until decades after he had benefited by her instruction. In a relentless attack on Stein in his late-life memoir, *A Moveable Feast*, an homage to Hadley in Paris and his regret that he ever left either the lovely city or the lovely wife, he suggests that Stein's work "went on endlessly in repetitions that a more conscientious and less lazy writer would have put in the waste basket."[8] This is good advice for the ordinary writer attempting to write clear, crisp sentences in logical sequence, but it is a deviously intentional misunderstanding of Stein's project. The deviousness becomes apparent when we know an unsavory backstory.

Years before writing his memoirs, Hemingway had been stung by a passage in Stein's 1933 *Autobiography of Alice B. Toklas*, Stein's autobiography written as though Toklas is telling the tale of their lives together. In this passage, the fictional Toklas reports that Stein and Anderson agreed one day that Hemingway was their creation, the two of them, and that as Hemingway had grown famous and ever more himself, they had grown "ashamed of the work of their minds." They had come to agree that Hemingway's writing revealed his childlike ability to perform what he could never understand—literary tricks and methods and concepts that they had taught him, fully understanding both what they taught and what they wrote. Unfortunately, they thought, Hemingway was unable to master the complexities of their writing.[9] Hemingway read this passage with understandable hurt and fury. He was so furious that he waited to serve his revenge ice cold. More than twenty-five years later, Hemingway retaliated in his own memoir with the comments about Stein's laziness, not to mention an anecdote that makes Stein seem the compliant sex slave to Toklas's domineering Svengali. In this tale, he claims to have dropped by 27 rue de Fleurus one day, unexpected, only to accidentally overhear Stein begging Toklas not to perform some unspeakable act of torture. Hemingway has Stein "pleading and begging, saying, 'Don't, pussy. Don't. Don't, please don't. I'll do anything, pussy, but please don't do it. Please don't. Please don't, pussy.'"[10] Whether Hemingway is writing history or fiction here, it is mean-spirited to share such a deeply private moment.

Stein's poems may be uninteresting and her novels unrewarding—and yet, it is worth remembering that dadaist and cubist art did not wish to render the real world clearly and credibly. Instead, the project of these abstract and ironic arts was to push readers and viewers into a new, freer form of consciousness. There was a psychoanalytical motive. The logic was something like this: the more that people forgot the ordinary world, with all its laws and habits and repressions, the better chance they had to imagine a new one freely—so freely, in fact, that they might actually imagine a world of more widespread peace, justice, and mental health. This is the psychological side of the modernist project, and it stood alongside the political side. Stein had gathered this notion, apparently, from her careful study of Paris's abstract arts. Hemingway did in fact learn that lesson, not only from Stein but from the many friends and rivals then steeped in Freudian theories, which were supposed to be socially as well as psychologically liberating.

Calling Stein a lazy writer, Hemingway seems to be rejecting her project and her influence entirely, but this is far from the truth. During the early days of 1922 he visited her apartment every few days, sometimes with Hadley along and sometimes on his own. He looked at Stein's magnificent Matisses and Picassos and Cézannes, the works she and her brother Leo had purchased cheaply before these painters gained their fame. And he listened to Stein as she told him her theories about the rhythmic seductions of the new prose and its ability to render human psychologies in an utterly new way. His early stories, the best ones he wrote in Paris, just a few months later, are filled with passages imitating or adapting Stein's language experiments. His own project seems to have been to employ a subtler version of Stein's nonrealistic expressions, retaining her literary-cubist effects while still trying to retain the reader's interest. He charms with musical-formal-Steinian repetitions, while keeping an engaging story alive.

Hemingway simply could not bring himself to write a weird sentence such as this one from Stein's *Three Lives*: "Mrs. Lehntman did not urge her to this thing nor even give her this advice, but feeling for Mrs. Lehntman as she did made even faithful Anna not quite so strong in her dependence on Miss Mary's need as she would otherwise have been." Yet he evidently admired musically repetitive passages such as this one, also from *Three Lives*:

Anna never liked her brother's wife.

The youngest of the two daughters was named after her aunt Anna.

Anna never liked her half brother's wife. This woman had been very good to Anna, never interfering in her ways, always glad to see her and to make her visits pleasant, but she had not found favour in our good Anna's sight.[11]

Within months of his first 1922 tutoring sessions with Stein, Hemingway was employing her methods. In the story "Soldier's Home," which he composed in 1923 and which we have analyzed as an autobiographical tale of a frustrated Great War veteran returning home to a pious Victorian household in the Midwest, he converts Stein's repetitions into something lovelier and more psychologically taut. The narrator shares the veteran Krebs's thoughts about local girls:

When he was in town their appeal to him was not very strong. He did not like them when he saw them in the Greek's ice cream parlor. He did not want them themselves really. They were too complicated. There was something else. Vaguely he wanted a girl but he did not want to have to work to get her. He would have liked to have a girl but he did not want to have to spend a long time getting her. He did not want to get into the intrigue and the politics. He did not want to have to do any courting. He did not want to tell any more lies. It wasn't worth it.[12]

This passage is phrased in the same manner as a subtle musical composition—as both Pound and Stein wanted it to be. Hemingway suggests the sense that Krebs is shell-shocked, both consciously and subconsciously unsettled, intellectually and socially disengaged somehow. Yet Hemingway avoids rendering his character as infantile or primitive, as Stein's sometimes seem. Krebs suffers from ordinary frustration, elected immaturity, and, probably, post-traumatic shock syndrome. He is in despair about his place in his suffocating community, correctly diagnosing a love relationship with a conventional local girl as a route into boring conformism and, thus, not "worth it." He is a bit ill, and his language reflects his condition. This is what interests

Hemingway, and it is what makes his work in 1920s Paris conspicuously, fascinatingly modern.

Of the many chapters Hemingway did not write for *A Moveable Feast* that I think we wish he had, the first for me opens in Stein's sitting room just as the spring flowers begin to bloom outside in the Luxembourg Gardens. It is May 1922, and Hemingway has begun to feel at home in Paris. Stein sits, enthroned as always, in a low armchair at one end of her massive library table fronting the fireplace. Hemingway sits at the other end of the table in a less regal chair. While Hemingway sips on a glass of Toklas's homemade *eau-de-vie*, Stein carefully explains the modern qualities, the discrete artistic experiments exemplified in the glorious paintings grouped from waist height to the high ceiling on every wall surface of that room. She shares every insight she has developed, along with those the artists themselves have shared with her. As James Mellow suggests, the Stein salon was the first museum of modern art, its

> principal attraction . . . the collection of Cézanne oils and watercolors, the early pictures by Matisse and Picasso, the paintings by Renoir, Manet, Gauguin and Toulouse-Lautrec, which she and Leo had had the funds and the foresight to buy. The walls of their atelier were hung to the ceiling with now-famous paintings, the double doors of the dining room were lined with Picasso sketches.[13]

And there was Hemingway—a young man in his early twenties with no more credential than an Oak Park High School diploma, a certificate of honorable discharge from the Red Cross, and a letter from Sherwood Anderson. He must have found it incredibly fortunate that he had privileged access to great masterworks of the century and to one of their best interpreters.

In this missing chapter of Hemingway's memoir, we would hear Stein explaining to young Hemingway Matisse's *Woman with a Hat* (1905), a shockingly vivid portrait in royal blues and acid greens and shades of rust and rose and mustard—and these colors are used to render a well-dressed woman's skin. One French art critic, Stein recalls with a laugh, had called the painting "a pot of paint . . . flung in the face of the public."[14] Matisse's wife is pictured wearing a large, elaborate hat, both her face and the decorations on the dark blue-black hat rendered in bright, unshaded and unmixed pigment streaks, yellow and red and indigo. Stein explains to Hemingway who *les Fauves* were, and why they enjoyed being called "wild beasts," why they had rejected Victorian standards of beauty, good taste, and representational idealism. She goes on to explain how modern writing must also be courageously experimental, informed by the best new theories of consciousness and perception, and freed from the tyranny of audience expectations. Perhaps she shares a pet theory with Hemingway, partly to flatter his ego: the idea that "[Picasso] and Matisse have a maleness that belongs to genius." She offers a broad hint about her own ego, and her sex too. *"Moi aussi* perhaps."[15]

Hemingway might have mused that it was a good thing Hadley had stayed home practicing her piano that day, so that she didn't hear that insult to women's intelligence. Then his attention is back with Stein as she sorts out the cubist tenets: the rejection of the routine world, the exploration of primitive types and postures, the openness to surprise in painting more "automatically," with less tedious attention to rendering detail, the playful tricks of warping space, creating surfaces for the display of color or pattern or calling attention to the idea that reality is made up of geometric solids and spatial planes, which in a painting are nothing but paint on canvas. She tells him there is something amazingly honest about admitting that paint and words create illusions, and that those illusions can tempt us into deeply false understandings of our world. "Notice, Hemingway," she urges him, "the next time you see *Three Women at the Spring*, how Pablo places all but one foot and one hand on exactly the same plane at the foreground of the picture. The girls reach and bend to do it, not for any ordinary purpose." She turns the lesson to a literary one: "This is the kind of creative play the casual reader will never notice consciously, but will instead feel. No effort is lost on the subconscious. Believe in that. Write for the fully invested, curious, searching mind, not the ordinary, bored, indolent one."[16] She promises to take Hemingway with her to La Lapin Agile, a cabaret on the Montmartre butte near the despised new Sacré-Coeur basilica, built to honor the reactionaries who had put down the Cummune. She wants him to meet Picasso at one of his soirees. She will be glad to give Hemingway the advantage of her introduction. Later, when Stein is finished with her lecture, he is allowed to study her paintings on his own. Hemingway cannot help but study the Cézannes. He responds to these paintings. He cannot help it.

≡ ≡ ≡

We do not have to imagine Hemingway's preference for the Cézannes in the early 1920s. He tells us about this passion in *A Moveable Feast*: "I was learning something from the painting of Cézanne that made writing simple true sentences far from enough to make the stories have the dimensions that I was trying to put in them. I was learning very much from him but I was not articulate enough to explain it to anyone. Besides it was a secret."[17]

Again, Hemingway's instincts were serving him well, for as French art historians Vincent Bouvet and Gérard Durozoi note, beginning around 1921, artists in Paris were starting to reject some of the crudity of cubism in favor of a "return to order." These artists found themselves offended at the boldest cubist experiments, its graceless repetitions in large patches of thickly applied paint, its stubborn fascination with geometry over against any other form, such as the long, organic curve of a woman's limb. Artists returning to order wanted to believe in artistic craft again, in the skill it took to render the world.[18] Cézanne may have been, as Matisse called him, "the father of us all," or as Picasso called him, "a mother who protects her children."[19] But that doesn't mean he would have been charmed by every move his artistic children made during the cubist and dadaist 1920s. Hemingway seems to have intuited, or perhaps even recognized consciously, that the most interesting modern art, such as Cézanne's, played with new methods for rendering the world—we will discuss his architectural combining of patches of unmixed paint and use of few, deliberate brush strokes—but still honored a coherent history of painting that tried to render the world realistically. In art as well as politics, Hemingway was thus a bit of a traditionalist.

This does not mean that in all things Hemingway preferred liberal reform to complete, sweeping revolution. He may have believed fervently in a revolution in Western literature and art, but a revolution that thinking people would recognize as the fulfillment of long-held ideals rather than the sophomoric imaginings of radical, unrooted new ones. In this sense, Hemingway's famous writing style becomes, perhaps, a model for his politics. He wanted to make things new, but he felt that traditions had some hold on him too, and he would never tolerate the chaos and loss of meaning of a runaway revolution. He was content with raising human problems into consciousness, which meant he had to be an artist of the materially real world and the psychologically astute world. Awareness leading to reform was revolutionary enough, and raising awareness was the core of Hemingway's resistance to the world of stupid patriotism, unnecessary war, routine domination, and widespread hunger.

It is not easy to pin down Cézanne's virtues, those things Hemingway learned from the great painter. Certainly, Cézanne received a good deal of extravagant praise, both during his lifetime and after. Baudelaire, for example, offers this ecstatic praise for Cézanne's work:

> Imagine a beautiful natural space where everything is greening, reddening, clouding, and shimmering in complete freedom, where all things are in constant vibration, variously colored according to their molecular constitution, changed from one second to another by the movement of shadow and light, stirred by an inner energy, that makes the lines flicker and fulfills the law of eternal and universal movement.[20]

In the scholarship on Cézanne, certain themes emerge: Incredibly few brush strokes. Solidity of the depicted object or body. Proof that Cézanne knew the full, dimensional conclusion of a painting even before he began it, something scholars see because Cezanne placed light shimmers in white and yellow paint before limning the object upon which the light shines. Evidently crude drawing in blue paint that magically outlines a three-dimensional object, such as a thigh or a mountainside. Implied awareness that he is not painting objects, but the shimmers of light reflecting from objects. Uncanny patience in producing art, patience necessary for genuinely intelligent art. Three pigments of blue purchased in the art shop mixed and cut to become sixteen colors of blue on the canvas. Human figures shown enduring, resting, never illustrating. Absence of satire, absence of comment, only existential waiting.

Many literary scholars have attempted to describe Hemingway's debt to Cézanne. They describe Hemingway's interest in Cézanne in terms I have used to describe cubism—planes and dimensions and color and volume and form. Some of these words Hemingway himself has used in talking about Cézanne—dimension, for example. Ronald Berman claims that Hemingway was after a corollary to the vertical tree forms in Cézanne's *Rocks-Forest of Fontainbleu* series.[21] Others list tenets that seem only to do with the visual arts, questions of volume, shading, and architecture. These are all concepts Hemingway had a full capacity to understand and probably to adapt to his writing about landscapes. But he was interested in people and their struggles to adapt to a violent modern world—so we are still left to wonder how Cézanne's priorities mapped onto his own.

Remembering that young Hemingway encountered Cézanne while under Gertrude Stein's tutelage during that spring and summer of 1922, we realize he had a choice to make. He could choose Stein's Cézanne, an experimenter with paints who called ordinary representation into question with his large patches of unrealistic paint, thickly and roughly applied. For Stein, Cézanne's way of painting was like automatic writing, completely spontaneous and unedited: "If the story does not come whole, *tants pis*," she once declared, "it has been spoiled." If Hemingway had made this choice, he might have also adopted Stein's own literary method— writing quickly and without revising, allowing the sounds of words and fixed psychological states to trump social meanings, demonstrating an aloof contempt for ordinary audiences. Alternately, he had the option of choosing his own Cézanne, whose landscapes depict the natural world solidly, even while the artistic process is evident in the patchy, faceted, thickly applied paint and repetition of geometric forms. That, of course, was Hemingway's choice. He chose a qualified realism, one that allowed him to show a modern artistic consciousness based in principled doubts about the beauty of the normal—because, after all, normal Christianity and governing and diplomacy had just given the world a cataclysmic war—yet he also chose for himself a realism that allowed him to identify with suffering people in the modern world. This will become clearer as we encounter some of his writings of the next few months, but we can look ahead briefly to Hemingway's full command of his modernist style.

One of the most important passages in *The Sun Also Rises* (1926) provides an example of Hemingway's most Cézanne-esque style. This is the paragraph-long tale of Vicente Girones, a local peasant who is gored to death in the running of the bulls in Pamplona during that year's *feria*, or carnival. The relevant passage describes both the dead man and his community's commemoration of his life:

> Later in the day we learned that the man who was killed was named Vicente Girones, and came from near Tafalla. The next day in the paper we read that he was twenty-eight years old, and had a farm, a wife, and two children. He had continued to come to the fiesta each year after he was married. The next day his wife came in from Tafalla to be with the body, and the day after there was a service in the chapel of San Fermín, and the coffin was carried to the railway-station by members of the dancing and drinking society of Tafalla. The drums marched ahead, and there was music on the fifes, and behind the men who carried the coffin walked the wife and two children. . . . Behind them marched all the members of the dancing and drinking societies of Pamplona, Estella, Tafalla, and Sangüesa who could stay over for the funeral. The coffin was loaded into the baggage-car of the train, and the widow and the two children rode, sitting, all three together, in an open third-class railway-carriage. The train started with a jerk, and then ran smoothly, going down grade around the edge of the plateau and out into the fields of grain that blew in the wind on the plain on the way to Tafalla.[22]

This is a key passage in the novel. Most of the novel involves the drunken and adulterous antics of young American and British expatriates, so this passage is Hemingway's opportunity to affirm faith and family and rural work and solidarity among fellow citizens as his emotional, moral, and political touchstones. He gives his most elegant and stately prose to a celebration of a peasant man's life by those who loved him.

Certainly the landscape in this paragraph is beautifully rendered, as Cézanne might have painted it, particularly the Pamplona plateau that the train circles and the grain fields that the track crosses. Also like Cézanne, Hemingway is able to show sympathy with ordinary working people, contrasted in *The Sun Also Rises* with the hard-drinking, promiscuous, damaged, flippant pretenders the novel's hero (or antihero), Jake, tends to hang around with. They are veterans of the war, so we have some sympathy for them. We hope these expatriate friends of Jake's, who live near him in Paris in order to engage in a frantic quest for fun and love, can find more meaningful lives. Reading this passage, we hope they can find lives like the abbreviated life of Vicente Girones, whose body travels through the fields he used to farm, past the church that celebrates both the fiesta and his life, in a train carrying the wife and children who love and mourn him, and the workers' societies that embraced him, protected his living, and now must embrace his memory and care for his family. This portrait is about the ancient church and community expressing its traditions of welfare and socialist dedication. The passage is both ancient and startlingly modern at once. Stein taught Hemingway to write with this serious artistry. On his own, he brought to his writing the sympathy for faithful laboring families.

≡ ≡ ≡

Hemingway learned a great deal about literary artistry during the first half of 1922, much of that learning coming from Gertrude Stein and, through a bit of deduction, from the fellow Catholic convert Paul Cézanne. This learning allowed him, for the first time, to lend sufficient dignity and psychological insight to his portraits of the people whose straitened lives concerned him and whose faith and hard work impressed him. In the meantime, he also learned much about the political organization of Europe, as did Quoc. The two of them spent 1922 learning about Dada and other brash, conceptual arts of Paris, learning about the Machiavellian tendencies of presidents and prime ministers negotiating the fate of nations, and learning how to improve their creative writing skills. As we are about to see, both of them also learned the skills of documentary journalism in a world beset by conflict and filled with instances of personal suffering. They were to seize the opportunity to make that broken world, with all its crying needs, known to the wider citizenry.

# 11

## THE STAR REPORTER

### HEMINGWAY IN 1922 AND EARLY 1923

I am a newspaper man living in Paris," Jake Barnes writes in a passage Hemingway eventually cut from *The Sun Also Rises*. "I used to think Paris was the most wonderful place in the world."[1] Jake is a bit of an antihero in the novel, which means that we have plenty of reasons to dislike and distrust him, but his interests and observations about Paris usually sync with Hemingway's. We might ponder what changed Jake's mind about Paris and its wonders. Maybe it was the experience of performing the journalist's work—examining closely the cynical, ugly reality behind ideal or prepared appearances.

We forget that like the fictional Jake Barnes, the very real Hemingway and Ho Chi Minh had their starts in Paris as prodigious journalists. Perhaps we tend to understand the two men's careers in reverse or retrospect, dwelling first on Hemingway's career as a Nobel Prize–winning novelist and great white hunter, and Ho's career as the scholar who led his people to decisive victories at war over the French empire and American superpower. Hemingway's scholars especially treat his days as a reporter in the early 1920s mainly as an apprenticeship phase, a time for him to develop a lean, elegant prose and glean a few exotic experiences to depict in his fiction. Ho's scholars also tend to dwell on his public appearances, those marking his political development, such as the Paris Peace Conference of 1919, where he first spoke for all Vietnamese people, and the Tours Congress of 1920, where he declared himself a communist and helped found the French Communist Party.

But both Hemingway and Quoc were very good journalists. They wrote vivid accounts of the pain ordinary people were suffering around the world. They addressed and assessed the European leaders then vying for political precedence and survival. And they wrote with an eye toward the improvement of the society they lived in. They were also very industrious, as good reporters must be. While both struggled to balance accuracy and objectivity with the seductively vivid story—or the convenient, persuasive lie—they usually wrote with a deep honesty and sympathy.

Arguably, in 1922 Hemingway and Nguyen Ai Quoc were two of the best and most important journalists in Paris. Certainly they were the most important newcomers to the profession, the co-rookies of the year. That year, Quoc wrote a number of important articles for the French Communist Party journal *L'Humanité*, and a few other left-leaning journals, but more importantly, in April he started up his own little magazine, *Le Paria* (*The Pariah*, subject of our next chapter). The magazine was a lot like the Lost Generation little magazines such as *Poetry, Broom, The Little Review*, or *the transatlantic review*, organs of literary and political manifestos and uneven, experimental fiction and poetry. Like these modernist little magazines, *Le Paria* was underfunded, brash, and brief—both in number of pages and in lifespan. It was also crudely written. During 1922 and 1923, however, *Le Paria* gave Parisians their best chance to understand what was happening in France's colonies. During the same period, Hemingway turned himself into a political reporter with real international credibility. He began to be a recognized expert on balkanized Europe and its tragedies—the homelessness, the violence, the abused and vulnerable women, the hungry children, the complacent men in high places. Hemingway was beginning to find more than the subject matter for his fiction; he was finding people in pain to care about and to document in an appeal to good conscience.

≡ ≡ ≡

During the first few weeks Hemingway lived in Paris, the winter of 1922, he wrote thirty important articles in sixty days for the *Toronto Star*. The years 1922 and 1923 were actually his full-fledged professional phase as a Paris journalist. They were only his freshman and sophomore years as a fiction writer—in other words, a time to practice fundamental skills rather than to demonstrate full professional competence. Hemingway came to Paris an experienced professional journalist with a brief career on the *Kansas City Star* to point to, yet we see in the first thirty stories, and then in the next few dozen after that, a growing awareness of a complex political Europe and a chaotic warring Middle East. We see him realize what complacent, rich old men in both regions were doing to the lives of ordinary working people. In 1922 and early 1923, Hemingway was figuring out both the governmental and the economic system that made colonialism and other ugly, unjust political institutions possible, and now, with the help of working reporters as well as the artists he consulted, he was learning the style of writing that, he hoped, would make a change in this international criminality.

Hemingway began writing newspaper stories in high school. The October after graduating from Oak Park High in 1917, he moved to Kansas City to cover a police reporter beat.[2] His wartime service in Italy and subsequent recuperating time in Michigan interrupted the journalism career, but by early 1920, while he worked his temporary job as companion to the Connable boy in Toronto, he began to submit stories to the *Toronto Daily Star*. Later that year, as we have seen, Hadley and Anderson helped him hatch his plan to move to Paris, and John Bone hired him as a foreign correspondent. Indeed, reporting for the *Star* was his main job once he arrived in Paris, and he worked hard at it.

Imagine a major metropolitan newspaper in North America today—the *Minneapolis Star-Tribune* or *Washington Post*, for example—sending a twenty-two-year-old high school graduate to Paris unsupervised, with an unrestricted charge to cover peace and treaty conferences as both sole reporter and columnist. This is just what John Bone of the *Toronto Star Weekly* and *Toronto Daily Star* did in late 1921 when he capitalized on Hemingway's move to Paris. Bone thought he was sending Hemingway to Europe on the Toronto paper's dollar and could therefore expect an attentive and obedient, if part-time, employee. In fact, Ernest and Hadley were headed to Paris with an income stream from Hadley's trust fund, a circumstance that gave young Hemingway the freedom to treat Bone as he treated nearly everyone else—with a maddening combination of charm and open contempt.[3]

During 1922 alone, Hemingway published travel writing from two trips to Switzerland, including the story of a walk over a mountain pass into Italy. He covered postwar peace conferences in Genoa and Lausanne. He reported on his insight that Afghanistan was going to be the site of East-West prestige conflicts. He rode the Simplon-Orient Express train to Turkey, where he telegraphed dispatches from fleabag hotels near the chaotic aftermath of the Greco-Turkish War. During 1923 he reported observations from northern Italy, where fascism was then hatching, and spent ten days in Germany, where he benefited personally from the terrible inflation he found there, eating wonderful meals and staying in luxury hotels at next to no cost, but also felt great pity for the German families in their economic suffering.

It may have been journalism rather than alpine sunshine that took the Hemingways from their small, dark apartment on rue du Cardinal Lemoine only the day after they moved into it to a resort hotel in Chamby-sur-Montreux, Switzerland. There, in a brief two months from early February to mid-April of 1922, Hemingway churned out those first thirty stories. Some are the predictable travel stories any young American in interwar Europe might write: stories about the scarcity of tourists in Switzerland that year, or about Paris as "rainy, cold, beautiful and cheap," or about the cast of characters wandering the lobbies of Swiss hotels, or about the thrills bobsledding and luging offer to the formerly uninitiated. One brief story describes a hat women have just taken to wearing in Paris, "a brown, mushroom-shaped affair with a girdle of stuffed English sparrows"—usually about "fifteen of them to a headpiece," he helpfully tells us. Even though he is writing from Switzerland, Hemingway describes the "strange-acting and strange-looking breed that crowd the tables of the Café Rotonde," and contrasts the American swells in Montmartre nightclubs with the French *apaches* (street criminals) who dance in *bals musettes* (dive dance halls), where the music is provided not by a jazz band but by a man playing accordion and stomping the floor with a booted foot and a "string of bells around his ankle."[4]

In one of these early, immature stories, Hemingway's *apaches* beat a tourist with a lead pipe wrapped in *Le Matin* and steal the little cash some North Americans are carrying after a long night in an extortionist nightclub. Trying out a technique he would use more effectively in his later career, he indicates (hilariously) that the *apaches* are speaking French by over-translating *"Moulin Rouge"* and *"n'est-ce pas, mon ami"* in one compact sentence spoken by a Parisian street tough: "The Red Mill holds him up worse than we did, not so, my pal?" A similar story explains the strange trousers Frenchmen wear, tight at the ankle and "balloon-shaped" around the thighs. Frenchmen hate these trousers too, Hemingway reports, but they cannot avoid wearing them because frugal wives buy these trousers for them. Hemingway the reporter was not above the lazy, sexist cliché, and you suspect he was sometimes moonlighting already, freely writing fiction on John Bone's salary.[5]

Hemingway shows more intellectual discipline and growth in a piece on Europe's struggle with inflation. "German Export Tax Hits Profiteers" explains very clearly how German inflation was then causing international difficulties, particularly with Switzerland. Because the Swiss currency remained relatively strong in the immediate postwar years, anyone holding that currency or another strong one, such as American or Canadian dollars, might travel into Germany, buy up goods, bring them back to Switzerland, and reap a financial windfall selling to the fiscally secure Swiss. Hemingway illustrates this problem concretely, suggesting that "a couple of Swiss" might bring two or three weeks' worth of their wages to Germany and, because of the extremely severe German inflation, buy out an entire clothing store. They might then open their own store in Basel (where Hemingway claims to have filed this story) or any other Swiss city, selling the quality German goods at less than half the going Swiss price for trousers, shirts, jackets, and ties—and still profit nicely. This exploitation of German suffering would thus harm not only the Germans, who would lose local businesses that provided employment and tax contributions to the nation's coffers, but also the nonexploitative Swiss clothing vendors, who would find that their own fair prices were being undercut by the exploiters. Thankfully, Hemingway reassures his readers, recently instituted export taxes and careful accounting of goods and cash at customs control points were preventing such piracy. But all of Europe was in an economically fragile, volatile situation.[6]

Remarkably, the most interesting and searching stories Hemingway wrote during his first eight weeks in Paris involve colonialism. He writes about characters and situations that, as we will see, had become Quoc's subject as well. In one of them, a March 25, 1922, story the Toronto editors titled "Black Novel a Storm Center," Hemingway reviews a novel by a French Guyanese *indigène*.[7] This is his lead:

> Paris.—"Batouala," the novel by René Maran, a Negro, winner of the Goncourt Academy Prize of 5,000 francs for the best novel of the year by a young writer, is still the center of a swirl of condemnation, indignation and praise.

Because Hemingway was notoriously jealous of any other writer's success (he had just endured Pound's "Bel Esprit" campaign on T. S. Eliot's behalf, and felt that his own talent was superior and deserved this funding), this lead would seem to set up a critical, even backbiting story. In 1922, he wanted nothing more than what Maran had just received—a novel under his belt, an audience for the novel, public acclaim, the approval of reviewers and peers, and a cash award. Yet Hemingway writes respectfully about Maran's novel, and observes that French colonialism is an assault on peace and community: "The preface of the novel describes how peaceful communities of 10,000 blacks in the heart of Africa have been reduced to 1,000 inhabitants under the French rule." Hemingway praises Maran for his vivid portrait of African village life. Along the way to that point, Hemingway makes unfortunate, stereotyping reference to "the big-whited eyes . . . the pink palms, and the broad, flat, naked feet of the African native," but he praises Maran for excellent writing: "You smell the smells of the village, you eat its food, you see the white man as the black man sees him, and after you have lived in the village you die there."[8] Clearly, to be in 1922 Paris was to know colonialism.

Hemingway's next 1922 destination was the Genoa Economic Conference of April, a summit meeting of European leaders attempting to get Europe's postwar economies back on a firm foundation.

Slyly, Hemingway opens his Genoa coverage with a reference to Machiavelli. He notes that the meeting hall where the first plenary session was held featured niches where busts of Italian greats were mounted, such as Columbus and Machiavelli. Columbus and Machiavelli, New World and Old: there is a self-reflexive hint here, as the young man from the New World meets up with European cynicism and *realpolitik*. As the conference opened it seemed that the Germans were the Machiavels. They were suffering terrible inflation, but the silver lining for them was that they were paying down huge war reparations with almost worthless marks. Taking further advantage of their position, and shocking the conference almost before it began, the Germans announced that they had signed an agreement with the Soviets, the Treaty of Rapallo, which was negotiated in the town where the Russians were lodged for the conference. In essence, the two former enemies forgave all war debts and granted each other favored diplomatic and economic status. Germany and Russia were wounded warriors at the time, but anyone could see what a colossus they might become in a few years, if allied under the effects of this treaty.

One of their longer-term and higher-order goals was to get all Allied nations to forgive all war debts and reparations, as Hemingway saw and cabled on April 14:

> Genoa.—"No country intends to pay its war debts; France does not intend to pay the United States; to pay Allied claims would make Russia a slave state; Russia will not calmly agree to pay what four years of war could not force from her; we must find a common basis" was the Russian delegation statement today. Russian counterclaims make the first big snag in the conference. Russians will offer a counterclaim for each Allied demand.[9]

Those were days when hard copy written in Europe took nearly two weeks to reach North America, so these brief messages, which crossed the Atlantic electronically via underwater cable, broke emergent news. Back in Toronto, John Bone would rewrite this brief report into a full story about German-Soviet scheming. (Indeed, Hemingway suspected that Bone rewrote the leads on such expanded stories and sold them to American newspapers under his own byline and for his own profit.) In a longer piece written three days later, Hemingway laid out a settlement in which Russia, as he called the Soviet Union, would continue to pay the czar's war debts, would have those debts adjusted for inflation and other relative factors, and would receive full diplomatic recognition. This would be "a wiping clean of the Bolshevik past," as Hemingway put it, which would lead to the USSR's good standing among European nations.[10]

Hemingway's Genoa reporting rested in an effective contrast he had worked up: British Prime Minister Lloyd George as the handsome hero of the conference and Mussolini as the wicked poseur. Employing this strategy, Hemingway risked oversimplifying or even distorting the moral and political content of England's and Italy's arguments, not to mention the stances of many nations that he does not personalize. But there is a wisdom in Hemingway's May 13, 1922, portrait, "Lloyd George's Magic." In this story Hemingway wants to show readers what kind of diplomatic talent can keep peace in mind, and lines of communication open. Written weeks after returning to Paris from Genoa, this story is half comic in its portraits of world leaders:

> Barthou, the Frenchman, looked like the left-hand one of the Smith Brothers of cough drop fame. Beneš, the Czechoslovak premier, looks exactly like a barber—a cropped-headed, rather sullen barber. Stambouliski, of Bulgaria, is a great, thick-bodied, black-headed, fierce-moustached, scowling Buffalo Bill; Viscount Ishii, a small cold-faced Japanese in a morning coat and silk hat; Walter Rathenau [of Germany], an egotistical, brilliant, perfectly dressed, hawk-faced, bald-headed scientist, contemptuous and confident.

To Hemingway's mind, Germany's Rathenau was the Machiavel among these other menials, entertainers, and pretenders. Rathenau represented the threat to the conference and its dream of peace through economic cooperation. Hemingway saw that the German's scheming with the Russians might very well blow up this conference and lead to even bloodier European conflict in the near future.

Yet David Lloyd George was there, a kind of gallant St. George. Hemingway seems to have loved Lloyd George. He tells us that Lloyd George cannot be captured in photographs, any more than movie stars can be, or "your best girl." Hemingway describes his hero almost rapturously:

> Lloyd George has no movie face. His charm, his fresh coloring—almost girlish—the complexion of a boy subaltern just out of Sandhurst [Britain's West Point], his tremendous assurance that makes him seem a tall man until you see him standing beside someone of average height; his kindly, twinkling eyes; none of these show in the photographs.

What did this paragon of human goodness do to save the conference? Nothing. And that is Hemingway's point, the important lesson he took away from Genoa. Nations, he saw, pursue self-interest cynically and with little thought to violent consequences. Or rather, they flirt with violent consequences, when it suits them, in order to secure economic benefits. No one at the conference, it seemed to Hemingway, was thinking about the young men who were scripted to die in the next war or the next revolution. Yet perhaps L. G. (as his aides called Lloyd George) was wiser than the others, because his choice to do nothing about the alarming Treaty of Rapallo saved the conference. "After an exchange of acrid notes between the Allies and Germany," Hemingway reports, "when an impasse was obviously reached and one side or the other must yield, L. G. simply considered the incident closed—and it was closed. All the flames died down and the conference went on with its work."[11] In the end, the Treaty of Rapallo did not lead to the setting aside of all claims to war debts. It did lead to an odd and threatening alliance between two nations moving, on entirely different tracks, toward totalitarianism, but Hemingway was not wrong to admire a leader who sought peace rather than national honor through war.

Of course, it's possible that Hemingway merely gave his Canadian readers—who were citizens of a British Commonwealth nation, after all—a British hero they could love. Hemingway was certainly capable of lazy reporting, and of the occasional lazy sentence, such as, "The bobbed-haired German had bobbed hair." He could also indulge in the bigotry of his day. Later that year, in an article titled "Rug Vendors in Paris," he would serve up some unfortunate anti-Arab prejudice while telling readers about a day on the streets of Paris when a Muslim street vendor from the colonies tried to sell him a rug of dyed goat, which the man passed off as Bengal tiger:

> "Ah yes, Monsieur," the rug vendor puts his hand on his heart, "it is a veritable tiger. I swear by Allah."
> "It is a goat," you repeat. "Stop this lying."
> "Ah yes, Monsieur," the rug vendor bows his head. "It is a veritable goat."[12]

Still, in his loving portrait of L. G., Hemingway seems interested in an existential mystery transcending his lazy prejudices: Why is it that some world leaders seem to care about peace and work for it selflessly and wisely, while others do not and apparently never will?

After a cold, wet trudge into Italy over the St. Bernard Pass with Hadley and a friend in May of 1922, Hemingway filed a few more reports that spring and early summer on the ominous gains Mussolini's black-shirted Fascisti were making all across Italy. In two articles, both published in Toronto on June 24, Hemingway treats Mussolini with some respect, describing him as a patriot, newspaperman, and former socialist who is now, through force of personality, in charge of half a million violent and loyal young men. Hemingway only hints at Mussolini's inner wildness, a suggestion he makes by picturing *Il Duce* twice "fondling the ears of a wolfhound pup." The other article is far blunter. Describing the young Fascisti rather than their leader, he writes, "They enjoyed hunting live Communists much more than going to school or working in their fathers' offices—and they intended to keep right on. So the Fascisti have kept on fighting, burning, pillaging anything resembling communism they can find." He closes his article by comparing these young men to "a three-year-old child playing with a live Mills bomb."[13] (The Mills bomb was a Great War hand grenade of British make.) Hemingway had absolutely no sympathy for knee-jerk, vicious anti-communists. His lifelong anti-fascism was crystalizing.

The most moving article Hemingway wrote in 1922 recounts his and Hadley's trip to the area north of Venice, the region where Ernest had served Italian soldiers as a Red Cross volunteer. He calls himself a veteran in this story but avoids telling the reader his real role in the war—that he was wounded while serving as a humanitarian volunteer, handing out candy and cigarettes, not carrying a weapon in defense of the Italian nation. He does describe the "neat, white scar" on his shin, which was won honorably enough. He does not plead for sympathy or praise, but only wants to recall important places in his life. His deeper attitude becomes clear when he tells us that "no one but a staff officer could love a battlefield." That is, only the planners can like the killing fields, never the foot soldiers who lived in the trenches and watched their friends scream in pain and, too often, die.

Then he recounts a series of disappointments. In spite of the mortal risks he once took on the Italians' behalf, they treat him rudely now, minimizing his wartime service. He shares a first-class train compartment with "evil-smelling Italian profiteers going to Venice for vacations." Seeing the town of Fossalta, where he had once moved around in trenches, keeping an eye on the Austrians, he is surprised to find completely rebuilt houses and no sign of the trenches. He takes a dig at the French and Belgians, remarking to Hadley that "some other nations were using their destroyed towns as showplaces and reparation appeals."

Then Hemingway writes a moving pair of paragraphs that reveal just how passionate he was in his hatred of war and hope for peace. The emotion of these paragraphs can't really be paraphrased:

> For a reconstructed town is much sadder than a devastated town. The people haven't their homes back. They have new homes. The homes they played in as children, the room where they made love with the lamp turned down, the hearth where they sat, the church they were married in, the room where their child died, these rooms are gone. A shattered village in the war always had a dignity, as though it had died for something. It had died for something and something better was to come. It was all part of the great sacrifice. Now there was just the new, ugly futility of it all. Everything is just as it was—except a little worse.
>
> So we walked along the street where I saw my very good friend killed, past the ugly houses toward the motorcar, whose owner would never have had a motorcar if it had not been for the war, and it all seemed a very bad business.

"Very bad business" here is not just a British idiom. (He and Hadley are accompanied on this trip by their Anglo-Irish veteran friend Chink Dorman-Smith, and Hemingway's magpie mind tended to pick up the lingo.) It is a hint that the hated profiteers are again on Hemingway's mind. Because he sees that the war brought only vain material gains to the people who endured it, he finds the new Italian houses ugly and the driver's new motorcar undeserved. Probably he saw that the conferences he had been attending in Switzerland and Italy were bound up with this materialist seeking, only on an international scale. He cannot believe that this is what his "very good friend" gave his life for—new cars parked beside a few ugly new houses, right where the trenches had been.[14]

Hemingway's most important year as a reporter concluded with his work in Anatolia, covering the aftermath of the Greco-Turkish War. This war epitomized the circumstances that would lead to a century of continuous, nearly permanent war in Europe and the Middle East—reminding us very much of our own world today—as elements of the defeated Ottoman Empire, Muslims under their secular-modernist-leaning Kemal Atatürk, started another war in order to drive Greek settlers off Anatolian lands. Turks considered these lands their own by Wilson's principle of self-determination, which they knew before Wilson wrote about it. The geopolitical prizes the great powers competed for were oil fields in present-day Iraq, Iran, and Saudi Arabia.[15] But the Greek government went to war for a swath of seaside farming land—and for national pride and control of the straits leading to Constantinople and the Black Sea. They were determined to colonize an Islamic land.

Greece had been granted Anatolian lands by postwar treaty, the Treaty of Sevres. Predictably, when perceived homelands were at stake, Turks, who had been part of the Central Powers coalition that had lost the Great War, did not feel remorseful or contrite. When the Treaty of Sevres turned out to be even harsher for the Turks and other defeated Ottomans than the Treaty of Versailles had been for the Germans, and when Greece sent troops into Anatolia to occupy Smyrna and other formerly Turkish cities in an effort to consolidate and extend treaty gains, Kemal Atatürk organized troops and fought back. He was successful. By the time Hemingway arrived in Constantinople in September, ready to make reporting trips west into Anatolia, Greek forces had been defeated, the Greek home government had fallen, government ministers thought responsible for the disaster had been executed, British naval vessels that had sailed to Smyrna to protect Greek refugees had been removed already, and a massive, brutal population exchange was underway.[16] Wilson could not have imagined that the ideal of self-determination he brought to Paris in 1919 would play out in this horrifying way.

Hadley did not want her husband to go to Turkey that autumn of 1922. In fact, she and Ernest quarreled so bitterly over the trip that she gave him the silent treatment for three full days before he left.

Meanwhile, he worked to secure the Greek, Serbian, and Bulgarian visas he needed so that each border check on the Simplon-Orient Express would go smoothly. Purchasing his train ticket, he spent more than $200 of the $500 advance money John Bone had sent him for this journey. Hemingway didn't realize it yet, but he was stepping into a conflict that his hero David Lloyd George had helped to create by promising Greek leaders Anatolian assets if they supported the Allies during the war and by encouraging the Greeks to build their "Christian Empire" through expansion across the Aegean. Lloyd George, like many leaders in his century and ours, wanted ready access to Mesopotamian oil. So did France. The Allies were not above using their people's Christian faith and fear of Islam as a pretext for these moves, but in this case only Britain aligned against Islam. As Hemingway reported, while Britain bet on Greek military superiority, France simply bought Kemal and, doing so, backed the right horse. Even though France had been bled white defeating the Central Powers, which included Turkey, the French now trained and supplied Atatürk's Turkish forces. Hemingway knew what he was witnessing. Former loyalties that had been trumpeted as noble had given way to Machiavellian pursuit of self-interest. This conflict was now about homelands and oil, not about fighting a war to end wars.

Hemingway's stories from Anatolia are incisive and opinionated both. They illustrate his geopolitical learning, which he took mainly from diplomats and ministers around him, and from the mostly unnamed journalists he consorted with. His stories at first note a traveler's reactions—that minarets appear dirty white from the train, or that Serbs who once lived in Boston speak perfect American street lingo when you meet them on a train. Some of Hemingway's stories, such as a report about a parade of refugees slogging along the Karagatch Road, found their way into his fiction almost verbatim, as we have seen.

Throughout these news stories, Hemingway portrays the Greco-Turkish War as a conflict between Christianity and Islam, the cross making way for the crescent, as he put it in one dispatch. He rarely refers to Greek and Armenian forces or refugees by their nationalities. He calls them Christians. Yet he recognizes some complexity in the situation, noting in another story that the conflict is between classes: "Bismarck said all men in the Balkans who tuck their shirts into their trousers are crooks. The shirts of the peasants, of course, hang outside." He then describes one of those who tucked in his shirt, a French-connected banker named Hamid Bey, who speaks for Atatürk as head of the Red Crescent. "What have the Christians to fear?" Bey asks. He falsely claims that the Turks have put down their arms, and that all atrocities have been committed by the Greek Christians, an accusation hotly debated even today. Hemingway knew that Armenians and others had been massacred, saw that Bey was a liar, and helped his readers to see it too.[17]

After a time in Constantinople, Hemingway began to explain to his readers a more subtle version of the events he was witnessing. He saw that the alliance the French had entered into with Kemal Atatürk was extremely dangerous for them, because the Turkish nationalist was also an ally of the Soviets. At stake were the Bosporus Straits, "Constan" (Constantinople) itself, the ethnic and religious identity of that Mediterranean land, and much of what we now call Arab oil. Receiving support from both France and the Soviet Union, Kemal would one day have to decide which nation represented Turkey's true interests, as Hemingway noted:

> Now, in the victorious Kemalist troops, French influence is at its height. I think it has reached the crest and will be on the downgrade from now on because of Kemal's affiliations with Soviet Russia. It is that which will sooner or later bring him into difficulties with France, and it is that which, next to the conflict between Islam and Christianity, makes the greatest danger to the peace of the world.[18]

The danger, as Hemingway saw it, was that France was allowing a Soviet-aligned "wedge" consisting of Turkey and Bulgaria to be hammered into the Balkans. This "not oversecure" situation, as Hemingway sarcastically put it, is like keeping a piece of dynamite under your bed, armed with a fuse. Later Hemingway realized that this conflict he was watching was no binary Christian/Muslim affair, fought to decide whether the liminal Anatolia, which the apostle Paul had visited often, would be an Eastern or Western possession. Atatürk, he realized now and reported to his readers, is more of a businessman than a "new Saladin," bent on ridding his lands of Christian crusaders. Many of the Kemalists, he writes, are "atheists and French Freemasons rather than good Mohammedans."[19] That Atatürk was no jihadist gave Hemingway little comfort. Atatürk remaining unaligned made the Turkish nationalists that much less pre-dictable in 1922.

Hemingway writes under the influence of his fellow reporter and friend (and eventually Hadley's second husband) Paul Mowrer, whose theories of balkanized Europe he had been reading. In his reporting, Hemingway applied both Mowrer's theory of balkanization and Wilson's theory of self-determination. Riding the train toward "Constan," Hemingway is struck by the resemblance of this country to the prairies of eastern Ontario. "It is hard to believe," he writes, "that this rich, pleasant farming country is the bleak-sounding Balkans. It is, though, and as you ride through it you can see how the love of the land can make men fight wars." This is Mowrer's influence, the product of his book, *Balkanized Europe*, which popularized the idea of nations becoming "balkanized," or endemically and competitively violent. Next comes Wilson's influence: "and there can never be peace in the Balkans as long as one people holds the lands of another." In another story he warns of the dangerous effects of the self-determination theory, noting that "it is hard for the racial fear to be quieted" and that, unfortunately, such hatreds cause "the innocent to suffer."[20]

Leaving Thrace, Hemingway offers a vivid description of refugees moving to a place where they were to be separated at a fork in the road, Greeks to one side and Turks to another. The fork in the road was, for Hemingway, both physical and existential. He describes a Turk who mistakenly took the wrong turn, was beaten by a Greek soldier with the butt of his rifle, panicked, ran, and was beaten further. The descriptions of suffering refugees on both sides of this conflict, their "bundles, bedsprings, bedding, sewing machines, babies, broken carts, all in the mud and the drizzling rain," are worthy of inclusion in his best stories. Writing vivid, concrete descriptions of such events was Hemingway's natural talent, the one he didn't need to learn when he arrived in Paris.

Hemingway closed out the impressive reporting of 1922 with a pair of dispatches from Lausanne, where another peace conference convened. There he learned from Lenin's foreign minister George Tchitcherin (Hemingway's spelling) just how convinced international diplomats were that another great war was in the offing. Hemingway notes the danger of a leader like Mussolini coming to power, as he recently had in

Italy. And then Chitcherin, he reports in an additional story, told him just how much the Soviet Union would sacrifice, in arms buildups and possibly in blood, to keep Western warships from crossing freely through the Bosporus and into the Black Sea. Hemingway noted that Chitcherin liked to parade in a military uniform that his wartime service had not earned. The man always wanted to be a soldier, Hemingway saw, "and soldiers make empires and empires make wars."[21]

Hemingway must have been amazed at what the craft of writing could teach him. For if he was not yet fully aware that colonialist competition and the arrogance of empire were at the root of the war that killed millions and almost killed him, he was after Genoa, Anatolia, and Lausanne.

# 12

## HUMANITY AND THE PARIAH

### QUOC IN 1922 AND EARLY 1923

**P**erhaps the most troubling moment in Ho Chi Minh's Paris education came when he decided he was not a citizen of the city any longer, or a guest of the French, but a pariah. From 1919 to 1922, he saw himself as a respected envoy of his Vietnamese people whose role left him free to take an active part in the country's debates about the future of the empire and its colonies in the quickly evolving postwar world. Quoc occasionally took part in these debates in the halls of government, as he had during the Paris Peace Conference, or in the offices of certain ministers of the colonies, but his main venue for broadcasting his political views was in the pages of local magazines. For like Hemingway, Quoc was a young but very promising journalist who balanced objectivity with his vision for a more just future.

Then, in the spring of 1922 Quoc ceased to be a regular contributor to *L'Humanité*, the newspaper of the French Socialist Party and, later, the French Communist Party, and began to publish his own little magazine, *Le Paria*. The titles of the two periodicals reflect the shift in Quoc's attitudes and favored doctrines at that time. He was beginning to feel less humane and hopeful, more estranged and angry. Trained in French Enlightenment philosophy and in love with the French and American Revolutions, Quoc had written and debated with an idealistic confidence in humanity, with a real hope for better conditions for workers around the world, who would gain, he hoped, broader rights through leaders' willing acceptance of reforms rather than through revolutionary war. He was especially hopeful that reforms would extend to the colonies and eventually result in Vietnam's liberation from French control. Quoc's articles in *L'Humanité* pleaded with his communist and non-communist readers alike, asking for sympathy and understanding for his cause, for a realization that human rights familiar to citizens of Western nations but almost never to indigenous residents of colonial lands must be extended to all people, regardless of their class or race. Because the concept of human rights is often thought to be a Western Enlightenment idea, Quoc's early stance during the Paris years is essentially a melding of Western liberal and communist ideals, and his role is not that of a pariah but of an idealistic seeker, a wholly human being insisting upon his unalienable rights.

*Le Paria*, on the other hand, was overtly "anti-West," as Quoc himself put it. In this sense, it was Dada-esque and, as we will soon learn, surrealist in a Parisian sense of the word. In the pages of *Le Paria*, in other words, Quoc willingly exposed the insanity of contemporary Western ways. He joined the dadaists in shoving French noses straight into the *merde*, the evidence of Western insanity now so obvious to us in the repeated orgies of violence at the Somme, Passchendaele, and Ypres— and continuing in the 1920s in Turkey and North Africa. In story after story, he showed the French what brutes they sent to manage the colonies in Vietnam and how incredibly far French behavior in Indochina was from any kind of "civilizing mission."

Quoc quickly saw that this tactic would get results. The fledgling magazine was soon so politically explosive that the French Ministry of Colonies purchased every copy its agents could lay their hands on, and announced that any colonial subject found reading *Le Paria* would be subject to immediate arrest.[1] Colonials arrested in France were usually either imprisoned without due process or deported to their native lands, regardless of mitigating factors such as a career or family in France, so both Quoc and his readers were upset, defiant, and determined enough to risk their freedom and their current daily lives by reading *Le Paria*.

In *L'Humanité*, Quoc had stated philosophical ideals or debated the realism of Marxist doctrines; in *Le Paria*, he documented French atrocities. He wrote in a controlled voice, but one that is clearly outraged. The men in the Ministry of Colonies knew that such testimony might expose the violent, coercive nature of the colonial project. French violence was an aspect of the colonies they denied existed—denied, perhaps, even to themselves. But Quoc was determined to get the real news out. Because Quoc's magazine was such a perceived threat to the French, the publishers, writers, and readers of *Le Paria* were indeed pariahs—the untouchables of establishment French society.

≡ ≡ ≡

Sadly, at the same time that reporting from war zones was helping Hemingway to open up to the world's political complexity, endemic violence, and resulting pain, Quoc's career in journalism was making him angrier and more politically volatile. The truly sad part of Quoc's adoption of the pariah persona is that it reflects his emotional hardening, the genesis of the ruthlessness we see in him as a military leader of the Viet Minh and Viet Cong later in the century. "You can kill 10 of my men for every one I kill of yours," he warned the French in 1946, as he arrived in Vietnam to begin his first revolutionary war, "yet even at those odds, you will lose and I will win." Two decades later he uttered a similarly chilling brag to an American journalist who asked how long the North Vietnamese would fight American troops: "Twenty years, maybe 100 years—as long as it took to win, regardless of cost."[2] This incredible determination did indeed have its costs. Ho's 1969 *Time* magazine obituary notes his responsibility for the human toll of the American Vietnam War: three million North and South Vietnamese soldiers and civilians dead by 1969, and many more horribly wounded or homeless or both.[3] Like Dr. Jekyll turning into Mr. Hyde, in 1922 Quoc was turning into Ho Chi Minh.

*L'Humanité* and *Le Paria* were very different periodicals, as different as Quoc was from Ho. *L'Humanité* was an established and successful newspaper, founded by socialist Jean Jaurès in 1904. Jaurès could be called a humanist-socialist, because he opposed militarism and tried hard to keep France and Germany from going to war in 1914. As war threatened, he attempted to start a general strike in both countries, a move he hoped would force French and German leaders to negotiate a sensible and peace-keeping settlement. But French nationalism was surging in 1914. Too many older French citizens recalled vividly their suffering and humiliation when France lost the Franco-Prussian War in 1871, and too many younger French had been trained in school to regard Alsace-Lorraine, a German possession since that war's conclusion, as rightfully French. Most felt Alsace-Lorraine's current attachment to Germany was a moral outrage. For decades, schoolchildren in France had been shown European maps with Alsace colored black. These kids were taught that the province was a "black stain" on their national pride, and that no French patriot should ever forget it. As a result of this kind of training in patriotism, the French rallied to the flag in 1914. Then, as now, some carried their patriotism to criminal extremes. Jaurès was assassinated in 1914 by a resentful young nationalist who had been trained to hate Germans. This young man admitted he was deeply offended that *L'Humanité* would argue for peace without altered national boundaries returning the custody of Alsace-Lorraine to the French.[4]

Quoc's stories for *L'Humanité* tended to have an intellectual, doctrinaire quality that emerged from the magazine's newly communist commitments. (The magazine became communist as a result of the same 1920 meeting he did.) Sometime in 1921, for instance, Quoc writes in that journal that it is "wrong to say that this country, inhabited by more than 20 million exploited people, is now ripe for revolution." It is also wrong, on the other hand, he continues, to think they are "satisfied with the regime." Quoc asserts that his compatriots were then gaining a new revolutionary consciousness: "The wind from working-class Russia, revolutionary China or militant India has cured them of intoxication. It is true that they don't get educated by books or speeches, but in another fashion." What he means is, the Vietnamese were not yet highly literate, but they were learning the lessons of their own painful experiences. Something inside them was "seething [and] rumbling," Quoc asserts, and those who knew of Lenin had come to realize that "it was up to the elite to hasten the coming of that moment" by continuing to prod the Vietnamese toward the time when abuses and injustices perpetrated by the elite would cause the former to "explode formidably." This, Quoc implies, is simply a rational prediction of the battle of classes Marx and Lenin foresaw.[5]

*Le Paria*, on the other hand, was a little magazine—closer kin to *the transatlantic review*, the little magazine Hemingway would soon edit in Paris, or to *The Little Review*, the magazine that was soon to publish Hemingway's prose poems for the first time, than to an established national political newspaper. These magazines were called "little" because they had few readers, though usually passionate ones. A little magazine usually began as a platform for a school of writers who wanted to make aesthetic and political declarations and to publish illustrative examples of each other's writing. Typically, a financial "angel" kicked off a little magazine's existence. For example, Hemingway's one-time friend Harold Loeb (Robert Cohn in *The Sun Also Rises*) financed *Broom* with his small inheritance. Typically, a little magazine would thrive for a few months, then perhaps merely survive on subscriptions and other meager sales for a few more months. (Some little magazines outperformed this model, surviving to our day and going strong, such as Chicago's *Poetry: A Magazine in Verse*.) Most of these little magazines published experimental fiction and poetry with little immediate commercial appeal—such as Hemingway's brief early prose poems and angry free verse poems. As Hemingway learned, the little magazines could make an unknown writer known to certain editors and other important literary contacts, both in Paris and in distant but oh-so-important New York. Little magazines could even begin to alter readers' tastes, creating acceptance and even demand for more eccentric modern experiments. As a result of such a shift in taste, established publishers such as Horace Liveright and Charles Scribner did indeed begin to publish modernist works, including Hemingway's, in the middle 1920s. This evolution in taste, initiated by the little magazines, is exactly how modernist writing became mainstream writing—and eventually even required reading in high schools—especially in the United States.

As a resident of a neighborhood with some of the best modernist bookstores, including Shakespeare & Company with its front window crammed with little magazines for purchase or in-store perusing, Quoc knew that the literary little magazine had many non-literary cousins, especially in revolutionary politics. Because little magazines were essentially lawless and could publish exactly what they wished, it took no special skill, Quoc saw, to organize such a magazine or indeed to write for one, so long as funds were available. And apparently Quoc's communist colleagues helped him raise funds for his efforts, so that was no problem. *Le Paria* was one of those seat-of-the-pants and fly-by-night operations, as Quoc's testimony confirms: "There was one time when I was the editor, chief treasurer, and distributor of *Le Paria* as well as the person who sold it. The comrades from Asian and African colonies wrote articles and solicited contributions and I did practically everything else." The title *Le Paria*—meaning, as we have seen, "The Pariah" or "The (Hated) Outcast"—is another clear indicator of little magazine DNA. Nearly every little magazine was presented by its editors as under-appreciated, boldly innovative, despised by the ordinary reader, and essential to the future of humankind.

There appear to be two main reasons for Quoc's involvement in *Le Paria*. First, he had grown frustrated with the French government's responses to his "Demands" and other entreaties. He was especially frustrated with Minister of Colonies Albert Sarraut, whose bullying and flattering in those required meetings of the previous two years Quoc found a maddening combination. Secondly, Quoc had begun to accept an argument his mentor Phan Chu Trinh had started making that year, which was that Quoc was not reaching his target audience. According to Trinh in a February 1922 letter to Quoc, the Vietnamese did not read French, or even *quoc ngu*, the now-established Vietnamese language in Latin letters that the French had imposed upon them in the nineteenth century. Vietnamese illiteracy was a real stumbling block to reforms. Obviously, Trinh argued, illiterate colonial subjects and expatriates could not be reached through intellectual arguments in French magazines, even simple Leninist arguments about the nature of economic classes and their inevitable conflict. Trinh argued that Quoc should leave Paris, return to Vietnam, and find ways to appeal to his fellow Vietnamese with his message of liberation. "I am convinced," Trinh wrote, "that the doctrine that you cherish so much can be diffused among our people. Even if you fail, others will take up the task." Trinh sugarcoated this bitter advice with a compliment, which is that he, Trinh, was a "tired horse," while Quoc was a "fiery stallion."[6] Still, the two comrades were drifting apart. Quoc seems to have concluded immediately that Trinh was wrong. Quoc still felt he needed to address colonized people directly from Paris, as he had been doing, with brief and intensely shocking tales that could be read aloud to groups both in the metropole and, once copies of these writings were smuggled into colonial Vietnam, in his own country. But Trinh was correct, he realized, in seeing that he was at a crossroads. He needed, he felt, to shift from writing reasonable demands or carefully crafted arguments or edifying instruction in class conflict. It was time to write unsubtle propaganda and provocations.

One of the earliest and most shocking of Quoc's *Le Paria* essays appeared in August of 1922 and was titled "Annamese Women and French Domination."[7] It is in fact the most stunning, provocative, and stomach-turning piece of colonial documentation Ho Chi Minh ever wrote. The essay begins, however, with a standard Leninist thesis: "Colonization," Quoc writes reasonably enough, "is in itself an act of violence of the stronger against the weaker. This violence becomes still more odious when it is exercised upon women and children." With this calm and rational introduction, he then proposes to review a "few instances" of eyewitness testimony to colonial "sadism." In fact, he describes just one situation in fewer than three hundred words.

In Quoc's prose poem, French soldiers arrive in an Annamese village, finding that most residents have already fled. The residents fear that any of them could be accused of being an anti-colonial rebel. Only two old men remain, along with one "maiden," and a mother suckling a baby and gripping her eight-year-old daughter by the hand. In a deadpan delivery, Quoc then describes a true horror. After interrogating these Annamese for a time, the French soldiers become furious about their failure to be understood, so they beat one man with their rifle butts and spend hours roasting the other alive over a wood fire. Meanwhile, other soldiers rape the two women and the eight-year-old girl. The mother escapes to become Quoc's eyewitness. While still hiding in the area, she witnesses a soldier stabbing the maiden, slowly and deliberately inserting and drawing out the blade, over and over again. Quoc's story concludes with this horrifying description:

> The three corpses lay on the flat ground of a salt-marsh: the eight-year-old girl naked, the young woman disemboweled, her stiffened left forearm raising a clenched fist to the indifferent sky, and the old man, horrible, naked like the others, disfigured by the roasting with his fat which had run, melted and congealed with the skin of his belly, which was bloated, grilled and golden, like the skin of a roast pig.

In the same issue as his horrifying "Annamese Women" essay, with its rapes, murders, and grilling of human meat, Quoc published an "Open Letter to Albert Sarraut."[8] The title implies a diplomatic political argument, but what Quoc offers this time is furious sarcasm. He begins by seeming to flatter Sarraut, who was proud of his reformist policies for the colonies. "We know very well," Quoc writes, "that your affection for the natives of the colonies in general, and the Annamese in particular, is great." He notes that the Annamese have experienced "prosperity and real happiness" under Sarraut. Then Quoc's tone shifts. This prosperity and happiness, he writes, is the result of "an increasing number of spirit and opium shops which, together with firing squads, prisons, 'democracy' and all the improved apparatus of modern civilization, are combining to make the Annamese the most advanced of the Asians and the happiest of mortals." Quoc next sarcastically congratulates Sarraut for his "fatherly solicitude" in granting each Annamite in Paris a "private *aides-de-camp.*" We realize what Quoc means by this when he refers to "novices in the art of Sherlock Holmes." He is talking about the police agents who haunt him and, he must realize, most other Annamite rebels. He then offers to save the indebted nation of France "some of the spending money that the proletariat has sweated hard for." He is willing to put the police agents out of work by reporting on his own activities. To that end, he summarizes his daily schedule:

Morning: from 8 to 12 at the workshop.

Afternoon: in the newspaper offices (leftist of course) or at the library.

Evening: at home or attending educational talks.

Sundays and holidays: visiting museums or other places of interest.

Quoc's report on his habits is clearly meant to ridicule the idea that he was a mere terrorist. On the contrary, his schedule of earnest and edifying activities mirrors that of a revolutionary hero of the French, Ben Franklin. It is a schedule that denies the French their favored thesis, which is that all Annamites were moral children in need of civilizing. It also happened that Quoc was telling the truth. This really was his daily schedule in 1922 Paris.

Usually, Quoc wrote brief, unsubtle, almost crudely violent articles for *Le Paria*. One describes a Vietnamese woman in Indochina who asked for her wages and for this effrontery was kicked until she bled. Another tells the tale of a cold-blooded shooting of "three natives" by a French settler who found native sheep in his olive grove. Yet another tells of the brutal beating of two North African men for eating "a few bunches of grapes" from a French plantation.[9] In each of these essays, his presentation is inartistic, even when judged as objective reporting, as this partial catalog from a story of that year illustrates:

A railway official beat a Tonkinese village mayor with a cane.

M. Beck broke his car driver's skull with a blow from his fist.

M. Bres, building contractor, kicked an Annamese to death after binding his arms and letting him be bitten by his dog.

M. Deffis, receiver, killed his Annamese servant with a powerful kick to the kidneys.[10]

Yet artistry is not Quoc's goal. Rather, he is giving testimony in a court of public opinion. He knows that accumulated evidence will win the day.

Most of the other articles are mainly tutorials on colonial economics and are not distinct enough from each other to bear summarizing, and anyway, very few are to be found in the scanty collections of Ho's writings now available. But one from August of 1922 serves as an excellent example of Quoc's style. In fewer than five hundred words, "Murderous Civilization!" tells the tale of a Cochin-Chinese railway worker named Le Van Tai, who was charged with overseeing four employees who were to close a drawbridge over a Vietnamese river whenever local trains needed to pass.[11] One day, all four Vietnamese workers were manning the bridge. None of them knew any French. One of them saw a train approaching, so he closed the bridge to river traffic just as a "government launch" expected to pass under the open span. The launch was bringing a white man—a "naval dockyard official," Quoc calls him—home from a hunt. The boat quickly docked, and the white man rushed up onto the bridge to berate the worker for delaying him. As the Vietnamese worker fled toward Tai's home for help, the white man pursued him, throwing stones. "When he heard the noise, Tai came out to meet the representative of civilization," Quoc writes sarcastically. The white man refused to listen to Tai and called him a stupid brute, and as Tai, who also spoke no French, pointed to the red signal that indicated a train approaching, the infuriated white man beat him and pushed him into a nearby brazier. Tai died six days later after "atrocious suffering" from his burns. Meanwhile, the Frenchman was not charged. Quoc calls the white Frenchman who perpetrated this outrage "M. Long's collaborator," a reference to the governor-general who succeeded Sarraut. In other words, this outrage was a sanctioned activity of official France. In his final lines, Quoc refers to a colonial exhibition then being staged in Marseille:

In Marseille, the official prosperity of Indochina is on display; in Annam, people are dying of starvation. Here loyalism is praised, there assassination is perpetrated! What do you say to this. . . . Excellentissimo Sarraut?

PS While the life of an Annamese is not worth a cent, for a scratch on the arm M. Inspector General Reinhardt receives 120,000 francs compensation. Equality! Beloved equality!

We do not need to know who M. Reinhardt was or why he received compensation. Quoc felt such situations spoke for themselves. He knew that Vietnamese sailors managed to get a few copies of *Le Paria* into the colony as each new edition was printed, and he believed that peasant farmers there would respond properly both to his atrocity stories, which were either real or realistic, and to his sarcasm. That is, these peasants in Vietnam would become enraged and radicalized and ready to fight for their freedom and for the values taught to them in their Buddhist, Confucian, and Catholic temples, churches, and homes.

Sometimes, Quoc's and Hemingway's journalistic interests merged. In December of 1922 Quoc showed in one compact *Le Paria* story that he shared Hemingway's interest in very specific events of the previous year. These included a boxing match involving a black Senegalese fighter (a bout Hemingway attended and Quoc probably did too), René Maran's stunning new novel about French colonial crimes in Africa, Kemal Atatürk's fight to restore Anatolia to Turkish control, and the weakening of the great empires as native ethnic resistance movements rushed into the power vacuum created by the Great War.[12]

In "About Siki," Quoc writes one of his characteristically angry and sarcastic stories about Amadou Mbarick Fall, otherwise known as Battling Siki, a boxer who fought the white French champion Georges Carpentier in the Buffalo Velodrome on September 22, 1922.[13] Hemingway attended the bout that evening just before boarding the Simplon-Orient Express for Anatolia the next day. (Hadley probably did not attend, because she was still furious at Ernest for taking on this reporting assignment and was still refusing to speak to him.) Hemingway witnessed such obvious and fascinating corruption that evening that he saved up the memory and used it to contribute to a 1925 story, "Fifty Grand," which is also about cheating in the boxing ring. Quoc may have attended the match too. We know he regularly covered boxing matches because in May he had attended Carpentier's fight with the Jewish fighter "Kid" Lewis and afterward had written a furious opinion piece for the magazine *Cinégraph*, decrying Franglais coinages he had heard sportswriters nearby using that night, such as "le manager," "le round," and "le knockout." In the *Cinégraph* article, he begged Premier Raymond Poincaré to ban non-French phrases from French sports stories—a very oddly Francophile thing for him to have done.[14] If nothing else, we see here that Quoc did love language, even the French language, enough to protect it from barbarous neologisms. He was a writer in the truest sense, even if his own prose was often ragged.

Quoc was exercised about the Siki fight for a different reason—namely, the French racism the event placed on display. Siki claimed after his fight with Carpentier that he had been paid to throw the match. He changed his mind, he claimed after the bout, as Carpentier beat on him unnecessarily and mercilessly. He concluded that the fix was bad. Though Siki had been bloodied—the *Chicago Tribune* Paris edition described him as an "ebony Tarzan stagger[ing] up with his face like a chocolate éclair smeared with catsup"—he gathered himself and began to brawl with Carpentier. Soon, he gained the upper hand. A referee later tried to throw the fight Carpentier's way, but three judges and the crowd would have none of that. They forced the referee to declare

Siki the rightful champion. Hemingway's companion at the fight, Lincoln Steffens, thought the fight was a perfect parable for the ways the white empires were bungling the fragile postwar peace and losing out to weaker, duskier, but more justified nations.[15]

Quoc loved this story, for obvious reasons. He wrote in his lead that whites are usually paid to "bash in the faces of the blacks." But the Carpentier-Siki match offered a reversal: "For once, a black has been paid to do the same thing to a white." He then makes an offhand remark that tells us a great deal about his commitments during those final months of his stay in Paris: "Being an opponent of all acts of violence, we [sic] disapprove of either procedure."

So Quoc was a self-proclaimed proponent of nonviolent direct action. He goes on after this declaration to note that Siki is a Frenchman but never recognized as such because of his color and his African place of birth. Quoc notes, in one brief sentence without helpful context, that the Siki story has followed on yet another illustration of French misdeeds abroad, which comes from "Maran's ironical pen." Here he refers obliquely to the popular African novel Hemingway also admired and reviewed positively for its surprising black authorship and anti-colonial message. Quoc suggests that both the novel and "Siki's gloves" have upset the assumptions of the "political sphere." He suggests that from "a colonial viewpoint, a Carpentier-Siki match is worth more" to him and his allies "than one hundred gubernatorial speeches to prove to our subjects and protégés that we want to apply to the letter the principle of equality between races." Finally, he takes a moment to renew his personal feud: "Isn't that so, M. Sarraut?"

Quoc concludes his story with the moral that a black athlete can never be forgiven in France for defeating a white one. Even if the athletes do not feel this way, the "chauvinism of others"—presumably white French citizens—makes this so. Then Quoc concludes with a series of images that hint at the worldview he and Hemingway were coming to share that year. British promoters were considering a fight in England involving Siki, but a ban on such fights was expected. Why? Because the British government could then "digest neither Kemal [Atatürk]'s croissant nor Gandhi's chocolate." Quoc ends his essay by asking, "Understand?" Perhaps we don't. He hints, apparently, that Kemal was feeding the French an indigestible deal for national independence in Turkey, and that Gandhi was doing the same to the British in India. A Siki bout in England might provide another unwelcome parable about the unexpected strength of colonials of color. From his writing desk in Paris, Quoc saw this as a hopeful sign for the Battling Sikis of his world.

After the Siki fight, Hemingway left for Anatolia, where he witnessed the refugee crisis that would first become the source of his best news stories of the decade and then of his best prose poems—including the one that caused his father to wish him dead. Quoc, who could not secure a passport from officials determined to keep him in immediate view, was forced to monitor these events from Paris. In "The Workers' Movement in Turkey," Quoc drops his sarcasm. He merely points out, as Hemingway had, that the Treaty of Sevres was unworkable and that Turks under Kemal were rising up in indignation. On the other hand, he is more direct about predicting an outcome. He believes he sees the signs of a coming class war. French capitalists are "penetrating peacefully into the Land of the Crescent." But workers in Constantinople have been organizing by the tens of thousands and Quoc is encouraged, as we will learn in the next chapter.

The stories Hemingway banged out on his Corona portable in 1922 expressed his sympathy for the refugees in Thrace and disgust for Russian and French *realpolitik* at the year's peace conferences. Quoc's stories that year show a similar spirit, that recognizably modern blending of disgust and hope. Yet Quoc's inner rage, which was becoming more obvious, set him apart, as did his dadaist rhetoric. In one particularly surreal essay of early 1923, "Menagerie," Quoc opens with the sarcastic "We have racked our little yellow brains in vain, yet we cannot succeed in discovering the reason which led the men and women of France to found the remarkable institution called the Society for Prevention of Cruelty to Animals."[16] In an effort to explain this odd failure of "yellow brains" to understand the existence of the French SPCA, Quoc launches into an extended metaphor in which the nations of the Paris Peace Conference are identified as animals: the English "Bulldog," French "Tiger," and "Muscovite Bear." These beasts had "come to tear away the entire structure of the Peace Conference." Quoc then describes "colonial beasts"—sparrows, parrots, watchdogs, and other metaphorical animals suffering at the hands of the French. He neglects to assign these animals a national identity. Quoc grows more vehement and less coherent as he goes. In the middle of one sentence he inserts a table listing the alleged payments made by each of fifteen French colonies for the peace conference. The costs add up to millions. He closes the essay by referring to Paris's great story of the day, a Doctor Voronoff who had been transplanting tissue from monkey testicles into the gonads of rich elderly men who hoped to be "rejuvenated." Quoc thinks the French SPCA might at least attend to such matters and put a stop to the suffering of these monkeys. But they will not. The rich must play their narcissist games unimpeded, he implies. It is a truly bizarre essay, but it arose from understandable feelings. It is a measure of Quoc's growing frustration in 1922 that for his byline he sometimes used the pseudonym Nguyen Ai Phap, or Nguyen Who Hates the French.

# 13

## SWITZERLAND AND PEACE IN OUR TIME

### QUOC AND HEMINGWAY IN

### LATE 1922 AND EARLY 1923

Oddly enough, in 1922 and 1923 both Quoc and Hemingway demonstrated that Switzerland had a magnetic pull on them. This was far from a coincidental matter of taste, a shared love of alpine country. Both men had come to regard the most famously neutral nation during the Great War as proof that national nonviolence was not only possible but rational. The prosperous country also seemed to be getting the postwar years right. Switzerland addressed two crucial public needs with a national health care system and provision of social security insurance; they allowed unions to negotiate workers' wages and working conditions; Swiss women had the vote; and the Swiss people controlled their own governmental fate with a parliament voted in by proportional balloting. Hemingway, if not Quoc, appreciated that the Swiss drank beer and wine copiously. Indeed, Hemingway seems to have viewed postwar Switzerland as a kind of playground for peaceable political anarchists like himself, a realm where personal liberty was guaranteed and meaningful work possible—and where one could go ahead and despise the profiteer. The skiing town of Chamby, with its community of traditionalist mountaineers, was one of his favorite places in the world. Meanwhile, Quoc—according to the minuscule scholarship we have available on him for any moment in his Paris residency—viewed the country as the birthplace of Lenin's Bolshevik revolution and an incubator of propitious class conflict. Most meaningfully, both saw Switzerland as an example of the international world's hope.

≡ ≡ ≡

Switzerland was, we recall, the Hemingways' very first side-trip destination from their first new home in Paris. Ernest and Hadley had made the small error, they discovered, of arriving in Paris in the dreary, muddy wintertime. On January 9, 1922, they had just moved into the apartment at 74 rue du Cardinal Lemoine, placing Hadley's inherited silver safely in its drawer, to her relief, when they sublet their apartment and headed to Switzerland the very next day for a few weeks of what they called "the winter sport." The Hemingways thought they might prefer the mountain sun and the deep, white snowfall in Chamby, a resort town near Montreux. They did enjoy the crisp, dry mountain weather, staying in Switzerland for a few weeks and then returning to Paris in late winter, eager to meet Pound and Stein finally, and then to see the city's boulevards in their April glory.

In November and December of 1922 Hemingway returned to Switzerland, not only to Chamby this time but also to Lausanne for the peace conference. As he monitored the creation of a treaty the Turks would honor, unlike the short-lived Treaty of Sevres, Hemingway was able to get away from crowded, official Lausanne for only a brief break at their now-favorite Chamby hostel, just a short climb above Montreux. Chamby had come to feel like a second home, a retreat from life's complications and draining tasks.

The only thing most Hemingway fans know about this Lausanne/Chamby trip is the story of the stolen manuscripts, which is the crisis of *A Moveable Feast*. Ernest and Hadley's letters tell an even more interesting story. In late November of 1922, exhausted by the Lausanne Conference, Hemingway wrote to Hadley in Paris, encouraging her to join him in their beloved Chamby to relieve his loneliness. Addressing Hadley as "Poor dear little Wicky Poo" and calling himself a "little wax puppy," two of the baby-talk nicknames he and Hadley used for each other, he pressed hard for this reunion even though Hadley had written him to say how ill she was with a cold. He frankly admitted to her that he wanted to arrange a meeting during the most favorable time in her monthly cycle for sex, "the most comfortable and jolly time for mums," as he put it in his letter.[1] Though she still felt ill, Hadley agreed to meet, and as she packed for Switzerland she planned a surprise for her husband. She knew that Ernest's new reporter friend and fellow boxing fan Lincoln Steffens, who was also covering the Lausanne Conference, was an important media figure. If she brought all of Ernest's extant writings to Lausanne, Ernest could ask Steffens to read and comment on his work, and hopefully even recommend the best stories to editors he knew.

Famously, of course, Hadley left her train compartment to walk the Gare de Lyon station platform in search of a bottle of water for the long ride to Switzerland, unwisely leaving a valise containing the manuscripts in the train compartment, and they were stolen while she was gone.[2] She was frantic, but the train left the station as scheduled, and there was nothing she could do. When she arrived in Switzerland, ashen, and told her young husband of her terrible bad luck, he was shocked and dismayed. He remembers the tale in *A Moveable Feast*: "It was true all right [that Hadley had lost both the original manuscripts and carbon copies] and I remember what I did in the night after I let myself into the flat and found it was true." He does not tell us the unspeakable things he did that night. Some biographers believe that Hadley's mistake doomed her marriage to Hemingway, though evidence of his resentment is scant and speculative. The Hemingways remained close. And there is this: Once Hemingway returned to Paris, he considered advertising a reward of only 150 francs (about $10) for return of the manuscripts. And he apparently offered no reward of any kind, as no advertisement has ever been found in Paris papers of the day.[3] Hemingway must not have found the loss too terribly tragic or defeating, but remembering the event in that way made for a great tale as he wrote his personal myth in later life. Indeed, just as Quoc had, Hemingway took the theft of his literary efforts in stride and, also like Quoc, took the opportunity to dedicate himself fully to a new writing style.

Yet there are much more important things to learn from the Lausanne trip. That is the moment, as we have seen, when Hemingway began to write news stories about neutrality, peace, diplomacy, and the conditions that lead to war, including class conflict and colonialism—ideas that would stay with him all life long as core political commitments. And it is where, under the spell of Swiss ways, he began to fashion an idea of working men and women at fundamental, secured peace.

Switzerland had been an island of peace in wartime Europe. Swiss leaders had zealously guarded the country's neutrality, its armed forces fluctuating from two hundred thousand men to just over twelve thousand, depending on borderland threats, which were rare even during the war. None of Switzerland's men in arms died in battle during the war, even though the easternmost trenches ended at the Swiss border. A few artillery shells did fall on Swiss ground, and tensions over these provocations could have drawn Switzerland into the Great War. The diverse Swiss population included both German speakers, who were often sympathetic to the Central Powers, and French and Italian speakers, who were often sympathetic to the Allies. But there was no Swiss overreaction, little ethnic polarization, and thus no bloodbath in Switzerland.

Indeed, Switzerland used its neutrality to perform some important humanitarian work. During the war, the Swiss Red Cross—the Swiss had founded the organization in the first place—tracked and fed thousands of prisoners of war on both sides of the conflict, and they handled mail between these prisoners and their families. The Swiss government suggested to both the Allies and the Central Powers that wounded soldiers unlikely ever to return to fighting should be repatriated through Switzerland. As a result, 8,700 German soldiers and 2,300 French soldiers made it safely home in this way. Swiss officials had to be creative about maintaining their neutrality. They rationed food so the Allies could be assured that the foodstuffs they exported to Switzerland would be just enough for Swiss consumption, never enough for an excess to be sold on to Central Powers nations—for if such an act of provocation had occurred, it might have caused the Allies to declare war on Switzerland. As a wartime officer in the European Red Cross, Hemingway was well acquainted with this heartening story.

Hemingway favored countries that had maintained wartime neutrality. It is no coincidence that in the summer of 1923 the Hemingways at first planned to visit Norway for its "wild country, pine forests and great trout streams," but then chose Spain instead.[4] Presumably Spain was preferable to Norway because it offered similar trout streams, mountains, and wild country, but also bullfights and a more direct train line from Paris. There was another reason: Hemingway ranked both Norway and Spain as among the neutral, peaceable nations during the Great War.[5]

As we have seen, Hemingway's 1929 novel, *A Farewell to Arms*, actually turns on the contrast between a deadly wartime Italy and sensibly peaceful Switzerland. Frederic Henry and Catherine Barkley, he a lieutenant in charge of an ambulance unit and she a volunteer nursing assistant in Milan, fall in love while Frederic recuperates from wounds under Catherine's care. Late in the novel the two face a deadly choice that the war had produced: Frederic, who barely escapes execution during his army's retreat from superior Austrian forces, may carry out his duties with an Italian army whose ineptitude and disorganization are likely to get him killed, or he can face a court martial and possible execution for desertion if he tries to flee those duties. In addition to these problems, Frederic is in love and cannot bear to be without his girl. So, fresh out of good options, he and Catherine row across Lake Como on a stormy night, evading Italian border patrols, to reach welcoming, tranquil Switzerland.

Unfortunately for them, Frederic and Catherine learn that their actions have deadly consequences in Switzerland just as they had in Italy, as Catherine and an unplanned baby die from complications during childbirth. Though rarely discussed, these complications during Catherine's labor include unprescribed, reckless use of anesthetic gas on Frederic's and her part. I read this as Hemingway's hint that his characters' entire Swiss life has been a kind of anesthetic or drug state, a delusional retreat from reality. So there is, for Hemingway, no peaceable land where people escape death for long, nor the existential consequences of their choices, nor the welcome and unwelcome duties that come with having a nation to love.

Still, Switzerland was a land where young men died mainly as a result of their own decisions rather than the decisions of calloused, privileged generals and government ministers—those Hemingway really seems to have hated. He loved Switzerland, for this reason and others. In January of 1922 he wrote giddy letters about Chamby/Les Avants to his family and Michigan summer friends, such as Kate Smith, the friend and probable lake-area lover whose invitation for Hadley to visit Chicago allowed Ernest and Hadley to meet. Switzerland emerges in these letters as a kind of paradise, an anodyne to modern sicknesses. "Paris got sort of damp," he writes to his mother, father, and siblings, "so we came down here in the Alps to get rid of our colds and get healthy." He describes bobsledding, and the "black forests of Pine trees," and the big mountain that loomed over their pension. "Snow is forty inches deep but you are never cold. Wear only sweaters and the air is bracing." He notes to his teetotaling family that he and Hadley "drink lots of milk all the time and both Hash [Hadley] and I are getting into splendid shape." To Smith he describes the same bobsledding, forests, and neighboring mountain and then brags, "We live in a chalet run by an english [sic] speaking Swiss named Gangwisch and have breakfast in bed and two enormous meals besides, Mrs. is a high grade cook and we rate meals like roast beef, creamed cauliflower, fried potatoes, soup before and blueberries and whipped cream after for two seeds [dollars] a day." Hemingway loves the fiscal situation, but international peace is never far from his thoughts. In the same letter to his friend Katy he parodies American jingoism in the popular wartime song "Columbia, Gem of the Ocean": "[Switzerland] isn nawthing [sic] to make a man cry the army and navy forever three cheers for the red white and blue!"

Hemingway then encourages her to read his *Toronto Star* articles about Switzerland—a good idea, for when we take his advice ourselves, we find a startling contrast to these giddy letters. The articles offer the same descriptions of the beautiful country and affordable fun, but there is hostility too, as Hemingway pictures Switzerland as a country invaded by wartime profiteers and an effete aristocracy. He seems deeply offended that the peaceful land, so recently committed to the work of compassion, a country that had moved wounded men of both warring sides from trench to home, would now serve the privileged ruling class that launched and benefited from a trumped-up war. In his early travel essays about his three weeks in Chamby in January 1922, Hemingway begins to show the awareness of the ills of colonialism that his *Toronto Star* stories show more definitely later that year.

In "The Hotels of Switzerland," published in the *Star* on March 4, 1922, Hemingway describes Les Avants as steep country above Montreux, dotted with "large brown hotels built on the cuckoo clock style." He combines elegant descriptions of mountains "as wild as the Canadian Rockies" with sophomoric remarks about the Swiss architectural style, which he compares with the "iron-dog-on-the-front-lawn" period of Canadian architecture." But Hemingway's tone grows harsher as he begins to describe the patrons in these hotels, mostly "utterly charming young men, with rolling white sweaters and smoothly brushed hair" who play bridge with old women for easy cash.

Hemingway's complaint is partly about class differences, a subject that often caused him to take his gloves off. "The French aristocracy that comes to Switzerland," he writes of the upper-class travelers who frequent the Les Avants hotels, "consists of very young men who wear very old names and very tight in the knees riding breeches with equal grace." Throughout his life, and especially during the bohemian Paris years, Hemingway was extremely hostile toward people who lived by graft rather than honest labor, who did not produce meaningful works, and who created an empty style rather than worthy art or argument. That same month (on March 5, 1922), he wrote his infamous article, "American Bohemians in Paris," which begins with the line "The scum of Greenwich Village, New York, has been skimmed off and deposited in large ladlesful on that section of Paris adjacent to the Café Rotonde." He describes the eccentric dress of this scum, and corrects his readers' suspicions that these are genuine artists. "They are nearly all loafers," he writes. So it is with the French aristocracy in Switzerland—and yet they are not the worst Europeans to visit the Swiss resorts. There are also the war profiteers "who, through some holdings or other in iron or coal, were enriched by the war." Hemingway insists that we notice the iniquitous exploiters who wanted war: "When the young men with the old names come into a room full of profiteers, sitting with their pre-money wives and post-money daughters, it is like seeing a slim wolf walk into a pen of fat sheep."[6]

"Fishing on the Rhone Canal," published as a news-and-travel story in the *Toronto Star* on June 10, 1922, makes a similar topical move from peaceful Swiss leisure to war-making. At first Hemingway seems to describe a day when he caught trout in the Rhone Canal, a yard-wide stream that empties into Lake Geneva just below Chamby. At one point in the story he stops fishing and lazily ponders the area scenery, wondering who lives in "four grey houses" and worships in "three grey churches" nearby. He tells us that when the sun goes down and moun-tain shadows cross the canal, the flies come out, the trout feed, and a fisherman can make wonderful catches—if crowds don't come and ruin his solitude. He decides to walk to the town of Aigle, which he has not visited before, and suddenly he thinks about others who made the same walk down this "white and dusty" road. They were warriors. "I thought of Napoleon's grand army," he writes, "marching along it through the white dust on the way to the St. Bernard Pass and Italy." He imagines Napoleon's "batman" (English military slang for personal aide) fishing for the emperor's breakfast in the canal he has just fished. Then the Romans and the Huns come to mind, an interesting thought because the wartime American epithet for the evil Germans was "the Huns." In a few concluding lines Hemingway promotes the peaceful, unspoiled, untrafficked current character of Switzerland, the "beer foaming out in great glass mugs," and the barmaid who "asks about your luck." But he can't help thinking that the trains that come into Aigle every two hours are bound to bring more assaults of the historical kind he has just imagined, or how those currently enjoying Switzerland's peace "wish they would never come." His sentence implies his firm knowledge that a new generation of warriors will come to ruin the nation's calm.

The "Rhone Canal" article reads like a very fine short story, moving as it does through concrete immediate experiences to historical reveries that raise existential issues of life and death, war and peace. What is striking about Hemingway's young mind is its precocious ability to connect, to rise above his own complaints about a war that nearly killed him to sympathize with local working people who also need and desire peace.

The most intriguing of the early travel-and-existence news stories Hemingway wrote from Switzerland, interesting because it cleverly evokes both colonialism and class conflict, is titled "The Swiss Luge." It was published in the *Star* on March 18, 1922. As Hemingway tells us, he and Hadley and their friends certainly enjoyed learning to ride the luge. For his Canadian readers he describes the luge as "a short, stout sled of hickory built on the pattern of little girls' sleds in Canada." The sledding in Switzerland is hardly childish, however. On Sundays, twelve funicular trains a day, packed with Swiss families, lift people out of the Lake Geneva valley to the alpine heights. There, lugers set out on a thrilling ride. "You go down a long, steep stretch of road flanked by a six hundred foot drop-off on the left and bordered by a line of trees on the right. The sled goes fast from the start and soon it is rushing faster than anything you have ever felt." Lugers must navigate icy turns and the too-common prospect of meeting hay sleds with huge "curved-up runners" carrying loads of hay "cut and cured in the summer" or "firewood and faggots cut in the forests." This portrait of Swiss luging suddenly becomes a parable about class conflict, as the lugers of the leisure class shout for the right of way to "the men with the hay and wood sleds [who are] tired of pulling their loads to one side."[7] Switzerland may have avoided fighting in the Great War, Hemingway hints, but he cleverly suggests that the Swiss will not avoid the coming collisions between capital and labor, the leisure class and the working class. Just as Quoc warned his readers in his *L'Humanité* articles, Hemingway warns his readers, albeit more subtly, that class conflict is all around us, especially when the elite express their privilege stubbornly and relentlessly.

Remarkably, Hemingway brings colonialism into this parable of class conflict. He does so by shifting his attention to a particular group of lugers, the "British colony," as he meaningfully calls them, who lived in chic apartments in Bellaria, along the shores of Lake Geneva. Particularly avid lugers, these Brits use the busy road from Chamby to Montreux because that run, when concluded, deposits them at their "comfortable apartment buildings just above the lake." This seems an innocuous remark until Hemingway describes a particular British luger:

> One wonderful sight is to see the ex-military governor of Khartoum seated on a sled that looks about the size of a postage stamp, his feet stuck straight out at the sides, his hands in back of him, charging a smother of ice dust down the steep, high-walled road with his muffler straight out behind him in the wind and a cherubic smile on his face while all the street urchins of Montreux spread against the walls and cheer him wildly as he passes.

The name of this particular ex-military governor is difficult to track down, and does not in fact matter. What does matter is the irony Hemingway sees, that it is not the children of laborers who get to have fun sledding, to feel the rush of freedom while at play. The ones who enjoyed the thrills are the privileged grown-ups who exploit and limit the freedom of colonized others in distant lands. (Imagine the play of the skinny, ill-clad, impoverished children of Khartoum on their dusty land.) Here, in a land known for never holding colonies and never fighting in modern wars, we find English colonialists enjoying a Swiss peace they did not work for, a peace that is in fact threatened by their participation in the economics of colonialism that took their nation, Great Britain, to war.

Switzerland is Hemingway's land of peace, but in his *Star* articles the nation's pacific social order is threatened by iniquitous invaders. A collision looms between privilege and want, capital and labor, the ex-military governors of colonies and the street urchins of Swiss cities—who will one day drive the hay sleds on Swiss roads as they labor each day and will, no doubt, stop cheering and enjoying the sight of colonial governors and other members of the leisure class flying by in their selfish obliviousness.

≡ ≡ ≡

Quoc was fascinated with Switzerland too—though as usual, we know far less about his particular adventures there. As part of his self-taught general education program in Paris, he traveled to Switzerland on a group tour sometime early in his stay in the city, perhaps 1920 or 1921. And then in the summer of 1923 he used another group tour headed to the Alps, a fictional one this time, as his cover story for his escape from Paris, a tale that enters this account soon enough. It is not difficult to imagine why Quoc loved Switzerland. He probably knew about the social welfare programs being tested there, but another moment in revolutionary history interested him more. As he and Hemingway very well knew, the Russian Revolution had received essential assistance from Switzerland. It was the land that provided Lenin with a haven he needed while he planned to get back to Russia—as secretly as Quoc was about to leave Paris—to spark the Bolshevik revolution.

For Quoc especially, then, Switzerland had special meaning as a peaceable land, more peaceable than Lenin's Russia and yet pivotal in supplying the world with a revolutionary philosophy and a method that Quoc had embraced at Tours when he voted into existence the French Communist Party. He connected the alpine nation with the origins of successful working-class revolution and personal liberty (at that time, before Stalin or the confirmed revelations of Lenin's murderous abuses). So it is more than coincidental that Quoc and Hemingway both found themselves fascinated by Switzerland. All around the world, people saw the country as deeply reasonable and invested in compassion and creative political-social change. For many, especially progressives in Paris, whether utopian or realistic, Switzerland was what modernity was about.

Both avid readers of newspapers, Hemingway and Quoc knew the story of Lenin in Switzerland, even though it was just coming out in 1922 and 1923. As we know, they also each worked in a community of experienced international journalists covering peace conferences and ongoing revolutions. So Hemingway must have known, and Quoc surely did, that in February of 1922 a correspondent for the *New York Times* named Karl Radek had scooped the story of Vladimir Lenin's secret journey from Switzerland, where he had lived in exile since the Great War began, to Petrograd, Russia, in 1917.[8] There he began to participate in and to direct the Russian Revolution. Radek's article gave the world the phrase "sealed train"—the tantalizing image of a train completely locked down so that no one could leave it or interact with people alongside the tracks during its course across Germany. This was a key German condition of the trip toward the Baltic seacoast: German officials were content to allow Lenin to destabilize the Russian empire, but not the German one. In return for helping Lenin travel through Germany to get back to Russia, German officials wanted Lenin—once he won his revolution—to return German prisoners of war held in Russia and to promise to work for a lasting peace between the two nations. During the war, but not after it, Germany stood to gain a lot from the czar's ouster.

In 1922, then, Switzerland was famous, or infamous, as a haven for revolutionists, which is part and parcel of Hemingway's and Quoc's attraction to the country. Anyone reading newspapers in Europe that year knew very well that it was in Switzerland that Lenin and Trotsky had planned the Russian coup d'état, and that their arrival from Zurich at Petrograd's Finland Station meant a new, more organized and purposeful phase of the revolution. (Lenin at the Finland Station quickly became an entire genre of Soviet painting.) This happy association between Switzerland and revolution—happy for Hemingway and Quoc in that day, at least—was about to become more complicated as they both witnessed the proceedings of the Lausanne Conference. Hemingway and Quoc saw that Switzerland, more than other wartime neutrals, such as Norway, the Netherlands, or Spain, had become the site for negotiations and accords nominally pursuing peace. Disappointingly, however, Lausanne in 1922 was like Paris in 1919 in actually inventing and establishing causes for further conflicts. Both Quoc and Hemingway paid very close attention to the Conference of Lausanne in 1922, and both were educated and disillusioned by its outcome.

As we have seen, Hemingway attended the Lausanne Conference as a reporter from November 1922 to January 1923, while Quoc, confined to France because he had no passport, monitored the conference from Paris. (He probably received intelligence from his boss and editor at *L'Humanité*, Marcel Cachin, who attended the conference and drew Hemingway's notice.) Both were intrigued to see how the great powers of Britain, France, and Italy would confront the outbreak of war between Greece and the Turkish rebels, an open conflict that had been caused by the postwar Treaty of Sevres.

Quoc also knew the lesson that Hemingway learned in Lausanne— that empires inevitably make wars. He watched the Lausanne Conference closely because he hoped in 1922 that a genuine proletariat would arise from among the Turkish workers who would be affected by the conference's treaty, that they would make revolution, that the revolution would lead to wider justice, and that justice would prevail and lead to peace. He knew that the Turks were a peasant population that, like his people in Vietnam, had no urban, industrial heritage and thus no trade unions or other early-stage Marxist sources of solidarity. He knew that Marx's theories depended upon industrial workers across Europe rising up to make revolution. It was Lenin's revision of Marx that suggested, to Quoc's joy, that peasant people, including colonial peasants, could take a role in this revolutionary process. Lenin made this argument in part because his own Russian people were rural peasants. He theorized that they could initiate a revolution in Russia's European west, but he also feared that if that revolution did not spread to Germany, France, and Britain through those nations' unions and socialist cells, as Marx predicted, then the Soviet Union would be a communist island in a hostile capitalist sea. So it turned out to be, for eighty-some years. Quoc knew these doctrines and believed in them, so he wrote about Lausanne not as a treaty conference—which he derisively refers to as "the Lausanne event," the word "event" implying that nothing official or decisive happened there—but as a momentary victory for reactionary capitalism.

Quoc rivaled Hemingway in his ability to explain such processes to ordinary readers, even if he lacked Hemingway's clever and allusive style. In "The Workers' Movement in Turkey," published in *L'Humanité* on the first day of 1924, Quoc explains to French communist readers that the recent Greco-Turkish War was really a bourgeois revolution of national independence. It is laudable, he suggests, that Turkish laborers have "torn up the odious Sevres Treaty," which had parceled out Anatolia and Palestine to victorious Allied nations. But now, Quoc argues, the Turkish proletariat has to push the process further, to "embark on another struggle: the class struggle."

Quoc describes the workers' situation in Turkey. They suffer the lack of unions. There are only corporations or "friendly societies," which raise awareness locally but do not interact from community to community. This means there is no common message circulating around Turkey, just local learning and planning. But there is hope. Recent strikes in Constantinople involved ten thousand workers, and these people came to realize that "organization and discipline are necessary in order to triumph."

Ominously, the Turkish government had recently shown signs of capitalist treachery. Two hundred and fifty delegates representing some forty-four thousand urban laborers and miners had recently voted to create a great federation out of local workers' societies. A frightened government refused to recognize the new federation. It was becoming clear that Turkish leaders valued working men as soldiers who could drive foreigners out of the country, as they had recently driven out Greek forces. But, unsurprisingly, Turkish capitalists did not want to see these same men organizing and bettering their economic situation in civilian life. These capitalists, Quoc warned, were "flirting with foreign capital," specifically with the large investments French bankers and businessmen were making in the country. Though the European empires had never succeeded in colonizing Turkey in the standard way, through occupation and economic and religious domination, they were about to make the same attempt through investment banking.

It was the Turkish workers' task to put a stop to these exploitative processes. These men and women, Quoc writes, have made the necessary first step in establishing a Turkish republic. But now they need to engage in the class struggle. "It will go on," he predicts.[9]

As we will see, it is a lovely irony that when Quoc eventually leaves Paris, he devises a Swiss cover story to get Sarraut's agents off his scent. Quoc had no practical reason to choose Switzerland, so his calculation was probably this: if Russia meant Lenin as ruthless revolutionary and political assassin, Switzerland meant Lenin as hopeful planner, working to create a just and peaceful country dedicated to material security for the awakened worker.

Like Hemingway, in other words, Switzerland had an almost mythical importance in Quoc's mind. Peace prevailed in Switzerland, in their time.

# 14

## ESCAPE FROM PARIS

### QUOC IN 1923

Coincidentally, Hemingway and Quoc each spent only about half of the year 1923 residing in Paris. For both, the year involved a few months of intense involvement in modernist arts and politics in the City of Light, and then a break from that work to honor other priorities. After a promising burst of writing during spring and summer, Hemingway moved reluctantly to Toronto in the early autumn for the birth of his and Hadley's first child, a move he had to make because she insisted that the birth occur in a North American hospital whose medical staff gave her confidence. Quoc's move was more permanent. He left town that summer to adopt as his academy an actual university in Moscow rather than his quasi-university of Paris. He would remain a thorn in the side of France's Ministry of Colonies during the 1920s and then again during peace negotiations on behalf of an incipient Vietnam in the 1940s and the republic Americans called North Vietnam during the 1950s and 1960s. But his presence in Paris from 1923 onward would be intermittent, and his voice would be heard mainly in some important new writings that appeared first in the City of Light. He would be present in Paris mainly as a voice in certain publications.

Yet it seems that in an important way, Paris traveled with both young men during their time away from its boulevards that year, prompting them to continue working on their own peaceable, provocative ways of resisting the values of empire and oligarchy. Indeed, Quoc was to learn before Hemingway did that Paris was "a moveable feast." He was the one who carried the values of Paris with him into a land of alien values—specifically, Soviet Moscow and then revolutionary Canton, China—and sent back messages that gave evidence of his commitment to Paris's creative, audacious, psychologically sophisticated new visions for a more equitable world. That story would unfold during the coming four years, a time when Hemingway stayed in Paris to refine his writing and ignite his amazing career, while Quoc visited the city and published important work there during the same period. And then Hemingway, too, would leave Paris and send back messages about the crucial things he had learned there.

≡ ≡ ≡

Quoc, who had grown disillusioned with French government leaders' refusal to seriously consider legal reforms in Indochina, or even to honor their own stated goals in the colonies, also grew more and more convinced during 1922 and early 1923 that Lenin and the Russian Bolsheviks had what he needed to liberate the colonies—not Marxist ideology but state power in service of anti-colonialism. Given the intransigence of French government officials whenever they met with the Annamite Patriots, Quoc realized that only a large, militarized nation-state like the Soviet Union could offer substantial and effective help to the Vietnamese in their campaign to accomplish that task. During the next two decades, he would look to both the Soviet Union and the United States for this powerful assistance. For now, Quoc continued to use the political little magazine Le Paria as a platform for his outrage, and he still believed that educating Vietnamese and French Parisians could lead to political solidarity and accompanying political pressure on France to liberate its colonies. But he could not quite believe in that happy outcome. And so for the time, he planned to train for a revolution in Vietnam, and he looked to Moscow for that training.

If Hemingway's 1922 was a time of accelerated learning, of accepting his role as student of Pound and Stein and certain experienced reporters working the year's peace conferences and the local wars they caused, then Quoc's 1922 was a period of mounting frustration with Paris's politics, which he found far too moderate—even the French Communist

Party. He also had to endure the hypocrisy of a nation that touted its Rights of Man yet treated him like a wayward boy.

Yet as angry and outcast as Quoc felt, his humanism never entirely evaporated, and in early 1923 he engaged in a civilizing mission of his own. Not only did he write and edit *Le Paria*, which is the act of an international Marxist revolutionary, but he formed a mutual aid society for the downtrodden Vietnamese workers still in Paris, which is an act of compassion and solidarity consistent with his Confucianism. The goal of this "Fraternal Association," scholar Sophie Quinn-Judge tells us, was "to unite the poorer Vietnamese manual workers in France," whom, she reports, one of Quoc's friends described as "badly paid, badly nourished, badly housed and sometimes scorned by their employers." Mutual aid societies were distinctly Vietnamese institutions. They offered a way for nearly powerless restaurant workers and domestic servants to provide emotional and material support to each other. These workers would meet in cafés on their few holidays and other days off (they worked six days a week and often moonlighted on Sundays for extra cash) to gamble, argue, talk politics, and give each other gifts and loans that would help them get by in their difficult lives in the city. Oftentimes these workers brought along their French girlfriends—who impressed the Vietnamese men if they had learned the techniques and etiquette of chopsticks and the rice bowl, the serving of others first, the distribution of the best morsels onto others' bowls of rice.[1] This is another important form of solidarity. Quoc taking a leading role in a mutual aid society of his own means that he sought not only to address the hearts and minds of Vietnamese workers in Paris, but also to feed their bodies.

Leading the Intercolonial Union was another layer of difficulty in Quoc's life in late 1922 and early 1923, but the work had its rewards. His material life improved when he moved in March of 1923 to his final Paris address at 3 rue des Marché des Patriarches, which became the official address of the Union and of *Le Paria*. (This move put him only a few hundred yards from the Hemingways again, who lived on the other end of the rue Mouffetard.) Quoc gained important experience in the next year and a half, working to keep national differences among the Union's Algerian, Indochinese, Caribbean, and leftist European factions from exploding into open conflict. Now Quoc was representing the world's colonials in general, not just the colonized Vietnamese, and the work was difficult. There were always tensions, followed by defections. Attendance at union meetings peaked at two hundred, but soon slipped to fifty or so at each gathering. In February of 1923 attendance bottomed out, with only twenty-seven members attending, including two women who were the French mistresses of colonial members.[2] It was not easy to lead such troubled and inconstant people.

≡ ≡ ≡

Throughout 1922 and early 1923, Quoc had been changing as a writer and provocateur. As his SPCA article illustrates, he was willing to explore new literary methods for satirizing the powers that be—for satirizing selfish wealth itself—and their dubious activities in Vietnam. He learned these methods from Paris's avant-garde writers, specifically from the surrealists, a group of politically serious Western communists who had broken off from Dada. No one in his immediate circle of Vietnamese comrades could teach these literary methods to Quoc or support him in his exploration of them, but discussions among the cultivated and arts-minded membership at the Club du Faubourg were teaching Quoc about the political possibilities for literature. Henri Barbusse was a member, and his anti-war novel, *Le Feu*, had raised public awareness of the near-mutiny in wartime trenches, of a continued revolutionary community in Paris, and of the war's brutality and futility. Quoc would continue to model some of his writing after Barbusse's, documenting conditions with outraged objectivity. But he also now employed the antic, sarcastic, absurdist rhetoric of the surrealists.

Quoc must have decided that his own rhetorical skill in French did not lend itself to the writing of novels, but he did evidently see possibilities in drama. When the puppet emperor of Annam, Khai Dinh, announced a planned visit to France in 1922, Quoc seized the opportunity for a specifically literary provocation designed to gain some press attention. He attacked the emperor in the pages of his magazine in August of 1922, calling him an ignoramus. Then he decided to write his first work of nonfiction, a play titled *The Bamboo Dragon*. We know almost nothing about the action of the play, except that it was a satire on the powerless puppet emperor. *The Bamboo Dragon* premiered at a festival sponsored by *L'Humanité* and the Club du Faubourg later that year. "Hardly Molière, *n'est-ce pas*," wrote Leo Poldes after he had seen the play's premiere, "yet carefully crafted, animated by a certain Aristophanic verve, and not lacking in scenic qualities." Because Aristophanes is known for comedies that engaged in bitter ridicule—even slander, according to Plato—*The Bamboo Dragon* seems to have had some Dada-esque qualities. Knowing what we do about Quoc, there was principled disrespect, resistance to the idea of "normal," sarcasm, earthy humor, probably even exposure of insanity and absurdity in official conduct. (The title itself is sarcastic, implying that France's favored Annamite king is a false dragon constructed of a common jungle weed.) Certainly there was Dada's implied passion for a very different world. Given the raw emotion and unflinching goriness of Quoc's magazine pieces, the ridicule is unlikely to have been subtle or complex.

Quoc seemed suddenly willing to try all kinds of new ways to reach a broader audience. Not only did he attend meetings of socialist and communist organizers in late 1922 and early 1923, but he even joined the Masons, attending at least one meeting of the Masonic Lodge at 94 Avenue de Suffren, just off the Champ du Mars with its iconic tower. Around this time, he also asked the editors of two established Parisian magazines whether they would accept his articles. He was ready to try anything to reach a broader audience—even rubbing shoulders with the bourgeoisie. He began to assess his Indochinese audience more carefully too. In May, just a few weeks before leaving Paris for good, he sent out a subscription advertisement for a new *quoc ngu* bimonthly newspaper called *Viet Nam Hon* (*The Soul of Vietnam*). He promised future readers "Asia, Europe, India and America all summarized in one paper."

In an unfortunately condescending note, he added, "Women and children will be able to understand."[3] Quoc surely meant well with that acid remark. He indicates that all of his audience, including the least literate, will find his new magazine edifying and interesting. Indeed, he is using this ad to draw even more of these illiterate and semi-literate people into his world of ideas. Yet perhaps he also reveals a bit of his own personal contempt here for the mere peasants, who lack his education and experiences, who are not yet acquainted with the doctrines of revolution and resistance that had come to move him.

In any case, all of these efforts came to little. There seemed to be no significant resistance movement coalescing among Paris's visiting workers from the colonies. Finally, when Quoc found these and almost all other avenues for effective resistance in Paris blocked, and when he had to admit this failure to himself, he decided to escape to Moscow. He hoped a move to Soviet Russia would open up new learning opportunities for him, and new ways to pursue his goals. He did not necessarily want to become a Bolshevik dedicated to expanding Soviet-style society to the rest of the world. Indeed, he soon told friends that he had no interest in residing in Moscow and wanted to move on to Asia proper after only a few weeks in Russia. But he did realize that the Soviets had developed sophisticated means to propagate revolutions, particularly in countries where the people were poor—such as his Vietnam. He wanted to learn these methods. He also desperately hoped that he would meet his hero, Lenin.

Ironically, of course, all of this travel away from Paris was Parisian to the core. It was Paris's libraries that had given him a broad and scholarly acquaintance with colonial abuses; it was in Paris that he read Marx (reluctantly) and shouted with joy when he encountered Lenin's thesis on the importance of the colonies for world revolution; it was in Paris that his youthful love of French and American civil rights flowered into a more mature commitment to developing and expanding those rights rather than assuming their guiding centrality; it was in Paris that President Wilson's indifference and Minister Sarraut's recalcitrance taught him that he had to up his revolutionary game; it was Paris's avant-garde arts that taught him skills he could use in his lifelong propaganda efforts; it was in Paris that he became a writer—the fundamental skill he would use for the next decades, until war caused him to learn and employ other, more deadly skills as a guerilla leader and commander-in-chief.

It does seem odd that Quoc would leave the city just as he advertised a new journal to be published there, with its experiment in using *quoc ngu* to address Vietnamese readers. Maybe he was tempted away by a sudden opportunity. There is speculation that a Soviet talent scout named Dmitry Manuilsky, who attended FCP conferences, may have noticed Quoc's talents in writing, organizing, and teaching and seen reason to recruit him as an Indochinese asset for the Comintern. (As we will see, the Comintern eventually recruits Hemingway too, though as a spy rather than an organizer.) But scholars agree that it is just as likely that Quoc made his own decision to trade Paris for Moscow and further points east. First, he could study in the so-called Stalin School or Communist University of the Toilers of the East (KUTV), whose goals he likely learned at FCP meetings: improving industry in communist countries; improving agriculture, especially through more efficient irrigation; establishing cooperatives of toilers locally; and then establishing Soviets, or planning councils, on a national scale. These are all humanist and positive revolutionary goals rather than bloody or expansionist ones. Quoc may have been particularly attracted to a fifth and final stated task of the KUTV—building national culture through general education and vocational training.[4]

Quoc did in fact fall in love with his new university and its curriculum, which was more formal and seemingly more relevant than his self-sponsored learning in Paris had been. The book he was to publish in 1924—more on that to come—contains a passage that promotes the KUTV as a kind of ideal college, one that provided Quoc and other students with good health care, meals, opportunities to grow and harvest vegetables, fine exercise facilities, and opportunities for women as well as men. Most importantly, Toilers U provided training for revolutionary cadres, teacher-coaches who lived among agitators and troops, helping them to sustain morale, do their duty, and exercise correct revolutionary goals.

≡ ≡ ≡

With the goal of enrolling in this university, Quoc planned his escape from Paris carefully. First of all, he had to keep the police agents in his midst, devious young Indochinese men living in his very home, from gaining any idea of his plans. Indeed, the most satisfying part of Quoc's escape from Paris—and it was an escape, because French authorities monitored and detained him in Paris as a kind of political prisoner—is the way he fooled his nemesis, the nearest thing this book has to a villain, that snitch and manuscript thief and apparent leader among Quoc's harassing agents, Agent Désiré. It seems that he told only one or two colleagues about his planned flight to Moscow—only those he required to help him get his light luggage to the train station on the day of his departure. Sometime in late spring of 1923 he told all of his comrades, both the true ones and the spies, that he had signed on for an eight-day tour with friends from the Club du Faubourg. They would visit the

French Alps in the Savoie region. Quoc then created a realistic cover story: He would have enjoyed seeing Switzerland, he told his associates, but he did not want to request a passport from the French because their likely refusal would be humiliating to him. On this tour, he told his roommates, he would visit the French Alps only.

On the final day of his physical residency in Paris, Quoc took a bus to a suburban cinema. Exploiting the dark in the auditorium and its multiple exits, he slipped out a back door during the show. He paused to make certain no one followed him out. Then he made his way to the center of Paris and the Gare du Nord, where he met a friend who had brought his luggage. Ducking into a restroom, Quoc changed into a business suit so he could pose as a well-to-do Chinese merchant, complete with a cigar as an appropriate prop.[5] He made his way to his train. Quoc's passport—we do not know who forged it for him—identified him as a Chinese citizen named Chen Vang, who was ticketed to travel first-class to Berlin, as businessmen typically traveled.[6]

Quoc's train travel across France and into Germany was uneventful, which means his tormentors in Paris were thoroughly fooled by the escape plan and the clever acting of his true friends. Apparently, the agents watching the theater Quoc snuck out of were unfazed when he failed to appear on the street with the other patrons at the show's conclusion. Perhaps the agents thought he had simply gotten past them in the exiting crowd and then, instead of returning home for ordinary farewells or to retrieve his luggage for the package tour, had left town for his holiday. Désiré, for one, was totally fooled by Quoc's story of a French mountain vacation. On June 15 he reported that Nguyen Ai Quoc had left Paris on June 13, leaving without luggage and implying to friends that he would not be vacationing for long. But this is a strange story for the agents to have accepted. It would be a very brief holiday indeed if it required no luggage at all. And hadn't Quoc told his circle that his tour would last eight days? Sometimes it seems that Sarraut's agents and his assistants in the Ministry of Colonies were less than professionally adept.

In Berlin, Chen Vang secured a visa or safe-conduct pass to the Soviet Union and a ticket on the passenger ship *Karl Liebknecht*, which was soon to depart Hamburg. Still using this alias in case trains to Russia were secretly monitored, which they almost certainly were, Quoc made his way from Berlin to Hamburg, boarded his ship, and sailed peacefully to the new Soviet Union. His ship docked in Petrograd on June 30, and he began his struggle to be recognized as a proper visitor to the USSR. After some weeks spent trying to pass muster with Russian border officials, who had no idea who Chen Vang was—or Nguyen Ai Quoc, for that matter—and may well have thought they had apprehended a French spy, he finally made his way to Moscow. There, Quoc was surprised by a rather chilly welcome. French communist propaganda had painted the Soviet Union as a kind of paradise for the incipient revolutionary, so it may have come as a shock to discover that the USSR embraced his presence as little as Paris had. If the Russians had recruited Quoc, no one had told the low-level officials who first greeted him. Poor Quoc may even have missed Paris a bit.

Back in Paris, Quoc's smokescreen continued to be incredibly effective. For weeks, no one questioned his absence. One day, the group of people still publishing *Le Paria* held an editorial meeting and got all those present, including the government's informers, to agree to a delay in sending the paper to the printers. Agent Désiré reported to his superiors, "They decided to wait for the return of Nguyen Ai Quoc for that." Quoc's friends must have done some good acting in that meeting. Then everyone sat back to continue waiting for Quoc's return. They waited and waited. Perhaps they had become lax because they were all delighted to have some time off, a bit of relief from spying duties for some and from magazine publishing for others. More weeks passed, and then it began to dawn on the Annamites, friends and enemies alike, that something was amiss. Quoc had spent a very, very long time hiking in the French Alps. It is not clear whether anyone thought to check on other members of the Club du Faubourg to see if some had returned from the eight-day holiday, or whether a tour group of club members had ever gone to the Savoie at all. It does not seem so. By now, with Quoc safely in Moscow, the main reason for any deception must have been to keep agents from knowing who was in on the escape and who was not.

That fall, while Quoc's fate was still unknown, his elder, mentor, and roommate Phan Chu Trinh wrote to reveal to one of the police agents, Nguyen Van Ai or Agent Devillier, that he had known about the agents' spying for quite some time. Trinh appears, however, not to have known Quoc's cover story or his true plans, because in his note he accuses Ai of complicity in Quoc's disappearance: "Why did you betray him, with your cowardly and underhand methods? He trusted you like a brother. . . . Why did you try to make trouble for him? I ask you for the truth, where did you incite him to go?" Of course it is possible that Trinh wrote this note to thicken the smokescreen that concealed Quoc's escape. But one thing we can detect with some certainty: Trinh really did despise the informers who had troubled and tormented Quoc.

It was not until October that Sarraut and his agents discovered where Quoc had gone. On October 11, Sarraut wrote to the Governor-General in Hanoi warning him that in tracking Quoc, he must now direct his attention to Moscow rather than Paris. French intelligence had finally discovered that Quoc was in the USSR. And this discovery was not made through great spycraft: some biographers suggest that the Ministry of Colonies only discovered where Quoc was when agents read his byline on articles he published from Moscow. (Quoc no longer needed to conceal his location.) Fooling Désiré and the other police agents, Quoc also fooled Sarraut, whose secret and underhand intelligence-gathering must have earned him an unpleasant and shaming surprise when he lost track of Quoc. It must have been humiliating to learn that Quoc had so easily escaped his French controllers. Sarraut had to take responsibility for the failure. According to one biographer, "It was Albert Sarraut himself who signed the secret telegram sent on 11 October 1923 to the Governor-General in Hanoi, to inform him that Nguyen Ai Quoc's tracks had been picked up in Moscow."[7]

Well into December, friends and agents still believed that Quoc might return to Paris from Moscow. How, the agents must have wondered, could a man choose the privations of Bolshevik Moscow over the joys of freedom-loving Paris? But by the end of the year, all of Quoc's friends and enemies finally gave up on that idea, and consequently, they gave up on ever seeing Quoc again. Some of them never did, including his closest mentor-comrade at the avenue des Gobelins, Phan Chu Trinh, who died of cancer in Vietnam in 1926. Upwards of 140,000 people attended Trinh's funeral, and as part of their commemoration of his life and as an antidote to their grief, they protested colonial oppressions.[8] Thanks to Quoc and the Annamite Patriots, anti-colonial pressure was building in Vietnam.

Then, Quoc had a terrible shock. When he finally settled in Moscow in the deep winter of 1923–24, he found that Lenin had just died. He attended his hero's funeral in subzero temperatures, reportedly suffering such severe frostbite that his hands showed scars for many weeks afterward. He found Lenin's death emotionally painful too. Quoc was bitterly disappointed and saddened. He eulogized the great Bolshevik in a widely published essay, in which he wrote, "[Lenin] was our father, teacher, comrade and advisor. Nowadays, he is the bright star showing us the way to the socialist revolution."[9]

Quoc had no way of knowing then that the fate of Lenin's body—which was put on permanent display to support national goals—would be his own body's fate in another forty-five years. In spite of his late-life insistence that his remains be cremated and his funeral ceremonies kept humble, his North Vietnamese handlers had uses for him even after his death. By that time, a true party cadre named Le Duan and a deeply ideological Chinese-style Communist Party were in charge of North Vietnam, even of Ho Chi Minh's remains. After his 1969 death, they brought Soviet embalmers to Hanoi to learn the art of indefinite preservation and display of a corpse. They also sent Vietnamese embalmers to Moscow for additional instruction. With the help of Soviet mausoleum architects, Vietnamese architects studied monuments such as the Great Pyramids and the Lincoln Memorial, and then finally they settled on a design that looked a great deal like Lenin's mausoleum in Red Square. "The facing was of gray marble," writes Duiker, "much of it quarried at Marble Mountain, a limestone outcropping south of Da Nang, where Viet Cong troops housed in a cave inside the mountain could watch American GIs swimming at famous China Beach, one of the most popular resorts in the area." Today, a visit to Hanoi is not complete without a viewing of Ho Chi Minh's body, and nowhere else in Vietnam is it so clear that the guards and functionaries present represent a hard, controlling, and insistently reverent regime. Patriotic Vietnamese visitors and Western tourists alike move in the silent line of viewers around Ho's body, under the eyes of stern guards who appear to mean business. Everyone present is careful to make no outward display of anything that might be interpreted as disrespect.

This was to be the trajectory of Quoc's life, as he slowly became Ho Chi Minh and, as a result, lost control over his own life and his own chosen forms of resistance. He would spend the next few years after Paris developing contacts with Asian communists who joined him in wanting to erase colonialism from the planet. He took up his organizing and propaganda work in China and in colonial Hong Kong. Sometime around 1940 he took the name Ho Chi Minh, He Who Has Been Enlightened, and early in 1941 he finally saw Vietnam again. This happened during the Second World War when he accepted help from American Office of Strategic Services (later, the CIA) agents, who hoped to exploit his nationalist reputation and the fervor of his Vietnamese followers in a campaign to get the occupying Japanese out of Vietnam. With their assistance, he slipped across the Chinese border and eventually made his way to Hanoi. He had been away from his country for thirty years.

With what must have been a divided heart, he then watched to see whether Germany would defeat France in this second world war of his lifetime, a defeat that would have created an opportunity for Vietnam to free itself of French control once and for all. He knew that a German victory would create a brief power vacuum for his forces to exploit in Indochina. Yet it must have been dreadful for him to contemplate a France permanently controlled by Hitler and his fascists, even if Ho had to recognize that as the price to be paid for his people's freedom. After all, he was still the Francophile who had complained in Paris that "le knock-out" ought to be outlawed because it was no true French word. Ho must have hoped France would win the war but then find itself too exhausted to fight for its Indochinese colonies.

When that very situation occurred in 1945, he turned to the same strategies he had used during his Paris years. Declaring in his Parisian propaganda rhetoric that "the French imperialist wolf was finally devoured by the Japanese fascist hyena," he tried—again—to build an alliance with the United States based in constitutional principles and Enlightenment-era human rights.[10] When it was time for Ho to assume leadership of the new Vietnamese nation on September 2, 1945, a culmination he had only dreamt of in Boston, London, and Paris, he stood in Hanoi's huge Ba Dinh Square as it filled with tens of thousands of cheering Vietnamese supporters. He was flanked by OSS soldiers and agents, later to be among the first agents of the new CIA. He then offered President Harry S. Truman, even if only implicitly, the same deal he had offered France during the 1920s. If he and the American people would treat Ho and his people as though they believed their own ideals of liberty and equality, he would make them an ally. He would enter into trade with them and commit to spreading those ideals to other lands alongside the American people. His speech that day, which quoted from one of the United States' foundational documents, came from his heart:

> "All men are created equal. They are endowed by their creator with certain unalienable rights; among these are life, liberty, and the pursuit of happiness."
>
> This immortal statement appeared in the Declaration of Independence of the United States of America in 1776. In a broader sense, it means: All the peoples on the earth are equal from birth, all the people have a right to live and to be happy and free.
>
> The Declaration of the Rights of Man and of the Citizen, made at the time of the French Revolution, in 1791, also states: "All men are born free and with equal rights, and must always remain free and have equal rights."[11]

Around that same time he signed an "appeal to the people" that stated that the Vietnamese must rise up and seize this moment. "Many oppressed peoples the world over are vying with one another in the march to win back their independence," he wrote. "We cannot allow ourselves to lag behind." He signed the document with a name he invented for Paris and would never use again: Nguyen Ai Quoc.[12]

≡ ≡ ≡

Phan Chu Trinh, who once called Quoc a "fiery stallion" and himself a "tired horse," deserves the final word on Quoc's trials in Paris, where conditions were more clement than in Moscow, and where Vietnamese loyalists earned less obvious scars than those on his frostbitten hands. Writing angrily to that turncoat agent he suspected of being responsible for Quoc's disappearance, Trinh gave a frankly critical, but in the end loyal, assessment of Quoc:

> Even though Nguyen Ai Quoc is young and he doesn't act on mature reflection, this is not important because he really has the heart of a patriot. He left his family and travelled to Europe and America, working miserably to educate himself, without any help

from anyone. . . . If he makes mistakes or not, that is not the question, because all the Vietnamese respect his ardent heart. . . . Let those who want to follow him follow, and those who don't can leave him alone to get on with his work.[13]

Quoc's leaving Paris was a blow to his community of French communists. Ever since he had launched *Le Paria*, Quoc had been involved in an international *Union Intercoloniale* and had become its indispensable leader. He had spent a great deal of time and energy making this union truly international and intercolonial. It was a loss to the Parisian resistance scene that his successors retreated to a solely Vietnamese movement. Trinh saw it: they had lost what Quoc had to offer, which was a broader vision and an ardent heart.

For Quoc, the first few months of his stay in Moscow involved both study and teaching at the Communist University of the Toilers of the East. This may or may not have been the life he planned for. There is still evidence to come, evidence that appeared first in Paris, for Quoc's continued belief in a nonviolent revolution of minds and subsequent peaceable agitation, such as street demonstrations and general strikes and even constitutions ensuring essential human rights and freedoms. These, he believed, should lead to reforms among the empires, France especially.

And the coming few years—a time when Hemingway still lingered in Paris—would show that even though he lived in Moscow and then Canton, Quoc still retained the Parisian way. He still recognized that the oversimple history of class conflict that his Soviet (now Stalinist) professors taught did not explain every worthwhile idea. Quoc saw that Parisian historians were more complex and often more honest than their Soviet counterparts. He saw that Western liberties were powerful and beautiful, even if they were denied to his own people, so he continued to push for constitutionally guaranteed freedoms in the French and American style. His writings from his Paris days, including *Le Paria* stories declaring himself nonviolent, and diplomatic messages to French ministers pleading for peaceful remedies for the injustices of Vietnamese colonialism, show that he still believed in negotiated settlement, mutual benefit, and a rejection of war, unless it was absolutely necessary. He saw that free artistic expression in a society that tried to protect free speech was more profound and persuasive than the naïve propaganda and pedantic realism in fiction and art then required in the USSR—celebrations of farmer-peasants at work and mixing in cooperatives and the like. He clung to his belief in the general welfare of people, as his aid society work revealed, a belief that seemed to emerge from French and American civil liberties and from his continued belief in Confucianism and Eastern modes of cooperation generally. He was no single-minded Soviet cadre, even if producing such men and women was the goal of his new university.

Though he and Hemingway were no longer neighbors, Quoc's story and its relation to Paris had not concluded in June of 1923. Paris would hold both young men in its grip for at least another three years. Just as Hemingway began to publish books of his own stories in Paris late in 1923 and throughout 1924, Quoc, too, would publish an important modernist book in Paris. It was the study of French colonialism that he had begun writing in the city but had lost to the agent-thieves who tormented him, stealing the manuscript from his desk and impeding his work as an anti-colonial rebel. In this book and in other ways, he would demonstrate that the Communist University of the Toilers of the East had not deadened the special humanitarian, anarchic, artistic spirit that he had learned in Paris.

# 15

## THE AMERICAN DADAS

### HEMINGWAY IN 1923

H emingway's reporting was growing both exciting and profitable in 1923, just before he and Hadley made a planned, but reluctant, September sojourn to Canada for the birth of their child. His fiction was coming along too, though the possibility of profiting by it seemed distant. He was just beginning to develop a Cézanne-esque style all his own, marked with obvious artistry yet dignified and realistic too, rich with implied meanings even though the concrete descriptions seemed primary. Readers of the little magazines and avant-garde presses of Paris that year, including some readers in New York and Chicago, would soon begin to realize that Hemingway had not only a compellingly modern prose style, apparently shaped by Sherwood Anderson's, Gertrude Stein's, and Ezra Pound's mentoring and the examples their writing provided, but also a sophisticated international political subject and a profound sense of compassion for his struggling characters. Moreover, Hemingway seemed to have a mature and informed class consciousness not evident in the best and most popular literary fiction of the day, such as Anderson's and Sinclair Lewis's. Avant-garde publishers in Paris were thrilled to see his work developing in this way, and mainstream publishers in America were coming to see that the modernist focus on the international world might be compelling to paying readers.

These traits that Hemingway developed in 1923 would soon make him an attractive property in the mainstream publishing world and give him the literary career he desired. He knew, however, that he was not yet ready for the mainstream publishers. At this early stage in his career he needed to pursue more modest publishing opportunities in the avant-garde English-language community of Paris.

His networking with local publishers was paying off in early 1923, and would eventually lead to a series of slim, elegant chapbooks he could show off. Yet he struggled to produce the new writing he wanted them to publish. He was so desperate to see his name in print that he even tossed off free verse poems that year. Meanwhile, all he could write in his concentrated new prose style were the brief vignettes about battle and refugees, and even those were accumulating very slowly. Early that year, Hemingway wrote six of these vignettes and immediately found a publisher, placing them in *The Little Review* along with a free verse poem based on a peace conference titled "They All Made Peace—What Is Peace?" With lines such as "But / the Armenians. How about the Armenians? / Well the Armenians," it was not much of a poem, even if it addressed his favorite topic, the struggle to produce international peace.[1] Wisely, Hemingway worked harder on writing and promoting his prose.

One day in February, visiting Pound in his new home of Rapallo, Italy, Hemingway met the editor of the annual *Best Short Stories* volumes, Edward O'Brien, who was so taken with Hemingway and his tale of the stolen manuscripts that he decided to publish a horse-racing corruption story titled "My Old Man" in his series. It was a remarkable offer because the story had not even seen print yet. Ironically, "My Old Man" is still a developmental story for Hemingway, very much in the Anderson style—talky and sentimental and emotionally tortured and centered on a confused boy's consciousness. Hemingway gratefully allowed O'Brien to publish it anyway. He needed all the attention he could get.

Hemingway was just then developing his own distinctive prose style, very different from those of his mentors. He was willing to employ subtle echoes of Stein's repetitions and Pound's concrete images and Anderson's psychosexual dramas, but he knew what he was trying to achieve for himself. His prose would be absolutely adult, free of sexual repressions and well-mannered speech, spare and simple in expression, intensely provocative. This was his new Parisian mode, a fiction he could not have developed in Chicago, where there was no cubism or fauvism or Dada or widespread understanding of the power of absurdity and provocation. If Anderson had shown that he could bring Freud's theories into literature, with his parochial characters battling emotional and psychological barriers to authenticity and bliss, then Hemingway would show that he could master Freud and Marx both. He would explore psychological wounds and other barriers to right action, but he would also focus more pointedly on a world of haves and have-nots, and he would drop subtle hints that he retained a quiet but very real Christian compassion for weak and suffering refugees and working people. The multiform arts of Paris had shown him that these new combinations were possible, and he was determined to be his own man.

During the spring of 1923 Hemingway felt increased pressure to get his prose poems onto paper. His journalist friend Bill Bird, another ambulance driver from the war and a near neighbor in Paris, had recently bought an antique hand press and installed it in a room on the Île Saint-Louis, in the shadow of Notre Dame on the neighboring Île de la Cité. Bird called his new venture the Three Mountains Press (or in his dadaist moments, the "three mountains press") and planned to launch it with a series of modernist books with Pound listed as general editor. Pound immediately insisted on a book series promising, outlandishly, an "inquest into the state of contemporary English prose," and he recruited such luminaries as himself (of course), T. S. Eliot, William Carlos Williams, Ford Madox Ford—and the non-luminary Ernest Hemingway.[2] It was a great favor and a huge gesture of confidence, but now Hemingway had to come through with enough prose poems for a not-too-thin volume. He knew that if he could write a few more prose poems in addition to those six in *The Little Review* "Exiles' Number," perhaps twelve more, he would see his name on a first book—or chapbook, anyway. When Bird and Pound put out ads for their book series, they had to list Hemingway's offering as "Blank," which was embarrassing. But he knew that one day he would produce those prose poems and would title the thirty-page book *in our time*—one of his favorite allusions from the Anglican Book of Common Prayer, with its morning prayer asking the Lord for peace in our time.[3]

The prose poem had been his favored form for a few months, as he struggled to write sentences as he never had before—not with relaxed and intuitive skill as he had in Chicago, but with the intense concentration

Stein demanded and the vivid, concrete imagery Pound favored. Hemingway found it necessary to spend hours trying to write only one sentence, and it had to be what he called a "true sentence"—whatever that meant in the realm of fiction. He usually wrote by a coal-fired iron stove in a cheap, rented garret in the neighborhood, an expense that he and Hadley found they could just afford. Later in life he described his writing process in those days:

> Sometimes when I was starting a new story and I could not get it going, I would sit in front of the fire and squeeze the peel of the little oranges into the edge of the flame and watch the sputter of blue that they made. I would stand and look out over the roofs of Paris and think, "Do not worry. You have always written before and you will write now."[4]

He had not written much before, certainly, but he did find that he could usually produce that sentence he needed, and then perhaps a few more before the working day was over. He found it essential to cut the moralizing Victorian talk as he created the modern image, the uninterpreted view or utterance of a baffled person dealing with a violent world. "If I started to write elaborately," he wrote, "or like someone introducing or presenting something, I found that I could cut that scrollwork or ornament out and throw it away and start with the first true simple declarative sentence I had written."[5] Writing this way was slow going. Hemingway was certain he would never write something as long and involved as a novel.[6]

Then he had another publishing offer early that year, one that he could not take quite so seriously as the "inquest" book. During the stay with the Pounds in Rapallo, a tennis-playing buddy of his and Pound's named Robert McAlmon showed up, talking of a fine opportunity. Because McAlmon had entered into a marriage of convenience with the poet Bryher, daughter of a wealthy shipping magnate and a bisexual woman who needed an excuse to leave her parents' home, he had money, which he chose to employ as a literary angel. The perfect manner of funding a little publishing house, which he called Contact Press, had fallen into his lap: he could tap his rich father-in-law for the work of anti-capitalist resistance. Another early believer in Hemingway's talent,

McAlmon offered to publish his best current stories and poems in one volume. Between *The Little Review* and *in our time* commitments and Hadley's innocent mistake leading to the theft of his work, Ernest didn't have much to offer McAlmon. But he had just received a few of his poems in the mail, returned by the editors of *Poetry: A Magazine in Verse* in Chicago, and he had the *inaccrochable* "Up in Michigan," which at Gertrude Stein's suggestion had been shut up in a drawer. By adding a recent composition, "Out of Season," and the story he had promised to O'Brien, "My Old Man"—which had been mailed to another editor during the time of the theft and apparently later rejected for that magazine—he would have just enough, he thought.[7] Indeed, these three stories and ten poems gave Hemingway the title for his first book, *Three Stories and Ten Poems* (1923).[8] This book would appear during the coming winter. Only a few people would ever purchase these two slim books of 1923, and only a few more would read the half-dozen prose poems he had placed in *The Little Review*. Together, these few works represented Hemingway's total literary output for the year. Yet he was beginning to have justifiable faith in his future as a modern writer. If Stein, Pound, Bird, O'Brien, and McAlmon saw promise in his small body of work, he could believe in it too.

Now Hemingway needed to find a new set of friends, whose worldviews were more like his own. He enjoyed the company and correspondence of Stein and Pound and Anderson, but Stein and Pound were rightists, at least one of them a proto-fascist, and Anderson was so psychoanalytical in his interests that he hardly seemed to care about people's material lives or the political forces that shaped them. Furthermore, Hemingway knew, he would need to develop his elegant, interiorized prose style further so he could articulate more clearly the pain his characters were enduring in class-driven, ethnically divided Europe. He needed a new set of mentors. Hemingway liked leftist writers with imagination and guts and unrepressed verbal talent, and in late 1922 or early 1923 he found two of them in John Dos Passos and e. e. cummings.[9] Both were Harvard-educated writers who, like Hemingway and Bird, had worked in the ambulance service during the war. Even more natural revolutionaries than he was, each had written an important book about the war. Both books impressed Hemingway, perhaps more than their authors did. He saw that he could learn something from friends like these without being required to worship at their feet.

In 1922, cummings had written an autobiographical novel titled *The Enormous Room*, which told the tale of his imprisonment for sedition during the war. During downtime in his wartime ambulance corps, cummings had written some unwisely frank letters home about his experiences in the European combat zone. He confessed to his family back in America that he hated all war, including this one, and did not see a compelling reason to hate Germans. French officials read the letters, which was their right within the military during wartime, and arrested and interrogated him. The most pressing question they asked him was whether he hated Germans. It was a kind of litmus test. To be pro-French in that day meant to hate Germans. (There is that madness again.) Cummings stuck to his guns and replied that he did not hate Germans, though he claimed that he did love the French very much—a passion that would alter after his imprisonment. For this answer and for the attitude it conveyed, he spent months in detention, in a room that he called "enormous" in his memoir-novel because it contained men of such diverse conscience, ethnic attachment, and political attitude.

Dos Passos had also written an important war novel. It was titled *Three Soldiers* (1921), a tale that follows three American soldiers of differing regional backgrounds through their experiences of the trenches. The three are threatened continually with poison gas, and they endure frontal assaults in the face of machine guns and other modern killing machines. They come to realize that modern values and modern machines both conspire against their freedoms and their lives. Important American reviewers had praised the novel for its honesty, which is to say for its willingness to sympathize with suffering soldiers rather than praise them in Victorian fashion for their noble sacrifices on behalf of the Western empires.

Hemingway read *The Enormous Room* early on in Paris, recording the comment that "it was one of the great books" (not just wartime books) soon after. He admired the effort the novel must have required: "cummings worked hard to get it," Hemingway said.[10] He read *Three Soldiers* no later than August of 1923, which we know because he wrote a letter that month using the novel to argue for blank pages to pad out *Three Stories and Ten Poems*. (Hemingway pointed out to his publisher Robert McAlmon that *Three Soldiers* had "8 blank pages without a goddam thing on them immediately after cover.") He called Dos Passos's novel swell, which was unusually glowing praise for an active competitor. Soon

Hem and Dos, as they called each other, were sitting in the Closerie des Lilas as the lilacs in the café's name bloomed around them, drinking vermouth cassis and reading favorite passages from the King James Bible to each other. Hadley later pointed out to literary scholars that beginning that summer, "John Dos Passos was one of the few people . . . whom Ernest could really talk to."[11] Cummings was an irregular visitor to Paris, which was one factor that prevented such a close friendship between him and Hemingway. But both cummings and Dos Passos wrote very irreverent modern poetry and shared a distaste for pious and oppressive governments, and Hemingway loved cummings's novel, so there was mutual respect.

Both Dos Passos and cummings had spent time in Paris and discovered Dada. Both quickly embraced its ethic of shocking but principled nonsense and naughtiness and linguistic liberty. Cummings hung around with Dada founder Louis Aragon, and because he and Dos Passos were sketchers and painters, they paid attention to dadaist collages. Both would bring the free association of collage to their poems and novels, embracing the freedom to place honest expression beside hackneyed patriotism for useful comparison. This was a method Hemingway used too, but mainly in his less accomplished poems. One result of this liberated poetry was cummings's anti–Great War poem "i sing of Olaf glad and big," a tender introduction to a conscientious objector and caustic exposure of a certain kind of patriotism:

> i sing of Olaf glad and big
> whose warmest heart recoiled at war:
> a conscientious object-or

Olaf is tortured cruelly for his principled nonconformism and opposition to war. Cummings does not spare the language of resistance and provocation then awakening Paris:

> Olaf (being to all intents
> a corpse and wanting any rag
> upon what God unto him gave)
> responds, without getting annoyed
> "I will not kiss your fucking flag"

Furiously patriotic soldiers torture him further for his stubbornness and insolence, abusing him with anal insertions of heated bayonets. Eventually, after much suffering, Olaf dies. Cummings ends the poem by asserting that Olaf "was more brave than me:more blond than you."[12] We readers are left to ponder whether Olaf might have been *both* more blond and more brave than we are, and whether principled scatological resistance might have an important role to play in securing peace. As for his dadaist development, Dos Passos would develop a technique for using "found" language from government documents, popular songs, ads, newspaper clippings, and more to expose the basic hypocrisy and madness of European and American leaders, a technique Hemingway would employ later, in 1924, as we will see.

Hemingway liked these friends and their anarchic artistic and political leanings. While cummings was a more casual and momentary friend, Dos Passos would be a close fishing and writing buddy for years, the friendship finally fracturing in Spain during the country's civil war, when the buddies quarreled over the question Quoc was pondering in 1923—just how ruthless a revolutionary should be. Soon enough, these fresh friendships in Paris led Hemingway into his own very personal dadaist phase.

≡ ≡ ≡

This phase was a bit like a college course can be—a time of intense investment and aroused curiosity that is, for better or worse, rather easy to move beyond. Certainly Hemingway's interest in Dada was short-lived. Such courses are important nevertheless as a time of preparation for even deeper ideas to come, and that is the benefit Hemingway received from Dada. That deeper, more authentic intellectual destination to come for Hemingway was called surrealism, an arts-and-literature movement founded by men (they were almost all men) who dropped out from Dada to rescue and develop its implicit leftist politics and social seriousness. In early 1923 Hemingway was just opening up to Dada, or at least to Dada's logic, if not to all of its childish antics. However, we will see that Hemingway could be plenty childish and antic.

As Quoc had learned already, Dada had set out to show that Western civilization, which claimed to have invented and developed rationality itself, along with artistic beauty and scientific rigor and the deep goodness of the Christian church, was in fact insane at its very core. This idea accorded with Quoc's experience of colonialism, as he watched the French Catholic fathers' gracious *mission civilisatrice* lead to French soldiers butchering and roasting Vietnamese children and old people. Nothing could be more insane than that. The dadaists, knowing that French patriots could find ways to ignore or excuse such madness, set out to show in antic ways that Western civilization did not deserve hushed respect. As we have seen, they would paint mustaches on the *Mona Lisa* if they felt like it or, better yet, hang an effigy of a Prussian soldier with a pig's head from the ceiling and call it an archangel.[13] Eventually, these artists believed, these provocations would help the European public see the madness undergirding their own lives: the worship of war, the idolatry of the rich, and the uniting of militarism and nationalism leading too often to war.

In their turn, the surrealists would merely develop the more serious side of this movement, beginning in 1924. They would provoke with strange and serious art rather than sophomoric jokes and tricks perpetrated upon live audiences, and they would begin studying Marxist theory and developing their own notably humane interpretations of Marxist action. It is not difficult to see why this evolution in the movement interested Hemingway more than Dada did. He was more serious himself, more interested in provoking with depictions of realistic violence than with absurd play. And he saw that Dada's dropouts were better grounded in both modern psychology and a Marxist reading of history. Surrealism was propagated by a group of Parisian communists, led by a writer and poet named André Breton, who believed that spontaneous art, dream states, unharnessed imagination, and intense solidarity with working people could bring about a world in which laborers made decent wages, but also gained the respect, time, support, and mental liberty needed to make art. Their vision was communist, but certainly not Bolshevik, which was anchored to a rigid and unrelenting celebration of manual work that the surrealists found idiotic.

Hemingway would hold himself back from some of these unrealistic hopes, but he liked the qualities he first found in Dada: the spirit of expedient anarchy, liberty from deadly governments, and the larger mission to correct a corrupt economy. The signs of his interest are clear. He and

Hadley began collecting certain surrealists' art as early as 1922, and by 1924 they would become avid collectors of both surrealist art and ideas.[14] They would have dear friends among the surrealists. Notably, just at the moment that these friendships flowered, Hemingway's own talent for writing crisp, fascinating, complex, and emotionally coherent stories in his new Parisian style would also suddenly blossom forth.

In 1924, surrealism would be a major fascination of Hemingway's, but in 1923 he simply imbibed Dada's spirit—its implicit argument, shared and amplified by psychoanalysis, that it was healthy to shed repressions. People who learned this Freudian lesson invited and accepted impulses in themselves that came from deep within, those inner wishes to act out and resist conformity and norms. This was a modernist interpretation of Freud, of course, an idea then finding mostly sexual expression. If it felt good, do it, the modernists felt. If you wanted more sexual partners, do that too, as acting on unrepressed desires was likely to make you happier and healthier. And then, the theory went, sexual liberty would lead inevitably to other liberties, such as the wish to take to the streets to criticize pious or violent or stupid national leaders—in other words, acts that could ripple outward and even change governments. Hemingway and other artists who held to more serious missions (even as they had no problem with the idea of greater sexual freedom) saw that repressions helped keep an unjust state in power. Patriotism was mostly repression, after all, of the will to live and of the need to resist others' mastery of our lives. At its worst, patriotism was a kind of demented, servile willingness even to die for the hollow mission of keeping profiteers in their habituated comforts and their sociopolitical privileges.

There is a story about Hemingway's reaction to a modern musical performance that tells us about his growth into dadaist ways at this time, and into Paris's unrepressed ways generally. Throughout the early 1920s, Stravinksy's *The Rite of Spring* had captivated intellectual Paris, and everyone who cared about the arts attended at least one performance. *The Rite*, a ballet and atonal orchestral concert about a distant time and place Stravinsky called pagan Russia, told the story of a primitive people (1920s costumes appeared distinctly Native American) embracing the creative power of spring. These pagan Russians welcome spring with dance, though the dance does not remain celebratory for long. Some kind of strange energy quickly turns the dance deadly serious when one girl, chosen merely by her own movements and the movements of the people, is selected for a special sacrifice that helps the oncoming spring: she must dance herself to death. *The Rite*, with its message that even art arises out of primitive superstition and love of death, was clearly another example of an art that had the capacity to unsettle its audiences, as the following tale illustrates.[15]

One evening, a Parisian audience grew restive while watching Nijinsky's choreography set to Stravinsky's insistent music. The scene was apparently in the "Sacrifice" half of the ballet, where the female lead, dressed in an indigenous-looking leather shift, dances herself to exhaustion in preparation for her death in a barbaric murder-sacrifice. The ballerina put the back of her hand next to her cheek and, while the one-tone quarter-note tom-toms pounded away and the other dancers stomped in a way no ballet had allowed before, she shivered rhythmically. Both the music and the choreography of pain were a calculated affront to the audience, as the patrons recognized. This was not the beauty of dance. It was a mock-seizure celebrating a barbaric act. From the balcony a patron called out, as though concerned for the ballerina's health, "A doctor!" Another, making fun of the way she caressed her own cheek while shivering, called out, "A dentist!" and another upped the comical ante with a call for "Two dentists!" The audience roared, half in approval of the comedians' shouts and half in outrage at the interruption of the performance.[16] Some viewed the interruption as rude, while others saw it as unrepressed.

Hemingway saw and heard *The Rite of Spring*—and behaved just as rudely at a similar performance of challenging new modernist music. One evening, he and Hadley attended a performance by their friend George Antheil, who lived above Sylvia Beach's bookstore. He was to become world famous as a composer of operas, symphonies, and sonatas, including the *Ballet Mécanique*. After listening obligingly for a time to his friend's recital of his own composition—a version of Stravinsky's intentionally dissonant, repetitive, tuneless modern music—Hemingway lost his patience. It was not that his traditionalist childhood training in the Beethoven and Mozart his operatic mother favored now led him to reject Antheil's outlandish music; it was that the music was not modernist *enough* for him. From his concert-hall seat he bellowed out, "I like my Stravinsky straight!" Characteristically, Hadley, who sat next to

Ernest that evening and recalled the moment years later, remembered no feeling of personal embarrassment or impatience with her ill-mannered first husband.[17] She probably realized that in dadaist Paris it had become proper to howl from the theater seats, to let those Western repressions evaporate, to express a heartfelt and spontaneous opinion no matter how rudely. Ernest was learning the liberty of resistance.

One of Hemingway's slim new books of 1923 conveys his more serious but equally obvious debt to Dada. The absence of uppercase letters in the title *in our time* is one indication of its Dada heritage, just as e. e. cummings's name is. (No "capitalist" letters!) Yet the clearest sign is the collage behind the title, Hemingway's name, and the publisher name, three mountains press. The collage consists of newspaper headlines and fragments of stories, clippings arranged chaotically in overlapping strata, their lines on many different planes. According to Martin Puchner, who rightly sees collage techniques in the poetry of Pound and Eliot and in the rhetoric of 1920s Marxist manifestos, the Dada collage "mimics the disintegration of society, capturing the effects of the modern metropolis that overwhelms the senses of humans with a torrent of simultaneous impressions."[18]

Hemingway might have agreed, but he had something less hysterical in mind too. Looking more closely, we see that Hemingway had chosen his clippings for the cover of *in our time* very carefully: they reflected his journeys as a reporter and the tragedies he had witnessed and covered—modern Europe disintegrating in the eastern Balkans, and because of that disintegration, the people suffering. The cover is an apt introduction to Hemingway's stories about refugees, political assassinations, and men at war. Hemingway benefited from the collage compositions then made fashionable by Dada. Hemingway's brief sketches in *in our time* can be read as independent prose poems, but their meanings sharpen and multiply when they are read as parts of a larger collage, one designed to intrigue and startle and produce accidental and intended new meanings through spontaneous juxtaposition. This we have seen by comparing the two prose poems about soldiers killing at Mons during the opening weeks of the Great War. Those prose poems may have combined Pound's imagist doctrines with Stein's repetitions and her characters' blunted affects, but the aura of nightmare and the invitation to explore connections more deeply after initial shock—that is pure Dada.

Hemingway apparently shed fewer repressions than his new American friends did. Dos Passos and cummings both took part in Dada's naughtier shedding of repressions in early 1920s Paris, appearing in tales of urinating on burning books in those days, or marching with dadaists through private Turkish baths, or witnessing friends spontaneously beating rumored police informants in the Dôme Café.[19] Hemingway did not take part in these adventures. Even before they would bring their baby son home to Paris in early 1924, the Hemingways were a close family, which meant that Ernest did not have time to become a mainline dadaist, to be out among the people turning them against their will into audiences for illogical edification.

Nor did he want to. He still embraced some of the more benign and arguably healthy repressions, such as favoring the company of his wife, accomplishing the long day's work writing and reading, and returning home to a meal prepared by the French maid and cook, Marie Cocotte. He enjoyed a walk to one of the iconic Montparnasse cafés, sometimes with Hadley and sometimes on his own, looking for specific artist and writer friends. He still sneered at the fakers and frauds among the café set, those who acted provocatively merely to gain some pathetic attention. But when he sat to write, he worked to provoke the complacent reader with violent scenes, powerful emotions leading to chaotic outcomes, unflinching portrayals of the cruelty of war, situations revealing the vanity of life itself, nightmares and frightening drug states, language too profane even for his world-aware editors, and subtle reminders that, after all, he was making this all up out of a free imagination. He had imbibed what Dada and other resisting arts in Paris had offered him.

As Hemingway himself put it that year, "How very much better dadas the American dadas."[20] What he meant is that postwar Americans, and especially veterans like him, already owned a proper sense of the absurdly humorous and the determinedly dissident. Better than the French dadaists around him, he was finding a way to convey that sense to the ordinary reader.

Now it was time for the Hemingways to leave Paris—though unlike Quoc, they left with real regret. In August, the Hemingways boarded a ship bound for New York with connections to Canada, where they would depend on the skills of the local maternity doctors and nurses. They chose Toronto because of Ernest's professional connection with the

*Star.* For a brief time, he would be a domestic reporter instead of a foreign correspondent. He and Hadley assured Parisian friends they would return in about a year, accompanied by a toddler but, they insisted, still determined to continue developing the arts of writing about the modern situation and performing on piano, just as they had been doing before this interruption. As it happens, they would be away from Paris for only four months, lonely that soon for the city's charms and disappointed that quickly with life in Toronto. Soon after returning to Paris, and after making some new friends among the European dadaists transitioning into surrealists, Hemingway would learn a lesson Quoc already had, which is that surrealist provocations could play a key role in his art of resistance. When he returned to Paris in the winter of 1924, he would put this new technique to work.

# 16

## A CRUCIBLE OF FRIENDS

### HEMINGWAY IN 1924

I t was hard work caring for a newborn on a rolling, pitching ship crossing the rough Atlantic during winter, so after spending more than a week sharing a small berth with their two-month-old son, John Nicanor Hemingway, whom they already called Bumby, Ernest and Hadley were exhausted. Yet in spite of their fatigue and the fevery colds they brought with them from Canada, they felt wonderful when the liner *Antonia* docked in Cherbourg in January of 1924. After all, they had a beautiful new son, they knew Paris so well that now they could find a nicer but still inexpensive apartment to rent, and they were about to be welcomed by a number of smart, affectionate, and talented friends. What's more, they were in full agreement that the time had come for Ernest to quit his reporting work so he could write full time.

Hemingway considered himself a modern artist now, a full-time literary writer rather than a reporter who wrote prose poems between reporting assignments for the *Star*. He still loved his reporting work, which brought travel and adventure into this life along with a bit of ready cash, but the months in Toronto had made him weary of the job. The main problem was his editor, Harry Hindmarsh. While working out of the *Toronto Star* offices, Hemingway had endured a series of the editor's petty and punitive assignments, which were apparently intended to humble the brash, expatriate scribbler—which seems to be how

Hindmarsh saw him. Ernest found it especially galling to have missed Bumby's birth in October while traveling to and from New York on one such assignment. Knowing that Hindmarsh was fully capable of playing his passive-aggressive games across the Atlantic via cable messages, Hemingway concluded that working as a foreign correspondent for the *Star* was no longer worth the trouble, even if it had given him invaluable subjects to write about and a grounding in international relations that would lend intellectual and political depth to his fiction.

With his days cleared, Hemingway could also devote time to the work that supported fiction writing, such as reading writers worthy of being emulated and, not least, learning and evaluating the insights of Paris's modernist artists, who were just then undergoing a shift in focus that interested him. Methods of resistance were undergoing refinement. Many vanguard artists in the city were steadily moving away from the brash, angry absurdities of Dada toward more intellectual celebrations of worker solidarity, unrepressed spontaneity, and dreams of peace. With so much to do and so much to learn, Hemingway had made up his mind: he would write no more news stories and magazine pieces—not until the current power dynamic with his editors had reversed. It would be the editors who would ask him to write feature articles, and it would be his byline rather than the headline that would sell their papers and magazines.

The year 1924, eleven months of which lay before him when his ship docked, would be a major step toward that kind of literary fame. By the approaching December he would be known to other professionals, if not to many ordinary readers yet, as one of the most adept and clever writers of English-language short stories. Throughout the year, editors, reviewers, and other knowing readers in Paris and New York would begin to circulate some of his stories, fresh off the pages of the little magazines *The Little Review* and *the transatlantic review* and his Parisian boutique chapbooks *Three Stories and Ten Poems* and *in our time*. Almost universally, these New York editors and reviewers would praise him for his clean, elegant prose and his nominally masculine perspective, which was an asset because, then as now, it was difficult to get men to read and purchase books.

Yet some editors had doubts about the marketability of his brief stories. After paying good money for a hardcover book, readers wanted reasonably long and rewarding plots, not the distilled adventures of his brief short stories, and certainly not a mere handful of Hemingway's interesting but elusive prose poems. Few readers could really figure out their meaning or intention. With his focus on war and refugee trains and bullfighting, his manuscripts in late 1923 were certainly exciting enough, but when his brief vignettes were collected between covers, the books looked decidedly thin. His talent for writing vignettes and prose poems was perfect for modernist collage effects and for revealing moral and psychological states of mind through selective hints and cues, but they matched up poorly with the literary marketplace. It was the modernist's dilemma: when you judged the quality of your writing by the paucity of readers who could understand the sophisticated moves you made, and when you pushed your prose too far toward esoteric poetry, you had trouble pleasing more traditionalist editors at major publishing houses, who served the large mass of ordinary readers with their ordinary expectations.

Then, as 1924 was about to end, Hemingway got his breakthrough. He received the Christmas present he most wanted: a book contract with a New York publisher. Two of Hemingway's literary friends had intervened on his behalf with the Boni and Liveright publishing house. Once again, Sherwood Anderson had stepped up to help him, along with a new Paris tennis buddy named Harold Loeb, who also published a little magazine called *Broom* and had a New York book contract of his own already for a novel weirdly titled *Doodab*. Together, the two pressed their editors at Liveright to take a chance on Hemingway, who had a bright literary future, they were certain. The Liveright people were not enthused about the profit they might realize from the thin book Hemingway offered them, a collation of his *in our time* prose poems and the new titled stories he was churning out that year, gems involving Nick Adams and his young veteran and expatriate foils. But Mr. Liveright himself made the decision to take Hemingway on, much as a wine connoisseur purchases "futures" bottles of previously unknown and untasted wine. His calculation was that Hemingway's prose poems might be nearly unmarketable currently, but that the young writer was surely going to develop soon into that more sophisticated and valuable commodity: the novelist. The price for signing Hemingway to a publishing contract was so modest that it was possible to write off small financial losses on this first book, which was a bit too experimental and strange for American tastes, just to lock Hemingway into a contract that gave Liveright the first crack at the next book. Liveright hoped the next book would be more standard, and it *would* be a novel if he had anything to say about it. As Anderson and Loeb had argued, young Hemingway seemed a good bet. His prose style and his international themes were impressive already. What Liveright did not realize is that Hemingway was quietly committed to his resistance project, his exposure of the calamities caused by profiteers and oligarchs and their governmental stooges. There would have to be a showdown between them.

Hemingway felt uneasy about meeting Liveright's longer-term expectations. Though his family and friends knew him as extremely confident in his talent, he nevertheless doubted he could write a novel. Because he was an experimental modernist who eschewed all played-out forms and practices, he was not even sure he *wanted* to write one. As late as the summer of 1925 Hemingway would claim that he "did not know how [he] would ever write anything as long as a novel," and he also complained that the novel as a genre was "an awfully artificial and worked-out form."[1] Hemingway found that it took incredible effort to get his new modernist prose onto the page, though he felt the effort paid off. He still wanted to give his readers distilled scenes conveying realistic psychological states revealing the troubled minds of wounded characters. And he wanted these scenes for their collage effects, which were important to him because they required his readers' active participation in the meaning-making. When readers discovered the echoes between and among stories and vignettes and scenes he so craftily wrought, they realized that their own commitments and emotions and logical calculations had become more consciously known to them. These readers didn't just discover the book's meaning or Hemingway's meanings but also the things they themselves found meaningful—such as, hopefully, peace and justice and kindness.

By the early months of 1924 Hemingway had adopted complex modernist aesthetics, the distilled, intense, allusive scenes that exposed and resisted the consequences of war and domination. He had begun to concentrate his meanings, as Stein so wisely urged him to do at their meeting in 1922, so that it often took him, in his words, "a full morning of work to write a paragraph."[2] This slow pace was not a cause for despair; experienced writers know that writing a paragraph per day can produce surprising results in a few months' time. And that year, Hemingway indeed showed he had the chops required to write his novel. He supplied proof of his talent by writing the stories and prose vignettes for a new book with a title he had already used (sans caps), *In Our Time*, a task he accomplished in record time. In the spring of that year alone, in a small bedroom study in his new apartment above a humming sawmill or at a lilac-shaded table in the courtyard of the nearby Closerie des Lilas café, Hemingway wrote "Indian Camp," "Cat in the Rain," "The End of Something," "The Three-Day Blow," "The Doctor and the Doctor's Wife," "Soldier's Home," "Mr. and Mrs. Elliot," and "Cross-Country Snow."[3] About half of the book's stories concerned an autobiographical character named Nick Adams, who grows up in the Michigan lake country during adventurous summers, avoiding the commotion of suburban Chicago with his overbearing Christian family. As he matures from precocious boy to smart young man, he learns to love the active life in the Michigan outdoors, and eventually begins to shift his attention from fun male companionship to more serious relationships with women. And then he goes to help the Great War and nearly loses all activity from the waist down when he is wounded during battle. Still recovering from these physical wounds and the mental wounds that came with them, he then moves to Europe for a bohemian life and a search for ultimate purpose.

So, in effect, Hemingway had already begun knitting together a novel-length and continuous plot in these stories, a chronicle of Nick's and his own most trying existential moments. The stories chart the emotional and intellectual growth and then the deadly trials of a smart boy from the Upper Midwest, a sort of typical American kid. (The surname Adams hints at Genesis and the idea that he is a representative creature of God.) In "Indian Camp," Hemingway portrays himself as a little boy accompanying his physician father on a call to an Ojibwe work camp, where he is stunned to witness both a bloody birth and a bloody suicide. In "The Doctor and the Doctor's Wife," a slightly older Nick must face up to his father's weakness in dealing with both his wife and some resentful Ojibwe neighbors, whose ire seems connected with the theft of the American Indians' pristine world during the previous century. As a teenager, Nick, in "The End of Something," first takes his male buddy's advice and breaks up with a Michigan girlfriend, and then, in "Three-Day Blow," engages in a drunken and conflicted attempt to justify and affirm this breakup in a discussion with the buddy, who tries to convince Nick that women and sex are inferior to masculine pursuits, such as adventure books, sports, liquor, hunting, and fishing. In "The Battler," Nick is a high school kid who sets out into the world on his own, riding the rails in the Upper Peninsula, meeting people living on the margins of society, such as a demented ex-boxer and his black caretaker. Nick is shocked to see that even ex–professional athletes living life as wandering toughs may also be interracial and homosexual lovers.

In the Chapter VI prose poem, Nick is wounded in battle, paralyzed temporarily by a bullet to the spine. Hemingway knew that this was a special moment, yet he was not quite sure why he had consigned it to the vignettes rather than making a longer, titled story of it. Later he would figure out why, and would make it a controlling element in the construction of this novel-in-stories.

Then there were stories that concerned characters only a bit like Nick, characters we might call his foils. In "Cat in the Rain," a young, male veteran simply called the American lives the expatriate life in European hotels, enduring the complaints of a wife who longs for a real home and some basic intimacy from her distracted husband. There were non-autobiographical satires too, all essentially introducing us to the problem of growing up in patriotic, Christian America and then taking up a new life as a world-aware modern relativist, acquainted with the horrors of war and desperate to find a more fulfilling and peaceable way to live. These characters struggle to find two things they know they will need in order to thrive and survive: a loving partnership and a meaningful vocation. They often seem balked or perversely unable to manage either one. Hemingway's characters often seem cut off from, or undeveloped in, nonerotic love. Their parents often seem unloving toward them, and their modern friends, who have all read Freud's theory that animal libido had replaced love, seem too cynical to believe in such an evanescent, spiritual thing.

Hemingway hints that these people should join him in a life of awakened political resistance to the values of a domineering plutocracy. Unlike their author, none of these characters explores radical political and artistic ideas, so they are unable to see that resistance to a cynical, empty, unjust, and unaware world is an act of love. In these stories, Hemingway was turning away, if only slightly, from the pregnant observations of his prose vignettes to the meanings that arise from extended literary story—meanings about existential and practical choices concerning vocation, work, national service, partnership, love, and home.

Yet the length of his narratives is only the most evident sign of Hemingway's growth. He was also testing and applying the more complex intellectual lessons he learned while writing these wonderful stories. These were lessons about a new kind of art that rejected serenity and social normalcy, an art that provoked and mystified and challenged readers to rethink what it means to live properly and rightly. During 1924, Hemingway immersed himself in talk about surrealist art, and he did so by making a new set of very dear friends. He still corresponded with his newswriting buddies and with Pound and Stein and Dos Passos, the friends of 1922 and 1923. But now he spent most of his time writing during mornings and then consorting during afternoons with a new group of young friends who not only shared his alarm at the ongoing evolution of Western civilization, as his old friends had, but also tended to view anarchic art and progressive politics as the necessary volatile compound that might explode into something world-altering. Hemingway and the new surrealist friends he made that year believed that through careful thinking and writing and painting, they could craft a more wholesome and emancipated world to live in.[4] It was an added benefit that, in doing so, they would remake literature and art at the same time, as well as gaining vaunted reputations for themselves.

≡ ≡ ≡

During this first year back in Paris from the unpleasant Canadian sojourn, Hemingway enjoyed visiting friends for exercise, usually afternoon tennis or boxing matches followed by a drink or two in a café. The talk over these drinks often turned to discussions of the new modernist aesthetics. Indeed, one of the reasons Hemingway was so productive in 1924 was that he had wonderful luck with his friendships that year. Hemingway was about to fall in with the French, Spanish, and American surrealists, who provided him with both support and key ideas about art and its role in resisting the war makers and profiteering oligarchs. For a number of reasons, Hemingway mentions only some of these friends in his late-life memoirs, but it is possible to knit together the network of friends and the ideas they are known for—the ideas Hemingway must have discussed over those drinks in the neighborhood cafés and then pondered on his walk home to Hadley and Bumby in their rue Notre-Dame-des-Champs sawmill flat.

Boxing lessons led to one of these friendships. Sometime in that spring of 1924 Hemingway began to walk after his morning writing session a few blocks westward from his apartment and favorite cafés to 45 rue Blomet, a run-down, Left Bank building consisting of four mismatched wings surrounding a cobbled courtyard that opened onto a series of large studios and workshops. There, in two roomy studios in number 45, one of them kept neat by a natty bachelor Spaniard and the other a chaotic mess of brushes and half-spent paint tubes and playing cards and chess pieces allowed to accumulate by a married French veteran, Hemingway gave boxing lessons to the surrealist painters Joan Miró and André Masson.[5]

Hemingway had met Masson—the untidy one—through Gertrude Stein back in 1922. She bought the young Frenchman's cubist paintings before anyone else did, and promoted his work avidly. She was eager for Hemingway to meet an artist of his own generation, just as she had met and befriended Picasso and Matisse during her first years in Paris. She encouraged Hemingway to purchase the art of his most promising contemporaries, buying while their works were affordable because they had not yet met commercial success. This is, of course, how she had accumulated her Picassos, Matisses, Cézannes, and Gauguins a generation earlier. Soon enough, Hemingway did purchase Masson's paintings. In 1923 he and Hadley even loaned their first Masson painting back to the artist for his first solo gallery showing. When they attended the opening evening of the show, they felt a bit in awe of the sight of their own painting hanging in a prestigious Parisian gallery.

Masson introduced Hemingway to Miró at the neighboring studio. The three became fast friends, and before long they could be seen together, walking the broad sidewalks of Montparnasse on their way to Hemingway's more serious boxing matches and paid sparring sessions. (Hemingway sparred with professional boxers, according to Miró, earning extra cash working as a practice opponent.) Miró liked to carry Hemingway's duffel bag, with its load of tennis shoes and towels and boxing gloves. Because Miró also liked to wear a dark suit, spats, a bowler hat, and a monocle in public, even to the gym, he was sometimes mistaken for Hemingway's butler—or so one of Hemingway's *Toronto Star* buddies, Morley Callaghan, once claimed. Miró was also tiny, and Hemingway very tall, so when they walked with an average-height person, such as the young, fit Masson, the three of them looked like stair steps.[6]

Friendship—or solidarity among workers and veterans and undervalued women—was an important element in the surrealist commitments of Miró and Masson. Indeed, and perhaps surprisingly, consorting with friends is what resistance was all about for the rue Blomet comrades. Their logic went like this: The only way to resist the dominant politics and economics of the day was for like-minded men and women to band together to find joy and love in each other's company, to assist each other in their callings, to promote the dignity of working people, to break down the logic of warring nationalism, and to satirize the claims of the rich and other controlling powers that be. Miró and Masson were like Hemingway in that they enjoyed learning from others and being near groups and schools and cliques of artists, who always seemed to engage in an energetic sharing of ideas. But they were also like Hemingway in living out an anarchic, independent spirit that kept them from assenting to any manifesto or doctrine. For a time, they had hung around with dadaists without taking the Dada label for their own work. Then, for months leading up to 1924, they had seen certain friends growing impatient with Dada pranks. Some of these friends, such as Dada founder André Breton, tried to convince them to join him in a more seriously communitarian arts movement called surrealism, but Masson and Miró resisted Breton's adamant attempts to recruit them. Even after they did sign on in 1924, a bit warily, they were able to deflect his hectoring about rigid adherence to the Marxist-Leninist doctrines he favored. Breton supported the Third International, which called for armed revolution when necessary, yet he declared again and again that surrealism was utterly independent and took no directions from either the Comintern or the French Communist Party. He saw himself as a member of the bourgeoisie who could only assist the proletariat's revolution by encouraging personal acts of resistance against dominant bourgeois values, especially patriotism and nationalism. Yet he was so prickly about his own ideas that he eventually purged almost all other members of his clique. In his mind, he *became* surrealism.[7] Miró and Masson, who deplored the idea of violence implied by the Third International and were wary of Breton's domineering and rigid personality, decided that uninhibited painting and writing and friendly discussion were revolutionary acts in their own right, a position that apparently felt right to Hemingway too.

Miró and Masson simply liked people, especially writers and artists who sided with workers and veterans, who believed that psychoanalysis was wise to call for fewer repressions and more spontaneity, who liked to create from imagination rather than observation, and who believed that they could promote mental and material peace. They had never been much interested in Dada, even if they understood and employed its absurdist logic. The dadaists did not grant art enough dignity, they felt, and the rue Blomet comrades were confident that they were creating beautiful, significant paintings that transcended dadaist playfulness. The surrealist artists and poets were also more interested than the dadaists were in a more serious assessment of Marxist and Freudian dynamics. Dadaist clowns perpetrating pranks might expose the madness underlying Western thought, but Miró and Masson wanted to understand what people might do to seize better material and emotional lives. They suspected that Freudian therapy and Marxist social transformations would lead to a more settled, nourishing world. For these and other reasons, Hemingway was interested in their opinions when he joined with them, after boxing, for a vermouth cassis and a discussion of these ideas.

And he loved the art they produced. He, too, felt that he was creating significant art, arational and provocative at times, yet still elegant, dignified, and moving. He was also interested in the more serious, complex, and personal dynamics of Freudian and Marxist ideas. He wondered, his stories of the time imply, whether his Lost Generation could ever defeat personal narcissism and the disabling effect of their post-shock nightmares long enough to fight for the rights and dignity of laboring people. But he felt that these surrealists were onto something, as they connected personal and political liberty with the unrestrained imagination, honoring of the subconscious, and repealing of certain social repressions. He learned, he confessed to George Plimpton late in his life, "as much from painters about how to write as from writers."[8] During the twenties, Masson and Miró were two of the most important of those painters.[9]

There is a story the surrealist artists liked to tell about what friendships meant to them. In the winter of 1917 a certain young German
soldier named Max Ernst, who would one day become a founding dadaist, served with German artillery troops assigned the task of shelling an
enemy trench about a kilometer away. Ernst and his fellow soldiers lobbed
shell after shell into those nearby French trenches, where, Ernst was to
learn after the war ended, a Frenchman named Paul Eluard manned
a parapet facing no-man's-land in anticipation of the German infantry attack that often followed on such a shelling. Somehow, both Ernst
and Eluard survived the war. In Paris just a few years later—around
1924, in fact—the two had become dear friends and both surrealists,
Ernst a painter and Eluard a poet. They had forgiven and embraced one
another as artists and friends. According to one scholar, they were part
of a friendship and a movement that was "taking on for them the form
and the potentiality of the total emancipation of man"—emancipation
through mutual forgiveness among former enemies and through mutual
solidarity as workers for a better world. This was about soldiers learning
to love instead of hate. For the surrealists, this story was a kind of parable
of what their commitments and art made possible.

Interestingly, Hemingway depicts the same kind of postwar friendship in the final chapter of A Moveable Feast—and he, too, seems interested in liberty through loving friendship. Describing the wonderful
time he and Hadley and Bumby had in the Austrian town of Schruns
one Christmastime, he remembers "the snow on the road to the village
squeaking at night" and the simple reverence of the locals, who always
greeted them with the wish for God's blessing, "Grüss Gott." He remembers the "country men in the Weinstube with nailed boots and mountain
clothes," many of whom had served in the same theater of war where he
had been wounded. He does not say so, but one of these Austrian men
may very well have fired the mortar round that nearly killed him. But
those days are over, Hemingway implies as he describes one of the Austrian men in particular:

Many of the young men had served in Austrian Alpine regiments
and one named Hans, who worked in the sawmill, was a famous
hunter and we were good friends because we had been in the same

part of the mountains in Italy. We drank together and we all sang
mountain songs.[10]

Hemingway implies that if all of Europe were like this mountain village
in Austria, where friendship, forgiveness, and working-class solidarity
prevailed, not to mention Christmastime reverence for God's love, there
might be a kind of international emancipation of people's spirits.

Among the surrealists who held up the Ernst and Eluard friendship
as a model for their artistic partnerships, Masson and Miró seem to have
taken the story most to heart. Masson in particular had a generous spirit
that drew others into his orbit. "Due to some alchemical accident that
you might call 'l'air du temps' ('something in the wind')," he wrote in his
memoirs, "my studio became the headquarters not of an organization,
but of a crucible of friends."[11]

Hemingway was one of the writers and artists whose ideas were
tempered in this crucible. He enjoyed the lively discussions and debates
about art at the two studios—this according to Hadley, whose memories
of Paris are sometimes more honest than her first husband's. But mainly
he knew kindred souls when he met them. Masson recalls that the painters and writers who gathered at 45 rue Blomet were a band of brothers: "Fanatics about our freedom," he writes, "we had a very pure sense
of friendship—each was what he was, accepted as such." These friends
gave each other "freedom of access too. That studio was open house at
all times. Of course there was a door, and a latch on the door, but no
key." Their artistic endeavors were pure as well, Masson reports, and
there were no concerns "with propaganda, no dissension, no intrigue, no
rivalry, no one-upmanship, no lying. The greatest brotherhood and trust
united these young people."[12] They were a lively bunch. Next door to the
studio was an integrated jazz bar called the *Bal Negre*, where the surrealists enjoyed rubbing shoulders with the colonized men and women then
living in Paris. This *bal* was the *indigènes'* own dive, a place where they
could share their native food and music and could learn jazz rhythms
alongside the international artists. As the name implies, the *Bal Negre*
was more Caribbean and African than Indochinese, but Quoc may have
visited for the international atmosphere and to spend time with members
of his Intercolonial Union. But if he did, unfortunately we know nothing about it.

When Stein learned that her prized young cubist painter Masson had joined up with Breton's surrealists, she was dismayed. She was fundamentally opposed to the surrealists' left-leaning ideas, for one thing, but she had also always regarded Masson as too much the anarchist to join any movement. She loved him for this courage—and because he was one of the few painters, she observed, who knew how to paint in white. She was correct about the courageous faith in anarchic independence. Masson believed that when people conducted themselves freely and spontaneously and when they pursued personal interests and talents unimpeded by any governmental or institutional coercion, then these compassionate libertarians coalesced into a healthier community, even a healthier civilization. Masson's anarchist yet compassionate spirit accorded nicely with Hemingway's.

If Quoc was Hemingway's unknown brother-in-arms, then Masson was the known one. Again, as with Quoc, the kinship began with a parallel experience of terror, a wartime wounding. While serving in the trenches with the French army, Masson had seen, as his friend Breton put it, that the Great War turned "aspirations [into] a cloaca of blood, stupidity, and mud." Masson, who was driven nearly to mutiny by his wartime frustration and exhaustion, became a true victim of the stupidity. One day late in the war, he was gravely wounded by a bullet to the chest. He nearly died of shock and blood loss. Stretcher-bearers could not move him under fire, so he had to lie on his back in a shell hole one whole night long, bleeding and suffering. During that long night, he watched "red and green rockets" shearing the sky over his head, "striped by the wake and the flashes of the projectiles." He wondered whether he would survive this display. He described his fear:

> To see all that, face upward, one's body immobilized on a stretcher, instead of head down as in the fighting where one burrows like a dog in the shell craters, constituted a rare and unwonted situation. The first nerve-shattering fright gives way to resignation and then, as delirium slips over you, it becomes a celebration performed for one about to die.

Masson did survive, but during his rehabilitation, still in French uniform, he continued to have difficulties. There was a spirit of mutiny in

French trenches later in the war, born of the blood, stupidity, and mud, and the freethinking Masson seems to have been swept up in it. Characteristically, his mutiny was personal and his resistance independent. While recuperating from his wounds in the hospital, he was insubordinate to a military official, so he was sent to an asylum, where he stayed until the war had nearly ended.[13]

Hemingway was also bullied by officious Italians during his convalescence, but there was one key difference between his experience and Masson's. Unlike Hemingway, Masson devoted himself to a specifically compassionate calling at the war's immediate end. Just after being freed from the asylum and discharged from the army, Masson brought his artistic skills to a pottery factory, where he helped disabled French veterans develop new work skills. The war had transformed Masson more quickly than Hemingway. He had swiftly become, in an odd combination, a soldier's soldier and a good Samaritan, and he hated the officer class. He felt so hostile toward the nationalism that had forced him into the trenches that he refused to call himself a Frenchman. He was, he said, a European. It took time for Masson to return to the art studio with a right spirit, and it also took time to accept the healing friendships that Hemingway and the band of surrealists introduced into his life.

In their memoirs of the rue Blomet years, both Masson and Miró mention Hemingway as a friend whom they recalled with special affection. A pair of his boxing gloves always hung on their wall, ready for the next coaching session. For his part, Hemingway bought significant artworks from both men, and he prized both the paintings and the friendships all his life long. He appreciated the tutoring they gave him in modern art as well. Hadley claimed in a late-life interview that "in those early years, Hemingway had been 'profoundly occupied' with the theories of Stein and Ezra Pound, and that Masson's paintings had been important for him" too. Most literary scholars would not place Masson, the surrealist painter, on a par with Stein and Pound, but Hadley said it was so.[14] Everything Hemingway was curious about in those days, Hadley remarked, was "grist to a superfine powerful mill"—that is, to Ernest's artistic imagination and amazing capacity to learn and to adapt that learning to his own work.[15]

Hemingway wrote warmly about Masson for years. In *the transatlantic review* that summer, he wrote an incredible compliment about

Masson's paintings—not those Hemingway owned, which he does not mention, but the ones he regularly saw hanging in Gertrude Stein's salon: though they hung beside "something like thirty of the best Picasso's [*sic*] in the world," Hemingway wrote, "[they] do not lose by the comparison."[16] Masson must have marveled at that line. In the 1934 book *The Green Hills of Africa*, Hemingway depicts a woman character he calls P.O.M. (it is a reference to his second wife, Pauline) comparing a beautiful stand of woods to a Masson painting that she and the narrator, her hunter husband, happen to own:

> "By God, isn't it a great looking country?" I said. . . .
> "The trees are like André's pictures," P.O.M. said. "It's simply beautiful. Look at that green. It's Masson. Why can't a good painter see this country?"[17]

In turn, Masson appreciated Hemingway's good taste in modern painting and his understanding of what the painters were trying to accomplish. "Those from the rue Blomet," Masson wrote about his friends, including boxing coach Hemingway, "were, from that moment of fusion, unconsciously but fatally prepared, by their way of life, for a dissident future."[18]

One of the convictions Hemingway, Masson, and Miró shared with other surrealists was a belief in the rights and integrity of the farmer-laborer class, which they saw as challenged by the aggressive iniquity of the ruling and profiteering classes. To put it baldly, it had been an oligarch's war and a farmer's and laborer's fight. This surrealist sympathy for the worker was a profound influence. So was the surrealist tendentiousness and willingness to shock. These friends worked on an art of resistance.

As much as he admired the Masson paintings he owned, Hemingway would turn his attentions to Miró's work in 1925, when a painting even more ambitious came up for sale at a price he felt he just might be able to afford. We will see how a surreal painting that lets us see through walls can, among many other things, express solidarity with poor farmers. But in 1924 it was Masson who fascinated Hemingway and who engaged in a friendship in which neither knew who was the mentor and who was the protégé. What the two men seem to have taught one another is that a credible art must ask more of readers than simple calm attention and respect. Art—real art—must challenge the viewer-reader to participate in the emotions that art produces in them. There is no other way for an art to produce serious philosophical reflection or resistance or mutiny or solidarity with others. And the most important emotion, necessarily leading to action, was love.

That, if we think about it, is the one element lacking in the *in our time* vignettes, and yet, perhaps thanks to Masson, fully present in the best titled stories of 1924: both erotic and nonerotic love. In his vignettes, Hemingway had already abandoned serenity and traditional literary language and form. His very brief portraits revealed the consciousness and (often balked) conscience of the viewer, who speaks about the witnessed horrors. Hemingway was bold enough to show us these horrors vividly, in gory detail. In the new stories, he may have moved marginally toward a more traditional short-story form. But more importantly, he had engaged in surrealist treatments of themes that were startling for his time—and sadly, perhaps also for ours: love across racial lines, love embracing various sexual identities, love leading to nonstandard homes and vocations, love upsetting the settled Christian traditions the patriarchs and oligarchs promoted, love departing from Victorian principles of nobility and chastity. At the heart of these stories is an implied need for credible friendships between and among modern men and women— the very blessing he was lucky enough to have experienced with Hadley and Masson and Miró and others.

# 17

## THE MIRACULOUS YEAR

### HEMINGWAY IN 1924

S ome of the stories Hemingway wrote in 1924 came to him so quickly that one biographer calls the year miraculous, but by late spring the writing had stalled.[1] Hemingway had written those Nick Adams stories, carrying his autobiographical character through his childhood and teen years in the Michigan lake country with his Victorian Christian parents, witnessing death and birth much too early as his physician father tended to an Ojibwe woman's difficult pregnancy; watching his father in racially charged disagreement with two Ojibwe men about valuable drift logs; breaking up with a girlfriend who is uncomfortably good at his favorite avocation of fishing; and setting out on his own first solo adventure riding the rails in the Upper Peninsula and meeting disturbing vagrants in their camp just before the war. Furthermore, as we have seen, he had found it possible to describe, in one of his prose poems, the terrible moment when Nick nearly lost his life to a war wound as he took a bullet to his spine in an Italian street battle. Hemingway had also written a series of stories that displaced his experiences as wounded veteran and young expatriate onto characters other than Nick. But now the final two stories for the book, which he thought should return to Nick as its central character, had become very challenging. Now he felt he had to say something important and definitive about expatriate life in Europe and all it had come to mean to him. He encountered problems that appear to have resisted solutions. Perhaps the fiction had simply become too personal.

Certainly, with the story "Cross-Country Snow," now the penultimate narrative in the book, Hemingway began to grapple with his own immediate dilemma, which had to do with his conflicted feelings after Hadley had announced her pregnancy only a few months before. Placing Nick Adams in the very same dilemma, reluctantly facing the loss of bohemian Europe at his pregnant wife's insistence, he now struggled to express an attitude or point of view on the vexing problem—vexing for him, at least—of finding a way to welcome a child into the world and then to balance the demands of that child's care with the freedoms that a modern artist and sociopolitical dissident required. It took him from late spring until late August to resolve the dilemma we find Nick pondering in "Cross-Country Snow"—and the result of this resolution was the surrealist masterpiece and denouement of the book, "Big Two-Hearted River," a fascinating meditation on the vocations of father and revolutionary.

☰ ☰ ☰

"Cross-Country Snow" is set in Chamby, the "cross-country" adjective referring both to the long mountain ski runs Nick and his friend George experience one beautiful, cold winter day and, it seems, to the international theme of the story—the necessity for both young men to cross borders into countries and states of mind they apparently do not find congenial. Specifically, a partly healed Nick is about to give up Paris and the Alps and Sion wine shared with buddies and steep climbs in funicular trains and the other benefits of Swiss expatriate life—utterly against his will—to take up fatherhood in the United States. For this reason he ponders, rather desperately, what it would mean to make art and resist injustice in more complacent and less liberating places than Paris and Chamby.

Hemingway cleverly conveys this reluctance of Nick's through his psychological denial. During a break for a snack in a rustic Swiss mountain café on an idyllic day, Nick fails to notice that a waitress is pregnant, even after she has made two visits to their table. He wonders why he is being so dense, then reveals to George that his own wife, Helen, is pregnant. As his denial of the waitress's condition hints, Nick is far from joyous about his news. He is upset. He feels he is about to lose this pleasant life—for how long, he seems not to know, for we are not told. Perhaps forever. Nick and George then discuss how Nick might adjust happily to life in the United States once his wife's pregnancy nears its term, once her medical needs close down his independent fun, and once the child's birth gives him consuming new responsibilities. "It's hell, isn't it?" George asks. Nick, who loves his wife and wants to love his unborn child, can only reply, "No. Not exactly."

Hemingway seems aware of how immature and self-involved this attitude really is, and he connects this self-centeredness with class conflict, as Swiss working men come into the cabin to have a glass of new wine and a piece of cake before they go back out into the cold to harness their horses for a few hours' more work. Nick and George are preoccupied with their discussion of their friendship's future, but one of them seems dimly to realize that these Swiss teamsters are models for a self-forgetting solidarity in a peace-loving culture. They embody something far more important than the feelings of privileged young expatriates letting go of their leisure pursuits. It is George who is dimly aware of such an idea as he gazes at the strong, contented working men and says, "I wish we were Swiss."[2] Nick, however, is far too deep in self-pity to respond, and the story ends with a final ski run after an agreement that, given the realities, they should make no promises to each other about renewing this Swiss life the two of them share.

Writing the sequel to this story, "Big Two-Hearted River," was equally difficult for Hemingway, probably because it was difficult for him to imagine a fulfilling future for Nick Adams in the United States, or anyplace where the bourgeois life was the norm and where smart, artistic friends were thin on the ground. Eventually Hemingway rode his wonderful talent to the ambiguous conclusion of "Big Two-Hearted River," in which Nick experiences an epiphany that allows him, perhaps, to welcome his pending fatherhood and get on with his vocation, which is certainly writing and, given autobiographical connections, might even be resistance writing.[3] To achieve this epiphany, Nick will have to enlist memories and dreams and mental imagery—undergoing the kind of dream state he had been learning about from his Freudian-Marxist friends in Paris.

"Big Two-Hearted River" is basically a fishing story recounting two days of Nick Adams's lone expedition along a river north of Seney,

Michigan. He appears to be on one last independent adventure before his child is born. It is a story so ambiguous and ambivalent that early readers thought there was no serious subtext, just a demonstration of how to fish skillfully for trout in Michigan's Upper Peninsula. As the story opens, Nick Adams jumps from a train car he has hitched. He gazes at some trout in a nearby stream, noting how fitted they are for this environment—a feeling he does not share with them, as Michigan feels alien to him now. He then hikes into the woods, takes a nap, and makes a camp. He fishes the next day in hot sun, making half a dozen exciting catches. He reassures himself that he has "many more days" to experiment with even more difficult catches. That, apart from some funny memories of fishing and camping with buddies in the woods when he was younger, is the content of the story.

But there are subtle marks of surrealist intent. Partway through "Big Two-Hearted River," Nick falls into a deep and prolonged daytime sleep. He has hiked far into the Michigan woods in search of a good fishing spot with a pleasant campsite, but exhausted from the long trip with a heavy pack, he delays finding the right campsite for this rest. He wakes belatedly to find that the air has cooled and the light is waning. He needs to hurry to set up that night's camp. From that moment on in the story, Nick enters a kind of dreamlike state. For the next few hours, past acquaintances appear in memories and the landing of trout has strange connotations suggesting deep emotional power and sexual meaning. Nick seems to be no longer in concrete Michigan trout-river country, but in a self-consoling reverie and mental search for meaning.

The story is widely understood as a revelation of Nick's damaged mental state. We know that Nick is both recovering from shell shock and bitterly upset to be back in Michigan because of his wife's pending childbirth, two factors that also affected Hemingway in 1923. Nick's thoughts and actions on the Big Two-Hearted River communicate his burden of anxiety and his need to find peace of mind, to enlist memories, ecstatic sensations, and hopes for an interesting near future—even as he sees nothing ahead of him but a life of bourgeois conformity. The stakes are high here. Nick knows that bourgeois normalcy, with its casual patriotism and bigotry and consumerism, tends to neglect questions of justice or interesting new theories of social organization. Nick does not see what he will have to live for.

The next day, Nick catches a series of fish, small and large, including one Freudian dream-fish that he pulls from a hollow log into daylight, like a child emerging from the birth canal, the line "pumping"—a word that, with the hollow log imagery, suggests either contractions or some memory of the ecstatic sexual release that engendered this emblematic birth. He gazes in wonder at this fish and another in a sack hanging from him like a belly, "two big trout alive in the water."[4] Recognizing the beauty of these squirming, living fish—powerful correlatives to his unborn child, and examples of life over against the wartime deaths that haunt him—Nick may have begun to find a route to peace of mind.[5] Catching the fish with the "pumping" line and then carrying it in a sack hanging from his belly, his unborn son becomes suddenly real to him. It is as though *he* carries the child now, rather than Helen, as though imagination has suddenly allowed him to enter his wife's mind. Finally realizing the miracle of this impending birth, he may be able to wake from the nightmare life that began when he said goodbye to his friend George in a Chamby ski hut. He may be able to begin a phase of his life after expatriate adventure. Perhaps he realizes that if proper solidarity in dissidence is a service to a broken world, then so is proper love in fatherhood—or that love of family can be the origin of love of community or class.

Now we understand the title of the story: What is big and two-hearted? A pregnant woman. Or a man who does not know which of two lives he really wants to live.

"Big Two-Hearted River" is an elegant, beautifully modern, and complex story about the possibilities of nonerotic love—a force Hemingway's surrealist friends believed had powers that reached beyond the bourgeois family. There was a chance that widespread nonerotic love could heal an entire society—feeding the hungry and housing the cold and giving hope to the depressed—even a society that had recently gone to war.

≡ ≡ ≡

In the early fall of 1924 Hemingway had this fine story under his belt, to his huge relief. But he still sought a New York publishing contract, and if he were to conclude a credible book with this haunting narrative, he had to consider a proper arrangement for all of the stories. It was a daunting task. After all, some of the titled stories involved Nick, while others merely echoed his problems in the experiences of other characters. These disparate stories had to be blended somehow, and interspersed among those prose poems. Nick Adams's maturation stories took up more than half of the book Hemingway imagined, and Nick's epiphany needed to be the denouement. Furthermore, Hemingway knew he would have to fill out the book with nearly every single piece he had written during the previous two years, yet without offering readers another ad hoc collection like those he had published in Paris. There would be no *Three Stories and Ten Poems* this time, no tacit admission that he was simply putting out what little writing he happened to have in hand.

He knew he needed to diagnose the deeper meanings in his own stories—including meanings that were not necessarily known to him as he wrote them. This was another lesson he was learning from writers among his new surrealist friends, who loved to engage in automatic writing—the acceptance as right and true whatever one wrote in a spontaneous, unedited session. The moderns believed that the subconscious was always at work, especially in the artistic life. It was inevitable, and in fact entirely desirable, that art would reflect subconscious desires, so it was unnecessary—indeed, harmful—to plan one's art before making it. Much better to let the subconscious lead to spontaneous expressions of unrepressed liberty and refreshment.

Hemingway knew that these new stories were mysterious and dreamlike enough to draw readers into serious reflection, and then maybe into the new perceptions that Freud and Marx wrote about: their dreams of healthier lives through desperately needed psychological and material changes. He knew there were meanings in the stories' echoes and resonances with each other, meanings that emerged from his own subconscious life so that even he might not recognize them yet. He realized, in other words, that the arrangement of the stories was part of his artistic task, and he knew he needed smart models for this.

Once again, it was through friendship and artistic conversation, this time among fellow Americans who were experimenting with post-dadaist and surrealist methods, that he found a valid and expressive form for his first American book. It was not quite Masson's collage, this form, nor Anderson's and Joyce's use of cityscape and neighborhood talk as an organizing principle. Hemingway saw that his interests in war, crime, bourgeois habit, class conflict, sexual love, nonerotic love, and friendship—even his fascination with bullfighting—might be collated into a literary arrangement capable of producing new meanings.

So he turned to Dos Passos, who, like Breton, Aragon, and other dadaists, was briefly fascinated with the prankster movement and then more seriously involved with the Russian model of communism and its implications for literature. Dos Passos loved the surprising and unscripted effects of collages, which he developed in *Manhattan Transfer* (1925) and perfected in his 1930s books, the *U.S.A.* trilogy. Each of these books included gatherings of selected quotations from political speeches, newspaper articles, and popular songs from a certain span of months, along with longer stories illustrating workers' lives and injustices perpetrated upon them. For example, there is this collation of headlines and popular music lyrics from his 1932 novel, *1919*:

*Newsreel XXVII*
HER WOUNDED HERO OF WAR A FRAUD
SAYS WIFE IN SUIT

Mid the wars great coise
Stands the red cross noise
She's the rose of no man's land

according to the thousands who had assembled to see the launching and were eyewitnesses of the disaster the scaffolding simply seemed to turn over like a gigantic turtle precipitating its occupants into twentyfive feet of water. This was exactly four minutes before the launching was scheduled

*Oh that battle of Paree*
*It's making a bum out of me*

BRITISH BEGIN OPERATION ON AFGHAN FRONTIER[6]

Whatever else this collection of songs and headlines and news story fragments means, it surely conveys the popular flippancy about war (the "battle of Paree") and colonialism ("AFGHAN FRONTIER"), and it reminds us that not all wounded veterans and Red Cross nurses ("noises") were as noble and respected as Victorian patriots then said they were.

In another stroke of good luck attached to an ambivalent experience, in that spring of 1924 Hemingway began, a bit reluctantly, to edit a little magazine. He was seeking a stronger network of supportive friends, but his luck was better than he could have imagined. As co-editor of the little magazine *the transatlantic review*, Hemingway published Dos Passos's fiction regularly that year, the time when Dos (as Hemingway called his friend) was writing the simpler collages of *Manhattan Transfer*, which interpolated song lyrics with descriptions of urban street life. Reading Dos Passos's dadaist fiction, Hemingway saw that he could exploit a similar interpolation of his prose poems and titled stories. Yet he could not merely become Dos's imitator. Already reviewers saw too much of Stein and Pound in his writing, and he hated that. He was going to need to develop his own collage form.

One day, Hemingway saw that one of his vignettes, the odd one out that concerned Nick's wounding on an urban Italian battlefield, might become the hinge or pivot on which the entire book turned. It made sense: the vignette depicted a young expatriate artist like himself, threatened by death in an absurd war. He was not sure why he had demoted Nick's wounding to a vignette in the first place, when all of the young man's other experiences occurred in titled stories. Probably it was because the wounding was so disturbing and profound for him, a strange echo of his own wounding in an Italian trench, and therefore difficult to express except fragmentally.

The vignette opens with concrete descriptions in an unemotional tone: "Nick sat against the wall of the church where they had dragged him to be clear of the machine-gun fire in the street. Both legs stuck out awkwardly. He had been hit in the spine." Heightening the strangeness of Nick's wounding—possibly his permanent paralysis or even his bleeding out and dying—Hemingway writes a series of brief, staccato sentences, some seeming absolutely out of place in such danger and distress: "His face was sweaty and dirty. The sun shone on his face. The day was very hot." Nick then shows a funny kind of courage by joking with another wounded comrade, an Italian named Rinaldi. "You and me we've made a separate peace," he jokes, using the phrase then describing the Bolsheviks' new withdrawal from the war. Rinaldi is not amused.

Closing out the vignette, Nick thinks to himself that "Rinaldi was a disappointing audience."

But just before that deflating line, Hemingway makes some pregnant suggestions. First, he offers emblems of the kinds of things young men like Nick lose when they fight for the values of empire: "The pink wall of the house opposite had fallen out from the roof, and an iron bedstead hung twisted toward the street." With this reference to a broken house and twisted bed, Nick acknowledges dimly that with his spinal injury he may have permanently lost these things: a home with his own family, and a sexual life with a chosen partner. Then Nick makes his joke about the separate peace, which may be Hemingway's hint that there are alternatives, sometimes revolutionary ones, to giving up your body for the nation-state.

To Hemingway, the arrangement of the total book now seemed settled. The five vignettes leading up to that moment would convey the international world at war, including the two Mons vignettes we have studied. There would also be a portrait of the field kitchen he had worked at while a Red Cross volunteer, and a picture of the shooting of Greek cabinet ministers held responsible for their nation's losses in 1922 Anatolia. Interpolated between these vignettes, the titled stories leading up to Chapter VI would offer an ongoing and startling contrast—that is, Nick's ordinary and necessary existential learning as a boy enjoying summers in the Michigan woods. He would see the miracle of life and the tragedy of death; he would learn how difficult it was to feel love authentically and to choose a real life partner; he would encounter poverty and homelessness and unusual love alongside Upper Peninsula rails. Nick's wounding would be the collision of these two worlds, the values of war and the values of natural maturation in tension, if not in open battle.

The key was the Chapter VI vignette about Nick's wounding. There the innocent American world of Nick's childhood merged with the violence of balkanized Europe, just as 1917 had seen green American troops merge with the exhausted French and English and colonial troops already in their trenches. This merger of American patriotism with European imperialism cost many lives, and nearly costs Nick his too, as he lies paralyzed in an Italian street. The vignette offers a chilling scene about what happens to cannon fodder—including smart, brave boys.

The second half of the book would take up the problems of continued maturation in a broken postwar world, using both Nick and a series of other, less astute characters as models. Hemingway saw that he could address the problem of modernity, which included knowing how to arrange a new personal life amid the swirl of modern psychological, political, and artistic theories, knowing what to work toward, and knowing what to resist or fight against. Nick, it turns out, makes many of Hemingway's choices, as we learn from "Cross-Country Snow." He moves to Europe and adopts the expatriate lifestyle, rejecting bourgeois America. If his foils in the book, other young veterans and would-be artists trying to keep loving relationships alive, are any indication of his mind—and they are—then the wounds he suffers seem to be changing Nick's political consciousness too. He no longer sees America as the essential realm of personal liberty, or the bourgeois American home as the be-all and end-all. He prefers the ways of the Swiss, with their dedication to peace, their social welfare schemes, and their worker solidarity.

The latter half of the book allows Hemingway to contrast Nick's seemingly wise choices with other models of European expatriate and postwar life. While in the titled stories, characters such as Krebs (that young veteran just home from war in "Soldier's Home") struggle with pious American parents, others, such as those named in the title "Mr. and Mrs. Elliot," struggle with questions of sexual identity and marriage, as Mrs. Elliot comes to realize she is gay. A young woman modeled after Hadley, also unhappy in a European hotel, longs for a bourgeois home in "Cat in the Rain," and a kid loses a dad who, out of love for this son, becomes a corrupt horse owner and jockey in France in "My Old Man." Meanwhile, vignettes about crime-fighting, capital punishment, and bullfighting suggest the cultural rituals that might either threaten or, more happily, lend meaning to these expatriates' lives. Bullfighting especially meant to Hemingway a world of courage and death redeemed by Catholic ritual. A final vignette about a reporter's chat with the deposed king of Greece titled "L'Envoi"—a poetic convention of adding a stanza to a poem to make a special comment—closes out the book by suggesting that all European refugees—those hungry, shocked, broken victims of balkanization—want to move, for better or worse, to America. "Like all Greeks," Hemingway writes, "[the deposed king] wanted to go to America."[7]

There would be no easy or definite interpretation for this moment, so that the book would close out with suggested questions: What is America, really? Why do people wish to live there? Why do others refuse to live there? Can Americans learn to tolerate new political commitments and sexual identities? How are Americans shaped by the immigrants and expatriates who come to the country's shores or the indigenous people who have been there for millennia? Is America destined to become as balkanized—and as violent—along ethnic lines as Europe had recently become? Is there another European and American war in the offing? Is there any way for young people to resist such a war or the values tending toward it? These are questions Hemingway's artistic friends were helping him confront and that he wished to raise in this important modernist book making its prayer for peace in our time.[8]

≡ ≡ ≡

For better or worse, Hemingway was about to turn away from these questions about the modern arts to more immediately personal ones. Like Quoc, he was about to be tempted away from Paris. Mr. Liveright's offer in December of 1924 to publish this new collage-novel titled *In Our Time* would reignite his wish for fame and profit. His new conception of himself as an internationally significant writer rather than as a Parisian progressive would have its costs—his happy marriage with Hadley being one of them. Less tragically, his friendships with the surrealists Miró and Masson would also erode. Hemingway's process of leave-taking from Paris would take much longer than Quoc's, but its unfortunate effect would be the same: Hemingway, too, would have to hoard memories of the Parisian hopes for peace, equity, solidarity, psychological health, occasional bliss, lively imagination, and resulting new patterns for coherent lives. He would have to keep Paris's lessons fresh and relevant as, like Nick Adams, he traveled far away from the city's lights to American shores.

# 18

## FRENCH COLONIALISM ON TRIAL

### QUOC IN 1925

I
n 1925 the black singer, dancer, and comedienne Josephine Baker
was all the rage in Paris. One reason for her popularity among the
French, apart from her bared breasts and tiny skirt ringed with whole
yellow bananas, was her charming performance of a little ditty titled "*La
Petite Tonkinoise*," or "The Little Girl from Northern Vietnam." The tune
became Baker's signature. Singing it, she took the role of the *petite Tonkinoise*, who sings like a little bird and enjoys it when her man—clearly
a Caucasian Frenchman—calls her his "little bourgeoisie." The word
"bourgeoisie" does not here indicate the Vietnamese girl's middle-class
status. It refers instead to her role as his housemate, with all that must
entail when a nonwhite colonial girl with no social power shares a home
with a colonizing white man. Apparently Parisians regarded such sexual
exploitation of the Vietnamese as entertaining. Baker's song helps that
medicine go down when the Vietnamese girl confesses that she is in
love with her sweet Frenchman. That affection between colonizer and
colonized could blossom, surely, but most Parisians probably found it
amusing, the idea of a silly Annamite girl believing she might unite in
loving partnership with a sophisticated and civilized Frenchman. The
poster advertising Baker's performance at the Folies Bergère depicts her
with squinting eyes and, for her performances as a Tonkinese rather than
African fantasy, an apparently traditional Asian beehive coif. She looks

more like a cinema vamp than a twittering bird, which was in keeping with the meaning of the naughty song. Annamite men were put to menial work in Paris, and Annamite women were taken to bed.

A black talent reinforcing French prejudices about the sexually exploited Vietnamese—something morally pregnant was happening in Paris that year, something Quoc and Hemingway might have been able to witness and turn to artistic provocation. But they were on to other things already. It was just about to begin: the difficult career each would soon take on; the continual, unpleasant interplay they had to endure between their political and artistic vocations—their Parisian wish to make the world a better place—and the personal frustrations and successes that would diminish their hopefulness and their investments in social change. By the 1930s, both would feel thwarted in their wish to improve the lives of others. It is not for this study to say, but it is possible that both also became less kind and less answerable to conscience over time, less idealistic than they had been in Paris.

For Quoc and Hemingway, things were about to get serious. The Paris of peaceable resistance to oligarchy, profiteering, bigotry, domination, and needless warring was growing less important to them. They were considering leaving Paris, physically or emotionally or both, to pursue more ruthlessly focused projects. Quoc's attention had turned to the east, toward Indochina and its mounting anti-colonial resistance movement, while Hemingway's attention had turned to the west, toward New York and its busy publishing houses, which had access to tens of thousands more English-language readers than Paris's boutique presses did.

Yet in 1925 they were still Hemingway and Ho Chi Minh in Paris—for a short time to come, anyway. That year, both distracted writer-dissidents celebrated their learning in Paris by publishing books they had recently struggled to finish to their satisfaction, and they published those books to Parisian audiences and vanguard tastes. Significantly, both books employ modernist-surrealist methods to make passionate calls for peace and social equity. Both books show us that Quoc and Hemingway had learned a very real and very sophisticated craft in Paris. The one thing both men learned there, and it was an art they would never abandon, was how to produce gripping writing peppered with intentional provocations, in service of human dignity and equity. To become such writers, they had had to learn and improve quickly. Quoc came to Paris a

semi-articulate immigrant with almost no writing experience after high
school, and Hemingway came with a bundle of manuscripts focusing on
sarcastic remarks about sports and gambling and ethnic groups. Both
would be internationally known artists before they left Paris, revealers
of the economic and political problems causing suffering in a deadly
modern world. In 1925, both of them still worked hard on their Parisian
vocations, singing songs more enlightening than *"La Petite Tonkinoise."*

≡ ≡ ≡

Quoc's *Le procès de la colonisation francaise* (*French Colonialism on Trial*),
published in 1925 or 1926, and Hemingway's *In Our Time* both appeal
to readers' consciences through vignettes—those carefully selected and
crafted specimens of violence and oppression rendered in precise, startling, and demotic prose. Both Quoc and Hemingway respected their
readers and met the challenges of addressing them. They knew they had
to bring conventional French and American patriots around to a renewed
respect for compassionate conscience, the kind of caring inner life these
people might have learned about in church or during school civics lessons. This compassion was the obverse of the violent, heretical holy-war
theology the French, Americans, and others had been bathed in since at
least 1914, when all the empires of Europe, and the United States too,
claimed to be on God's side in a crusade against evil. Quoc knew he had
an additional audience to address: the mostly homesick Annamite men
who worked in their truck garages and restaurant kitchens and photo
retouching studios by day and gathered together in mutual aid societies in the evening to help each other survive Paris. Building solidarity
and renewing a love of Vietnam among such men, and among the few
Annamite women who also lived in France, was vitally important to
Quoc. In *French Colonialism on Trial*, he addressed both audiences with
shocking, modern outrages committed in that warm, beautiful, green
country of his.

Most of Quoc's daily activities during 1925, as opposed to the central
acts of his vocation, occurred in Canton, China, where he had moved
the year before. It was an eventful year for him, as he organized a revolutionary youth league, published a weekly journal titled after the league,
and married Tang Tuyet Minh, a Chinese midwife and student. Like

Hemingway's marriages, beginning with his marriage to Hadley, this one would not last long. Quoc told comrades he wanted to marry a Chinese woman to help him with the local language and to take care of his house-keeping needs—rather practical, if coldhearted, reasons. It seems Quoc reserved his passion mainly for his revolutionary work, so throughout his adulthood women came into his life and left shortly after—taking his children with them, when there were children. A friend found Tuyet Minh for him. She was a young Catholic daughter of a Chinese mer-chant's third concubine, and she became homeless when her father died. Quoc refused to honor Chinese custom by paying a dowry for a wife, so Tuyet Minh's dire financial situation suited him. During their time together, Quoc tried to teach his Chinese wife core Leninist doctrines, but she lacked interest in such things. Failing to interest her in his life's work, Quoc gave up on both the teaching and the marriage. Some reports claim that this marriage produced a daughter, but that is uncertain.[1]

As this marriage commenced in 1925, Quoc worked in the Comin-tern offices writing brief articles and preparing reports on the situation in Vietnam, basing his writings on intelligence he must have learned from informers and *émigrés*, some of them back in Paris. The work was tedious and he must have longed for the active ferment of Paris.

Then Quoc made a significant literary and anti-colonial splash in the City of Light that he could not witness. He finally published his study of French colonialism, a new version of the book Sarraut's nefari-ous agents, Désiré and the rest, had stolen from his desk in 1922. *Le procès de la colonisation francaise* was published in Paris by the Librairie du Travail (Workers Library), and there the book found its first audi-ence. How large an audience, or how enthusiastic, we do not know. Even calling the work a book is actually a bit generous, just as it was generous to call *Three Stories and Ten Poems* or *in our time* genuine books. One scholar, Sophie Quinn-Judge, who saw the typescript of *French Colonial-ism on Trial* in the Comintern archives before it was finally published in English in the early 1990s, called the manuscript a brochure. She describes the text of *Le procès* this way: "It included a brief section on Vietnam's history and geography, as well as chapters on the confiscation of Vietnamese land by the unscrupulous French administration." The book does much more, as we will see, but Quinn-Judge is correct about the manuscript's odd brevity. Quoc's strenuous daily researches in the

Bibliothèque Sainte-Geneviève in 1922 would seem to have led to a long, detailed tome. We might wonder where all that scholarship on French colonial policies went, and all those examples of racist outrages and dubious military actions that Quoc collected during his first year in Paris.

The answer is that Quoc had learned in Paris to write like a modernist artist rather than a traditional realist historian. His "brochure," which eschews legal and political arguments and detached descriptions of misdeeds in favor of emotionally charged provocations, is actually a compact, hard-hitting book and a clear sign of Quoc's modernist learning in Paris. Like Hemingway, Quoc now practiced compression in his writing, and tried to involve his readers through psychologically realistic situations and documented absurdities and outrages. Both Hemingway and Quoc had learned that explaining ideas to readers or embodying ideas in unrealistically emblematic characters, as Victorian writers tended to do, was simply a far weaker strategy than presenting brief and challenging images, pictures of behavior arising from complex and sometimes contradictory ideas. Because the artist was committed to a deep honesty, these might be either the corrupt ideas of the Victorian world or the more hopeful and revolutionary ideas of modernism. In either case, it was important to convey personal history as it actually occurred, even if personal history failed to illustrate perfectly prized doctrines or noble behavior. As he composed *Le procès de la colonisation francaise*, Quoc also knew that his largely illiterate audience of Vietnamese workers would likely need to listen to this book rather than read it. Therefore, the book had to be brief, it had to be vivid, and it had to be emotionally charged.

Quoc also apparently believed that the book needed to offer no noticeable ideology accompanying the shocking scenes. There is no mention of Leninist doctrines as the outrages unfold (apart from a brief coda), and no promotion of an inevitable history in which the working class would flip the current power structure, gaining the powers then concentrated with the wealthy and their political friends. And then there is the reason for selecting the outrages. The appeal is mainly to moral conscience, not to Marxist doctrine, so the outrages seem to address a Confucian sense of compassion much more than Leninist doctrines predicting that workers will rise up as a revolutionary class.

Now that we have access to *Le procès de la colonisation francaise*, we can see that indeed the marks of modernist Paris are all over the book.

And it *is* a book; if *Procès* is a brochure, then so is Hemingway's *In Our Time*. In truth, the book reads like the editorial pages of a little magazine—in the sense that it is brash, unrepressed, inelegant, circuitous, sarcastic, single-minded, and often openly insulting. Though the book opens with the ploy that Quoc is putting French colonists on trial for crimes—calling certain criminal French people to account before "the Tribunal of History"—that approach quickly breaks down.[2] In his erratic, disorganized, poorly proofread way, Quoc simply documents outrages he has heard from his fellow *indigènes*. Such stories take up all but the final pages of the book, which is where Quoc finally declares his political allegiance in the clearest terms we will witness during his Paris years.

If we require a usefully brash, unrepressed, and politically committed passage from a standard modernist little magazine for comparison with Quoc's writing in 1925 to confirm that his prose is definitely modernist in the Parisian mold, we can turn to Hemingway himself. He provides a usefully unrepressed little magazine passage that shows the kinship. In October of 1924 in a famous editorial for *the transatlantic review* on the relative merits of T. S. Eliot and the recently deceased Joseph Conrad, Hemingway writes, "If I knew that by grinding Mr. Eliot into a fine dry powder and sprinkling that powder over Mr. Conrad's grave Mr. Conrad would shortly appear . . . I would leave for London early tomorrow morning with a sausage grinder."[3] Eliot was supposed to be Hemingway's friend, so this is just one of many vicious put-downs of rival writers he wrote during his career, an acid remark arising from his sometimes fragile personality. But it is also characteristic of little-magazine rhetoric—which is to say, the rhetoric of Lost Generation Paris. It is purposely immediate, uninhibited, unedited, sarcastic—mean, even—and verging on surreal. It violates good manners and risks childishness to make an impact. It is language no Victorian would ever use.

Quoc employs similar shocking sarcasm and bitter irony in his *Procès* when on his very first page he describes the benefits of French civilization: "This is true," he writes. "French colonialism brings us the railroad, the electric trolley, radio (not counting the Gospel and the Declaration of the Rights of Man); only, the question is, who forks over to pay for these marvels?" He answers his question with another question, clearly rhetorical: "Is it the blacks of Sudan and the yellow of Annam, or the conquistadors with pink faces, who steal their lands and their herds, and who steal the fruit of their work, after having massacred their countrymen?" In calling all European imperialists conquistadors and mass murderers he associates the ordinary colonizer with the most brutal and sanctimonious of historical examples, and he does not spare the sarcasm.

In these two examples we see that Paris had given Quoc and Hemingway remarkably similar interests and writing tasks. Hemingway went over the top rhetorically in defense of Conrad and his modernist fiction about a suffering colonized world. Hemingway loved novels such as *Lord Jim*, with its tale of a guilty sailor expiating his sins by living among and even marrying into a South Seas tribe, or *The Heart of Darkness*, with its alarming portrait of a megalomaniac European coming to dominate a group of Africans far from any white civilization. Because he has a point to make about Conrad, Hemingway seems not to give a damn about Eliot's feelings. In *Procès*, Quoc goes over the top in a similar way to show the suffering colonials themselves that he knows their plight and wishes to remedy it, and he does not give a damn about the ordinary French patriot's sense of his nation's greatness. In the end, neither Quoc nor Hemingway can avert his eyes from suffering in the colonized world, so both of them repress good manners and tell it like it is.

*Procès* is a cumulative nightmare of atrocity stories. It is also a sly juxtaposition of French colonial rhetoric—the French "big words," Hemingway might call them—and horrors perpetrated in the colonies of Sudan, Syria, Morocco, Martinique, and, mainly, Annam. The surrealist effect is truly unsettling. Quoc catalogs case after case of horrifying maltreatment of colonized people. At first he documents the relatively mild issues of forced labor, heavy taxation without representation (six Annamese in the governing council, he shows us, always losing contested votes to the eighteen ethnic French also present), forced purchasing of French alcohol by all Annamites regardless of their age, and legal sales of opium pushed upon the *indigènes* until French government quotas are met.

Soon, however, he moves to describing rapes, beatings, and casual shootings, among other horrors. There are the Moroccan women who were stripped naked and paraded through a village in order to coerce their men to surrender for compulsory military service. "A woman who carried her baby on the back," Quoc writes, "had to beg permission to have a free hand to keep her child balanced. Two old people dropped from starvation on the run; the young girls, terrorized by such cruelties, had their period for the first time; a pregnant woman gave premature birth to a stillborn child, and another gave birth to a blind child." There is the cinema owner beating pedestrians bloody to keep the doors of his Saigon movie house clear for the use of more valued white patrons. There are the routine shootings of native people, sometimes because they fled arrest for possible malingering or smuggling, sometimes because they happened to be in the way of French shipping or leisure travel, sometimes because they were unfortunate enough to stand along the shore as Frenchmen sailed by with weapons in their hands and decided it would be fun to see which of them could "knock over" the most Annamites in ten shots.[4]

Such murderous cruelty is horrible enough, but perhaps the most surreal of Quoc's passages appears in a chapter titled "Clericalism." The chapter is a description of crimes committed by French missionary clergy. In an earlier chapter, Quoc has already described one appalling missionary ("ah, yes! A sweet apostle") who, suspecting that a native Christian seminary student had stolen a small sum of money from him, tied up the student, suspended him from a frame, and beat him senseless. Quoc accuses this missionary priest-professor of repeating these beatings until the student was nearly dead. "Perhaps he is dead today," Quoc conjectures.[5] Later he describes further incongruous acts on the part of clergy. He tells of heavily armed priests on search-and-destroy missions in rebellious Annamite areas, or other priests burning a village for its failure to pay its "taxes," which must mean obligatory church offerings, to the local parish. "Another," Quoc writes, "has sold a native catholic [sic] girl to a European for 300 francs." As usual, Quoc does not spare the sarcasm:

> If paradise existed, it would really be too confined to accommodate all these brave colonial apostles; and if the unfortunate Christ crucified had returned to this world, he would be disgusted to see the manner in which his "faithful servants" observe the holy poverty: The catholic [sic] mission in Siam owns 1/3rd [sic] of the cultivatable land of the country. That of Cochinchina, 1/5th [sic]. That of Tonkin 1/4, only in Hanoi, plus a small fortune of close to 10 million francs.

None of this wealth was rightfully earned, writes Quoc: "It is useless to say that the largest part of these goods are acquired by unknowledgeable and unavowed means." Later he uses a biblical metaphor to argue that "the annamite [*sic*] peasant is crucified by the bayonet of capitalist civilization and by the cross of prostituted Christianity."[6]

Quoc portrays French government officials as equally iniquitous. His old enemy Sarraut makes more than one appearance in *Procès*, usually playing the role of Quoc's voice of hypocrisy, the preacher of hollow French idealism. Quoc refers to Sarraut as the "little father of the natives (according to what he says), [who] adored the Annamites and was adored by them." But then Quoc deconstructs Sarraut's self-declared reputation, quoting the Minister of Colonies in an actual letter to colonial administrators, urging them to impose alcohol and opium quotas on Annamite villages. This work, he declares, is "for the greatest good of the interests of the Treasury"—but it is not, we recognize with Quoc, for the greatest good of the Vietnamese people. Such policies can only lead to addictions, suffering, crime, and other rips and tears in the social fabric. Pushing his ironies further, Quoc expresses his sarcastic hope that Sarraut will have a very long life—a sarcastic wish because it was clearly not kindly meant. Because Sarraut's letter reveals that he is quite literally an opium pusher—a vocation that is strangely legal in Indochina, where the locals must purchase opium by quotas, but absolutely illegal in France—he has earned a prison sentence, according to French home law, of "at least *one million three hundred fifty thousand* (1,350,000) months in prison *each year*, because every year he sells to the Annamites more than *one hundred fifty thousand* kilos of opium."[7] Quoc's promiscuous use of italics indicates his anger and agitation.

Much of *Procès* is undocumented, and some of it—such as the Moroccan woman giving birth to a blind child after French torture—is hard to accept as true. (The torture is easy to accept, but not the blind infant as its result.) However, Quoc does occasionally try to prop up his veracity by claiming to quote from French sources. One such source is the travel diary of a colonial soldier, clearly white, who tells an appalling tale about Vietnamese boat merchants. Tourists in Vietnam today are often taken to such floating markets on the Mekong River or its tributaries; it is an opportunity to buy fresh fruit or even a can of soda in an incredibly exotic and scenic locale. Apparently, such markets were active in the early twentieth century too, because Quoc reports that white soldiers, including the one he cites, enjoyed buying from water-going junks selling fruit and shellfish, small household items such as "pipe stems, pant buttons," and even "butts of cigarettes." Sadly, whenever soldiers felt they may have been cheated in these transactions, Quoc notes, they taught lessons in "commercial honesty to the natives."

These were appallingly harsh lessons. Quoc allows the colonial soldier to tell one such story of lesson-giving in his own voice, with its own moral inflection: "At other times, funny story, some drivers throw a bucket of boiling water on the spines of the unfortunates." The soldier continues:

> Just below me an Annamite, BURNED FROM HEAD TO FOOT, absolutely mad, wants to throw himself into the sea. His brother, oblivious of the danger, drops the oar, grabs him, and forces him to spread out on the floor of the sampan. The struggle, which did not last two seconds, is just over when another bucket of water, with a sure hand, SCALDS THE SAVIOR IN HIS TURN. I saw him rolling in his boat, his flesh bright, with cries not at all human! And this makes us laugh, this seems extremely funny to us. WE ALREADY HAVE THE COLONIAL SOUL.[8]

"Funny story." It is sometimes difficult to tell whether Quoc's French is up to the task of telling these stories accurately or, indeed, whether he is simply writing fictional hyperbole.[9] Certainly this is one tale that confuses us with its moral point of view: Does the soldier regret or celebrate these despicable acts and attitudes? Is he confessing the warped "COLONIAL SOUL" he has attained to his shame, or is he merely telling a "funny story"? Quoc's carelessness keeps us from answering these questions.

Yet Quoc is sometimes entirely believable. For example, he presents a typical interview protocol for French immigration officials to use with Annamites seeking entry to France. The questions reveal France's ingrained attitudes of white, Western superiority:

A—Your wife and children, do they speak French?

B—Do they dress like a European?

C—Do you have furniture at your house?

D—And chairs?

E—Do you eat at the table or on the mat?

F—What do you eat?

G—Do you eat rice or bread?

Real French people eat bread, not rice, it seems, and the choice has moral implications. The list of questions is longer yet. Item K asks for "Your religion?" which prompts Quoc to wonder, in sarcastic prose, whether these "nosy imbeciles" will take their questions an ill-mannered step further: "A little more, and these gentlemen will ask if our wife made [love] to us?"[10]

In his final two chapters, which he titles "The Russian Revolution and the Colonial People" and "Proletarians and Peasants of the Colonies," Quoc finally gives Lenin his due, which is to say he lays out more of Lenin's doctrines than just that central insight—central to Quoc—that there ought to be colonial involvement in revolution. In these chapters, Quoc suggests that the Russian Revolution taught the world an important lesson, which is that it is a waste of time to "make nice platonic speeches and to vote humanitarian motions in favor of oppressed people." (So much for the "Demands of the Annamite Patriots.") Lenin's revolution "teaches them to fight."[11]

This is one of Quoc's more literate and seemingly sincere passages in this untamed and often ungrammatical book. The pressing question it raises, though, is what Quoc means by "fight." Lenin was perfectly clear about his own willingness to use brutal, bloody mass violence. It may be, then, that Quoc's celebration of Lenin's call to fight implies his support of weapons in the hands of Vietnamese workers and blood in the streets. But before we arrive at such a conclusion, we should consult Quoc's own life in Paris. He had just spent his entire three years in the city making such Platonic speeches and voting for such humanitarian motions, first as a French Socialist and then as a nonviolent French Communist. Indeed, he had been a humanitarian to his Parisian end, writing provocative anti-colonial stories and working to create and maintain his colonial workers' aid society.

As if to demonstrate where his own heart was in this question of violent and nonviolent methods, he then describes the important work of his Communist University of the Toilers of the East, work he describes in remarkably Platonic and humanitarian terms. He describes the school, now his alma mater, in words that sound much like a modern-day admissions brochure. He lists the current enrollment of 1,025, "of which 151 are young girls" and (only) 895 are communists, a conspicuous suggestion that freedom of conscience and both gender and intellectual diversity were elements in the university's work. He promotes the courses in "social science, mathematics, historical materialism, the history of the workers [sic] movement, natural science, the history of revolutions, political economies, etc.," a weird brew of liberal arts disciplines and courses in Leninist indoctrination. Quoc also offers peasants interested in enrolling access to "a movie house," which is open two days a week, two libraries containing forty-seven thousand volumes, and lecture halls full of "daily papers and magazines." There is an on-campus journal to write for, free medical care, "vacation colonies" with nine houses, and a campus farm with thirty cows and fifty pigs.

Clearly, Quoc does not steel students for a boot camp or for bloody revolution in this passage. Rather, he entices them with the things he had in Paris—access to a wide variety of readings, support for learning, enough fresh food to eat, an attitude of a healthy mind in a healthy body, and the peace required for study. (Of course, Toilers U was about to become known as the Stalin School, so Quoc was lucky to have left it just before its spirit was probably about to change sharply.) As for the remark about the futility of "humanitarian motions," within a year we will see Quoc make just such a motion or plea to the people of Paris in full sincerity. There are still signs in 1925, and there will be for some time after, that Paris has not been displaced in Quoc's mind by Moscow or Canton. Paris's peaceably provocative modernist values, and even its Enlightenment constitutional and religious idealism, lived on in him still.

Publishing *Procès* in Paris, Quoc was not just mopping up unfinished business from his socialist days so he could get on with the planning for revolutionary war. He was still largely committed to his Parisian mission, his urgent appeal to individual consciences rather than chilling warnings to the doomed aristocracy and bourgeoisie that they were about to be swept away by inevitable revolutionary processes. Quoc had yet one more Parisian plea to make, one that would show how perfectly content he was to see France existing as a robust capitalist trading state within its current representative democratic form of government—if only Quoc's country might gain its independence. This plea also reveals his willingness to see Vietnam in a negotiated trade relationship with France—if only he could one day see his country governed by the Vietnamese themselves. If Quoc showed willingness to be a Leninist in 1925, then he would also show a willingness to be a capitalist in 1926, so long as Vietnam gained its freedom. And he would address this wish to Parisians.

# 19

## BUYING *THE FARM*

### HEMINGWAY IN 1925

That same year of 1925, Ernest Hemingway sent his own clear signals about his political commitments, which also involved a strong interest in the anarchic arts of political unsettling. He sent this signal when he bought *The Farm*, a Joan Miró oil painting in the artist's early surrealist style, a canvas depicting in bold colors a strange catalog of objects to be found on an early twentieth-century Spanish farm. This purchase was far more than a matter of liking the artist's style or aesthetic, the striking colors or the rural Spanish theme or the very modern abstraction. (We have to remember how new and startling abstraction and expressivism were in the 1920s.) It was a chance for Hemingway to show his kind, politically minded, anarchic, gregarious surrealist friends that he took their work seriously. He already owned Masson paintings in a surrealist mode, and he wrote extraordinary compliments about his friend André's work in *the transatlantic review*. Now Hemingway made a purchase at the very margins of his and Hadley's personal budget to show just how much he admired the surrealist mission—perhaps even to signal that he practiced surrealist methods himself—and to secure for himself a symbol of his admiration and of their mission that he could display and ponder his whole life long.[1]

The farm Miró depicted in the painting was a special one, the one he grew up on in Mont-roig del Camp, near Barcelona and the

Mediterranean coast. The depicted objects include a stone house-barn and a cutaway of another outbuilding filled with tools—the outline of its walls traced in a bold red line so that viewers can see through them, in effect—all displayed against a background of tilled and planted fields and gardens. All of these objects are gathered together beneath the wiry branches of a scraggly but geometrically stylized tree in the center of the canvas. There is a cartoonish quality to these objects in unmixed bold colors (though it would be an adult's cartoon) and a hyper-regular pattern to the tilled earth, like the vegetables in a Grant Wood garden. An intensely blue sky dominates the top half of the canvas, while a rich rust-brown earth occupies the lower half. The two yellow-white stone buildings interrupt the border between these two fields of contrasting color with complementary glowing rectangles—large, bright, flat patches of buff buildings set against the deep blue sky and the rust-colored field.[2]

*The Farm* is a loving picture of a childhood home, and a reference to the honorable work that went on there. Miró shows that he, too, does honorable work, transforming a jumble of farm implements and outbuildings into a startling comment on the solidarity the artist feels with people tied to the land, to their tools, to home, to the hues of home country, and to a deep ethnic culture. He also shows that his imagination transcends the capacities of mere photography or any other form of realistic inventory. Here we see that surrealism could be congenial to a dignified writer such as Hemingway. There is no need for unreality in an alien, science-fiction style. There need be no warping of space or suspending of gravity or turning of solid objects into fluid ones. There simply needs to be an artistry of unrestrained imagination, a willingness to look through the walls of ordinary perception.

By mid-November of 1926 Hemingway would wheel the large canvas, about four and one-half feet square and someday to be worth millions of dollars, in a hand cart across Montparnasse to deliver it to Hadley in her new single-woman's apartment, not as a birthday gift this time but as a share of her divorce settlement.[3] Hadley watched Ernest from her window and noted that he wept throughout this chore, whether for the loss of the picture or of the marriage or both. She recalled him "weeping down the street and I know he was very sorry for himself."[4] It is a vivid scene, capable of pleasing both those who admire Hemingway for his artistry and personal liberty and those who condemn him for his excessive masculinity. But this vivid moment should not supplant an understanding of the painting itself, which was a calculated artistic statement, both for Miró and for Hemingway, about core political and existential values. *The Farm* represents Hemingway's fullest interest in the surrealist movement.

≡ ≡ ≡

Joan Miró came to Paris in 1920, attracted to the artists then interested in the cubist and dadaist movements and in abstract art generally. He had met Picasso a few months earlier, and knew that his fellow countryman was a master to learn from. Yet like Hemingway, he came to fauvist, barbaric, modern aesthetics primarily through the art of Paul Cézanne. It is not clear precisely what drew Miró to Cézanne, but *The Farm* provides a hint. It is much more realist and referential—as the objects seem real even if the space doesn't—than the two paintings to follow in his career, both of which pleased the true surrealists (read: Breton and his ilk) much more. In *Carnival of Harlequin* (1924), for instance, the surrealists loved the total abandonment of natural space or earthly gravity, and also the private code of the *Miró-Monde* (Miró world), the visual "rhyming" (say the baffling art historians) of cube, sphere, insect, ladder, etc., all floating in relief against a backdrop of color rather than a world of earth and sky.[5] Gérard Durozoi aptly notes that Miró "engendered a universe swarming with shapes, graphic signs, animals, aggressive or ironic people; the world depicted was of an astonishing richness and effervescence." As Breton declared, Miró was "the most surrealist" of them all.[6]

*The Farm* was less surreal but no less revolutionary. The painting clung to certain realist themes—the recognizable European place, the worker's life evoked through agricultural objects, the theme of healing fecundity in the natural world. Yet there is the evident stylizing of the Spanish farmers' world, and there is the childlike move to make walls invisible. It is not surprising that these themes and aesthetic methods pleased Hemingway. He, too, liked to slyly reveal what was inside people as he described them bodily and the world they occupied vividly. *The Farm* certainly must have reminded him of his own work, his particular combination of shock at absurd modern acts of violence rendered in elegant and traditional prose. There was also his love of rural, Catholic Spain. Perhaps Hemingway had little time for the wacky *Miró-Monde*—but we don't know that. In fact, he seems to have loved artistic experimentation and abstraction, especially during the Paris years. And we should not close down the possibility that he recognized in *Carnival of Harlequin* that the *Miró-Monde* is, among other things, a fellow Catholic's celebration of Mardi Gras and all the mysteries that Lent and Easter conjure up in Christian believers like him and Miró.

Both Miró and Masson were at the heart of the surrealist movement, so they were surrounded by writers interested in their work and what it meant. Some of these writers adopted a kind of resistance work best described as the writing of dream states through automatic writing and the dreaming of political states through Marxist doctrines. The combination seems odd, but there was a coherent logic. The surrealists believed so much in psychoanalytical doctrines that they regarded dreams, which Freud called the "royal road to the unconscious," and automatic writing, which eliminated the repressions that might come from excessive planning, as central to human freedoms. The idea, again, was that dreams and spontaneous expression reveal authentic desires while the conscious life and ordinary, tame expression are likely to be riddled with repressions taught to us by the powers that be. The surrealists also believed in Marxist-Leninist solutions to political problems, because these solutions harnessed the immediate needs and wishes of working people in the interest of their own mental and physical health. However, for some surrealists there was a caveat. Breton and his followers, including Miró and Masson, could never see themselves following Comintern orders. Nor could they see themselves killing for justice. So they preferred to think of Leninism as a condition that might be brought about simply by wider understanding of personal liberties and the friendships (or solidarity) that might result.

As we have seen, the surrealists were part of a movement that dreaded the ordinary—both exterior habits and interior consciousness—for in the previous decade, ordinary ways of thinking about civilization had led to the Great War bloodbath and tens of millions dead. For Spaniards and Frenchmen and their friends in 1925, the horror seemed to be starting up again in North Africa with the Rif War, as French ministers and generals used increasingly brutal means to control North Africans in their colonies. The surrealists were desperate to find an alternative to these ongoing colonial wars and the serial wars of balkanized Europe. They were on a quest to find a new consciousness somewhere—anywhere such a new consciousness could be found—even in dreams and spontaneous artistic eruptions.

The worst thing you could call a surrealist was "bourgeois"—and for a political reason. The surrealists hoped for a revolution with anarchic qualities. They wanted the overthrow of accepted middle-class, or bourgeois, ideals—nationalism, patriotism, piety, empty tradition and expression, artistic reproductions of the way things were and supposedly ought to remain. They hoped for a revolution that would both feed the hungry poor, including those of Indochina and Africa, and give all people a realm of freer thought and action. This is why the surrealists and their sympathizers like Hemingway often seemed so contrary, tendentious, and insubordinate. They distrusted all authority, even leftist authority, and wanted to remain free of those who could sentence them to death, either during wartime or in a courtroom whose laws tended to stack up against them. And the surrealists knew how much worse the laws stacked up against colonial people. They voiced their attitudes toward the then-expanding Rif War in Morocco boldly, as Dada cofounder and later surrealist Louis Aragon does here: "Any idea that gives legitimacy to a war must be condemned; since there are men being sent to die [in Morocco] in the name of France, may this idea, like all nationalist ideas, disappear from the face of the earth."[7]

Hemingway agreed, as his flirtation with Dos Passos's and cummings's dadaism and his interest in Masson's and Miró's surrealism suggest. (As we will see, he would also plant a pregnant reference to the Rif War in his next book.) Surrealism may have split off from Dada in an effort to be more serious, more revolutionary in a Marxist sense. But that does not mean the surrealists toed any communist line. In fact, in an illustration of their independence from the Comintern, in 1925 they entered into a kind of feud with Quoc's own newspaper, the communist organ *L'Humanité*. Quoc was, of course, in China by that time, but it is intriguing to think that if he had still been in town, he might have debated the surrealists more flexibly and creatively than his former colleagues were about to. In any case, the argument, which was a bit esoteric, was about whether the communist commitment to exclusively material things such as food and clothing and housing and work led to or followed from surrealism's explorations of a kind of spiritual life, that of the creative, unfettered conscious and properly honored subconscious awareness. The surrealists were certain their experiments with mind and art were a gateway to liberation. Art, they insisted, should be neither tit-illating diversion for the bourgeoisie nor lockstep illustration of Comin-tern doctrine. Apparently, French communists at *L'Humanité* disagreed, believing that artistry was basically frivolous, and that work and room and board were primary.

Breton and his friends diagnosed an intellectual rigidity in the French Communist Party, an element they loathed. They accused *L'Humanité* of being "puerile, bombastic, uselessly *cretinizing.*" A revolution of obedient cretins obeying the Comintern, they argued, was no revolution at all— just the adoption of a new totalitarianism devoid of creative, human-ist care. Because Lenin was the real author of Comintern policies, they disliked him intensely. "The revolutionary flame burns where it wants to," according to Breton, "and it is not up to a small group of men, *in the period of expectation in which we live,* to decree that it is only here or there that it will burn." Because of this fiery independence of the French surrealists, the Soviet politburo overruled the FCP's offer of admission to Breton and his comrades, who were also denied full membership in the Third International.[8] With his Parisian ties and continued interest in the revolution's status in all European and Asian cities, Quoc was sure to have known about this *contretemps.* What side was he on?

One sign of Hemingway's probable stance in this argument is conveyed by his friend Masson, who was among those who deplored *L'Humanité.* In a letter to a friend, he complained bitterly about the mag-azine's shortcomings:

> For six months I've been reading *L'Humanité* closely, and not with-out some anger, but no surprises. The same prejudices are spread out there in "better" or "worse" form than those of the Bourgeoisie— the same disapproval of anything that is unusual or strange, the same artistic and literary rubbish and the same Religion of work.[9]

Masson went on to say that he felt little choice but to support the FCP, because it was the only truly revolutionary party in France, but he implied that his heart just wasn't in it. He did not want to consign workers to a world governed by the "Religion of work." He wanted to liberate them into new ways of thinking and producing and partnering. The proletariat must gain power, Masson thought, but he wanted more than a fairer redistribution of the people's wealth. He wanted to forge a new world, peaceful and imaginatively governed. So, if we think about it, did his friend Hemingway, whose characters of those days always prefer the free and creative bohemian life to a life of bourgeois duties, good manners, and regular hours. Being a bohemian in Paris could be more than a style—it could be a vocation.

In a 1934 article for *Cahiers d'Art*, Hemingway told readers for the first time why he purchased *The Farm*. He starts out sincerely but then becomes a bit coy. He knew before making the purchase, he states, that Miró was a hardworking painter who had "very little to eat." So Hemingway's purchase was partly motivated by a wish to see a hungry artist finally paid for his work. He also knew that the large painting had taken nine months of very hard work to produce, and that "no one could look at it and not know it had been painted by a great painter." He tells about rolling dice with his buddy, horse-racing reporter Evan Shipman, for the right to buy the painting, then, after winning, frantically borrowing money from friends to make the last payment before the dealer's deadline lapsed. Hemingway was very happy to have *The Farm* hanging above his bed, even if he owed money on it. Miró, for his part, was very happy for his friend and boxing coach to be the painting's owner. In this article Hemingway then names one additional reason for buying *The Farm*: the fact that it "has in it all that you feel about Spain when you are there and all that you feel when you are away and cannot go there."[10] It is a coy way of taking sides with Miró's anti-fascists in the coming Spanish Civil War.

Here he hints at the powerful ideas embodied in *The Farm*, including its celebration of an ancient, reverent, and loving Catholic workers' culture. Hemingway's fascination with surrealism extended to its core ideals, which, admittedly, he may have adopted only in part. He profited from surrealism's interest in dreams and mental illness or psychological damage—profited literally, in the sense that his new stories were finally making money. He also chose surrealism's interest in abstraction, strangeness, shock, and psychological complexity, knowing that these traits represented a kind of resistance to the unjust ordinary.

We should remember that these were the days of the so-called "American scene" novels, with Sinclair Lewis's *Main Street* on the best-seller lists. Hemingway admired Lewis (or understood the benefit of his blessing) enough to allow his blurb to appear on the back cover of *In Our Time*. Hadley reported that Hemingway studied *Main Street* (1920) very carefully, which he probably did because Lewis's novel was a model for him of the huge bestseller. But by December of 1925 Hemingway was writing letters making fun of both *Main Street* and *Babbitt* (1922). He resented Lewis's recent successes and denigrated the novels' oversimple, realistic treatment of American middle-class life. He knew that such novels, with their evocation of the normal, did little to resist tyranny.[11]

Hemingway knew what was missing in *Main Street* and other "American scene" novels. They lacked an awareness of the full psychological and ideological effects of the Great War, not to mention the civil and colonial wars that raged in the Balkans and in Morocco and, to a lesser degree, in Indochina in that day. These home-grown American novels lacked the capacity to shock. They were psychologically interesting, but not complex or provocative or bold enough. They lacked the strangeness the surrealists called for, the haunting qualities that Hemingway had recently learned to deliver in his own fiction. They ignored trauma.

Hemingway knew he could unsettle complacent minds with a more sophisticated fiction. In "The Battler" (1923), for instance, he employs a stunning provocation that seems, at first, to have nothing to do with war or class conflict. A teenage Nick Adams has been thrown from a train he is riding on some sort of break from home. He walks for a time and then spies a fire. Approaching an encampment in a clearing, he finds a beat-up man who reveals, soon enough, that he is a retired boxer named Ad Francis. Nick has heard of him. Clearly brain-damaged, this strange man encourages Nick to throw rocks at brakemen on passing trains in retribution for the insult of being thrown off his ride. Ad seems ready for violence himself, as he takes inexplicably sudden offense if Nick so much as looks at him for too long.

Then, a black man comes into the firelight. He greets Nick, introduces himself as Bugs, and offers to share a meal of hot fried ham and runny egg sandwiches. Soon, and for no apparent reason, the ex-boxer becomes agitated and threatening. He takes terrible umbrage at Nick's presence. The story begins to be deeply provocative. Bugs strikes Ad behind the ear with a blackjack, rendering him unconscious. Yet this violence appears to be an act of love, a way of relieving the brain-damaged ex-fighter from his agitation. Bugs then tells the tale of Ad's brief marriage to a woman who may or may not have been Ad's own sister. The ambiguous reference to sexual taboos suggests to us that Bugs and Ad may also be passionate partners—a clear sin in 1920s America.[12] At the very least, they are a total reversal of America's racial dynamics, the black man very physically in charge of the white one. A confused and wary Nick decides to be on his way.

That story must have unsettled American readers' attitudes toward race and sexual identity in the middle 1920s. Careful readers would have recognized the symbolism of an out-of-work young man throwing rocks at the employees of America's richest men, the railroad barons, or of the poorest working American, the black man, offering food to a hungry young white man. There is a parable of class-related violence and cross-racial solidarity in the brief story. Hemingway wrote "The Battler" in a surrealist mode of psychological and political complexity. It is about the American scene, but not the normal one.

Or there is the scene from *The Sun Also Rises* in which Jake gets drunk on absinthe and submits himself to a beating at the hands of his friend Robert Cohn, who is offended because Jake has pimped the woman they both lust after, the beautiful Lady Brett Ashley, to a bullfighter in tight pants named Pedro Romero. That scene surely unsettled ideas of faithfulness, sobriety, and courage among American war veterans. Or there is the surreal scene in *A Farewell to Arms* in which a wounded Frederic Henry rides on a stretcher in an ambulance carrying him away from the battlefield. He is forced to listen to a stream of blood hitting the floor as a fellow wounded soldier bleeds out and dies. That scene took care of the settled idea that it is sweet and becoming to die for your country—or that "our boys" always received the very best medical care from the ministering angels and manly saints of the Red Cross.[13]

These unsettling scenes mean little if they do not accomplish the surrealist task—revealing bourgeois values as threadbare and deeply relative, far from the settled core values French and American patriots claimed they were. Hemingway recognized the central contradictions of the routine common sense of his day. One such contradiction troubled him especially: the idea that young men should die in service of the continuing material comforts of older citizens. His interest in Conrad's colonialist writings also suggests that he found another idea contradictory: that colonial subjects should die for France while few of the French would ever die for them. Hemingway was interested in a worldwide revolution, but his form of resistance took him to the cafés to write rather than to the streets to demonstrate. He hoped for the anarchic, peaceable, and culturally awakened revolution that most French communists then hoped for and that the surrealists modeled for him. The revolution had to create a community in which their kind of politics, writing, and art would be properly understood and honored.

When he bought *The Farm*, Hemingway showed plainly enough that he was no longer the intuitive Wobbly of 1920 who saw revolution as revenge upon people like his parents. Paris had worked its ways on him, helping him grow from such a naïve anti-establishment impulse to a fuller, richer philosophy of intellectual resistance to political complacency. As we have seen, Hemingway's journalism in the 1920s was politically alert. He noted and despised the rise of fascism in Italy, the destabilizing effects of European inflation, and, especially, the fascinating and somewhat alarming political project just underway in Russia. He was no one's fool or dupe. He recognized the dangers of Leninism, yet he knew in his heart that working people and colonial subjects were being unjustly vaporized in the furnaces of capitalist wars. He discussed these issues over boozy lunches with Miró and Masson, who decried the Comintern's regime of control yet hoped for a workers' revolution—if only such a revolution might remain open and intellectual and imaginative enough, not tied to the current cretinizing worship of work the Bolsheviks celebrated. Hemingway certainly lifted his glass in agreement.[14]

Hemingway wrote stories, such as "The Revolutionist," about the naïve belief in inevitable revolutions in Western Europe. The story begins with a brief conversation on board a train car in 1919, in which a naïve young Menshevik revolutionary, a mere kid who wrongly believes that revolution is about to take Italy, expresses his hope for a communist Europe.[15] The narrator, who represents Hemingway's way of thinking, withholds comment.

"But how is the [communist] movement going in Italy?" [the kid] asked.

"Very badly," I said.

"But it will get better," he said. "You have everything here. It is the one country every [communist] is sure of."

I did not say anything.[16]

Hemingway's narrator likes the revolutionary kid, but does not share his hopes for a communist Italy. He withholds comment because he does not want to destroy the boy revolutionist's hope.

Not that Hemingway believed revolutions were impossible. He felt, in fact, that revolution in Italy had been narrowly averted just after Caporetto, that disastrous Italian defeat in November of 1917 that he describes so brilliantly in *A Farewell to Arms* (1929). A few years after writing that novel, he came to believe that ruthless suppression in the nation's capital of the Bonus marchers, dirt-poor vets asking for early payment of a bonus they had earned by fighting in the Great War, had only just averted a largely justified revolutionary moment in the United States. Hemingway supported the Bonus Army, felt that the Depression was reason enough for them to receive their Great War veterans' bonuses early, and was outraged when many of them, who had moved to Florida for work, died for lack of proper shelter during a Keys hurricane in 1935. Considering himself their loving comrade, Hemingway helped clean up their bodies from the beaches and mangrove forests in his Keys neighborhood. He hated the government that had failed these men and allowed their deaths, as he argued in "Who Murdered the Vets?" which appeared in the leftist *New Masses*.[17] He hated any government that failed to take care of its people.

Hemingway also honored his surrealist roots when he had the courage to portray political revolutionaries as credible, well-meaning, justice-centered people. There are examples from throughout Hemingway's career.[18] For instance, the communist Nelson Jacks in *To Have and Have Not* (1937) is sober, realistic, and truthful. He tells Richard Gordon, who is modeled after Dos Passos, that his left-leaning fiction is "shit," apparently because Gordon has failed to show the "discipline and abnegation to be a Communist." He has not taken the road Jacks has, to Washington to march with the veterans who desperately needed their bonuses if they were to eat or have shelter, or to other nations where workers were oppressed—"Mexico, Cuba, South America, and around." Hemingway's novels always tell the truth about ambiguities, so the ordinarily flawed Jacks is no hero. But this is not to say Hemingway was apolitical. Literature is diminished when put to merely political uses, Hemingway saw, just as an education is squandered when its focus turns from the burden of mortal consciousness to mere professional training. The trick was to combine practical, political, aesthetic, and existential purposes. As the surrealists taught him through their fight with *L'Humanité* and elsewhere, the arts should unsettle assumptions and activate creativity, not reeducate according to rigid or complacently accepted doctrine, tradition, or habit.

Buying *The Farm* was all the things the biographers say it was—a sad gesture of waning love for Hadley, a source of tension during the divorce agreement, a canny "futures" investment in modern art, an exploitation of runaway French inflation by a somewhat economically fortunate young American, an act of friendship with and support for a hungry Spanish artist. But these are trivial rather than consequential matters. We want to know what Hemingway cared about in his gut. We want to know what he was willing to train and work for.

Viewed in that sense, buying *The Farm* was also Hemingway's acknowledgment that he worked for left-leaning political solutions in a Parisian anarchist mode.[19] From 1925 onward, many of Hemingway's books would include passionate, justified communists, fighting to make sure the hungry poor had decent homes and enough to eat. The books that do not portray communists at work, such as *The Sun Also Rises*, offer passages that celebrate Miró's people—workers and farmers with coherent, fulfilling lives. Hemingway did not love big government of any kind, certainly not Soviet forms of social control or even FDR's work-welfare programs. He had no sympathy for totalitarian states or even nanny states. He hated what American conservatives sloppily call communism, which is really fascistic totalitarianism. Like his antihero Robert Jordan in *For Whom the Bell Tolls* (1940), he was "not a real Marxist." Hemingway and his character Jordan were too constitutionally French and American for that: "You believe in Liberty, Equality and Fraternity," Jordan thinks. "You believe in Life, Liberty and the Pursuit of Happiness."[20]

Hemingway hoped and dreamt of a more socialist America under its original constitution, a fuller realization of democracy in which genuine freedoms, such as these constitutional freedoms of France and the United States, would be preserved and celebrated and fully honored. He believed in the state the surrealists dreamt about, and recorded on their dreamlike canvases—one in which citizens would be utterly creative and free, responsible for each other's welfare, and together dedicated to the idea that no one should have to die for anyone else's material advantage nor drone away at work for another man's or woman's unearned wealth. That is an ideal he bought into when he bought *The Farm*.

≡ ≡ ≡

Still, Hemingway was clearly conflicted about his future as a writer. Even if he retained these deep commitments to progressive or revolutionary politics and to the arts that might emerge from revolutionary hopes, he still wanted fame. During this pivotal year of 1925, the very embodiment of this hope for fame would come into his life and enter his heart— the famous and briefly wealthy F. Scott Fitzgerald.

He met Fitzgerald on an April day when the famous American writer drank himself into a fugue state in Montparnasse's Dingo Bar while Hemingway, who had just been introduced to Fitzgerald, watched in appalled fascination. Like most of the interactions between Scott and Hem (as the two soon came to call each other), especially the interactions that first came to our attention in *A Moveable Feast*, this one may be mythical—designed by Hemingway to emphasize, perhaps wishfully, his sobriety and industry as contrasted with Scott's dissipated personality. But the insecurities giving rise to that contrast were Hemingway's late-life ones. In 1925, he was simply pleased to have made the acquaintance of a man who published routinely and easily in the *Saturday Evening Post* and with the prestigious Scribner publishing house, both serving up slick entertainments to the huge American reading audience and paying authors well. If Scott happened to drink hard, that was fine with Hemingway. He did too, in spite of his stories claiming otherwise. And besides, drinking hard and appearing in public a bit drunk were simply two of those liberties the moderns believed emerged from the healthily unrepressed unconscious.

Scott, who was visiting Paris with his wife, Zelda, to explore the expatriate zeitgeist after a hard period of writing, seems to have needed a male friend, and he liked Hemingway immediately—that much is true. So within days of their meeting, Scott invited Ernest to travel with him by train to Lyon to retrieve the car he and Zelda had abandoned on a recent trip when the weather turned bad for driving. We know the story is based in fact because scholars have found a cable message Hemingway wrote that spring about catching a particular train for Lyon, a cable he drafted on the back page of a book Fitzgerald had lent him. Whether each and every event in the tale actually happened in time and space or only in Hemingway's imagination, on the other hand, we can only guess.

As *A Moveable Feast* presents the episode, Fitzgerald is an unbelievably feckless clown. In the meeting to make plans for the trip, he wrongly accuses Hemingway of intentionally denying facts about their previous meeting. "There's no use to make mysteries simply because one has drunk a few glasses of wine," he scolds. "Why did you want to make the mysteries? It isn't the sort of thing I thought you would do." Hemingway is stunned at this treatment, but claims he so wanted to know a more experienced writer with an impressive publishing history that, in spite of these antics, he was willing to make the trip to Lyon with Fitzgerald. Then Scott fails to show at the Gare de Lyon for the departing train, so Hemingway is forced to spend precious funds saved for his and Hadley's planned trip to Spain on the train ticket Scott was supposed to provide. He rides the train alone, wondering where Scott has gotten to. He checks into the luxury hotel Scott had mentioned back in Paris, but once again, his inconstant new friend fails to show. He does finally appear the next morning and, predictably, fails to take any responsibility for the confusion. Indeed he scolds Hemingway again for failing to wait for him in Paris so they could travel together as they had planned.

The trip back to Paris unfolds as a moral fable. Hemingway finds lovely foods and wines wherever he goes, purchasing these things cheaply and knowledgeably on the genuine French economy, while Fitzgerald merely abuses alcohol in a nonstop bender, purchases food from the kitchens of luxury hotels at inflated prices, and then neglects to savor excellent French delicacies. Scott is also an outrageous bully of restaurant waiters and hotel staff, and his hypochondria reveals a deep narcissism. He has the soul of an oligarch, if not the income.

And yet, Hemingway could not ignore the one valuable thing his new friend Fitzgerald had in 1925: talent as a writer. When the two finally did return to Paris with the Fitzgerald car, Scott had a surprise for Hem. He had a fresh, new copy of his latest book for him. It was titled *The Great Gatsby*, and Scott hoped Hemingway would give it a quick read. After reading the novel, Hemingway dwelt for a moment on his awe at the talent that could produce that book:

> When I had finished it I knew that no matter what Scott did, nor how he behaved, I must know it was a sickness and be of any help I could to him and try to be a good friend. He had many good, good friends, more than anyone I knew. But I enlisted as one more, whether I could be of any use or not. If he could write a book as fine as *The Great Gatsby* I was sure that he could write an even better one.

What goes unsaid, of course, is that Hemingway would have to compete to write "an even better one," a novel better than any sequel Fitzgerald might craft. Suddenly, there was a shift in his attention. There was the threatening chance that Hemingway would cease finding his best models for fiction in surrealist paintings and doctrines, that his models for good writing now might be found where Scott published, in New York.

As if to prove that profit was indeed now his main concern, and New York his focus, Hemingway then shed Sherwood Anderson in a conniving bid to change publishers. He did damage to his friendship with Gertrude Stein in the same blow. When Stein refused in 1925 to review *In Our Time*, a snub that enraged Hemingway, and when reviews began to mention her and Anderson a bit too often for Hemingway's comfort, he went after both of them. Anderson's friendship he sloughed off in the more dramatic and decisive fashion, satirizing the Chicago mentor's latest novel, *Dark Laughter*, in a shocking, unfunny, book-length ad hominem attack. In this book, which he titled *The Torrents of Spring*, Hemingway wrote and published an entire novel's worth of ironic attack on Anderson's recent work. *Torrents* actually had two purposes in reality, only one of which involved letting the world know that he did not in fact admire and imitate Anderson's more primitivist and sentimental work. The more important purpose of that book was to force the Boni and Liveright publishing house to release Hemingway from their contract, which entitled them to his next book. Giving them a book-length attack on one of their authors, and a subpar book at that, should do the trick, Hemingway seems to have calculated. Sadly, he had meaner motives in mind too. As Hemingway wrote to Ezra Pound, he also wanted to "destroy Sherwood and various others." The kind-hearted Hadley hated *Torrents*—probably because she hated the idea of destroying her friend Sherwood.

Ironically, Hemingway shed Anderson by writing a mock-surrealist work. *The Torrents of Spring* presents absurdly unrealistic situations and dialogue. One character, for example, collects material for short stories by "drinking on the railroad tracks" and watching trains go by. All this silliness for no larger purpose than to tell Anderson, a good friend who deserved gratitude rather than critique, that his recent work was not quite up to par. The mock-surrealist passages, none of which deserve further summarizing, seem to serve no more meaningful purpose. After receiving a letter from Hemingway attempting to justify the book as a message to a beloved but faltering writer who needed the critique, Anderson wrote a rebuking reply. He told Hemingway to grow up and reform his ways: "Come out of it man." And he denigrates *Torrents* as an undignified work with a "smarty tinge."

Then Anderson cut Hemingway to the quick: "You always speak to me like a master to a pupil. It must be Paris—the literary life. You didn't sound like that when I knew you."

# 20

## LEAVING PARIS TO CREATE SOMETHING

### QUOC AND HEMINGWAY FROM 1926 TO 1928

I n his move to Soviet Russia in the summer of 1923, and then to revolutionary China a few months after that, Quoc seemed to have rejected hopeful, peaceable, socialist reformism for a more brutal ethic of violent, expansionist revolution. In *Le procès de la colonisation francaise* he expressed strong support of Bolshevism, at least in its educative form, which he believed much more humane than Western civilization as practiced by the empires. In that book, he also called on colonial and European youth to get on board the Third International. Yet in 1926 he returned his attention to Paris, joining up in an effort with his former Annamite Patriot comrades, who were still socialists working for legal reforms in the colonies. These reforms, they felt idealistically, should be voted in by French voters or mandated by enlightened government ministers using their rightful powers, and the reforms should lead to reasonable living and working conditions for Vietnamese people at home and abroad. Quoc was in full agreement. Together with certain key Annamite Patriots, he prepared and presented an important petition to the new League of Nations. There were no threats in the petition, either direct or implied, not even threats of walk-outs or strikes in support of the petition's pleas. It was all about making peace through international negotiations and agreements. Unbelievably, the petition also declared—or perhaps conceded—that France should remain a representative democracy with a robust free-trade, capitalist economy.

In similar fashion, Hemingway's fascination with New York publishers seemed to have doomed his friendships with Miró and Masson and his commitment to the Parisian arts scene generally. But that is not completely so either. As his friendship with F. Scott Fitzgerald deepened, and as he learned from Scott and from his editors in New York the art of profiting financially from his writing, he developed a new circle of friends who were less deeply invested in social equity and the dignity of working men and women. These new friends included an attractive fashion writer named Pauline Pfeiffer, the woman who would become his next wife, and Gerald and Sara Murphy, arts mavens and owners of a villa on the Riviera and a schooner they called the *Weatherbird*, who were soon to be boosters of his career. Though they had nothing against Hadley, the Murphys thought Pauline a more suitable wife for an up-and-coming writer, and Pauline thought the Murphys people who knew just how to live. As Hemingway moved into the Murphys' and Pauline's orbit, he apparently agreed. Yet in 1927 he followed up the huge success of his first novel, *The Sun Also Rises*, with an entirely different plot, setting, and set of characters. Gone were his most sexually charged and least valued friends, drinking hard and misbehaving during self-indulgent travels. He began to write a novel in which an experienced resistance-fighting father, known to the US government as a dangerous labor agitator, takes his teenage son from their beloved Michigan woods on a journey to Europe to join in a real, live shooting revolution.

Quoc's and Hemingway's evolving worldviews leave us with a key question: Just how important was the Paris of 1921 through at least 1928 in shaping these men's understandings of their work, specifically that part of their work that involved resistance to tyranny, bigotry, economic exploitation, warmongering, and arbitrary exercise of power? As it happens, in 1926 and 1927 Quoc and Hemingway provided strong evidence for their continued love of Paris's arts of resistance, as Quoc, the communist, affirmed constitutional democracy and Hemingway, the farmer-labor democrat, affirmed revolutionary effort.

≡≡≡

Quoc, it turns out, may have left Paris much more reluctantly than Sarraut's agents or even his own friends had known. There are signs that he may even have regretted the decision. When Quoc arrived in Moscow, he first mourned the death of his hero Lenin, earning those frostbitten hands in the process. Strangely enough, those injuries set the stage for Quoc's relations with the new Soviet roommates already in his assigned Comintern lodgings. In an extremely rare personal story from his life, Quoc's Moscow roommates reported to their supervisors that one day in January of 1924, he spoke to them about his grief over Lenin's death. He threatened to go out in minus-40-degree weather to attend a memorial service, perhaps a viewing of Lenin's body, and they advised him not to go—or at least to wait until they could scrounge some warm clothes for him. Quoc, of course, did not listen. Without warning and without the warm clothes, he soon disappeared. He was gone all day. "Somewhere around ten at night," one roommate reported, "I heard a soft knocking on the door." Quoc entered the room, his face, ears, and fingers blue with frost. "He was trembling from the cold," continued the roommate, "as he explained that he could not wait until tomorrow to pay homage to"— and here we learn the nature of Quoc's love of Lenin—"the best friend of the colonial peoples." He asked for and was given hot tea.

This spirit of mutual care and good feeling between Quoc and his Soviet comrades did not last long. In the coming weeks, Quoc began complaining to his Comintern handlers about his housing. Those kindly roommates had turned out to be quite unpleasant to live with. Quoc was kept awake by their talk and the persistent noises from the street and even unfamiliar Russian insect sounds. He blamed the Comintern. Ever the principled agitator, he withheld five rubles per month to protest his living conditions. Eventually, he was given another room, perhaps just to quiet his continual complaints.[1]

Then, in the late spring of 1924 he began telling people very frankly that he had never intended to stay in Moscow anyway, either to work with the Comintern or to attend the Communist University of the Toilers of the East. He had come to Moscow believing he was merely to stay over briefly so he could meet Lenin. Then, with Soviet support that he felt he had been promised, he would move onward toward Southeast Asia and his homeland. But the Comintern neither shared this understanding nor cared to oblige him by meeting his schedule. So, a few weeks later he felt compelled to write a strong letter pressing again for his way. In this letter of early summer 1924, he complained that he had been in the city for nine months, six of which constituted a delay in his mind. Next, he set aside the standard Soviet counterarguments that he expected to hear from his superiors: All the Toilers University training and talk of workers' organizations and secret societies mattered little to him because Vietnam had not yet reached a level of prerevolutionary preparation in which such organizations existed. It was a country of isolated and illiterate peasant farmers. He made no bones about his lack of loyalty to larger Comintern goals, to revolutions in Germany or the former Ottoman Empire. He knew what skills and dispositions he needed if he were to make a difference in Vietnam, and after his time of growth in Paris, he believed he had them in hand. Moscow, therefore, had nothing very important to offer him. He wanted to get to East Asia to "study the [Vietnamese] situation in a careful manner." If there was no revolutionary organization evolving there, that was no problem, for he would work, he wrote with unmistakable emphasis, "to CREATE SOMETHING."[2]

Quoc wanted to find contacts in Vietnam who would enter into cooperation with the Comintern, an organization he still represented in spite of his differing goals. He still believed that only the Soviets and their allies were likely to provide the arms and monetary assistance his people needed for a Vietnamese revolution. Quoc would have preferred American aid, but Wilson had closed that door. (World War II would see American OSS agents opening that door again by a crack.) In the time leading up to that Soviet-assisted revolution, Quoc wanted to study the economics and politics of the colony in more detail to find organizations that might be incipiently revolutionary, and to organize a system for the distribution of propaganda. He demanded a stipend that would allow him to make these travels and do this work. At first, the Comintern did not respond to his request for funded travel. He cajoled and complained for a few months more, even running an errand to the far end of Siberia to earn his superiors' deeper trust. Finally, in October of 1924 his plan was funded at a budget of $100 USD per month.[3] This Comintern stipend turned out to be crucial to his work. Indeed, he probably lived on Comintern stipends until at least 1945, when he began working with an OSS unit called the Deer Team and then, as the war ended, became Vietnam's first prime minister.

In 1924, however, he was just learning how to earn his revolutionary pay. He had been approved for an assignment in China involving clandestine recruitment in the Asian colonies. Just as he had done in Paris, and for the same reasons, he left Moscow furtively, catching a train from a major Moscow station and lying to friends about his plans because he hoped to avoid any interference or intelligence-gathering by enemy agents then in the city.[4] By November, he was living in Canton (present-day Guangzhou). He would return reluctantly to Moscow in 1928 for a brief period after counter-revolutionary nationalist forces in Canton cleared out most communists from that city, but from 1924 onward, Quoc lived mainly in Asia, including Hong Kong and Siam and Ceylon (present-day Thailand and Sri Lanka, respectively), Singapore, and other sites where he made and worked his best contacts in Vietnam.

It would appear that by late 1923 Quoc had moved into the orbit of Comintern disciplines, or at least those he believed relevant to revolution in Vietnam. Furthermore, it would appear that he had left behind Paris's more peaceable, creative, psychologically realistic, and humane resistance hopes and techniques. But it is not so. There are definite signs in 1926 that his wide-ranging, multiform learning in Paris was still active and operative, still shaping his revolutionary vocation. He still retained a flexible mind, creative hopes for change, and a love of peace—each a hard-won benefit of the Parisian curriculum of the 1920s. These Parisian values, including the value of constitutional language as a stay against arbitrary exercise of power, are central to Quoc's final act in 1926 Paris.

Sometime in early 1926 or just before, the League of Nations announced that its delegates and other interested parties would convene in Paris that summer. It would be a modest reprise of the 1919 Paris Peace Conference that had given him his first diplomatic role. Seeing another opportunity to appeal to reasonable, progressive people who had ready access to powerful leaders, Quoc and certain Annamite comrades living in both Vietnam and Paris wrote a petition to present to the convention. Bizarrely titled "Screams to the League of Nations," this document was in fact very close kin to the 1919 "Demands" document that the Annamite Patriots had addressed to the Paris Peace Conference leaders. It was a call for a list of civil rights reforms in Annam/Vietnam and a proposal for the country to immediately become a self-governing nation—but not under the Comintern or the USSR. The "Screams" petitions called for a democratic constitution. Quoc was not in Paris to present the "Screams" petition—he would run a small Comintern errand there in 1928 but remained in China during 1926—but his signature was appended to indicate co-authorship, and he was certainly present in argument and in spirit.[5]

Quoc's petition appealed to the Western powers' declared belief in justice for all people, regardless of race, creed, or sex. In the petition's pleas, Wilson's doctrines of self-determination were evident too, along with bohemian Paris's insistence on the possibility of local and international peace:

> On behalf of the true friendship that exists between the French and Vietnamese peoples, on behalf of the interests of both countries, on behalf of peace in the Far East and in the world, on behalf of the sacred principle of the right of self-determination for peoples, a principle proclaimed right after the Great War by the Allied Forces, including France, we demand, in the presence of the Society [League] of Nations, the complete and immediate independence of the Vietnamese people. Once our country is free, we commit ourselves to:
>
> 1. Pay, in money or in kind, in a certain number of yearly installments, a part to be determined from the war debts taken out of France from America and England.
> 2. Conclude a treaty of political and commercial alliance with France.
> 3. Draft a political and social constitution, inspired by the principles of sovereignty of the people, of respect for ethnic minorities and respect for work. That constitution shall serve as a basis for the creation of the Federal Republic of Indochina.
> 4. Build up a national army, according to our traditional system of militia, that shall be responsible for internal order and external security.
> 5. Send a delegation to the [League] of Nations on the same footing as Siam and China.
>
> Hanoi, 25 July 1926                    Paris, 30 August 1926[6]

With this document, Quoc, along with his mentor from Vietnam, Phan Boi Chau, and his Parisian roommate Phan Chu Trinh, offered France a rock-bottom deal, beginning with huge concessions. They pledged that France might retain every fiscal benefit of a colonial relationship, including tax revenues crucial for the repayment of French war debts and trade revenues they had exploited for decades. Furthermore, France would welcome into the world of nations another democratic republic aligned with French values and, presumably, ready to fight as its ally. However, Quoc then turned the bargaining screw to a definite sticking point. He insisted that France must relinquish control of Indochina immediately so that Vietnam and the other Southeast Asian colonies might control their own destiny and evolve toward the defense of their own interests. There seemed to be a long-game plan. Vietnam would defend its own borders in the short term and then defend its economic interests down the road.

At this moment in August of 1926 Quoc set aside the goal of a complete halt to the economic exploitations of colonialism, negotiating instead for a halt to the spiritual oppressions and indignities of colonialism. His proposal for a new model of economic cooperation might lead to future economic autonomy for Vietnam, he and his friends hoped, commencing once France's war debts were retired, but for now what he wanted was an independent nation and France's renunciation of the cruelest and most oppressive habits of colonialism—the raping and murdering and insulting and bullying and thieving. Quoc wanted the worst Frenchmen and -women out of Vietnam.

Amazingly, there is not a hint of Leninism in the deal. Considering that Quoc was writing from the Sino-Soviet inner circle in Canton, and that he lived among comrades still committed to serial armed revolutions until the world was a communist paradise, this is a strikingly peaceable, reformist approach. There were actually positive repudiations of communist ideals in Quoc's proposals, such as his call for a republican, or representative, form of government for an independent Vietnam and for cooperation in international trade. It was a deal any democracy-loving capitalist could embrace.

Driving this petition were Quoc's special skills, including his most reasonable writing—not the undisciplined, sarcastic prose he employed while describing abuses and atrocities, but the kind he used only in the highest diplomatic negotiations. With the vision of Vietnam led by the Vietnamese, he also demonstrates his Confucian respect for Asian moral maturity. He blends this respect for Asian ways with a somewhat countervailing respect for established French leaders and their ideals, even though they are in the opposition. This petition shows us that no matter how ruthless Ho Chi Minh would eventually become—and the degree of this ruthlessness and communist dogmatism is still a hotly debated subject—the young man who left Paris was a thoroughgoing humanist in a blended East-West mode who continued to display a preference for, if not a dedication to, democratic forms of government.

Some students of the history of anti-colonialism note the importance of Quoc's so-called constitutionalism, which I have mainly expressed as ideals he imbibed through his study of Enlightenment philosophers such as Montesquieu, Rousseau, Franklin, and Jefferson. These ideals, reinforced and reinterpreted by socialist bohemians in Paris and even by certain essentially nonviolent communists there, still had a purchase on him in 1926. Those who call Quoc a constitutionalist note that the texts of modern constitutions, especially those of the United States and France, "establish legal restraints on arbitrary power." As Son Ngoc Bui of the Center for Asian Legal Studies argues, constitutions like the one Quoc demanded in the 1919 "Demands" document and the 1926 "Screams" petition would "oppose arbitrary colonial rule (condemnation of political activity, special oppressive courts, and arbitrary decrees) and call for fundamental values of modern constitutionalism (namely legal equality, civil liberty, the rule of law, and democratic participation)." In other words, Quoc was opposed to totalitarianism; he wanted to fashion a Vietnamese government like those of the Great War's victorious democratic Allies. As Bui puts it, "He did not employ the soviet idea of constitution as a weapon for class struggle but as a framework to preclude despotism, to realize rule of law, and to protect liberal rights."[7]

It is dismaying to ponder the costs French officials incurred for their nation and for others, including the United States, by refusing to consider seriously this proposal to the League of Nations. Some sixty thousand French and French Foreign Legion troops died fighting Ho's Viet Minh during the early 1950s, desperately trying to retain French control of Vietnam. Some fifty-eight thousand American troops and support personnel died throughout the 1960s and early 1970s fighting his regulars and Viet Cong guerrillas, desperately trying to prevent another communist domino from toppling. It could have gone another way. If French and American leaders in the late 1940s and early 1950s had come to regard Ho Chi Minh as a pro-trade socialist rather than a Maoist or Stalinist communist, they might have allowed him to win a fair and open election in 1954 Vietnam, an election the West promised at the Geneva Convention that year but which Presidents Eisenhower, Kennedy, and Johnson would not allow because they could not countenance a communist, however popular in his own nation, winning a legitimate electoral victory.

Ho's 1926 proposal to the French is a small chapter in the long story of the divided heart of Quoc/Ho Chi Minh. This is the story of a Confucian altruist and nationalist who was trained in the French Enlightenment classics to love human rights—at war psychologically with the communist soldier and propagandist trained in the Stalin School to be ready to fight, and fight ruthlessly. American patriots who regard Ho as a moral monster should reread the Declaration of Independence, which declares in no uncertain terms that when colonial subjects find their natural civil rights violated by a tyrant, it is their duty to take up arms and resist the tyranny.[8] Ho believed something similar, but like any sensible, balanced person, he looked for humane alternatives first. Once the 1926 "Screams" proposal to the League of Nations was ignored by League officials, Ho had no alternative but to strive for revolution. As late as 1945, on the day he took control of the Vietnamese government, he still held out hope for US support, reading to a huge crowd that day from the Declaration of Independence as a sign of that hope.

This book is not about Ho Chi Minh after 1926, but it is important to note that Quoc's Paris education did give him a flexible, creative mind, and a lifelong dedication to humanist goals, if not humanist methods. North Vietnamese and Viet Cong brutality and atrocities surely did occur during the Vietnam War, and ought to be condemned, just as the My Lai massacre and prisoner killings and other American misdeeds should be. Yet Ho Chi Minh may not have been responsible for most of his warriors' misdeeds. As filmmakers Ken Burns and Lynn Novick argue in their documentary series on the Vietnam War, North Vietnamese hardliner Le Duan appears to have used and abused Ho's reputation for loving both independence and the Vietnamese people. Le Duan surely was a ruthless, ideological tyrant, and his methods—which he deployed under the cover of Ho's love of country—led in the middle 1970s to a totalitarian Vietnam abusing and starving its own people. Le Duan's reeducation camps were a horrifying violation of the civil rights Quoc loved, and his land reform policies led to widespread starvation. Only recently have Vietnamese lives improved significantly as the people's liberties have been widened and as Vietnam has joined in trade and other acts of common cause with the world's more liberal nations—an effort the Vietnamese call Doi Moi, or "open door." Quoc had opened that same door in 1926 with his "Screams" petition, but none of the right people would walk through it.

It is hard to imagine Ho presiding over a harsh, controlling, totalitarian Vietnam. Whatever his revolutionary sins, he does seem to have weighed even small ideological excesses as memorable and regrettable. In one poignant moment, an elderly Ho recalled behaving badly in Moscow during the days of his revolutionary fervor there, probably in 1924. He scolded a woman he saw on the street clad in stylish shoes and a silk dress. Quoc approached her and told her that such finery constituted theft from hungry working people. She replied defiantly that she had made the clothing herself, and she asked Quoc a pointed question: "Is it really so bad that young people now have the chance to eat and dress well?"[9] Ho Chi Minh later realized that his needless scolding of this woman arose from ideological rigidity, the kind Paris's arts community in the 1920s abhorred and called the religion of work.

Quoc had choices, and so did the Vietnamese people who knew him. As we have seen, Ho Chi Minh struck many throughout his life as "part Gandhi and part Lenin."[10] We know how Quoc came over to Lenin's side in 1922, but he could have come over to Gandhi's side instead. During the 1920s the most activist and world-aware Vietnamese were as interested in Gandhi's nonviolent direct action as a proper form of anticolonial resistance as they were in Lenin's Third International. "Marxism in its Bolshevik form was attractive," the French historians Brocheux and Hémery write, "but many were passionate about Gandhi . . . as well as about Sun Yat-sen and Lenin."[11] Clearly, Gandhi represented a real choice for Quoc. The entire literate world knew of the Amritsar massacre, Gandhi's Non-Cooperation Movement, his arrest on charges of inciting violence, his imprisonment, and then, two years later, his early release. Most knew of his twenty-one-day fast in 1924, and his campaign the following year for Indians to release themselves from British economic dependence by spinning their own cloth. Watching Gandhi, many learned the practice of nonviolent direct action. Later civil rights leaders such as Martin Luther King knew of the deep spiritual roots of Gandhi's efforts, which mirrored in many ways Ho's respect for the humanitarian ethics of Confucianism.[12] In other words, Paris and other cosmopolitan centers had the example of Gandhi's nonviolent direct action available to them, and they had evidence of its virtues and of its effectiveness. But for some tragic reason, Ho Chi Minh eventually followed Lenin and Mao into the logic of his own "people's war." He came to believe—reluctantly, one hopes—in bleeding an enemy dry on one's own soil so that, while your own people bleed too, they finally secure the national autonomy and the economy they think they want.

≡ ≡ ≡

Knowingly and unknowingly both, Hemingway had also begun to take his leave of Paris in 1926. It is a tale of seductions—of the attractiveness of New York publishers, of a certain pretty female American fashion writer, and of well-meaning, wealthy friends who wanted the best for him. In the spring of 1925, the Hemingways befriended Pauline Pfeiffer, the trim fashion writer who knew how to look good in Paris's couture, and Gerald and Sara Murphy, friends of Fitzgerald and Dos Passos who lived on Gerald's father's Mark Cross leather-goods money while Gerald painted modernist stage sets for Diaghilev and his *Ballet Russe*. Sara kept house. It was to be a new crucible of friends with values quite different from those of Miró and Masson.

Just months after receiving Miró's *The Farm* as a birthday gift in November of 1925, Hadley felt she had to ask her husband a bit desperately for something more—a hundred-day hiatus in his affair with Pauline Pfeiffer. Hadley had suspected since a March trip to Schruns for some late-season skiing that there was some kind of dalliance going on between her new friend Pauline and her husband, but knowing Ernest's flirtatious nature, she was not concerned. She and Pauline remained friends. Speaking to Pauline's sister Jinny one day, Hadley mentioned casually that she thought Ernest and Pauline got along well. Jinny's grave reply that "they're very fond of each other" struck Hadley as an announcement. She knew suddenly that her marriage was in trouble. In fact, Hadley later admitted that, hearing Jinny's confirmation of the affair, she knew immediately that she had already lost the battle to keep Ernest.[13]

But she worked to save the marriage anyway. During that summer's trip to Pamplona and a side trip to visit the Murphys in the south of France, Hadley was forced to treat Pauline as a valued and welcome friend. There are photographs of Pauline sitting at a Pamplona café table with the Hemingway group of half a dozen friends, including the Murphys, all of them in their natty traveling tweeds and ties and scarves. Pauline sits with her shoulder leaning up against handsome and grinning Ernest's. Meanwhile, Hadley sits further away from him on his other side, smiling uneasily. "I should have said to her, 'No, you can't have my husband.' But I didn't," Hadley told a biographer later in her life. One day in Antibes, visiting the Murphys at their villa, Hadley felt unable to prevent Pauline from joining her and Ernest in bed one morning for a shared breakfast, served by a shocked Marie Cocotte. "We all behaved badly that summer—like silly children," Hadley admitted.[14]

The hundred-day hiatus was her strategy for appealing to more mature impulses in both Pauline and Ernest. Hadley knew that in spite of the seemingly carefree intimate play the three of them engaged in, Pauline was a devout Catholic racked with guilt over destroying a marriage to take Ernest for herself. He clearly felt guilty too, perhaps because of his own Catholicism but likely for more ordinary ethical reasons. People in his family did not divorce. Hadley hoped that over a few weeks' time, this guilt on both of their parts would put a stop to the affair.

Hemingway neither ended the affair nor recognized his continuing love for Hadley. Or rather, if his longing for Hadley while writing *A Moveable Feast* in the late 1950s is to be believed, it took him decades, rather than a few dozen days, to realize that he had thrown away a profound and precious life with her. In *A Moveable Feast* Hemingway blames the breakup of his first marriage, which he had come to regret deeply, on John Dos Passos, who had brought destructive, wealthy friends into Hemingway's life—namely, Gerald and Sarah. They were good friends of Fitzgerald's too. In the memoir, Hemingway calls Dos Passos a "pilot fish," and the Murphys "the rich."

The Murphys' greatest sin, he wrote in the late 1950s, was their flattery, their excessive praise for his writing, which caused him to lose proper perspective on his life and career.[15] He indicts the Murphys in a passage he cut from *A Moveable Feast* for "[backing] me in every ruthless and evil decision that I made."[16] These rich friends loved Pauline (even little Bumby could tell that by contrast they found his mother dowdy and unsophisticated), and they felt Hemingway was too great an artist and public figure for such a humble, much older, and unstylish woman as Hadley.[17] In a September 1926 letter to Hemingway, Gerald Murphy lectured him on Hadley's unfortunate "slower and less initiative [tempo] than yours," and encouraged him to set aside qualms about "Hadley's comfort, [and] Bumby's." Hemingway honored this hard advice from Murphy during his breakup with Hadley, and he even accepted Murphy's gift of $400, enough to fund nearly half a year of frugal living and writing time in Paris.[18]

Hemingway had begun a novel that spring, even though he had recently derided novels in general, claiming they were outmoded and unfit for his careful, distilled style and painstakingly slow writing process. The Murphys were well aware of his surprisingly good progress on the novel because they spent much of May and June hosting Hadley and Bumby at their villa so Ernest could write uninterrupted. Actually, because Bumby had been diagnosed with whooping cough, Hadley and Bumby were given another villa near the Murphys' Villa America. Not only did the Murphys pay for the villa rental and send fresh garden vegetables and chickens over for Hadley to cook for herself and Bumby, but they generously paid the doctor who attended the little boy too. As Hadley remained in her gated home, accepting these gifts through wrought-iron bars as her tipsy friends came for a ritual happy-hour visit each day, cocktail shakers and glass for her in hand, Ernest was in Madrid.[19] He was at a crucial point in his revisions, he said, and wanted to see the San Ysidro bullfights.[20] The latter half of his new novel was all about bullfighting. Once Bumby was well enough, the little boy went off in the care of Marie Cocotte while the Murphys, Hadley, Pauline, and others joined Ernest in Pamplona for the *feria* and to pose for that interesting photograph.

Ernest's novel was titled *The Sun Also Rises*. It is the story of a Great War flying veteran named Jake Barnes, who suffers the effects of a very special wound. His penis has been shot off, but not his testicles (anatomy that Hemingway had to describe much more obliquely in 1926), so that he possesses the hormones that produce desire but not the anatomy needed to assuage it. He is tormented by longing for the beautiful, sexy, and sexually demanding woman he is in love with, Lady Brett Ashley. She is a dissipated and privileged English expat compensating madly with alcohol and affairs for the loss of a true love, an English soldier who died during the war. She loves Jake now but has accepted the modern Freudian view that her urges simply must be satisfied. Because Jake cannot satisfy them, he must be only a very dear friend to her—a situation they both find agonizing. It is tempting to call this situation surreal, except that such wounds and disabilities and frustrations were all too common after a war that involved millions of soldiers trying to survive the disabling effects of highly mechanized and explosive warfare.

The novel can be read in various ways—feminist or psychoanalytical or historical or political—many of which are compelling. But it is especially intriguing to read it in light of Hemingway's association with Masson and Miró and surrealist doctrines. The novel is a bit like Miró's *The Farm*: it sets up a contrast between the startling modern and the nourishing ancient. Hemingway gives us one set of values to embrace or reject—the chaotic and dissipated ways of a group of Anglo-American expatriates who make Paris their home or pied-à-terre and spend their time mostly drunk, scrapping, taking lovers, and frantically seeking various fun diversions. Hemingway knew such people, and indeed, the novel is a roman à clef, or a novel with a key, based on living characters who can be identified by name.[21] Jake and Brett are caught in the swirl of these activities, though they both seem to desire something deeper. Then Hemingway offers us a contrasting set of values—the ancient and nourishing ways of the Catholic Spanish farmers and laborers who come to Pamplona partly for the carnival fun and the bullfights and partly to honor San Fermín. The most devout of these Spaniards perform acts of worship and celebrate the liturgical carnival of the *feria*. These people know how to live with some generosity and grace. In one lovely little scene, dirt-poor peasants give wine and marinated tuna and onions to expats who, given their wealth and privilege, should be giving to the peasants instead. One of Jake's more opaque friends calls the food an hors d'oeuvre, but Brett, who is sharper and more class-conscious, tells him to stop eating the peasants' dinner.[22]

At the center of this contrast, in Hemingway's novel if not in the actual *feria*, is the *corrida*, the battle between matador and bull. This contest conveys important things about Spanish rituals of courage in the face of death, but also suggests that even in ancient Spanish custom there is selfishness and possessiveness and arrogance. *The Sun Also Rises* is a smart, balanced, properly ambiguous performance. It is a novel that helps the reader believe in Hemingway's good and generous heart, even though his treatment of Hadley as he finished revisions on the novel argues for his self-centeredness.

As for the most important surrealist doctrine, the creative imagination in service of human need, the novel does not disappoint. In its concluding pages, Jake is forced to imagine a creative form of care on Lady Brett's behalf, as her entirely sexual relationship with a handsome young bullfighter breaks down and she finds herself utterly abandoned, broke, and alone. Jake reluctantly finds a way to be her loving friend in spite of her many betrayals of his love during the *feria*. His kindness has religious overtones, which is not surprising, given Hemingway's own religious journey in those days. As Michael Reynolds suggests in his book on this period, "Hemingway was now powerfully drawn to the Church's ritual as well as its power and dogma, to its humbling cathedrals as well as its insistence on mystery and faith."[23] He was also drawn to the theology of love, to *caritas*, as his Samaritan role in Brett's rescue indicates.

Just after the Murphys departed Pamplona that summer, Hadley went home to Paris to ponder her options. She even left Bumby in Brittany with Marie Cocotte and her husband, Tonton, lengthening by many weeks the time she was without her son. She was clearly distraught. She and Ernest talked seriously later that summer, during a trip to Spain that he used to proofread the galleys for his novel. In August they returned to Paris, this time to separate residences. Hadley still fought for her marriage. In November she arrived at the strategy of the hundred days, but even before the hiatus expired, she saw that her wish for a repaired marriage was hopeless. In early November she spent a weekend in meditation and prayer in the cathedral city of Chartres, and, feeling some peace and resolution, she then wrote Ernest to cancel the agreement and accept the divorce.

"Come to see Bumby as much as you want," she insisted in a note to Ernest. "He is yours as much as mine—and take him out sometimes if you feel like that kind of thing—so that he will know you are his real papa. Drop in and see me if you want and—let's be impersonal."[24] (By "impersonal," she seems to mean friendly, above recent bitter quarreling.) Later there were more tensions, some of which would reveal interesting things about the Hemingways' faith lives, which they talked about rarely but apparently hewed to fiercely. When Hemingway suggested that he and Pauline, as Catholics, wanted Bumby to join their Left Bank parish of St. Sulpice, Hadley objected strongly: "He belongs to the Episcopalian Church by baptism & I hope will grow up free of judgment and full of faith in these matters. He can make up his own mind when he's eighteen and be as many Catholics as he wants then."[25]

In a gesture surely born of guilt and generosity both, Ernest offered Hadley all the royalties *The Sun Also Rises* would earn in perpetuity. Editing the book then for final publication, he could have had no real idea just how popular it would become. As the novel was an immediate bestseller and a modern classic, devoured by college students and back-packers in Paris and Pamplona alike from 1926 to this day, the spark that caused the running of the bulls in Pamplona to explode in the popular imagination and become a tourist's bucket-list item, these funds would make Hadley financially comfortable for the rest of her life. As for this willingly lost income, Hemingway may have been simply generous, or he may have had great confidence in his continued earning power as a writer. Or he may have felt that Pauline's family money—she had a doting Uncle Gus who sat on a pile of pharmaceutical profits—was a hedge against future financial reverses. Her money certainly did change Hemingway's life. After honeymooning in Le Grau-du-Roi and Pam-plona and Madrid and Santiago de Compostela on Pauline's funds in the spring of 1927, the new Hemingways moved on to the seaside resort of Hendaye, in the very farthest southwest corner of France, where the country is bounded by Spain to the south and the Atlantic to the west. There, amid France's rebellious Basque people, and perhaps prompted in part by their attitude toward government, in September of 1927 Hemingway started a new novel.

Looking past the unaccustomed luxuries he was then experiencing, he began to write what the scholars call the revolutionist novel.[26] The book is the clearest sign that Hemingway still dwelt on the question his surrealist friends continued to raise: whether some sort of smart, creative, iconoclastic, worker-centered revolution was still possible in the modern world; indeed, whether such a revolution could even be imagined in the fog of imperialist and consumerist propaganda. Hemingway told friends that the novel would be his *Tom Jones*—like Henry Fielding's 1749 picaresque novel, a lightly plotted series of adventures that satirize society by focusing on an intuitively gifted outcast from that society. (Hemingway loved another picaresque novel, *The Adventures of Huckleberry Finn*, which he believed to be the origin of all modern writing.) Hemingway's outcasts would be a father and son who traveled from Michigan to Europe in order to take part in a revolution they hoped would create a kind of workers' paradise, or at least a more humane and equitable society. He called the novel *A New-Slain Knight*, and he intended it to illustrate how the lake country of northern Michigan could produce a genuine revolutionary, a man so threatening to the powers that be that the State Department would refuse him a passport. The book also illustrated how the politically naïve could be tutored by the veteran revolutionary, as the revolutionist father raises a teenage son so tough and politically willing (if not politically astute) that he becomes his father's revolutionary apprentice. This father and son combined Hemingway's own dearest interests: love for family and friends, love for the natural world, love for a country's future, and love for revolutionary consciousness and determination. The book was to be modernist to the core, free of moral judgment and complex in its treatment of social ills, examining even criminality as a result of economic inequities.[27] It was to be deeply autobiographical too, an opportunity for Hemingway to tell further stories about his childhood summers in Michigan while adding a kind of wish-fulfillment element, converting his pious, conservative, patriotic, teetotal Victorian father into a hard-drinking modernist progressive, ready and eager for revolution.

Hemingway worked on this novel throughout 1927, writing twenty-two chapters before he lost momentum on it, or perhaps lost faith in its premise. He could not seem to get his father-and-son revolutionists onto a boat bound for Europe.[28] Where, after all, would they go to find a proper revolution to support, and would that revolution be a fictional one or some actual political crisis then occurring in time and space?

Meanwhile, he found himself distracted by both the most favorable and the most dismissive reviews of *The Sun Also Rises* and of the collection of stories that followed close on the novel, *Men without Women* (1927). Now that he was an emerging literary star, he had to deal with many offers from magazines and publishing houses, and he took pleasure in telling editors who had formerly rejected his work that he now had little interest in their needs or their tastes. Already he saw that he would not need to depend on Pauline's money after all.

In October of 1927 Hemingway wrote to his new mother-in-law that he could not decide whether to return to the States before or after the traditional Christmas-through-February sojourn to the Alps. Thinking about his stalled progress on the novel, Hemingway wrote to Mrs. Pfeiffer about the reasons he could not promise to bring her daughter home to her by Christmastime. It all had to do with the demands of composing: "You see when you are not working for anyone, but only in your head, and not writing down something that has happened but making it all up entirely, you get careful about going to new places while the work is going on because if one morning the head doesn't work and you can't make anything up, you are through."[29] Hemingway knew that the next new place in his life was to be Piggott, Arkansas, the Pfeiffers' hometown. He also knew that he wrote and felt better in apartments and inns where the views were spectacular, the food and drink interesting and ample, and the privacy congenial to the sexually hungry. This letter may have been a first move in prepping the Pfeiffer family for a rejection of life in Piggott.

But in January of 1928 Pauline discovered she was pregnant, and like Hadley in 1923, she insisted on a return to North America for the birth of the child. This time Hemingway welcomed the decision. He and Pauline wanted to get home to the United States as badly as Quoc wanted to get to East Asia, and their gaze to the west was as ardent as his was to the east. "I should have gone to America two years ago when I planned," he wrote to his new Scribner editor Max Perkins, whose partnership with Hemingway had been efficiently brokered by Fitzgerald after the *Torrents* debacle. "I was through with Europe and needed to go to America before I could write the book that happened there."

It turned out he could not write the book anyway. In March of 1928, still in Paris in his and Pauline's rue Ferou flat, he suffered a large

C-shaped cut on his forehead when a skylight fell on his head. Using his bathroom after waking late at night, he had pulled the chain for the skylight in the dark, thinking it was the flush chain for the toilet. The whole metal and glass skylight came down upon him. Coming home from the emergency clinic, high on painkillers and likely concussed, he suddenly realized he wanted to write a different novel. It would be about the war, and eventually it would be titled *A Farewell to Arms* (1929). He knew there would be revolutionary themes in the new war novel too, including persuasive and likeable Italian communist soldiers. But Hemingway was now free of the troubling rewriting of his relationship with his father, and free of portraying characters modeled after himself as doctrinaire, committed revolutionaries. He would still ponder revolutionary questions about the demands of patriotism versus the wish for revolutionary change, but he would do so less overtly than he was attempting in the revolutionist novel. He could play with the leftist trench mutinies rumored to have happened during the war, and he could explore Switzerland again, as a peaceful island in a warring world.

Later that month, the Hemingways sailed on the *Orita* for Havana, where they were to catch the ferry for the ninety-mile trip to Key West. They could just as easily have sailed for New Orleans, another southern port handy to Arkansas. Then they would have needed no ferry transfer—and Cajun foods might appear in the Hemingway cookbooks instead of tropical rum cocktails. But Havana was the destination on the tickets they purchased. They were to pick up a new Ford coupe on the Key West docks, a gift from Uncle Gus. They were to drive the Ford to Arkansas to complete their journey to their new home. But the car was not ready when they arrived, so Hemingway and Pauline were stranded for a few weeks in Key West. Before long, they met people they liked, invited friends to visit them, and enjoyed the deepwater fishing these friends offered in return. Hemingway fell in love with a dive bar called Sloppy Joe's, a far cry in style from Montparnasse's Select or Dôme, but friendlier perhaps. He realized, to his surprise, that he wrote well in the exotic, tropical backwater, with its carnival-like main street entertaining sailors from the local submarine base. So he and Pauline decided they would make their next home in the Florida Keys.

Hemingway gave up Paris for Key West just as he gave up *A New-Slain Knight* for *A Farewell to Arms*. The novels are nearly as different from each other as the cities are and were. We do not know just what story would have evolved if Hemingway had finished the picaresque novel about radical revolutionaries. Yet this is one of the many moments when Nguyen Ai Quoc's hopes and dreams illuminate a dark, neglected corner of Hemingway's writings. During the weeks just prior to sailing for Havana with Pauline, working on his revolutionary-father novel, Hemingway read a number of books that delved into the colonial experience, including *Lawrence and the Arabs*, *Recollections of the Irish War*, and *The Riddle of the Irish*.[30] Clearly, the ills of colonialism were in some way going to become a concern of one of his revolutionary characters, perhaps the father, who was supposed to be a veteran of twelve revolutions. Hemingway's love for the colonial writers Kipling, Conrad, and Joyce had finally borne not just exotic adventure tales but politically progressive fruit. Still, in spite of this new material, Hemingway could not push the novel forward into a revolutionary situation in Europe. It appears he simply could not imagine a European place or time for his father and son to take up their revolutionary and anti-colonial work. Maybe Hemingway could not imagine the two with weapons in their hands.

Just as Quoc carried Paris with him to Canton and sent messages back to the City of Light about his continued commitment to his education into creative and peaceable revolutions, Hemingway brought Paris to Key West and wrote material that showed he retained his own revolutionary worldview. Once he began writing *A Farewell to Arms*, Hemingway found he could devise a quieter, subtler revolutionary subtext. His antihero, Frederic Henry, is conspicuous for his lack of revolutionary fervor—or even the compassion required to work effectively as a combat medic and ambulance driver. Though Frederic experiences the near-mortal wounding his author endured, and though he discusses revolutionary politics with Italian workers who had been drafted into his unit during the Great War and now considered committing politically motivated mutiny, he eventually builds a fantasy of a personal, sexual "separate peace" with his lovely English medical aide and lover, Catherine Barkley.

Far too many readers believe, mistakenly, that Hemingway desired and endorsed such a private union and rejection of the social world. This separate peace is, in fact, a satire on any fantasy of non-involvement in the lives of others. After escaping the war and brutal proto-fascist Italian military police, Frederic and Catherine end up in Hemingway's beloved Chamby, enjoying Switzerland's peace in their time. Catherine is carrying their child. They enjoy the quiet, the deep snow, the skiing and sledding, the chocolate, the kirsch and beer, and, especially, the time for each other. When it is time for their child to be born, they travel down the mountain to Montreux for the delivery—following the luge tracks, we know, of the colonial ex-military governor of Khartoum.

The situation ends tragically. For this and other sad reasons, *A Farewell to Arms* should be read as a satire on the hope for peace sought in merely bourgeois terms—peace with one's family, peace through consumer goods and creature comforts, peace through fantasies of merely private satisfactions. Most readers dwell instead on Frederic's love for Catherine and the tragic nature of her death. Some praise Frederic for his stoicism in the midst of loss and grief. But once we realize how often Hemingway thought about colonialism and progressive solutions to such geopolitical travesties, we can see the novel's hints that a life of commitment and resistance is essential. Like most sensible people in his day and ours, Hemingway hoped for modern, creative solutions to broad social injustices such as hunger, poverty, and stolen liberty, and he still knew that a retreat into craven pleasures—sex and food and drink and money and fame and power and diverting fun—were no substitute for this vocation.

# 21

## WHAT SHOULD ONE LOVE?

### QUOC AND HEMINGWAY DURING

### AND AFTER PARIS

A s late as the middle 1920s, anyone in Paris, Quoc and Hemingway included, could board a northbound bus to make a visit to a less fortunate city, one that had been completely destroyed during the Great War. The tragic Belgian city of Ypres was still in ruins. It remained a pile of rubble well into the decade. In one 1922 picture postcard of Ypres we can see that the only restored, weather-tight building in the central city is the Hôtel-Restaurant Excelsior, a minimal, temporary, and new two-story wooden barrack fronted by a large cobbled parking area for the touring cars and cabs that brought sightseers to town. Surrounding this rectangular building are acres of rubble, formerly the homes, shops, and public buildings of the town, including its immense, beautiful, medieval Gothic structures, St. Martin's Cathedral and the Cloth Hall. We see open touring limousines in the parking lot outside the Excelsior, Citroëns marked *Agence Rayo*, each carrying about a dozen passengers, including women in belted jackets, skirts, and large hats and men in suits, ties, and flat straw boaters. These people seem to be having a good time. Smaller private cabs park alongside.[1] We see no sign of the Vietnamese men who went out to the trenches surrounding the town each day to search for bodies—or, to be more accurate, decaying parts of bodies. The Vietnamese laborers worried that the improperly buried and remembered dead might become malign ghosts. But they did the work anyway.

Almost everyone in Paris in the first half of the 1920s wanted to visit the Ypres Salient, an area of military activity people had read about so often during the war, the site of savage fighting because it was a favored wartime route for the Germans on their way to Paris, which they were determined to possess and occupy, and for the Allies to drive toward Germany.[2] In 1914 the still-mobile armies struggling for control of Paris stalled in and around Ypres, where they dug their first trenches. Neither the Allies nor the Central Powers accomplished a breakthrough in the Salient. Instead they fought in bloody stalemate, on essentially the same ground, about one or two awful battles per year from 1914 to 1918. The area in and around Ypres became a muddy, churned-up hell, littered with bits of barbed wire, lost and broken weapons, shell fragments and unexploded shells, and chunks of human bone. Even today, munitions experts remove tons of unexploded ordnance from the local battlefields every year. Farmers plowing fields often find human remains.

Poison gas was first used by the Germans in Ypres, the very first cloud drifting toward Allied soldiers on April 22, 1915. At first the troops who had just taken over for the British in the area judged the cloud to be beautiful and harmless. According to one of them, it looked like "mists seen over water meadows on a frosty night." The first soldiers to breathe in these mists were from colonial North Africa. These unfortunate men, Algerians called Turcos and Zouaves, numbered around fifteen thousand. Standing on parapets along the front edge of their trenches, they gazed curiously at the head-high cloud until it arrived at their front lines. Then they breathed in the beautiful cloud, trying to judge its character by its strange aroma. Nothing happened at first. Slowly the men became aware that their skin and lungs were beginning to hurt. Soon enough the pain grew intense, and it dawned on them that they had been badly burned, not only on their exposed skin but under their clothing and boots and in their lungs as well. They didn't know it yet, but as historian S. L. A. Marshall puts it, all these soldiers had ahead of them was "slow death, excruciating invalidism, and shock panic."[3] If enough gas made it into the lungs, within a few days, suppurating chemical burns caused the victims to drown in their own fluids. Non-mortal burns to the skin and eyes could not be bandaged and caused extreme pain. Nurses reported that soldiers hospitalized with bullet or shrapnel wounds normally tried to be stoic about the pain, but chlorine and mustard gas victims could not stop screaming.[4]

If we ask what lessons were learned from this horror, the answer is discouraging. In 1924, within a year of the time Quoc and Hemingway lived and worked and learned near each other in Paris, both studying the ills of French colonialism among other modern problems, the French and Spanish used mustard gas against colonial Riffian rebels in Morocco. Some of these rebels were probably among the *Turcos* and *Zouaves* who first experienced weaponized chlorine gas in Belgium a few years earlier, when they were considered heroes of Greater France. If the victims in Morocco were not the same North Africans, then they were their younger brothers and cousins. Arguably, the Riffians still fought nobly for France's future in 1924, just as they had during the Great War. Now they were engaged in principled revolt, trying to realize the French ideals of *liberté, égalité*, and *fraternité* for their own people. Through their acts of resistance in North Africa's colonies, they were trying to widen, not negate, these French values, as Hemingway saw when he referred obliquely to the problem the Rif War had become for defenders of empire in his 1926 novel *The Sun Also Rises*.[5] His main character, Jake Barnes, refuses a friend's urging that he tease a local waitress about the "jam" the French and their Spanish allies have gotten into in the Riff. Apparently reluctant to tease a girl whose brother might be awaiting a gas attack there, he demurs.

For the French and the residents of France's colonies, peace was proving elusive. We know now that the Riffian rebellion was only one of the wars, including another catastrophic world war, that would convulse Europe and its colonies during the twentieth century, one after another. Prescient observers in the 1920s saw these conflicts coming, which is why there was an acid joke going around Paris during the 1919 Peace Conference that Quoc attended. As dubious treaties with Austria, Hungary, Bulgaria, and the rest of the Hapsburg Empire were beginning to be debated in early spring, people said that the Council of Four—Wilson, Lloyd George, Clemenceau, and Orlando—seemed to be preparing "a just and lasting war." Many witnesses to this failed peace conference apparently thought their leaders had also learned too little from the past few years.

Ho and Hemingway seem to have been sharper, and they worked harder to learn. They came to Paris sharing a widespread belief that the Great War was an attempt by anti-modernists to resist modern changes that might erode their wealth and power. Certainly there is evidence that anti-progressivism was one factor motivating those who favored the war. A British field marshal named Lord Roberts thought war was the only way to cleanse "the great human rottenness that is rife in our industrial cities"—a clear condemnation of working people's ways.[6] Before he lost a son to the war and softened his views, Rudyard Kipling saw the war as a healthy lesson to irritating progressive "shouters and marchers," who wanted better pay rather than the defense spending he thought far more important. As war loomed, Kipling even worked to get his son quickly into Sandhurst, England's elite national officer training school, a decision he regretted deeply once his son was killed leading troops in battle.

Just before the war, Scotland Yard assigned a former colonial official named Basil Thomson to the task of surveilling anyone who threatened the status quo. Soon he had agents attending meetings of potential strikers, opening the mail of suffragettes, and monitoring the Labour Party. He remarked to a friend once that "unless there were a European War to divert the current [of such progressive efforts], we were heading for something very like revolution." An army officer of the time expressed a similar worry, writing in a letter to a trusted friend, "A good big war just now might do a lot of good in killing Socialist nonsense and would probably put a stop to all this labor unrest."[7] British Prime Minister David Lloyd George, whose diplomacy encouraged Hemingway so much at a postwar Italian peace conference, uttered an even more disturbing remark one day during the war. He declared that he would arrest and charge anyone who published the Sermon on the Mount if it "interfered with the war effort."[8] These reactionaries were aided and abetted by people such as Clarence Hemingway and Sarraut, who simply could not imagine or accept a world that was much changed from the one they grew up in. Judging by Clarence's distaste for his son's writing about refugees and Albert Sarraut's condemnation of Quoc's writing about colonial abuses, these nationalists would not even accept a change in the manners that helped preserve the world they knew and loved. It is hard to see how such men honored the gospels, which they claimed to love and to teach.

One sign of the futility of this reactionary attempt to quash progressive change is that in the immediate postwar years, 1917 to 1923, almost all of Europe's nations still flirted with social and political unrest verging on revolution. As a result, all across Europe women got the vote, affordable medical care was made available to more people, and unions gained the right to bargain with the executive class for better wages. Historian Arno Mayer goes so far as to claim that 1914 was not just the beginning of the First World War, but the beginning of a new Thirty Years' War in Europe, continued clashes between such humanitarian progressives, the reactionaries and fascists who opposed them, and hardcore revolutionaries who hated liberal reformism and fascism both and, for better or worse, insisted upon an utterly new world.[9] These conflicts continued until the Second World War ended and the Cold War, with its nuclear weapons and its threat of "mutual assured destruction," imposed a fearful and uncharacteristic discipline on the warring nations. As we have seen, these reactionaries, modernists, and revolutionaries all had robust colonies in Paris, so it was a particularly good place to receive an education.

As Quoc and Hemingway monitored these processes from Paris during the 1920s, they saw that a middle way was most consistent with their humanism, which arose from and continued to be fed by their faiths. As usual, they looked to Switzerland as their model for an ongoing, experimental process designed to lead to an outcome they could embrace.

In 1918 Switzerland seemed poised for its own revolution, as a general strike spread across the country. When the government called up four military units one day and four more the next, nominally to quell foreign political agitators taking advantage of wartime tensions but really to put down the domestic rebellion, Swiss workers rebelled. From the traditional Swiss perspective, military involvement in political debates was a suppression of their rights to organize and speak out. It was a counterrevolutionary, reactionary attack on their liberties. All the Swiss wanted, the workers claimed, was redress for the suffering they had undergone since the war—four long years when prices tripled, wages fell by 30 percent, and farmers took cynical advantage, reaping huge profits. To signal their opposition to a government doing little to solve such problems and punish such abuses, labor leaders called a general strike. The strike gained enthusiastic participants in German-speaking eastern and northern Switzerland, where railroads were shut down, preventing most residents from going to work. Worker participation was more modest in the South and West, where Italian- and French-speaking Swiss workers were in the majority. Yet in the end, with the Swiss a peaceably divided citizenry of sincere constitutionalists, there was no national crisis or civil war between the North and South. Labor organizers who argued for a radical over-throw of the government never galvanized enough support for that truly revolutionary goal. Rather than a revolution and a new economy, work-ers merely wanted better lives within the current political and economic scheme. Like Quoc as he expressed himself in his 1926 "Screams" peti-tion, they wanted democratic government, but they also wanted govern-ment to be interested in their welfare. They wanted an end to profiteering but did not insist upon the dissolution of the moneyed classes.

In Norway in the early 1920s, something similar happened. It was another outcome for Quoc and Hemingway to admire, as they had admired that nation's neutrality during the Great War. Suffering Nor-wegian workers caused another revolutionary political crisis, but it, too, failed to lead to the adoption of a Soviet-style communist system. Just as in Switzerland, too few Norwegians were willing to endorse the Third International. Indeed, some unionized Norwegians, otherwise sympa-thetic to a dramatic shift in political power toward the working man and woman, considered revolutionary deaths in Russia to be evidence of barbarism, and so they refused to affirm the Third International's call to violent revolution. The Lutheran Norwegians had their own tradi-tional views on the meaning of communal justice. One socialist editor went so far as to suggest that in Scandinavia, communism should be redefined. In Norway at least, he argued, the word had come to mean pacifism and Christian love.[10] Norwegians simply were not attracted to Moscow's more violent definition. The Norwegian idea of communism came to involve free schooling for the nation's children, from kinder-garten through university; government-funded pensions that would let Norwegians live out their post-working lives with dignity; and clinics and hospitals that would never turn any of them away for lack of money or for any other basically selfish or elitist reason.[11] It should be no sur-prise to us that, just before adopting Spain as his personal near-utopia, Hemingway planned to fish and travel and explore in Norway.

As a result of this peaceable European moderation, Bolshevism did not spread, and the Soviet Union remained isolated, a strange experimental nation with only a few reluctant satellite states nearby. The "Bolshevik autumn" was not beautiful enough for 1920s Europe, as McDonald notes: "If thousands of workers and intellectuals outside Russia welcomed the Bolshevik autumn with fervor and anticipation of general revolution, many others among the ranks of the socialist parties and unions regarded the Soviet experiment with skepticism and suspicion."[12] The socialist skeptics won the day because they exercised reasonable humanitarian judgment.

Quoc and Hemingway came to Paris to learn the history, the politics, the artistry, and the philosophy—maybe even the theology—of such humane judgment. Because they had been not only offended by the empires but nearly killed by them, and then made to suffer under them, both men cared about the task of lessening human pain. They also learned to ask the right questions. As most of us do, they learned this critical thinking through sustained, idealistic, intellectual study as young adults. "I have not had the good fortune to follow courses at the university," Quoc wrote in 1920. "But life has given me an opportunity to study history, the social sciences, and even military science." He knew that his learning had prompted him to ask some very important questions: "What should one love? What should one despise?" he asked. "For we Vietnamese, it is necessary to love independence, work, and the motherland."[13]

*What should one love? What should one despise?* It is hard to think of better guiding questions for an education, or better ways to phrase the attitudes Ho and Hemingway brought to Paris.

≡ ≡ ≡

Quoc's remark shows us that he viewed his studies in Paris as deeply personal and deeply ethical both. He acknowledges that he searched for a meaningful life serving others with passion. The route to that passion and that mission, he saw, was wide-ranging learning. He lists history, the social sciences, and military science as his major subjects in Paris, but we know he also read literature, looked at art, attended various performances of music and dance, debated and discussed contemporary ideas of the popular culture, and was an astute student of political philosophy. His acquaintances reported that whenever he had time, he walked to the

Sorbonne, where he read Shakespeare, Dickens, Hugo, Zola, Tolstoy, Lu Xun, Barbusse, and others.[14] Biographers report that he also studied the scriptures concerning Christ and the Buddha, and we know that his father, as a professional scholar of Confucianism, trained him as a practical theologian and believer.[15] Quoc updated these ancient teachings about human justice by reading Marx and Lenin, and biographer Jean Lacouture reports that a socialist named Vaillant-Couturier read aloud to him from the writings of the first anarchist Pierre-Joseph Proudhon and from the works of archetypal historian of the French Revolution Jules Michelet.[16]

More than any other aspect of Paris, Quoc said, he loved his freedom to read. He was grateful for "[the city's] libraries, its museums, and its books on various subjects [that] could be read by anyone without official restrictions."[17] He received his library card from Marx's grandson Jean Longuet, and then spent long hours in the library at Sainte-Geneviève and the Bibliothèque Nationale. French undercover police knew that Ho was working on the exposé *The Oppressed,* so they tracked his borrowing in the library. As we have seen, he checked out thirteen books on Indochina, including histories of the tax revolts he had witnessed firsthand, and studies of agriculture and finance in the colony.[18]

His varied learning was not confined to reading. He traveled throughout France, on socialist or communist business and for pleasure, but also signed up for popular commercial tours of Italy and Switzerland.[19] Historians of the Club du Faubourg record that he went to theater performances, art exhibitions, and salons, and note Quoc's interest in practical science, which led him to a session on aeronautics at Le Bourget airport, where Lindbergh would conclude his unprecedented transatlantic flight in 1927.[20] Even though he was teased in Paris for his basic language skills and for his shyness and acquaintances once called him "the mute of Montmartre," Quoc loved attending discussions at the Club du Faubourg. Apart from debates noted already between Christians and Bolsheviks, the club hosted discussions of both traditionalist and avant-garde intellectual life, including novels, painting, and theater. We know that Quoc attended lectures on reincarnation and the occult, subjects that had just become fascinations of the many people who had lost young loved ones during the war and wished, however desperately, to hear from them again.[21]

Thanh/Ba/Quoc certainly epitomized a pattern of learning and enlightenment that his generation of Vietnamese revolutionaries underwent, if they were lucky. In *Vietnamese Tradition on Trial*, David Marr argues that from 1900 onward, three generations of Vietnamese dissenters laid the groundwork for the Vietnamese people's anti-colonial revolutions under Ho Chi Minh. First came the scholar-gentry, trained in traditional Confucianism (or, we might add, Vietnam's even more sweeping Buddhism) but intrigued by the works of "Montesquieu, Rousseau, Smith, and Spencer"—that is, open to learning about secular liberal government, Romantic idealism, free-market capitalism, and the survival of the fittest. Marr claims that this generation understood such intellectual works "only vaguely." The scholar-gentry gave way to the intelligentsia of the 1920s, young men and women who knew neo-Confucianism only slightly and wanted Western learning to open the door to greater freedoms and eventually to an independent Vietnam. Marr makes a startling remark about the intellectual bridge these young Vietnamese students had to cross: "Their parents still believed in ghosts, arranged marriages, and strict social harmony," he writes. "However, in school, and increasingly through extracurricular means, they learned of cameras, germs, atoms, galaxies, free love, class struggle, and biological evolution."

This was Nguyen Ai Quoc's generation. Loving both modern intellectual concepts *and* their parents' ghosts, arranged marriages, and deep respect for family and neighbor, Quoc's generation required a framework for reconciling these two worlds. They came to love the liberal arts and sciences. Marr sees that this is so: "They wanted to look further, to explain the contradictions, and to fashion a new consciousness for themselves and for the Vietnamese people at large." Some second-generation intellectuals willingly signed on with the Viet Minh and their later iterations. Drawing on their broad intellectual training, they became the conscience of the revolutionary movement, even as they served as its troops or led as its officers.

Marr's third generation of Vietnamese dissenters were frustrated with temporizing and delay. They preferred action to theorizing, and sought to transcend the patient, thoughtful intellectuals in their circle. Some began to believe, with Lenin, that the conscience itself was an impediment to change, a useless construct that tended to block bold action. These revolutionaries may have had intellectual training in both classic Western and Confucian works, but they came to celebrate single-mindedness, not democracy and community. They became the "edu-cated cadres" (as Marr calls them) of the Viet Minh, the Indochinese Communist Party, and, eventually, of the Viet Cong and the North Vietnamese people and its army.[22]

In the revered Vietnamese novel of the American war, Bao Ninh's *The Sorrow of War*, we see that Vietnamese troops loved and learned from their cadres, who practiced kindness and support much more than they taught Lenin or Mao.[23] But some of the cadres grew more ideologi-cal and calloused. They cajoled and bullied those who were not, in their views, fervent enough about Vietnamese liberation, as Le Duan bullied Ho. These cadres were the kind who, after the Vietnam War, celebrated the reeducation camps.

Quoc was much more the second-generation intellectual than the third-generation party cadre. It does seem that sometime in the early 1950s, after both France and the United States disappointed him by brushing off his constitutionalist pleas, he became more frustrated and ideological in the Leninist stripe, more of the Party cadre. So even though we should admire his learning in Hue and Paris, and should respect tes-timony that he was a charming, gentle, thoughtful fellow throughout his long life, there is also evidence that he came to regard compassion as sometimes quaint and outmoded, especially in the midst of a patriotic war. Some historians would go further: as one historian of Vietnamese students in France puts it, Quoc and others in his generation learned a very hard and very modern lesson—"not only the organizational and intellectual skills to lead, but the ideological motivation to carry out, amongst their own people, political murders by the thousands."[24]

≡ ≡ ≡

Hemingway's Parisian curriculum was just as ambitious, and just as deeply tied to ethical expression and action. Biographer Jeffrey Mey-ers proposes that Hemingway entered into his own period of intense study in Paris for narrow personal reasons, because he envied university-educated buddies:

Hemingway soon found that many of his friends had graduated from Ivy League colleges and were extremely well educated. Pound had been at the University of Pennsylvania; Stein at Radcliffe; Dos Passos and Waldo Pierce at Harvard; Bill Horne, Strater, Loeb and Fitzgerald at Princeton; MacLeish, Murphy and Donald Stewart at Yale. Hemingway, who was highly intelligent, began to educate himself with an intensive course of reading.[25]

Hemingway surely knew that as a writer he was competing with trained and clever minds, and he was certainly competitive, but he trained himself for greatness and effectiveness rather than for competition with talented locals. He was more inclined to keep up with the Joyces and Eliots than with the Ivy League. He wanted to say something important to the world, not just prove himself to talented and well-educated peers, so he did study hard, and when he read and debated and visited galleries and attended shows, he sought out deeply intellectual materials, and he took them seriously.

Hemingway spent his Paris years reading avidly and with purpose. Sylvia Beach's Shakespeare & Company lending library at first supplied him with the works that Beach, along with Pound, Stein, and others, recommended to him. Unfortunately, Hemingway's and Hadley's lending cards for Shakespeare & Company have not yet been found, but we can track much of his reading through his letters, memoirs, and allusions to books in his writing. He read Tolstoy, Dostoevsky, Turgenev, Stendhal, Flaubert, Maupassant, Kipling, Conrad, Joyce, D. H. Lawrence, Twain, James, Crane, Anderson, and Eliot. Of course he read Stein and Pound. He read lowbrow too, devouring Georges Simenon's Detective Maigret novels, a gaucho novel by W. H. Hudson, Owen Wister's *The Virginian*, and Marie Belloc Lowndes's Jack the Ripper novel, *The Lodger*, which he and Stein both loved. Like Quoc, he read Barbusse to know more about the French soldier's miserable experience in wartime trenches.[26]

Yet he was not after merely literary training, as the following incomplete list of his reading in the 1920s attests. There was psychology: We know that he read Havelock Ellis's psychology of sex, with its ethic of almost total tolerance for sexual identities and practices. He read William James's *Psychology*, which was probably in his library because Stein had studied with the Harvard professor James while she attended Rad-cliffe. There was history: Just as Quoc researched every source he could find on French colonialism, Hemingway tried to figure out what the war had been about and how it had been fought. So he read all the early histories and memoirs of the war he could find, as well as the war fiction in both English and French, such as Tolstoy's *War and Peace* and Clause-witz's *On War*. There was political philosophy: He owned a copy of the *Communist Manifesto*, alluded to Machiavelli, and talked with political journalists such as Paul Mowrer about balkanized Europe. He found art wherever he looked: There were, of course, the Cézannes and Matisses and Picassos at the Musée du Luxembourg and at Stein's apartment, but he also gazed at the classic paintings and sculptures at the Louvre, and at the brash new works he saw in the studios of Miró, Masson, Man Ray, and Picasso. There was classical music: Not only did Hadley celebrate his return to her in 1922 Switzerland after one of his reporting trips by playing Bach-Busoni *Chaconnes* for him, works that she prac-ticed and practiced beforehand, but the two of them were also interested in the tuneless, seemingly disordered music of the moderns, including Stravinsky. Hemingway was good friends with Virgil Thomson and George Antheil, who would both become world famous and important modernist composers. There was scripture and theology: Hemingway quoted from both the King James Bible and the Anglican *Book of Com-mon Prayer* in his early works—indeed he framed those works in biblical terms with his titles and epigraphs, taking his title *In Our Time* from an Anglican prayer and his title *The Sun Also Rises* from Ecclesiastes. He took George Borrow's *The Bible in Spain* to Pamplona with him.

There was his special Pound curriculum in Western Civ. Pound and Eliot believed in writers they called the Tradition: there were Homer, Catullus, Ovid, Chaucer, Dante, Villon, the metaphysical poets, Flau-bert, and Stendhal.[27] Pound was so specific in his directions that he listed Henry James novels Hemingway was encouraged to read and others he was directed to ignore. Pound once chided Hemingway for complaining about the time he spent reading a James novel Hadley had liked but that he found boring. If Hemingway was going to ignore his syllabus, Pound declared with some asperity, then he could expect to experience further unpleasant consequences.

Pound proved that a deep and rigorous education in Western thought, especially one lacking proper humane and spiritual guidance, can lead to error, injustice, bigotry, and tragedy. Hemingway avoided Pound's virulent bigotry and mistaken hatred of America, but he, too, became a more hardened man as his life proceeded. While there is nothing wrong with altering affections, his serial marriages and affairs hint at an increasingly careless disdain for women's dignity, if not actual misogyny. His novels after the 1920s tend to promote a sentimental heroism in his central male characters, rather than the full, complex intellectual engagement in life's difficulties and opportunities that we see among both men and women in *In Our Time* and *The Sun Also Rises*, and already waning in *A Farewell to Arms*. Beginning sometime in the 1930s, Hemingway seemed to buy into his own press, which often referred to a "Hemingway code" of "grace under pressure." Such a code may be present in his work, but it explains far too few of his meanings, especially in those wonderful works he wrote in Paris.

Then there is his work as an agent for the Soviets. According to Soviet files, agents approached Hemingway in 1940 after three events that encouraged them: There was his 1935 diatribe against the federal government for leaving Bonus Army marchers vulnerable to the hurricane that killed many of them; then there was his support for the Soviets during the time of their support for anti-fascist Republican forces during the Spanish Civil War; and finally there was an anti-fascist speech he made at Carnegie Hall in 1937.[28] The files show evidence that he signed on as a rather benign Soviet agent, a sort of cheerleader for further worker-centered policies and anti-fascist efforts, and talent scout for other new propaganda assets like him. Yet Hemingway's flirtation with totalitarian communism is no more encouraging than Quoc's. It is one thing to support the Soviet Union during the part of World War II when the Soviets were America's allies, but quite another to continue that work during the USSR's Cold War aggressions, as Hemingway apparently did. (This is not to imply that being an American patriot in that day was either innocent or un-complex.) He seems to have become a kind of Party cadre too, in a distinctly underhand way.

≡ ≡ ≡

While careful students of Ho Chi Minh and Ernest Hemingway will find plenty of evidence of humane feeling in both men after 1928, it still seems that in leaving Paris both renounced the quieter and perhaps more important benefit the city had provided: a community of helpful, supportive mentors and critics. Each lost his crucible of friends. For the rest of their careers, Ho and Hemingway would more or less go it alone. Other people in their lives became adjuncts and assistants to their projects, rather than strong, influential peers. Lacking the helpful, humane counsel they needed, both Ho and Hemingway developed their characteristic single-minded, self-regarding ruthlessness.

If it is true that a liberal arts education is supposed to make us more alert to others' needs and creative in meeting them, less likely to push for personal advantages or to accelerate the pace of change or to angle for profit at others' cost, then in an important sense Ho's and Hemingway's Paris educations had at least partly failed. But failure, as we know, is the most normal and the most interesting story. And there is nevertheless a hopeful character to both Ho's and Hemingway's farewells to Paris. They had fought a good fight in resisting tyranny and bigotry, and, for a time, they had largely chosen humane things to love and to despise. They left Paris to continue their resistance against those forces that waste lives and ignore poverty and consume selfishly and hate difference and make unnecessary war. That resistance is difficult work to sustain artfully, and if they were not completely successful at it, perhaps we can understand and forgive.

# NOTES

## CHAPTER 1

1. These were popular contemporary interpretations of the time, since challenged by scholars.
2. I mean the future Ho Chi Minh. Please see the Preface for help with Ho Chi Minh's pseudonyms, particularly Thanh, Ba, and Quoc.
3. Ezra Pound wore a scarf in 1920s Paris that captures this zeitgeist: knitted into the scarf was the motto "Make it new."
4. Adam Hochschild, *To End All Wars: A Story of Loyalty and Rebellion, 1914–1918* (New York: Houghton Mifflin Harcourt, 2011), xi–xx.
5. Not until 1939 did the Great War become the First World War, in caps.
6. Princeton historian Arno Mayer makes this case most strongly, though many other historians I cite, including Peter Englund, Adam Hochschild, Philip Jenkins, and others, note the insincerity of the most avid war makers in their articulation of the war's real purpose.
7. In those days it wasn't important to secure fuel oil for cars and trucks, which were few, but for battleships. And "to trump" had fewer meanings.
8. James Mellow, *Charmed Circle: Gertrude Stein & Company* (New York: Henry Holt, 1974), 370–72. In the midst of this same passage, Stein suggests that Hitler should receive the Nobel Prize—but I choose not to cite it as a serious remark because she made it impishly and some have argued she was being ironic and deliberately provocative.
9. Nicholas Reynolds, *Writer, Sailor, Soldier, Spy: Ernest Hemingway's Secret Adventures, 1935–1961* (New York: William Morrow, 2017), 81 and 221–22.

## CHAPTER 2

1. William J. Duiker, *Ho Chi Minh: A Life* (New York: Hyperion, 2000), 17.
2. Duiker, *Ho Chi Minh*, 23.

3. Pierre Brocheux and Daniel Hémery, *Indochina: An Ambiguous Colonization, 1858–1954* (Berkeley: University of California Press, 2011), 5.
4. Duiker, *Ho Chi Minh*, 23.
5. Duiker, *Ho Chi Minh*, 41.
6. Pierre Brocheux, *Ho Chi Minh: A Biography*, trans. Claire Duiker (New York: Cambridge University Press, 2007), 6.
7. EH to Hemingway Family, 10 October 1918, in *The Letters of Ernest Hemingway*, eds. Sandra Spanier and Robert W. Trogdon, vo. 1, *1907–1922* (New York: Cambridge University Press, 2011), 147.
8. In American higher education today, we tend to teach communication first, independent of "content," and teach critical thinking as a fetish, as though it exists apart from clear thinking about intellectual content.
9. Duiker, *Ho Chi Minh*, 39.
10. David G. Marr, *Vietnamese Tradition on Trial, 1920–1945* (Berkeley: University of California Press, 1981), 74.
11. Michael Reynolds, *Hemingway's Reading, 1910–1940: An Inventory* (Princeton: Princeton University Press, 1981), 39–43.
12. EH to Clarence and Grace Hall Hemingway, 16 September 1915, in *Letters of Ernest Hemingway*, 1:22.
13. Mary V. Dearborn, *Ernest Hemingway: A Biography* (New York: Knopf, 2017), 79.
14. Duiker, *Ho Chi Minh*, 35. Both Brocheux and Duiker tell essentially the same story of the May 1908 near-tragedy, but the quoted chant is from Duiker.
15. All the Hemingway biographies tell essentially the same core story about this day, then launch into doubts and discrepancies that do not concern this telling.
16. Ted Brumback to Clarence and Grace Hall Hemingway, 14 July 1918, in *Letters of Ernest Hemingway*, 1:115.
17. EH, *A Farewell to Arms*, Hemingway Library Edition (New York: Scribner, 2012), 47.
18. Kenneth Schuyler Lynn, *Hemingway: The Life and the Work* (New York: Simon & Schuster, 1987), 99.
19. EH to Hemingway Family, 18 October 1918, in *Letters of Ernest Hemingway*, 1:147.
20. EH, *Farewell*, 161.

## CHAPTER 3

1. EH, "Soldier's Home," *In Our Time* (New York: Scribner, 1925/2003), 69–77.
2. EH, "Soldier's," 69.
3. EH, "Soldier's," 71.
4. EH, "Soldier's," 71.
5. EH, "Soldier's," 75.
6. EH, "Soldier's," 74–77.

7. EH, *In Our Time*, 21.
8. Gioia Diliberto, *Hadley* (New York: Ticknor and Fields, 1992), 243.
9. Wilfred Owen, "Parable of the Old Men and the Young," *Poetry of the First World War: An Anthology*, ed. Tim Kendall (New York: Cambridge University Press, 2013), 171.
10. Alice Conklin, *The French Republic: History, Values, Debates*, ed. Edward Berenson, Vincent Duclert, Christophe Prochasson (Ithaca: Cornell University Press, 2011), 173–74.
11. Pascal Blanchard, quoted in Clea Caulcutt, "Paris's Forgotten Human Zoo," *Visiting France* RFI, modified March 2, 2011, https://tinyurl.com/q2ajzub.
12. Caulcutt, "Forgotten."
13. Brocheux and Hémery, *Indochina*, 192.
14. Jules Francois Camille Ferry, "Speech Before the French Chamber of Deputies, March 28, 1884," *Discours et Opinions de Jules Ferry*, ed. Paul Robiquet, trans. Ruth Kleinman, https://tinyurl.com/y6bwsfw9.
15. Duiker, *Ho Chi Minh*, 34.
16. Brocheux and Hémery, *Indochina*, 192–93. This discussion includes the material on *tutoiement*.
17. He is father of the aviator Roland, who invented a way for World War I machine guns to shoot through airplane propellers without destroying them, and whose name is honored on the French Open tennis stadium.
18. Brocheux and Hémery, *Indochina*, 193.
19. Duiker, *Ho Chi Minh*, 39 and 50, for both of these drowning atrocities.
20. Marcel Duchamp, quoted in Leah Dickerman, ed., *Dada* (Washington: National Gallery of Art, 2006), 290. Subsequent chapters will describe the Dada movement in much more detail.

## CHAPTER 4

1. Duiker, *Ho Chi Minh*, 37.
2. Duiker, *Ho Chi Minh*, 40.
3. Duiker, *Ho Chi Minh*, 43–44.
4. Duiker, *Ho Chi Minh*, 44–53. This passage includes Ba's departure from Saigon through his stay in the United States.
5. Duiker, *Ho Chi Minh*, 52.
6. August Escoffier, *Memories of My Life* (New York: Van Nostrand Reinhold, 1997), 114.
7. Escoffier, *Memories*, 219.
8. Escoffier, *Memories*, 94.
9. Jean Lacouture, *Ho Chi Minh: A Political Biography* (New York: Random House, 1968), 10.
10. Duiker, *Ho Chi Minh*, 51–54.
11. Escoffier, *Memories*, 150.
12. Escoffier, *Memories*, 20–40.

13. Escoffier, *Memories*, 38.
14. Escoffier, *Memories*, 40.
15. Escoffier, *Memories*, 63.
16. Henry Du Pré Labouchère, "From Zoo to Table," *Lapham's Quarterly*, https://tinyurl.com/y5eszsry.
17. Alistair Horne, *Seven Ages of Paris* (New York: Vintage, 2002), 260.
18. Escoffier, *Memories*, 148.
19. Escoffier, *Memories*, 98–99.
20. Escoffier, *Memories*, 148, for the comment on socialism and quotation of Jesus's love command in Matt. 22:39.
21. Escoffier, *Memories*, 149.

## CHAPTER 5

1. Michael Reynolds, *The Young Hemingway* (New York: W. W. Norton, 1998), 99. Reynolds is better than most of the EH biographers at noting the importance of this moment for Ernest's career aspirations, and it is he who makes the observation about journalism and the literary life, and who lists relevant authors.
2. Keneth Kinnamon, "Hemingway and Politics," *The Cambridge Companion to Hemingway*, ed. Scott Donaldson (New York: Cambridge University Press, 1996), 159. Kinnamon notes that generations of Hemingway scholars have missed or minimized this vote.
3. EH letter to F. Scott Fitzgerald, 12 April 1931, in *Ernest Hemingway: Selected Letters, 1917–1961*, ed. Carlos Baker (New York: Scribner, 1981), 339.
4. Kinnamon, "Hemingway and Politics," 161.
5. "Preamble to the IWW Constitution," Industrial Workers of the World: A Union for All Workers, https://tinyurl.com/y2btogu9.
6. Industrial Workers of the World, www.iww.org.
7. Kinnamon, "Hemingway and Politics," 160.
8. James R. Mellow, *Hemingway: A Life without Consequences* (New York: Houghton Mifflin, 1992), 131.
9. Reynolds, *Young Hemingway*, 193.
10. Reynolds, *Young Hemingway*, 133–35.
11. Mellow, *Hemingway*, 120.
12. And now we know the likely origin of Ernest's idea for Krebs's dilemma in "Soldier's Home."
13. Isaac Don Levine, *The Russian Revolution* (New York: Harper & Brothers, 1917), 255 and 258.
14. Levine, *Revolution*, 265.
15. Levine, *Revolution*, 267. The italics are mine.
16. Levine, *Revolution*, 275–78.
17. Kim Townsend, *Sherwood Anderson* (New York: Houghton Mifflin, 1987), 80–81.

18. Sherwood Anderson, *Sherwood Anderson's Memoirs: A Critical Edition*, ed. Ray Lewis White (Chapel Hill: University of North Carolina Press, 1969), 315.
19. They were to become Hemingway's friends too.
20. Anderson, *Memoirs*, 315.
21. Anderson, *Memoirs*, 317.
22. Anderson, *Memoirs*, 353.
23. Hemingway and the Smith brothers ran a kind of liberal arts college in their apartment at 63 East Division Street. Not only did they have Levine and Anderson for dinner, but Hemingway met poet Carl Sandburg there, and it was not unusual for the men of the club to attend a classical concert, such as the Rachmaninoff concert after the Levine dinner.
24. In any case, he knew it by February of 1922.

## CHAPTER 6

1. David Halberstam, *Ho* (New York: Rowman & Littlefield, 2007), 43.
2. It could have been early 1919. Scholars argue about the precise date of Ba's arrival.
3. Halberstam, *Ho*, 8.
4. Duiker, *Ho Chi Minh*, 109.
5. Sophie Quinn-Judge, *Ho Chi Minh: The Missing Years* (Berkeley: University of California Press, 2002), 12.
6. David Andelman, *A Shattered Peace: Versailles 1919 and the Price We Pay Today* (New York: Wiley, 2014), 125.
7. Brocheux, *Ho Chi Minh*, 21.
8. James Brogan and Gil Jackman, *La Vie de Paris* (Bloomington, IN: iUniverse, 2008), 37.
9. Duiker, *Ho Chi Minh*, 64.
10. Son Ngoc Bui, "Anticolonial Constitutionalism: The Case of Ho Chi Minh," *Japanese Journal of Political Science* 19, no. 2, 208–9.

## CHAPTER 7

1. Duiker, *Ho Chi Minh*, 61.
2. Cosana Maria Eram, "The Autobiographical Pact: Otherness and Redemption in Four French Avant-garde Artists" (PhD diss., Stanford University, 2010), 20.
3. Janine Mileaf and Matthew S. Witkovsky, "Paris" in Leah Dickerman, *Dada* (Washington, DC: National Gallery of Art, 2005), 350.
4. Quinn-Judge, *Ho Chi Minh*, 29.
5. Quinn-Judge, *Ho Chi Minh*, 32.
6. Quinn-Judge, *Ho Chi Minh*, 29.
7. Brocheux, *Ho Chi Minh*, 22.
8. Quinn-Judge, *Ho Chi Minh*, 28.

## CHAPTER 8

1. Reynolds, *Young Hemingway*, 177.
2. In a story Hemingway never published, probably because of its sexual frankness, his autobiographical character Nick Adams has sex in the Michigan woods with a girl named Kate. Philip Young published this tale as "Summer People" in his 1972 collection of the published and previously unpublished Nick Adams stories: EH, *The Nick Adams Stories*, ed. Philip Young (New York: Scribner, 1972), 217–28.
3. EH to Hadley Richardson, 23 December 1920, in *Letters of Ernest Hemingway*, 1:258–59.
4. EH to Grace Quinlan, late July 1921, in *Letters of Ernest Hemingway*, 292–93.
5. *Letters of Ernest Hemingway*, 1:304n.
6. *Letters of Ernest Hemingway*, 1:309n.
7. French: *Tous les jours à tous points de vue je vais de mieux en mieux.*
8. Indeed, Duiker only refers to Marie in a footnote, never once in the text of his excellent book: Duiker, *Ho Chi Minh*, 593n.
9. Duiker, *Ho Chi Minh*, 593n.
10. This we know because she later supplied the insider's report on Quoc's activities.
11. Duiker, *Ho Chi Minh*, 64.
12. Margaret MacMillan, *Paris 1919: Six Months That Changed the World* (New York: Random House, 2007), 65.
13. Duiker, *Ho Chi Minh*, 72.
14. Walden Bello, *Ho Chi Minh: Down with Colonialism* (New York: Verso, 2007), 2.
15. Duiker, *Ho Chi Minh*, 71.
16. Quinn-Judge, *Ho Chi Minh*, 30.
17. Duiker, *Ho Chi Minh*, 76.
18. A. J. Langguth, *Our Vietnam: The War 1954–1975* (New York, Simon & Schuster, 2000), 34.
19. Duiker, *Ho Chi Minh*, 76–77.
20. Brocheux, *Ho Chi Minh*, 21.
21. Duiker, *Ho Chi Minh*, 79.
22. Duiker, *Ho Chi Minh*, 82.
23. EH to Sherwood and Tennessee Anderson, 23 December 1921, in *Letters of Ernest Hemingway*, 313.
24. MacMillan, *Paris 1919*, 67.
25. Christopher Lasch, *The American Liberals and the Russian Revolution* (New York: Columbia University Press, 1962), 198.
26. Lasch, *American Liberals*, 208.

## CHAPTER 9

1. Reynolds, *The Paris Years* (New York: W. W. Norton, 1989), 33.

2. Nancy L. Green, *The Other Americans in Paris: Businessmen, Countesses, Wayward Youth, 1880–1941* (Chicago: University of Chicago Press, 2014), 124.
3. Green, *The Other Americans,* 124.
4. Quoted in John Cohassey, *Hemingway and Pound: A Most Unlikely Friendship* (Jefferson, NC: McFarland, 2014), 7.
5. EH, "The Passing of Pickles McCarty or The Woppian Way," unpublished manuscript quoted in Richard Willing, "Hemingway Manuscript Revealed," *The Washington Post,* April 4, 1977, https://tinyurl.com/y4eounn3.
6. EH, *A Moveable Feast* (New York: Touchstone Books, 1964/1992), 108.
7. Ford Madox Ford, "Ezra," in Eric Homberger, ed. *Ezra Pound* (New York: Routledge, 2009), 223.
8. Humphrey Carpenter, *A Serious Character: The Life of Ezra Pound* (Boston: Houghton Mifflin, 1988), 403–4.
9. Mellow, *Hemingway,* 152–53. The meeting is common knowledge, but Mellow emphasizes Hemingway's deference.
10. Ezra Pound, "In a Station of the Metro," *Poetry: A Magazine in Verse* 2, no. 1 (Spring 1913): 12.
11. T. S. Eliot, *The Waste Land: A Facsimile and Transcript of the Original Drafts Including the Annotations of Ezra Pound* (New York: Harvest Books, 1971), 2–35.
12. Carpenter, *Serious Character,* 187.
13. Ezra Pound, "A Few Don'ts by an Imagist," *Poetry: A Magazine in Verse* 1, no. 6 (March 1913): 200–202. The three traits of imagist verse are Pound's too, from "A Retrospect," but reported by F. S. Flint in a companion essay to Pound's titled "Imagisme," 199.
14. EH, *In Our Time,* 13–157.
15. EH, *In Our Time,* 29.
16. EH, *In Our Time,* 37.
17. EH, *Moveable,* 107–8.
18. Carpenter, *Serious Character,* 612–13.

## CHAPTER 10

1. EH, *Moveable,* 15.
2. Reynolds, *Paris Years,* 4.
3. She tells the tale of her French and Vietnamese servant woes in her famous cookbook: Alice B. Toklas, *The Alice B. Toklas Cook Book* (New York: HarperCollins, 2010), 167–99.
4. Gertrude Stein, excerpt from *The Making of Americans* in *Selected Writings of Gertrude Stein,* ed. Carl Van Vechten (New York: Vintage, 1990), 309.
5. Malcolm Cowley, *Exile's Return: A Literary Odyssey of the 1920s* (New York: Penguin Classics, 1994), 148.
6. Janet Malcolm, "Strangers in Paradise," *The New Yorker,* November 13, 2006, https://tinyurl.com/y3hx8xvu.

7. Gertrude Stein, *Wars I Have Seen* (New York: Random House, 1945), 48.
8. EH, *Moveable*, 18.
9. Gertrude Stein, *The Autobiography of Alice B. Toklas* (New York: Vintage, 1933), 216.
10. EH, *Moveable*, 118.
11. Gertrude Stein, *Three Lives* (New York: Mondial, 2007), 18 and 29.
12. EH, "Soldier's Home," 71.
13. James R. Mellow, "The Stein Salon Was the First Museum of Modern Art," *New York Times*, December 1, 1968, https://tinyurl.com/y32oh9t5.
14. Nearly every Matisse biography, gallery brochure, or curator's description employs this quotation, the words of art critic Camille Mauclair.
15. Stein's comments here are cribbed from her own words, reported by John Richardson in "Picasso and Gertrude Stein: Mano a Mano, Tete-a-Tete," *New York Times*, February 10, 1991, https://tinyurl.com/yxn89rpt.
16. This is imagined instruction, in keeping with claims she makes in print in slightly different terms.
17. EH, *Moveable*, 13.
18. Vincent Bouvet and Gérard Durozoi, *Paris Between the Wars, 1919–1939: Art, Life, and Culture* (New York: Vendome, 2010), 193–99.
19. Patrick O'Brian, *Picasso: A Biography* (New York: Norton, 1976), 156.
20. Alex Danchev, *Cézanne: A Life* (New York: Pantheon, 2012), 339.
21. Ronald Berman, "Recurrence in Hemingway and Cézanne," *The Hemingway Review* 23, no. 2 (Spring 2004): 21–36.
22. EH, *The Sun Also Rises*, Hemingway Library Edition (New York: Scribner, 2014), 158.

## CHAPTER 11

1. EH, "Appendix III" in *Sun*, 277.
2. A few of his *In Our Time* prose poems reflect this time reporting on the Kansas City criminal underworld.
3. For example, Hemingway complained bitterly to Bone, who was his managing editor, about assistant editor Harold Hindmarsh—who, because he was married to the daughter of the *Star*'s owner, was not inclined to take a younger journalist's crap. This conflict led to Hemingway's resignation from the *Star* in December of 1923. Hemingway felt even greater freedom dealing with Frank Mason, who ran a Paris news service Hemingway moonlighted for (very unethically, because he reported the same stories to more than one paper), using the byline John Hadley. When Mason withheld a paycheck from Hemingway, awaiting receipts that would clear the financial books, Hemingway cabled him, "SUGGEST YOU UPSTICK BOOKS ASSWARDS HEMINGWAY." Because cables charged by the word, changing "stick the books up your ass" to "UPSTICK ASSWARDS" cleverly saved Hemingway four words in his telegraph charges. Many of Hemingway's early critics loved these linguistic tricks of compression.

4. EH, various stories in *Dateline: Toronto*, ed. William White (New York: Scribner, 1985), 87–116.

5. EH in *Dateline*, 117–18 and 105–6.

6. EH in *Dateline*, 96–97.

7. I reserve one such story for my "Switzerland and Peace in Our Time"—for thematic reasons.

8. EH in *Dateline*, 112–13.

9. EH in *Dateline*, 135.

10. EH in *Dateline*, 139.

11. EH in *Dateline*, 166–68.

12. EH in *Dateline*, 188–190.

13. EH in *Dateline*, 172–75.

14. EH in *Dateline*, 176–80.

15. As mentioned in a previous note, unlike today, early automobiles were not using up much fuel, but leaders worried about fueling their oil-fired battleships.

16. As I have noted, Hemingway included a prose poem about the execution in *In Our Time*, and early in the 1930s he added the story "On the Quai at Smyrna" to the book because it depicts the incredible suffering around those British naval vessels.

17. EH in *Dateline*, 220–21.

18. EH in *Dateline*, 234.

19. EH in *Dateline*, 235.

20. EH in *Dateline*, 227–29.

21. EH in *Dateline*, 299.

## CHAPTER 12

1. It is odd that the Ministry of Colonies did not simply shut down *Le Paria*'s offices and presses. Perhaps Sarraut, like many conservative nationalists today, wanted to preserve the appearance of a free press while working furiously to suppress inconveniently true stories.

2. Stanley Karnow, "Ho Chi Minh," *Time*, April 13, 1998, https://tinyurl.com/y5whn3gp.

3. Just as Ho Chi Minh died in 1969, a decisive plurality of Americans found fifty-eight thousand US deaths in Vietnam unacceptable.

4. In 1920, when French socialists and communists divorced in Tours with Quoc's blessing, custody of *L'Humanité* went with the communists. That the magazine publishes today is evidence of its firm foundation in French society, and of the continued attractions to European readers of post-Soviet communism.

5. NAQ, "Indochina" in Bello, *Ho Chi Minh*, 3–4.

6. Duiker, *Ho Chi Minh*, 82, and Quinn-Judge, *Ho Chi Minh*, 38.

7. Bellow, *Ho Chi Minh*, 10–11.

8. NAQ, "An Open Letter to M. Albert Sarraut, Minister of Colonies" in Bello, *Ho Chi Minh*, 13.

9. NAQ, "The Civilizers" in *The Selected Works of Ho Chi Minh* (New York: Prism Key Press, 2011), 15, and Bello, 16.

10. NAQ, "Racial Hatred" in *Selected Works*, 17.

11. NAQ, "Murderous Civilization!" in Bello, *Ho Chi Minh*, 14–15.

12. NAQ, "About Siki" in Bello, *Ho Chi Minh*, 18–19.

13. Bello, *Ho Chi Minh*, 18–19.

14. Brocheux, *Ho Chi Minh*, 21.

15. Reynolds, *Paris Years*, 73–74.

16. NAQ, "Menagerie" in Bello, 20–22.

## CHAPTER 13

1. EH to Hadley Richardson Hemingway, 28 November 1922, *Letters of Ernest Hemingway*, 1:371–73.

2. Yes, coincidentally, both Quoc and Hemingway had important manuscripts stolen while living in Paris. But coincidences should not concern us. Experiencing the thefts turned out to be far less important to them than their having a chance to rethink what it means to write for their audiences.

3. Reynolds, *Paris Years*, 91. Reynolds, with his unmatched command of detail, points out that Hemingway paid just as much for a month's ski pass later that winter.

4. EH to Grace Hall Hemingway, 10 January 1923, in *Letters of Ernest Hemingway*, 2:4.

5. Hemingway aficionados may note that in the winters of 1924 and 1925, Hadley and Ernest chose the Austrian resort towns of Schruns and Goschurn over Chamby. But Switzerland is merely a long ski run away from Schruns and, as Reynolds notes, this was a change made in order to exploit Austrian inflation.

6. EH in *Dateline*, 103–4 and 114–16.

7. EH in *Dateline*, 110–11.

8. Ironically and coincidentally, Radek would become Quoc's Comintern boss in a few more months, as both of them tried to spread the Bolshevik revolution into Germany.

9. HCM, "The Workers' Movement in Turkey" in *Selected Works*, 59–60.

## CHAPTER 14

1. Vietnamese men in Paris often had French girlfriends for heartening reasons of cross-racial affection, but also because there were far fewer Vietnamese women than men living in the city.

2. Duiker, *Ho Chi Minh*, 79.

3. Quinn-Judge, *Ho Chi Minh*, 39.

4. J. V. Stalin, "The Political Tasks of the University of the Peoples of the East: Speech Delivered at a Meeting of Students of the Communist University of the Toilers of the East," in *Works*, Vol. 7 (Moscow: Foreign Language

Publishing, 1954), 135–54, Marxists Internet Archive 2005, https://tinyurl.
com/y5uehr8k.
5. Duiker, *Ho Chi Minh*, 86.
6. Brocheux, *Ho Chi Minh*, 23. To me, the forged passport indicates a sophisticated organization behind Quoc's escape. It seems unlikely to have been his
own personal project. Yet the weeks in Petrograd imply that Quoc was not
expected in the USSR—or even especially welcome there—so it is hard to
judge which organization was helping him.
7. Quinn-Judge, *Ho Chi Minh*, 46.
8. Brocheux and Hémery, *Indochina*, 308.
9. NAQ, "Lenin and the Colonial Peoples" in Bello, 38.
10. Duiker, *Ho Chi Minh*, 296.
11. Duiker, *Ho Chi Minh*, 323.
12. Duiker, *Ho Chi Minh*, 306.
13. Quinn-Judge, *Ho Chi Minh*, 41.

## CHAPTER 15

1. All of these prose and free verse poems I've just mentioned appeared in the
"Exiles' Number" issue of *The Little Review* 9, no. 3 (Spring 1923).
2. Reynolds, *Paris Years*, 80.
3. Episcopal Church. *The Book of Common Prayer and Administration of the Sacraments and Other Rites and Ceremonies of the Church: Together with the Psalter
or Psalms of David according to the Use of the Episcopal Church* (New York:
Seabury Press, 1928), 30. The relevant evening prayer reads as follows: "Minister: O lord, show thy mercy upon us. Answer: And grant us thy salvation.
Minister: O Lord, save the State. Answer: And mercifully hear us when we call
upon thee. Minister: Endue thy Ministers with righteousness. Answer: And
make thy chosen people joyful. Minister: O Lord, save thy people. Answer:
And bless thine inheritance. Minister: *Give peace in our time, O Lord.* Answer:
For it is thou, Lord, only, that makest us dwell in safety. Minister: O God,
make clean our hearts within us. Answer: And take not thy Holy Spirit from
us." Emphasis mine.
4. EH, *Moveable*, 12.
5. EH, *Moveable*, 12.
6. EH, *Moveable,* 156. He also writes this confession to Max Perkins more than
a year later, in his first letter to his new editor, 15 April 1925.
7. Smith in Scott Donaldson, ed., *The Cambridge Companion to Ernest Hemingway* (New York: Cambridge University Press, 2002), 42.
8. The lazy title probably also hints at his minimal interest in McAlmon's Contact Press. EH, *Three Stories and Ten Poems*, reprint ed. (New York: Dover
Publications, 2019).
9. Ironically, both would become Republicans during the Cold War—to
Hemingway's disgust.

10. Mellow, *Hemingway*, 275. EH biographer Jeffrey Meyers suggests that the notoriously envious and competitive Hemingway only praised three books disinterestedly in his whole life: *The Enormous Room*, Dinesen's *Out of Africa*, and Orwell's *Homage to Catalonia*. Jeffrey Meyers, *Hemingway: A Biography* (New York: Harper & Row, 1985), 170.

11. Diliberto, *Hadley*, 124.

12. The odd typography is cummings's: e. e. cummings, *100 Selected Poems* (New York: Grove Press, 1994), 37–38.

13. This was a widely discussed exhibit at the Berlin Dada Fair of 1920, a work by John Heartfield (originally Helmut Herzfeld) and Rudolf Schlichter from that year. See Dickerman, *Dada*, 101.

14. More on this in the next two chapters.

15. Igor Stravinsky quoted in Pieter C. Van den Toorn, *Stravinsky and the Rite of Spring: The Beginnings of a Musical Language* (Berkeley: University of California Press, 1987), 26–27.

16. This scene is described in a documentary film: Perry Miller Adato, *Paris: The Luminous Years: Toward the Making of the Modern* (New York: WNET/PBS, 2010).

17. Alice Sokoloff, *Hadley: The First Mrs. Hemingway* (New York: Dodd, Mead, 1973), 74.

18. Martin Puchner, *Poetry of the Revolution: Marx, Manifestos, and the Avant-Gardes* (Princeton: Princeton University Press, 2005), 160.

19. The tales I cite here can all be found in the "Death of Dada" chapter of Malcolm Cowley, *Exile's Return: A Literary Odyssey of the 1920s* (New York: Penguin, 1994), 148–70.

20. EH quoted in Irene Gammel, *Baroness Elsa: Gender, Dada, and Everyday Modernity: A Cultural Biography* (Boston: MIT Press, 2003), 364.

## CHAPTER 16

1. EH to Maxwell Perkins, 15 April 1925, *Letters of Ernest Hemingway*, 2:318.

2. EH, *Moveable*, 156.

3. It is because of this incredible production that the late Paul Smith, founding president of the Ernest Hemingway Society, called 1924 Hemingway's "miraculous year." Smith, "1924: Hemingway's Luggage and the Miraculous Year" in Donaldson, *Ernest Hemingway*, 36.

4. Yes, this is a far cry from that cliché about Hemingway's work, that he wrote about "grace under pressure."

5. Why is it that Hemingway dwelt on Pound and Stein in *A Moveable Feast*, but not André Masson or Joan Miró? There are a number of credible reasons, but the two most important are these: First, *Moveable* is a book dedicated, in large part, to put-downs of rival writers and to a settling of scores. Hemingway enjoyed putting down the fascist and crypto-fascist Pound and Stein—especially Stein, who had insulted Hemingway as a dunce and an artistic fraud

in her memoir, *The Autobiography of Alice B. Toklas* (1933). Second, and more important, Hemingway could not write about his friendship with the surrealists Masson and Miró because they had been communists during the 1920s, and Hemingway wrote *Moveable* during the days of the House Un-American Activities Committee (HUAC), the Hollywood blacklist, and the Cold War standoff with the Soviets. Because Hemingway was a Soviet agent from 1940 onward, he had to conceal his true commitments to the revolutionary emancipation of the working class or risk blackballing, public shaming, and possibly even charges of treason.

6. Morley Callaghan, *That Summer in Paris* (Toronto: Exile Editions, 2002), 159–64. The stair steps are also Callaghan's imagery.

7. For a discussion of these values of Breton's see Pierre Taminiaux, "Breton and Trotsky: The Revolutionary Memory of Surrealism," *Yale French Studies*, no. 109 (2006): 52–66.

8. EH quoted in George Plimpton, "Hemingway: The Art of Fiction," *The Paris Review* 18, no. 21 (Spring 1958): 74.

9. Hemingway also admired and learned from painters he never met, including Cézanne (as we have seen), Pieter Breughel, Francisco de Goya, Andrea Mantegna, and, of course, Picasso. One of his best Key West friends, Waldo Peirce, was a muralist in a historical and realist mode.

10. EH, *Moveable*, 202.

11. Mary Ann Caws, *Surrealism and the Rue Blomet* (New York: Eykyn Maclean, 2013), 43.

12. Caws, *Surrealism*, 98. Of course, to contemporary ears, this language that excludes women is problematic. And it is true that women in Paris had to foster their own arts, as, for example, Shari Benstock shows in her *Women of the Left Bank: Paris, 1900–1940* (Austin: University of Texas Press, 1986).

13. William Rubin and Carolyn Lanchner, *André Masson* (New York: Metropolitan Museum of Art, 1976), 30–31.

14. Mellow, *Hemingway*, 152.

15. Mellow, *Hemingway*, 152.

16. Mellow, *Hemingway*, 255.

17. EH, *The Green Hills of Africa*, Hemingway Library Edition (New York: Scribner, 2015), 66.

18. Caws, *Surrealism*, 43.

## CHAPTER 17

1. Smith in Donaldson, "Hemingway's Luggage," 36–54.

2. EH, *In Our Time*, 111–12.

3. Most professional critics see postwar anxieties in Nick across the stories set in the early 1920s, just after the war. Many of these critics discuss obsessive behaviors apparently linked to post-traumatic shock, most showing up in "Big Two-Hearted River." Fewer of them read "Snow" and "River" as they should,

as stories about these anxieties shaping Hemingway's and Nick's shared view of a possible future involving fatherhood, marriage, and the writing career—all the elements of his dream life that might now have to be conducted in places less congenial and progressive than Paris or Chamby or Schruns.

4. EH, "Big Two-Hearted River: Part II," *In Our Time*, 154.
5. Not to press the symbolism too hard, but the fish, or *ichtus*, is also a symbol of the life-giver, Christ.
6. John Dos Passos, *1919* (New York: Mariner Books, 2000), 168.
7. EH, *In Our Time*, 157.
8. Episcopal Church, *Book of Common Prayer*, 30.

## CHAPTER 18

1. Duiker, *Ho Chi Minh*, 143. Tang Tuyet Minh may actually have been more attached to Quoc than she was willing to admit. Brocheux reports that Minh tried to write to Ho after he became president of North Vietnam. Communist Party cadres, seeing no advantage in the traditionalist Vietnamese people knowing that Uncle Ho had a history of abandoning wives and his own children, made her cease and desist. They bribed her to keep her story to herself. I write "wives and . . . children" in the plural because in Hong Kong, in 1931, Quoc married a second bride, a young Vietnamese girl he had just met named Minh Khai. We know nothing more about that relationship or its outcome, except that it did not last. See Brocheux, *Ho Chi Minh*, 181.
2. Nguyen Ai Quoc (Ho Chi Minh), *French Colonialism on Trial, or the Case against French Colonialism*, trans. Joshua Leinsdorf (Paris: Workers Library, 1926), 1.
3. Reynolds, *Paris Years*, 226.
4. NAQ, *Trial*, 4–22.
5. NAQ, *Trial*, 25.
6. NAQ, *Trial*, 43–45.
7. NAQ, *Trial*, 42.
8. NAQ, *Trial*, 24.
9. Fiction writers, the Hemingway of Paris days included, often write hyperbolic tales. It is their right.
10. NAQ, *Trial*, 37–38. Showing unusual restraint here of all places, Quoc spells "love" with only a lowercase *L* and an ellipsis.
11. NAQ, *Trial*, 53.

## CHAPTER 19

1. He did. He and his ex-wives competed, probably with more politeness than they felt, for possession of *The Farm* throughout his life.
2. The painting is now owned by the National Gallery of Art. Though it is not on view in 2019, the Gallery has published an online rendering: https://tinyurl.com/y3j8p2u2.

3. All of the Hemingway biographers I cite—Carlos Baker, Michael Reynolds, James Mellow, Jeffrey Meyers, and Kenneth Lynn among them—treat the purchase of *The Farm* as an interesting element in the Hemingway marital breakup. Mary Dearborn alone notes that the painting was purchased with money that might have dressed Hadley more fashionably, as Harold Loeb's lover Kitty Cannell suggested curtly at the time: "And it's her money!" Hadley's biographer Gioia Diliberto also tells the tale.

4. Mellow, *Hemingway*, 340.

5. The Knox-Albright Gallery in Buffalo, New York, holds the painting, and presents an image of it online at https://tinyurl.com/y792q4wf.

6. Gérard Durozoi, *History of the Surrealist Movement* (Chicago: University of Chicago Press, 2002), 118.

7. Durozoi, *Surrealist Movement*, 129.

8. Durozoi, *Surrealist Movement*, 129–34.

9. Durozoi, *Surrealist Movement*, 136.

10. EH, "The Farm," *Cahiers d'Art* 9 (1934): 28.

11. See, for example, EH to F. Scott Fitzgerald, 15 December 1925, in *Letters of Ernest Hemingway*, 2:445–47.

12. EH, *In Our Time*, 53–62.

13. EH, *Sun*, 150–56, and *Farewell*, 52.

14. Hemingway's politics are a bit of a conundrum. Prior to the recent revelation (or much wider understanding) that Hemingway willingly signed on as an agent for the Soviet Union in 1940 and continued in that role well past the time when the United States and the Soviet Union fought fascism as allies during the Second Word War, his biographers mostly projected political attitudes onto him. A more objective biographer, Keneth Kinnamon, demonstrated in 1996 just how wildly differing these opinions could be. Carlos Baker and Scott Donaldson regard Hemingway as a conservative Republican, Kinnamon reports. Neo-conservative Kenneth Lynn views Hemingway as naïvely wrongheaded and a "communist dupe." James Mellow sees Hemingway as an individualist first and a liberal second. Jeffrey Meyers claims Hemingway was "basically bored with politics" and half-hearted about class struggles, and Michael Reynolds agrees that Hemingway was essentially apolitical, even though in his youth he was profoundly influenced by Teddy Roosevelt's courage and love of the natural world. Kinnamon then presents a convincing chain of evidence showing that, as he writes in his final line of the essay "Hemingway and Politics," "Ernest Hemingway was always on the left." And it is true: During and after Paris, Hemingway supported a democratic version of socialism with an intense emphasis on individual liberty. He hoped that the two could be combined. Politically, he was a surrealist. Today we might call him a Social Democrat, which means, in essence, that he resisted capitalist wealth only when it subjected working people to deadly costs resulting from their poverty or abuse or their military service in unjust wars. See Keneth Kinnamon, "Hemingway and Politics," in *The Cambridge Companion to Ernest Hemingway*, ed. Scott Donaldson (New York: Cambridge University Press, 1996), 149–69.

15. EH, *In Our Time*, 81–82.
16. EH, *In Our Time*, 81.
17. Kinnamon, "Hemingway and Politics," 153.
18. I share Kinnamon's view of certain key characters, and I use his examples here. See "Hemingway and Politics," 163–64.
19. Hemingway wrote to Dos Passos in 1932 with a direct message to this effect: "I suppose I am an anarchist." See Kinnamon, "Hemingway and Politics," 162.
20. Quoted in Kinnamon, "Hemingway and Politics," 165.

## CHAPTER 20

1. Duiker, *Ho Chi Minh*, 97.
2. Duiker, *Ho Chi Minh*, 102.
3. Duiker, *Ho Chi Minh*, 103.
4. Duiker, *Ho Chi Minh*, 104.
5. Bui, "Anticolonial Constitutionalism," 197–221. For the story of the "Screams," see 209–10.
6. HCM et al., "Screams to the League of Nations," quoted in Truong Bun Lam, *Colonialism Experienced: Vietnamese Writings on Colonialism, 1900–1931* (Ann Arbor: University of Michigan Press, 2000), 236–37.
7. Bui, "Anticolonial Constitutionalism," 208–9.
8. From a transcription of the original Declaration of Independence published by the National Archives: "But when a long train of abuses and usurpations, pursuing invariably the same Object, evinces a design to reduce them under absolute Despotism, it is their right, *it is their duty,* to throw off such Government, and to provide new Guards for their future security. Such has been the patient sufferance of these Colonies; and such is now the necessity which constrains them to alter their former Systems of Government." (Emphasis mine.)
9. Duiker, *Ho Chi Minh*, 123.
10. Duiker, *Ho Chi Minh*, 576.
11. Brocheux and Hémery, *Indochina*, 307.
12. Duiker describes Ho's recitation of Confucian humanitarian sayings as late as 1965. See *Ho Chi Minh*, 555.
13. Diliberto, *Hadley*, 217.
14. Diliberto, *Hadley*, 212–23.
15. EH, *Moveable*, 208–10.
16. Mellow, *Hemingway*, 334.
17. Hadley was eight years older than EH.
18. In 1935 and 1937 the Murphys lost two of their three children to untimely deaths by disease, and Hemingway found that he loved them as friends after all, that he could comfort them in their incredible grief—a moment in his life he seemed to have forgotten as he wrote his memoirs.

19. Reynolds, *Hemingway: The Homecoming* (New York: W. W. Norton, 1999), 37–46.

20. Amanda Vail, *Everybody Was So Young: Gerald and Sara Murphy: A Lost Generation Love Story* (New York: Broadway Books, 1998), 174–75.

21. If you have the list of actual persons corresponding to characters, that is. They are available online.

22. EH, *Sun*, 126.

23. Reynolds, *Homecoming*, 35. As I do, Reynolds regards the Paris episode in Hemingway's life as all but concluded in 1925 and the remaining years a kind of important coda, demonstrating commitments learned.

24. Diliberto, *Hadley*, 242.

25. Diliberto, *Hadley*, 251.

26. Reynolds, *Homecoming*, 148, for one example.

27. Reynolds, *Homecoming*, 148–49.

28. Reynolds, *Homecoming*, 145–57, and Mellow, *Hemingway*, 359–60.

29. Reynolds, *Homecoming*, 145.

30. Reynolds, *Homecoming*, 163.

## CHAPTER 21

1. For a copy of this photograph taken by Paul Reed and titled "Ypres: The Early Pilgrims, 1922," see *GREAT WAR PHOTOS WW1 Photos Centenary Website: 2014–2018*, https://tinyurl.com/y5yalqxq.

2. Scott Fitzgerald even includes a touring group's visit to the trenches, already decaying and covered over with new grass, in his 1934 novel *Tender Is the Night*. We don't know that either Hemingway or Quoc made the trip to Ypres—but then, both of them had many experiences that are never recorded in the letters and journals that serve as scholarly sources.

3. S. L. A. Marshall, *World War I* (New York: American Heritage, 1985), 167.

4. Tim Cook, *No Place to Run: The Canadian Corps and Gas Warfare in the First World War* (Vancouver: University of British Columbia Press, 2000), 153.

5. EH, *Sun*, 92.

6. Quoted in Peter Englund, *The Beauty and the Sorrow: An Intimate History of the First World War* (New York: Alfred A. Knopf, 2011), 284.

7. Quoted in Adam Hochschild, *To End All Wars*, 70–71.

8. Hochschild, *To End All Wars*, 223.

9. See Arno Mayer, *The Persistence of the Old Regime* (Brooklyn: Verso, 2010), 329.

10. Stephen McDonald, "Crisis, War, and Revolution in Europe, 1917–1923," in *Neutral Europe between War and Revolution, 1917–1923*, ed. Hans A. Schmitt, ed. (Charlottesville: University Press of Virginia, 1988), 235–52. For the reference to one Norwegian's definitions of *barbarism* and *Christian love*, see 164–66.

11. Most Norwegians would not have called these policies communism because they realized that such policies actually helped keep a robust capitalist economy in place (it has) and kept the Soviet barbarism at bay (it did).
12. McDonald, 243.
13. Duiker, *Ho Chi Minh*, 73.
14. Duiker, *Ho Chi Minh*, 56.
15. Brocheux, *Ho Chi Minh*, 11.
16. Lacouture, *Ho Chi Minh*, 20–23.
17. Duiker, *Ho Chi Minh*, 34.
18. Brocheux, *Ho Chi Minh*, 29.
19. Duiker, *Ho Chi Minh*, 77.
20. Brocheux, *Ho Chi Minh*, 21. This page also refers to Quoc's commercial tours.
21. Claire Lemercier, "Le Club du Faubourg, Tribune Libre de Paris, 1918–1939," March 13, 2006, https://tinyurl.com/y3wu3qm5.
22. Marr, *Vietnamese Tradition*, 8–15.
23. Bao Ninh, *The Sorrow of War* (New York: Riverhead Books, 1996).
24. Scott McConnell, *Leftward Journey: The Education of Vietnamese Students in France, 1919–1939* (New Brunswick: Transaction, 1989), xiii.
25. Meyers, *Hemingway*, 72.
26. See Reynolds, *Hemingway's Reading*, 39–43, for all references to the books he read or owned or both—though references to his reading occur in so many biographies that this is common knowledge requiring no citation.
27. Reynolds, *Paris Years*, 29–30.
28. Nicholas Reynolds, *Writer, Sailor, Soldier, Spy*, 76–77.

# BIBLIOGRAPHY

Note: The alert reader may notice that I discuss certain events, especially in Hemingway's life, without citing a source for that information. The reason is that all citation systems, including the Fortress Press favorite and mine, the Chicago Manual of Style, allow for "common knowledge." That is, there is no need to offer a source for widely known information (the Great War ended in 1918) and information that appears in three or more books on the subject (Hemingway moved to Paris with Hadley in December of 1921). Choosing one source to cite of the many available would be silly and arbitrary. Given the wealth of sources on Hemingway's life and relative paucity of sources on Ho's, readers will notice that I cite almost all information on Ho's life while citing only a few little-known details on Hemingway's.

## HEMINGWAY BIOGRAPHIES

Baker, Carlos. *Ernest Hemingway: A Life Story*. New York: Charles Scribner's Sons, 1969.

Dearborn, Mary V. *Ernest Hemingway: A Biography*. New York: Knopf, 2017.

Kinnamon, Keneth. "Hemingway and Politics." In *The Cambridge Companion to Hemingway*, 149–69. Edited by Scott Donaldson. New York: Cambridge University Press, 1996.

Lynn, Kenneth. *Hemingway*. Cambridge: Harvard University Press, 1995.

Mellow, James R. *Hemingway: A Life without Consequences*. New York: Houghton Mifflin, 1992.

Meyers, Jeffrey. *Hemingway: A Biography*. New York: Da Capo, 1985.

Reynolds, Michael. *Hemingway: The Homecoming*. New York: W. W. Norton, 1999.

———. *Hemingway's Reading, 1910–1940: An Inventory*. Princeton: Princeton University Press, 1981.

———. *The Paris Years*. New York: W. W. Norton, 1989.
———. *The Young Hemingway*. New York: W. W. Norton, 1998.
Reynolds, Nicholas. *Writer, Sailor, Soldier, Spy: Ernest Hemingway's Secret Adventures, 1935–1961*. New York: William Morrow, 2017.

## HEMINGWAY'S WRITINGS

Hemingway, Ernest. *Dateline: Toronto: The Complete Toronto Star Dispatches, 1920–1924*. Edited by William White. New York: Scribner, 1985.
———. *A Farewell to Arms*. The Hemingway Library Edition. New York: Scribner, 1929.
———. "The Farm." *Cahiers d'Art* 9 (1934): 28.
———. *The Green Hills of Africa*. The Hemingway Library Edition. New York: Scribner, 2015.
———. *in our time*. Paris: Three Mountains Press, 1924. PDF. https://tinyurl.com/y6b6x6go.
———. *In Our Time*. New York: Scribner, 1925.
———. "In Our Time" and "They All Made Peace—What Is Peace?" *The Little Review* 9, no. 3 (Spring 1923, Exiles' Number): 5–9.
———. *The Letters of Ernest Hemingway*. Edited by Sandra Spanier and Robert W. Trogdon. Vol. 1, *1907–1922*. New York: Cambridge University Press, 2011.
———. *The Letters of Ernest Hemingway*. Edited by Sandra Spanier and Robert W. Trogdon. Vol. 2, *1923–1925*. New York: Cambridge University Press, 2013.
———. *A Moveable Feast*. New York: Touchstone, 1964.
———. *The Nick Adams Stories*. Edited by Philip Young. New York: Scribner, 1972.
———. "The Passing of Pickles McCarty or The Woppian Way," unpublished manuscript quoted in Richard Willing, "Hemingway Manuscript Revealed." *The Washington Post*, April 4, 1977. https://tinyurl.com/y4eounn3.
———. *Selected Letters, 1917–1961*. Edited by Carlos Baker. New York: Scribner, 1981.
———. *The Sun Also Rises*. The Hemingway Library Edition. Supplemented with early drafts and deleted chapters. Edited by Seán Hemingway. New York: Scribner, 1926/2014.
———. *Three Stories and Ten Poems*. Reprint ed. New York: Dover Publications, 2019.

## HO CHI MINH BIOGRAPHIES

Brocheux, Pierre. *Ho Chi Minh: A Biography*. Translated by Claire Duiker. New York: Cambridge University Press, 2007.
Duiker, William J. *Ho Chi Minh: A Life*. New York: Hyperion, 2000.
Halberstam, David. *Ho*. New York: Rowman & Littlefield, 2007.

Lacouture, Jean. *Ho Chi Minh: A Political Biography.* New York: Random House, 1968.

Quinn-Judge, Sophie. *Ho Chi Minh: The Missing Years.* Berkeley: University of California Press, 2002.

## HO CHI MINH'S WRITINGS AS NGUYEN AI QUOC

Quoc, Nguyen Ai. "Demands of the Annamite People." Quoted in Sophie Quinn-Judge, *Ho Chi Minh: The Missing Years.* Berkeley: University of California Press, 2002: 12.

———. *Ho Chi Minh: Down with Colonialism!* Edited by Walden Bello. New York: Verso, 2007.

———. *La Procès de la Colonization Francaise (French Colonialism on Trial, or the Case against French Colonialism).* Translated by Joshua Leinsdorf. Paris: Workers Library, 1926.

———. "Screams to the League of Nations." Quoted in Truong Bun Lam, *Colonialism Experienced: Vietnamese Writings on Colonialism, 1900–1931,* 236–37. Ann Arbor: University of Michigan Press, 2000.

———. *The Selected Works of Ho Chi Minh.* New York: Prism Key, 2011.

## HISTORIES OF INDOCHINESE COLONIALISM

Brocheux, Pierre and Daniel Hémery. *Indochina: An Ambiguous Colonization, 1858–1954.* Berkeley: University of California Press, 2011.

Marr, David G. *Vietnamese Anticolonialism, 1885–1925.* Berkeley: University of California Press, 1971.

———. *Vietnamese Tradition on Trial, 1920–1945.* Berkeley: University of California Press, 1981.

McConnell, Scott. *Leftward Journey: The Education of Vietnamese Students in France, 1919–1939.* New Brunswick: Transaction, 1989.

Peters, Erica J. *Appetites and Aspirations in Vietnam: Food and Drink in the Long Nineteenth Century.* New York: Rowman & Littlefield, 2012.

Robson, Kathryn and Jennifer Yee, ed. *France and "Indochina": Cultural Representations.* New York: Lexington, 2005.

Rosenberg, Clifford. *Policing Paris: The Origins of Modern Immigration Control Between the Wars.* Ithaca: Cornell University Press, 2006.

Truong Buu Lam. *Colonialism Experienced: Vietnamese Writings on Colonialism, 1900–1931.* Ann Arbor: University of Michigan Press, 2000.

## OTHER WORKS

Adato, Perry Miller. *Paris: The Luminous Years: Toward the Making of the Modern.* New York: WNET/PBS, 2010.

Andelman, David. *A Shattered Peace: Versailles 1919 and the Price We Pay Today.* New York: Wiley, 2014.

Anderson, Sherwood. *Sherwood Anderson's Memoirs: A Critical Edition.* Edited by Ray Lewis White. Chapel Hill: University of North Carolina Press, 1969.

Bao Ninh. *The Sorrow of War.* New York: Riverhead, 1996.

Benstock, Shari. *Women of the Left Bank: Paris, 1900–1940.* Austin: University of Texas Press, 1986.

Berman, Ronald. "Recurrence in Hemingway and Cézanne." *The Hemingway Review* 23, no. 2 (Spring 2004): 21–36.

Bouvet, Vincent and Gérard Durozoi. *Paris Between the Wars, 1919–1939: Art, Life, and Culture.* New York: Vendome, 2010.

Brogan, James and Gil Jackman. *La Vie de Paris.* Bloomington, IN: iUniverse, 2008.

Callaghan, Morley. *That Summer in Paris.* Toronto: Exile Editions, 2002.

Carpenter, Humphrey. *A Serious Character: The Life of Ezra Pound.* Boston: Houghton Mifflin, 1988.

Caulcutt, Clea. "Paris's Forgotten Human Zoo." *Visiting France.* RFI: issued February 16, 2011; modified March 3, 2011. https://tinyurl.com/q2ajzub.

Caws, Mary Ann. *Surrealism and the Rue Blomet.* New York: Eykyn Maclean, 2013.

Cohassey, John. *Hemingway and Pound: A Most Unlikely Friendship.* Jefferson, NC: McFarland, 2014.

Conklin, Alice. *The French Republic: History, Values, Debates.* Edited by Edward Berenson, Vincent Duclert, Christophe Prochasson. Ithaca: Cornell University Press, 2011.

Cook, Tim. *No Place to Run: The Canadian Corps and Gas Warfare in the First World War.* Vancouver: University of British Columbia Press, 2000.

Cowley, Malcolm. *Exile's Return: A Literary Odyssey of the 1920s.* New York: Penguin Classics, 1994.

Cummings, E. E. *The Enormous Room.* New York: Dover, 2002.

———. *100 Selected Poems.* New York: Grove, 1994.

Danchev, Alex. *Cézanne: A Life.* New York: Pantheon, 2012.

Dickerman, Leah, ed. *Dada.* Washington: National Gallery of Art, 2006.

Diliberto, Gioia. *Hadley.* New York: Ticknor and Fields, 1992.

Dinesen, Isak. *Out of Africa.* New York: Modern Library, 1992.

Donaldson, Scott. *The Cambridge Companion to Ernest Hemingway.* New York: Cambridge University Press, 2002.

Dos Passos, John. *1919.* New York: Mariner, 2000.

Durozoi, Gérard. *History of the Surrealist Movement.* Chicago: University of Chicago Press, 2002.

Eliot, T. S. *The Waste Land: A Facsimile and Transcript of the Original Drafts Including the Annotations of Ezra Pound.* New York: Harvest Books, 1971.

Englund, Peter. *The Beauty and the Sorrow: An Intimate History of the First World War.* New York: Alfred A. Knopf, 2011.

Episcopal Church. *The Book of Common Prayer and Administration of the Sacraments and Other Rites and Ceremonies of the Church: Together with the Psalter or Psalms of David according to the Use of the Episcopal Church.* New York: Seabury, 1928.

Eram, Cosana Maria. "The Autobiographical Pact: Otherness and Redemption in Four French Avant-Garde Artists." PhD diss., Stanford University, 2010.

Escoffier, Auguste. *Memories of My Life.* New York: Van Nostrand Reinhold, 1997.

Ferry, Jules Francois Camille. "Speech Before the French Chamber of Deputies, March 28, 1884." *Discours et Opinions de Jules Ferry.* Edited by Paul Robiquet. Translated by Ruth Kleinman. https://tinyurl.com/y6bwsfw9.

Gammel, Irene. *Baroness Elsa: Gender, Dada, and Everyday Modernity: A Cultural Biography.* Boston: MIT Press, 2003.

Green, Nancy L. *The Other Americans in Paris: Businessmen, Countesses, Wayward Youth, 1880–1941.* Chicago: University of Chicago Press, 2014.

Hochschild, Adam. *To End All Wars: A Story of Loyalty and Rebellion, 1914–1918.* New York: Houghton Mifflin Harcourt, 2011.

Homberger, Eric, ed. *Ezra Pound.* New York: Routledge, 2009.

Horne, Alistair. *Seven Ages of Paris.* New York: Vintage, 2002.

Jenkins, Philip. *The Great and Holy War: How World War I Became a Religious Crusade.* New York: HarperOne, 2015.

Karnow, Stanley. "Ho Chi Minh." *Time,* April 13, 1998, https://tinyurl.com/y5whn3gp.

Labouchère, Henry du Pré. "From Zoo to Table." *Lapham's Quarterly.* https://tinyurl.com/y5eszsry.

Langguth, A. J. *Our Vietnam: The War 1954–1975.* New York, Simon & Schuster, 2000.

Lasch, Christopher. *The American Liberals and the Russian Revolution.* New York: Columbia University Press, 1962.

Lemercier, Claire. "Le Club du Faubourg, Tribune Libre de Paris, 1918–1939," March 13, 2006. Translated by David Crowe. https://tinyurl.com/y3wu3qm5.

Levine, Isaac Don. *The Russian Revolution.* New York: Harper & Brothers, 1917.

Lynn, Kenneth Schuyler. *Hemingway: The Life & the Work.* New York: Simon & Schuster, 1987.

MacMillan, Margaret. *Paris 1919: Six Months That Changed the World.* New York: Random House, 2007.

Malcolm, Janet. "Strangers in Paradise." *The New Yorker,* November 13, 2006. https://tinyurl.com/y3hx8xvu.

Marr, David G. *Vietnamese Tradition on Trial, 1920–1945.* Berkeley: University of California Press, 1981.

Marshall, S. L. A. *World War I.* New York: American Heritage, 1985.

Mayer, Arno. *The Persistence of the Old Regime.* Brooklyn: Verso, 2010.

McDonald, Stephen. "Crisis, War, and Revolution in Europe, 1917–1923." In *Neutral Europe between War and Revolution, 1917–1923,* edited by Hans A. Schmitt, 235–52. Charlottesville: University Press of Virginia, 1988.

Mellow, James R. *Charmed Circle: Gertrude Stein & Company.* New York: Henry Holt, 1974.

———. "The Stein Salon Was the First Museum of Modern Art." *New York Times*, December 1, 1968. https://tinyurl.com/y32oh9t5.

O'Brian, Patrick. *Picasso: A Biography*. New York: Norton, 1976.

Orwell, George. *Homage to Catalonia*. New York: Bibliotech, 2018.

Owen, Wilfred. "Parable of the Old Men and the Young." In *Poetry of the First World War: An Anthology*, 171. Edited by Tim Kendall. New York: Cambridge University Press, 2013.

Plimpton, George. "Hemingway: The Art of Fiction." *The Paris Review* 18, no. 21 (Spring 1958): 85–108.

Pound, Ezra. "A Few Don'ts by an Imagist." *Poetry: A Magazine in Verse* 1, no. 6 (March 1913): 200–2.

———. "In a Station of the Metro." *Poetry: A Magazine in Verse* 2, no. 1 (Spring 1913): 12.

"Preamble to the IWW Constitution." Industrial Workers of the World: A Union for All Workers. https://tinyurl.com/y2btogu9.

Puchner, Martin. *Poetry of the Revolution: Marx, Manifestos, and the Avant-Gardes*. Princeton: Princeton University Press, 2005.

Richardson, John. "Picasso and Gertrude Stein: Mano a Mano, Tete-a-Tete." *New York Times*, February 10, 1991. https://tinyurl.com/yxn89rpt.

Rubin, William and Carolyn Lanchner. *André Masson*. New York: Metropolitan Museum of Art, 1976.

Sokoloff, Alice. *Hadley: The First Mrs. Hemingway*. New York: Dodd, Mead, 1973.

Son Ngoc Bui. "Anticolonial Constitutionalism: The Case of Ho Chi Minh." *Japanese Journal of Political Science* 19, no. 2, 197–221.

Stalin, J. V. "The Political Tasks of the University of the Peoples of the East: Speech Delivered at a Meeting of Students of the Communist University of the Toilers of the East." In *Works*, vol. 7. Moscow: Foreign Language Publishing, 1954: 135–54. Marxists Internet Archive 2005, https://tinyurl.com/y5uehr8k.

Stein, Gertrude. *The Autobiography of Alice B. Toklas*. New York: Vintage, 1933.

———. *Selected Writings of Gertrude Stein*. Edited by Carl Van Vechten. New York: Vintage, 1990.

———. *Three Lives*. New York: Mondial, 2007.

———. *Wars I Have Seen*. New York: Random House, 1945.

Taminiaux, Pierre. "Breton and Trotsky: The Revolutionary Memory of Surrealism." *Yale French Studies*, no. 109 (2006): 52–66.

Toklas, Alice B. *The Alice B. Toklas Cook Book*. New York: HarperCollins, 2010.

Townsend, Kim. *Sherwood Anderson*. New York: Houghton Mifflin, 1987.

Vail, Amanda. *Everybody Was So Young: Gerald and Sara Murphy: A Lost Generation Love Story*. New York: Broadway Books, 1998.

Van den Toorn, Pieter C. *Stravinsky and the Rite of Spring: The Beginnings of a Musical Language*. Berkeley: University of California Press, 1987.

# ACKNOWLEDGMENTS

So many people gave me generous and essential help on this book. I begin with the most important: my wife, Katie Hanson, and my adult children, Michael, Tyler, and Emily Crowe. Their main contribution was their loving support for the things I like to do—such as holing up in my study to write and revise my latest book project. The three Luther College English majors, Katie, Michael, and Emily, gave good advice on cover fonts and colors, and the Luther bio/chem major, Tyler, sent texts that kept me current on Minnesota team scores as I wrote. I love you, all four.

I thank my dear friend and longtime pastor, Peter Marty, who also happens to serve as the publisher of *The Christian Century*. One day, he recommended me to the *Century's* book review editor, Elizabeth Palmer, as an avid reader of Christian and other faiths' fictions who might review some new interfaith novels. Thanks to her welcome, I wrote a few *Century* book reviews during the past two years, with Elizabeth's wise editorial guidance, and one or more of these caught the eye of my editor at Fortress Press, Emily Brower. On a delightfully surprising day, Emily contacted me to ask whether I had any book projects in mind. Well, yes, I replied. I have a book in draft—a series of essays about Hemingway and Ho Chi Minh in Paris that have not yet found favor with a literary agent.

I have Emily Brower to thank for a number of things. First of all, I believe she has excellent judgment in English prose. Secondly, she clearly went to bat for me and my manuscript with the people at Fortress. Thirdly, she has worked very hard to prompt and push me to transform those essays—which I thought were the solution to the disparity of information available on the Paris experiences of Hemingway (too much information) and Ho (too little)—into what I hope is a clear and cohesive story about the two men evolving from their teenage traumas to their international reputations. I am grateful to Emily for her sound literary judgment and smart, clear advice as I carried this book through multiple revisions.

My best friend and best colleague at Augustana (after my wife) is Professor Jason Peters. A prolific writer himself, he is the only person other than my editor, Emily, who read draft chapters of this book, and amazingly, he volunteered to do it. Jason helped me see the difference between effective passages and ineffective ones, and he boosted my confidence with his approval of a chapter about Marie Cocotte's retired sergeant-major husband, Tonton, an interesting but eccentric chapter since cut as a little darling.

I thank my colleague Ann Ericson for asking me to take part in Vietnam Term, her brainchild and the reason I traveled in Vietnam three times, getting to know more each time about Uncle Ho and the nation he created. It was while teaching Tim O'Brien, Graham Greene, and Bao Ninh in Vietnam that the idea for this book came to me, and that would not have happened without Ann's idea for a study-abroad program visiting Saigon, Hue, Danang, Hoi An, and Hanoi.

I thank the research librarians and circulation and interlibrary loan staff in the Thomas Tredway Library at Augustana College, whose work gives the Augie faculty and students access to every single book we can ever need or want—and in only a day or two. Specifically, I thank Christine Aden, Sally Cobert, Sherrie Herbst, Donna Marie Hill, Vicky Ruklic, Stefanie Bluemle, Anne Earel, and Connie Ghinazzi. Before she retired, library director Carla Tracy also gave me enthusiastic help and support.

Finally, I thank two faculty committees at Augustana. I am grateful to the Faculty Research Committee for granting me funds to travel to the Hemingway Collection rooms in the John F. Kennedy Library in Boston. That was my chance to see the Massons Hemingway bought in Paris and to read Tonton's Christmas greetings to his little pal Bambi, whom his parents, Ernest and Hadley, called Bumby. And thank you to the Faculty Welfare Committee, specifically Deb Bracke, Mariano Magalhães, Joe McDowell, Doug Parvin, John Pfautz, and Mike Wolf, for releasing me from one of my assigned courses this past winter to carry this book through its penultimate revision. Thank you also to Interim Provost Wendy Hilton-Morrow, who watches a tight budget carefully and must have pulled the trigger on my course release.

I am tempted to thank the English professors who became my mentors at Luther College in the late 1970s and early 1980s, but instead I will offer up the claim we learn to say and to mean on that lovely campus: *Soli Deo Gloria.*

David W. Crowe
June 2019

# INDEX